Bleeding Kansas,
Bleeding Missouri

Bleeding Kansas, Bleeding Missouri

The Long Civil War on the Border

Edited by
Jonathan Earle and Diane Mutti Burke

University Press of Kansas

Published by the University Press of Kansas (Lawrence, Kansas 66045), which was
organized by the Kansas Board of Regents and is operated and funded by Emporia
State University, Fort Hays State University, Kansas State University, Pittsburg State
University, the University of Kansas, and Wichita State University.

Library of Congress Cataloging-in-Publication Data

Bleeding Kansas, bleeding Missouri : the long Civil War on the border / edited by
Jonathan Earle and Diane Mutti Burke.
pages cm
Includes bibliographical references and index.
ISBN 978-0-7006-1928-3 (hardback)
ISBN 978-0-7006-1929-0 (paper)
1. Kansas—History—1854–1861. 2. Kansas—History—Civil War, 1861–1865—
Social aspects. 3. Missouri—History—Civil War, 1861–1865—Social aspects.
4. Borderlands—Kansas—History—19th century. 5. Borderlands—Missouri—
History—19th century. 6. Slavery—Political aspects—Kansas—History—19th
century. 7. Slavery—Political aspects—Missouri—History—19th century.
I. Earle, Jonathan Halperin, editor of compilation. II. Burke, Diane Mutti, editor of
compilation.
F685.B65 2013
978.1'03—dc23   2013020161

British Library Cataloguing in Publication Data is available.

Printed in the United States of America

10 9 8 7 6 5 4 3

In memory of Michael Fellman

1943–2012

CONTENTS

PREFACE AND ACKNOWLEDGMENTS

The genesis of this project began with a long-ago conversation lamenting the fact that the paths of scholars of nineteenth-century Missouri and Kansas rarely intersected, and their work seldom crossed "the border." These artificial academic silos made little sense to us; as residents and scholars of the region, we strongly believed that the academic discourse shouldn't stop at a manmade state line. We decided to figure out a way to stimulate scholarly conversations that would emphasize the importance of the Civil War story in the border region and to help forge connections across both real and imaginary divides.

This is how one historian of northern antebellum politics employed by the University of Kansas and a historian of slavery in Missouri employed by the University of Missouri–Kansas City hoped to facilitate such a conversation and so convened an unusual group of distinguished experts on both histories who met in two intellectually nurturing conferences to present new research on the conflict on the western border. This group of scholars first gathered in the spring of 2011 at the Hall Center for the Humanities at the University of Kansas to present their preliminary findings. Instead of papers read from a podium, the draft papers were precirculated and workshopped for two full days. The entire group then reconvened at the Kansas City Public Library in the fall of 2011 for two and a half days of public presentations of revised scholarship. The outpouring of interest from the general public on both sides of the state line was nothing short of inspiring. Nearly 300 people attended Michael Fellman's keynote address on the first evening of the Kansas City conference, and the same number stuck around during the two full days of presentations. To hear academics present their research! This is not entirely surprising given the fascinating topic, the sesquicentennial of the Civil War, the relevance of guerrilla warfare to America's present-day military conflicts, and the intense level of historical education and interest locally, but to us this attention and the quality of the scholarship produced merited a wider diffusion of the findings. Hence, this volume.

A number of regional institutions, as well as supportive individuals, played key roles in bringing this top-notch public programming and scholarly content to a greater audience. The Border Wars Scholars Symposium and Public Conference were in the planning stages for many years. We carefully structured the scholarly content of the volume, making sure that we invited scholars who represented the histories of both Kansas and Missouri and whose work was chronologically expansive. We also leveraged the financial and logistical support of our universities, as well as historical and cultural agencies and historical-minded philanthropic foundations in the region. This project would not have come to fruition without their tremendous support.

Special thanks go to Victor Bailey, the director of the Hall Center, for hosting the Lawrence workshop, as well as to Ted Wilson and Jennifer Weber for allowing our group briefly to take over their running Seminar in Peace, War, and Global Change. Jeanie Wulfkuhle of the Hall Center deftly organized all of the details for the two lovely days that the border war scholars spent at the Hall Center.

The 2011 Border\Wars Conference at the Kansas City Public Library helped to launch the region's commemoration of the Civil War sesquicentennial. Although located in Missouri, the library remains the intellectual and cultural heart of the Kansas City region, and was the perfect place to host such a conference. Early in the planning stages, we approached library director R. Crosby Kemper III, and he enthusiastically agreed both to host and to financially support the project. We owe a tremendous debt of gratitude to him and to KCPL director of public affairs Henry Fortunato, who helped to make the public conference a smashing success. Todd Boyer and the able library staff managed all of the logistical pieces of the conference, including operational details, travel arrangements, and publicity.

It is a pleasure at long last to acknowledge the tireless work of Judy Billings, former director of Freedom's Frontier National Heritage Area, who has long supported this project. With the financial support of the Freedom's Frontier board, Judy agreed to host dinners for the scholars in both Lawrence and Kansas City. She also introduced us to Mary Cohen, who provided generous and timely financial support for the project through the Barton P. and Mary C. Cohen Charitable Trust. Julie McPike and Fred Conboy of FFNHA have continued to offer aid and sustenance to the project after Judy's retirement.

The history departments at both the University of Kansas, chaired by Paul Kelton, and the University of Missouri–Kansas City, chaired by Gary Ebersole, lent their support to the Border Wars project. The UMKC Bernardin Haskell Lectures Fund, through the support of Deans Karen Vorst and Wayne Vaught, underwrote Michael Fellman's keynote address at the Kansas City conference. The UMKC High School/College Partnerships program also hosted a luncheon for the local teachers who attended the conference in Kansas City, where they learned from the scholars how best to teach about the Civil War in this region. UMKC colleagues John Herron, Louis Potts, Mary Ann Wynkoop, Cynthia Jones, and especially Amy Brost, generously helped with various organizational aspects of the public conference. Lastly, as part of its mission to promote new scholarship of the region, UMKC's Center for Midwestern Studies lent financial support to both the conference and the production of this volume.

We are grateful to Gary Kremer, director of the State Historical Society of Missouri, who supported this project from the start and who helped fund the Kansas City conference, and to Gary, Virgil Dean, and William Piston, who joined us in Kansas City to serve as moderators of panels at the conference.

We also would like to thank Fred Woodward, the director of the University Press of Kansas, who took a chance by publishing yet another example of that dreaded product of academic publishing: the coedited anthology. The collection benefited greatly from the thoughtful comments provided by William Piston and Kenneth Winkle, both of whom supported publication and provided excellent constructive criticisms. Larisa Martin and Carol A. Kennedy helped get the book out on a timetable that neither of us had seen in academic publishing.

Thanks to both Leslie Tuttle and David Burke for graciously putting up with the dozens of phone calls, emails, and meetings that were necessary to organize two conferences and edit this volume. We often joked that we put about as much work and planning into organizing this project as we would a decent-sized wedding. As a seasoned volume editor, Leslie deserves special thanks for steering us away from potential pitfalls and providing always-sound advice for moving the process forward.

Finally, this project would never have come to fruition without the intrepid band of border wars scholars. To our delight, each fully bought into both the concept of the project and the process we laid out for it. Nearly every scholar who we approached agreed to participate, and in the end fifteen historians, including the two of us, twice took time out of their busy teaching and research schedules to travel to "the border" to present original work about this region's history. Each worked countless hours on multiple drafts of their essays and graciously submitted to a vigorous peer-review process at both the Hall Center symposium and at the University Press of Kansas. There was not a single slacker in this group—each pulled his or her weight and met numerous deadlines. It was a joy to work with them, and we are so grateful for the new friendships that we forged along the way.

A somber note marred the preparation of this volume when Michael Fellman died unexpectedly in June 2012. We invited Michael to deliver the keynote address for the conference because we wanted to recognize him as one of the first scholars to examine the Civil War on the border in all of its complexity. We rightly believed that he would provide an excellent and unique perspective on the state of the scholarship that has been produced since the publication of his path-breaking book, *Inside War*, almost a quarter century ago. As he did with all his passions, Michael enthusiastically dove into the project, participating at every stage at a level seldom seen from senior scholars. He closely read each of the essays and actively engaged in the process of peer review. He also gamely produced an original piece of scholarship specifically for the conference. In short, he was a mensch, and we will miss his historical insights, his caustic wit, and his unique combination of worldly pessimism about "the way things are" and a *joie de vivre* those who had the pleasure of knowing him found inspiring. It is to his memory that we dedicate this volume.

JE and DMB

Bleeding Kansas,
Bleeding Missouri

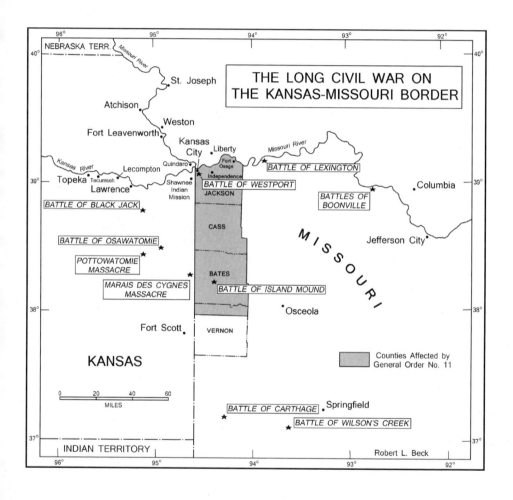

THE LONG CIVIL WAR ON
THE KANSAS-MISSOURI BORDER

NEBRASKA TERR.

St. Joseph

Atchison

Weston

Fort Leavenworth

Kansas City

Liberty

Missouri River

BATTLE OF LEXINGTON

Quindaro

Fort Osage

Lecompton

Topeka

Tecumseh

Lawrence

Shawnee Indian Mission

Independence

BATTLE OF WESTPORT

Columbia

JACKSON

BATTLE OF BLACK JACK

BATTLES OF BOONVILLE

CASS

MISSOURI

BATTLE OF OSAWATOMIE

Jefferson City

POTTOWATOMIE MASSACRE

BATES

MARAIS DES CYGNES MASSACRE

BATTLE OF ISLAND MOUND

Osceola

Fort Scott

VERNON

KANSAS

Counties Affected by
General Order No. 11

0   20   40   60
MILES

BATTLE OF CARTHAGE

Springfield

BATTLE OF WILSON'S CREEK

INDIAN TERRITORY

Robert L. Beck

Revisiting the Long Civil War on the Border

Jonathan Earle and Diane Mutti Burke

Forest Hill Cemetery is a sprawling necropolis located in Kansas City, Missouri, less than two miles from the Kansas state line—a border that is almost meaningless today but that 150 years ago formed a porous and portentous boundary between slavery and freedom, North and South, Union and Confederate. There, a short walk from the graves of notable Kansas Citians including jazz-age mayor Tom Pendergast and Negro Leagues baseball greats Satchel Paige and Buck O'Neill, is an impressive monument to fallen Confederate soldiers from the Battle of Westport, which was fought on these very grounds. The Civil War battle, often called "the Gettysburg of the West," was the largest military engagement this side of the Mississippi (30,000 men were engaged on October 23, 1864), and represented the turning point of Confederate General Sterling Price's Missouri expedition.

Although there are Union dead also buried at Forest Hill, few would be able to find their markers. This is because sites like Forest Hill and the Confederate Memorial State Historic Site an hour east of Kansas City in Higginsville are 100 percent dedicated to the "Lost Cause." Indeed, the markers at Forest Hill are dedicated to telling the story of Confederate General Jo Shelby's Last Stand that, during the Battle of Westport, allowed General Price's army to escape the battlefield. Shelby himself also retreated that October day, and when the Confederacy began to topple he buried his battle flags in the Rio Grande and, with 600 fellow militants, entered Mexico to plant the gringo colony of "Carlota" near Vera Cruz. After the dismal failure of the colony, Shelby returned to the border region (settling in rural Bates County, Missouri) in 1867. Shortly before his death in 1898, Shelby apologized for his role in the border conflict to the Kansas historian William E. Connelley, saying "I went there to kill Free State men. I did kill them. . . . I am now ashamed of myself for having done so, but then times were different from what they are now." Interestingly, the former Confederate went on to endorse the violence committed by his abolitionist foes: "I say John Brown was right. He did in his country what I would have done in mine in like circumstances. Those were the days when slavery was in the balance and the violence engendered made men irresponsible."[1] Despite this unusual recantation, Shelby's final resting place is a stone's throw from the towering monument to the Old South at Forest Hill.

A bookend of sorts to the imposing Confederate monument in Kansas City is the more modest "Quantrill Monument" in Lawrence, Kansas', Oak Hill Cemetery, closer to the west than Higginsville is to the east. This monument was erected in 1886 and according to the front of the marker is "dedicated to the Memory of the One Hundred and Fifty Citizens who Defenseless Fell Victims to the Inhuman Ferocity of the Border Guerillas [sic] Led by the Infamous [William Clark] Quantrell [sic] in his Raid upon Lawrence August 21, 1863." Just as Missouri Lost-Causers continued to celebrate the Confederacy in what was, of course, a border state that never left the Union, the citizens of Lawrence refused to forget the raid by Confederate guerrillas led by Quantrill who massacred a lion's share of that antislavery town's male population.

These memories preserved in stone reflect Kansans' and Missourians' postwar interpretations of the history of the Civil War on the border. Perhaps it is understandable that emotions were still raw in the years directly after the war, but it is more difficult to comprehend how such a simple view of the conflict—all white Missourians supported slavery and the Confederacy and all white Kansans were freedom-loving abolitionists who were victimized by Confederate guerrillas—to some degree persists 150 years later. Missing from this memory is the complex story of the earlier history of the two states and the violent conflict that erupted along the political line that divided them.

Beginning in the years following the War of 1812, settlers from Kentucky, Tennessee, and Virginia flooded into the bottomlands of the Missouri River, bringing with them the cultural values of the Upper South. Many also brought their slaves. During the following decades, these upland Southerners established a society in their western world with small-scale slavery at its core. Over time the population of the state became increasingly more diverse, however, as German and Irish immigrants and settlers from northern states moved into the region. Many of the new arrivals had a different vision for Missouri, encouraging early industrial development in St. Louis and promoting new railroad ties that would connect western Missouri to the Northeast and the Upper Midwest.

As the nation grew, tens of thousands of people passed through western Missouri on the way west on the Santa Fe, California, and Oregon Trails. The Kansas-Missouri border became a bustling crossroads where merchandise, cultures, and beliefs mixed and changed to take on a character of their own. But when Congress opened up white settlement across the state line in Kansas in 1854 this cultural and political diversity took on a new resonance. Americans held divergent visions for the future of the new Kansas Territory, largely based on their beliefs about liberty and freedom. Settlers possessing these conflicting ideas flocked into the territory, some traveling from nearby Missouri and the border South and others from as far away as New England in a literal playing out of the policy Stephen A. Douglas called "popular sovereignty."

Bitter feuding turned to open hostilities on the Kansas-Missouri border well before the firing on Fort Sumter. Violence first erupted in Kansas as free soil and proslavery settlers vied to stake land claims and erect a new territorial government. The nation watched as the residents of Kansas Territory and Missouri attempted to resolve the question of the extension of slavery that had so long stymied elected leaders in Washington. When proslavery congressman Preston Brooks beat Massachusetts senator Charles Sumner unconscious for innuendo within his speech "The Crime against Kansas," even the halls of Congress were no longer safe from the forces unleashed on the border.

Free soil forces eventually won the battle and Kansas joined the Union as a free state in 1861, but only after southern members who had long blocked its applications for statehood resigned their seats. Still, bitter memories of the border's violent conflict simmered beneath the surface and, after the Civil War began, erupted in an even more virulent form. It was now Missouri's turn to bleed as the growing internal divisions existing before the war and the presence of hostile forces on the western border turned the state into the scene of vicious guerrilla warfare. Western Missouri civilians—both black and white—were caught in the crossfire as Union and Confederate troops fought for control of the state and Bushwhackers and Jayhawkers ravaged the countryside.

The experiences of Missouri and Kansas residents during the era of the border war is a window on the issues and circumstances that shattered the union during the Civil War. After all, it was on the Kansas-Missouri border that Americans first grappled with the problem of liberty and slavery face to face—some even shedding blood in the interest of their cause. What was it that made the Civil War—including its prelude in "Bleeding Kansas" and long postbellum memory—so unique on the Kansas-Missouri border? Why did it become, in the words of the late historian Michael Fellman, the worst guerrilla war in American history? After all, the men and women on both sides of the border spoke the same language, worshiped the same God, and lived under the same flag. As Fellman wrote in his astonishing contribution to this collection—his last piece of scholarship in a much-lauded career—the war "became an endless cycle of robbery, arson, torture, murder, mutilation, an endless cycle of revenge and revenge and revenge. While using the most brutal and ruthless physical means, men and women . . . victimized one another, lied, dehumanized their enemies, lost all empathy and retreated into numbness, and buried their consciences behind a high, hard wall of utter antipathy." Indeed, the war on the border became a true *bellum omnium contra omnes*—a war of all against all, a conflict Thomas Hobbes memorably gave to human existence in the state of nature in his 1651 masterpiece *Leviathan*. Could a society so fragmented by ideology and violent conflict ultimately reconcile and rebuild upon different lines?

Books on the Civil War take up row upon row on library shelves, but the real estate devoted to the war in the trans-Mississippi West is relatively modest. Geographically distant from the major theaters of war and so considered a marginal story by many, the border region by and large has received limited attention from national Civil War scholars. In most people's minds, Gettysburg and Antietam win out over Wilson's Creek and Westport in significance. Even so, throughout the years a number of academic and professional writers have focused their attention on the political and military history of the conflict in the region, as well as the guerrilla conflict that raged along the border.

This focus on the history of the war on the Kansas-Missouri border developed within years of the war's end, although much of it was largely confined to the actual residents of the border region. A number of former border war participants, including politicians, such as Kansas governor

Charles Robinson, and guerrilla warriors, such as John Edwards and Cole Younger, published personal accounts of their wartime activities in an effort to shape the history to portray their side in a favorable light. Historians Wiley Britton and William Connelley also worked to define the early historical understanding of the military operations in the border region, as well as the first comprehensive account of William Quantrill's wartime activities.[2]

The first substantial scholarly treatments of the border conflict were not written until after the Second World War, however, when historians such as Richard Brownlee, Albert Castel, Jay Monaghan, and William Parrish published political and military histories of the Civil War in the border region, with a special focus on guerrilla leaders and their activities. Others, such as Alice Nichols and Allen Crafton, explored the history of the Kansas Territorial conflict and the state's involvement in the Civil War. The market for books on Missouri's Confederate guerrillas has endured to this day. In recent decades, the publication of guerrillas' original accounts, as well as histories of the conflict by authors such as Donald Gilmore, Thomas Goodrich, Edward Leslie, and Albert Castel, have added to the growing literature on the border conflict. By and large, these books profiled key border war personalities—all who were white male political or military leaders—and significant events and military actions such as Quantrill's Raid on Lawrence and General Thomas Ewing's General Order No. 11. Few of these works married the story of the political and military conflict along the border with the social history of the diverse people who lived in the region. In addition, this scholarship rarely examined the history of the region as a whole and instead concentrated the story on one side or the other.[3]

A few scholars have been willing to cross over both historical and geographic lines. These newer studies are increasingly expansive and use the conflict along the Kansas-Missouri border as a lens through which to examine the larger issues facing the nation during this crucial period in American history. Michael Fellman's foundational *Inside War*, published in 1990, was one such early effort to bring the story of Missouri's guerrilla conflict into the national scholarly conversation about the Civil War. Traditionally, social and military historians ran along parallel tracks, rarely making the crucial connections between the experiences of those living on the home front and of those fighting the war or between high politics and the power struggles of everyday people. Fellman artfully connected the military, social, and political history of the war in the region as he explained how young men might engage in violence against perceived enemies with whom they shared much in common. As he suggested in his symposium keynote address, this essential question continues to plague us today as Americans find themselves immersed in yet another in a long list of military engagements dominated by guerrilla insurgencies.[4]

More recently, there has been a resurgence in the study of the Civil War on the western border in part because of this contemporary resonance but also because of an emerging recognition by scholars that it is crucial to integrate the social, military, intellectual, and political history of the era in order to fully understand the conflict. The Kansas-Missouri border region, where warfare daily seeped into everyday life, is a wonderful laboratory for examining the interplay between these important historical forces. As Christopher Phillips explains, so much of what the Civil War eventually became—a "total" war in which the army engaged the civilian population—was in play along the border from the earliest days of the war. As a number of historians, such as Nicole Etcheson, Jonathan Earle, and Tony R. Mullis, make clear, these issues were put into motion on the prairies of Kansas even before the "actual" war began.[5]

In the last decade, scholars have increasingly worked to connect the conflict along the Kansas-Missouri border to the story of the larger war. An examination of warfare in the border region is an excellent vantage point for understanding the political and social conflicts that shook the nation during the era of the Civil War. Liminal geographic spaces increasingly have intrigued historians. In the Kansas-Missouri border region, diverse people with divergent ideas lived among one another and worked to create homes and communities in spite of their differences. Eventually their visions for the future of the region collided and virulent violence erupted. Both Stanley Harrold and Daniel Sutherland profiled the Kansas-Missouri border conflict in their comprehensive studies of how political conflict turned into violence in America's border regions, through their examination of the fight between antislavery and proslavery forces in the years before the war and the emergence of guerrilla warfare during the war itself. Other scholars explored how the region's border location influenced the way that residents lived and how they engaged in the violent conflict that engulfed their region. Diane Mutti Burke examined the ways in which slavery developed differently in Missouri because of its border location. Kristen Tegtmeier Oertel described how the activities of Native Americans,

African Americans, and white women influenced the emerging political conflict in Territorial Kansas, while LeeAnn Whites argued that secessionist women provided crucial material support for Missouri guerrillas. Christopher Phillips, Mark Geiger, T. J. Stiles, and Aaron Astor also described the motivations and politics of Missouri's southern sympathizers, and William Piston and Louis Gerteis examined the military history of the region along with social analysis of the soldiers who fought and the communities that supported them. With the exception of Jeremy Neely, who explored the Civil War history of the Kansans and Missourians who lived in the counties straddling both sides of the state line, few scholars have attempted to explore the many connections between border residents.[6]

Over the years, historians of Missouri and Kansas have written about the Civil War along the border, but few have attempted to examine the region in conversation with each other. *Bleeding Kansas, Bleeding Missouri* brings together the efforts of fifteen scholars who are interested in expanding our understanding of the history of this important region, as well as describing the ways border residents interacted. Taken together, the essays examine the history of the region holistically and in all of its complexity by focusing on the experiences of the diverse people who lived on both sides of the state line. These essays define both what united and what divided the men and women who lived in the region and how their political disagreements ultimately disintegrated into violence. They also present the story from a number of angles—military, social, intellectual, and political. Lastly, the collection traces the history of the conflict from its earliest days until well after the physical war was over, when the memory of the conflict was shaped by border residents' contemporary concerns.

We have divided the collection into three sections. In Part I, "Slavery and the Politics of Law and Order along the Border," the essays examine how the border region was transformed by the conflict over the status of slavery in Kansas Territory. Kristen K. Epps, in her essay "Before the Border War: Slavery and the Settlement of the Western Frontier, 1825–1845," describes the society that developed on what was initially the western edge of white American settlement. Slavery figured prominently in the region and, even though it operated on a smaller scale, was an economically and socially flexible institution that was essential to the developing border communities. In "The Goose Question: The Proslavery Party in Territorial

Kansas and the 'Crisis in Law and Order,'" Nicole Etcheson explains why western Missourians and their proslavery counterparts in eastern Kansas were so threatened by the growing presence of antislavery forces in Territorial Kansas after 1854. Many border residents sincerely believed that free soil settlers were defying the law when they challenged the existence of Kansas' proslavery legislature. Both Kristen Tegtmeier Oertel and Pearl T. Ponce explore how the emerging conflict on the Kansas-Missouri border took on a larger national significance. In "'Nigger-Worshipping Fanatics' and 'Villain[s] of the Blackest Dye': Racialized Manhoods and the Sectional Debates," Oertel shows how both Northerners and Southerners used gendered and racially charged language to vilify—and ultimately dehumanize—their political enemies, and Pearl Ponce, in "'The Noise of Democracy:' The Lecompton Constitution in Congress and Kansas," describes the interplay between local and national politics as the conflict over the Lecompton Constitution erupted on the national stage.

What began as a low-level conflict along the border erupted into full-scale warfare during the Civil War. In Part II, "Making the Border Bleed," the authors explore this transition to total warfare. In "The Illusion of Security: The Governments' Response to the Jayhawker Threat of Late 1860," Tony R. Mullis examines the response of the army to the violence perpetrated by free soil guerrilla forces against proslavery settlers in southeastern Kansas in 1859. They never fully arrested the violence, but military leaders nonetheless learned important lessons that they later employed against enemy secessionist guerrillas in Missouri during the Civil War. Jonathan Earle, in "'If I Went West, I Think I Would Go to Kansas': Abraham Lincoln, the Sunflower State, and the Election of 1860," explores the connection between the conflict over the status of slavery in the territories and the national political scene through an examination of Lincoln's 1860 trip to Kansas—the territory, and the political issue—that brought him back into national politics in the decade before the Civil War.

Other contributors examine the wartime experiences of the diverse people who lived along the Kansas-Missouri border. In "'A Question of Power Not One of Law': Federal Occupation and the Politics of Loyalty in the Western Border Slave States during the American Civil War," Christopher Phillips describes the dilemmas faced by the Union soldiers as they attempted to control and subdue the state. Although Missouri was technically loyal to the Union, a large segment of the civilian population was hostile to what they saw as an illegitimate military occupation. It was necessary to crush the enemy guerrilla insurgency while at the same time trying not to alienate a civilian population that supported it. In "'Slavery Dies Hard': Enslaved Missourians' Struggle for Freedom," Diane Mutti Burke explores how military occupation, guerrilla violence, and the initiative of enslaved Missourians ultimately resulted in the destruction of border slavery. In the final essay in Part II, Joseph M. Beilein Jr. describes the strong economic, political, and social connections between male guerrillas and the women who supplied them in "The Guerrilla Shirt: A Labor of Love and the Style of Rebellion in Civil War Missouri."

Violence decreased after the war's end, but border residents' traumatic wartime experiences left many scars. In Part III, "The Border Reconstructed and Remembered," the collection's authors explore the ways in which border residents rebuilt their society after the war and how they remembered it decades later. Both black and white Missourians struggled to reconstitute their social, political, and labor relations in the aftermath of emancipation. Aaron Astor, in "The *Lexington Weekly Caucasian*: White Supremacist Discourse in Post–Civil War Western Missouri," describes the ways in which white Missourians clung to the racial sensibilities of slavery in spite of Union victory and the rise of the Republican Party in Missouri, while in "'We Promise to Use the Ballot as We Did the Bayonet': Black Suffrage Activism and the Limits of Loyalty in Reconstruction Missouri," John W. McKerley describes how black Missourians worked to create a new political reality in the state. In "'A Little Different than in Alabama': Sectional Narratives and the Rhetoric of Racist Violence," Brent M. S. Campney shows that Kansans also wrestled with racial politics as they fashioned a new society and government after statehood was achieved. White Kansans proudly celebrated their free state origins at the same time that discrimination increased against black Kansans.

Only when Missourians and Kansans eventually embraced a common vision for their region—one based on shared agricultural practices, ideas about economic development, and racial inequality—could white residents on both sides of the border reconcile. Even as they increasingly were aligned socially and economically, white Missourians and Kansans still imagined that they were divided and found the explanation for their differences in the historical border conflict. In "The Quantrill Men Reunions: The Missouri-Kansas Border War, Fifty Years On," Jeremy Neely explains how white Missourians overwhelmingly embraced their Confederate past as they overlooked both the violent activities of irregular Confederate guerrillas and the reality that Missouri officially remained in the Union. For their part, Lawrence citizens were horrified by these annual celebrations of the men who massacred the male citizens of their town. Perhaps in an effort to reconcile and channel their historic animosities, the conflict was transferred to the gridiron during these same years. Jennifer L. Weber explores the ways in which the history of the border war has been used to explain the intensity of the sports rivalry between the University of Missouri and the University of Kansas in "'William Quantrill Is My Homeboy': Or, The Border War Goes to College."

In the final analysis, while unable to examine all aspects of the history of the Kansas-Missouri border war, we have attempted to tell the story of a people, who, although they perceived their differences were many, in reality shared much in common. Even today the belief in the differences lingers—as fans taunt one another across fields of play and as politicians lure companies back and forth over the state line—in spite of the fact that socially, culturally, ethnically, and politically they are remarkably similar. The Kansas-Missouri border continues to have cultural resonance in ways that seem disconnected from Civil War history but just under the surface remain firmly tied to the violence that plagued the region for nearly two decades.

Chapter 1

"I Came Not to Bring Peace, but a Sword": The Christian War God and the War of All against All on the Kansas-Missouri Border

Michael Fellman

On September 16, 2001, visibly and appropriately grieving, George W. Bush stood beside his wife Laura on the White House lawn, and, without a script, articulated his deepest feelings about the heinous attacks of September 11. These "Islamic fascists" are "a new kind of enemy," he said; they are "barbarians" without "remorse." Then he promised an American "crusade" against them.

Muslims around the world, the vast majority of whom were moderate and peace loving and as appalled by these attacks as he, who rejected the notion of jihad—the Islamic version of holy war—nevertheless were deeply offended by the reference to the Crusades. Blessed by popes and marching behind the cross, over several centuries pious Christian warriors fought brutal, sometimes genocidal wars of conquest against Muslims in the Holy Land (and for that matter European Jews and heretical Christians as well). Nearer our own times, almost certainly without realizing it, Bush's sensibility about the crusades and American mission had been filtered through the lens of nineteenth-century romantic imperialism, particularly the fervent ideology that accompanied French invasions into Islamic lands. For example, when he saw Horace Vernet's huge and heroic painting of the French assault on Constantine in 1837, one observer declared, "We find here again, after an interval of five hundred years, the French nation fertilizing with its blood the burning plains studded with the tents of Islam. These men . . . are resuming the unfinished labors of their ancestors. Missionaries and warriors, they every day extend the boundaries of Christendom." And in 1860, sending French troops into the Levant, Emperor Louis

11

Napoleon charged them: "You are leaving for Syria. . . . On that distant soil, rich in green memories . . . you will show yourselves to be worthy descendants of those heroes who carried the banner of Christ gloriously in that land."

Although he had been quite true to the ongoing energy contained in the crusading spirit of romantic imperialism, Bush soon dropped this vivid metaphor from the rhetoric he used when expanding the war on terror. Nevertheless, in that declaration on the White House lawn, for a moment, with candor freed from political censorship by anger, he had once again raised the banner of holy war against a barbarian enemy, a Christian war against Islamic Others who had declared holy war against the American people. Subsequently, the United States led invasions of Afghanistan and Iraq.[1]

Far from creating the ideology of Christian war, President Bush unconsciously had reiterated a set of beliefs that lies deep within the history of European religion, beliefs that European colonists brought with them when they settled the American wilderness and conquered its native peoples.

After centuries of crusades, and prior to romantic imperialism, came the European wars of religion, including the horrific Thirty Years' War of the early seventeenth century, in which Catholics and Protestants, all charged to their tasks by their clerics, put one another to death by the millions. Louis XIV, with the possible exception of Napoleon the biggest mass murderer prior to Hitler and Stalin and Mao, would repeat this history later in the seventeenth century in France when he consolidated royal power through foreign wars and the persecution of French Protestants.

In Great Britain, the centuries-long invasion of Ireland by England, which included the ethnic cleansing and colonization of Ulster, climaxed with the anti-Catholic holy war of Oliver Cromwell. In 1649, after slaughtering 2,800 men, women, and children in Drogheda and another 1,500 in Wexford, Cromwell declared that he had been God's minister, doing justice to God's enemies: "God, by an unexpected providence, in His righteous justice brought a just judgment upon [these barbarous wretches], and with their bloods to answer the cruelties which they had exercised upon the lives of divers poor Protestants."[2] The English colonists of North America brought these attitudes and experiences to bear against the Indians in the New World, against whom they warred with righteous, racist ruthlessness.[3]

These imported bedrock beliefs served as moral grounding for a deep tribalism that antedated Christianity. This flexible faith, wielded by a people who believed themselves God's chosen people, added ethical weight to their acts of slaughter against those they were certain were God's enemies.

In my recent book, *In the Name of God and Country: Reconsidering Terrorism in American History*, I studied the concept of Christian holy war in the nineteenth century, climaxing in the American invasion of the Philippines, the first colonial war of a sort that Americans have continued to fight. But in this essay I will focus primarily on the border war in Missouri and Kansas during the American Civil War, thinking back through some of the most haunting events I related in my book *Inside War: The Guerrilla Conflict in Missouri during the American Civil War*. I have never been able to put these accounts out of my mind. Neither have I been able to erase the horrific stories related to me over many years by several combat veterans, particularly from the war in Vietnam, nor their permanently stricken faces when they recalled memories that had seared them for life, nor what I have read in the psychiatric literature concerning the treatment of young men such as they who have committed atrocities—a far more common practice in all wars than we would like to acknowledge.

The border war right in the American heartland was, unfortunately, only one in a seemingly endless sequence of such wars—it is exemplary but not unique. No more restrained than other warriors engaged in irregular warfare, Americans during the Civil War did not escape the most horrendous forms of warfare, so characteristic of our species.

I do not have the space in this essay to convey the depths to which this guerrilla war descended, which are spelled out fully and painfully in *Inside War*. It became an endless cycle of robbery, arson, torture, murder, mutilation, an endless cycle of revenge and revenge and revenge. While using the most brutal and ruthless physical means, men and women reconstructed their personalities, their psyches, and their emotional lives. They victimized one another, lied, dehumanized their enemies, lost all empathy and retreated into numbness, and buried their consciences behind a high, hard wall of utter antipathy.

You will have to bear with me as I mention just a few of the practices of soldiers on both sides of this war—nearly all of whom were white, Protestant farmers who shared cultural values as they did ethnicity and language. These were not strangers from across the sea, but neighbors much like one's own, whom guerrilla warfare turned into violent enemies of an alien race.

In 1863, a Union spy who bludgeoned his enemy to death with a plowshare—reversing the biblical admonition—had gone on to literally deface Alfred Bolan, guerrilla captain in southern Missouri, a ferocious killer who had bragged of slaughtering forty Union men. Union troops and local civilians from miles around came to Fordyce to view his mangled remains that were put on public display. "His hair was all matted with blood and clotted over his face, rendering him an object of disgust and horror," Timothy Phillips, an Iowa soldier, reported. "Yet there were hundreds of men who gloated over him . . . there had perished a monster, a man of blood, of every crime, who had no mercy for others and had died a death of violence, and today hundreds gaze upon his unnatural carcass and exult that his prowess is at an end."[4] Note that Phillips used an odd construction ("there had perished") as if the Union spy had acted only as the vessel of impersonal divine retribution.

Killing was insufficient—mutilation of bodies, and almost certainly torture before death, became standard rituals practiced by both sides in this war. I will trouble readers with one example of the many I found. Union Colonel William Penick, stationed in Independence, Missouri, ten miles from Kansas City, reported the discovery of the bodies of five of his men killed during one week of January 1863, in separate incidents. "They were all wounded, and killed afterwards in the most horrible manner fiends could devise. All were shot in the head, and several of their faces were terribly cut to pieces with boot heels, Powder was exploded in one man's ear, and both ears cut off close to the head."[5]

Seeing their comrades defiled that way, infuriated Union troops responded in kind when enemies fell into their hands. Take for example the orders of General Clinton B. Fisk, who admonished one of his colonels about a captive: "Try the bushwhacker by drumhead court-martial tonight, and let every soldier in Macon shoot him if he is guilty, which he doubtless is." And, elsewhere in Missouri, Webster Moses, a Kansas cavalry sergeant recorded in his diary that his unit had captured "a few Rebs" one night, "who are next morning hung and shot at the same time."[6]

This behavior goes beyond execution of captured enemies. Such ritualized collective slaughter was intended to completely dehumanize the Other, deface him, desecrate the container of his soul while tearing his body to pieces, in the tradition of torturing and then drawing and quartering and disemboweling enemies practiced by European governments over most of premodern history. This was an aesthetic of obliteration. It would have been enough for a firing squad to kill a prisoner, for a bullet in the head to kill a downed fighter in the field. But more than killing was wanted: all in one's group were to draw together in this socialized drama of revenge. Doubtless such actions bonded the men practicing them, debasing the foe, exalting the brotherhood, exactly the analysis Iowa's Private Timothy Phillips gave when gazing with his fellows at the bloody carcass of Alfred Bolan.

Blood sacrifice has deep roots in Christian history, going back to the times of Manichaeism, where the Devil was the other all-powerful one, as powerful as a non-omniscient God, to be contested through holy combat. This was an early Christian heresy, an alternative religion denounced by the Catholic Church, but when over the centuries the lust for vengeance was the paramount goal, it resurfaced time after time in differing forms.

If not consciously religious, at the very least this spiritually freighted absolute dualism served as a proxy for religious practice during this guerrilla war. For example, when he prepared, in his official capacity, to send Colonel Charles R. Jennison's especially notorious regiment of Jayhawkers into darkest Missouri, Kansas governor John J. Ingalls was pleased to predict that this Union unit would take no prisoners, and would not be inhibited by "red tape sentimentalism," the normal limitations of civilized warfare. Ingalls labeled them "a band of destroying angels."[7] He was both horrified and thrilled by what he imagined would happen, and Jennison's men acted exactly as he anticipated. I do not believe his use of the term "destroying angels" was ironic: these Kansans were bringing the exact opposite of a reign of peace, and of course their Missouri Confederate guerrilla enemies operated under the same license.

Most of Jennison's band and most Missouri Confederate guerrillas were brutal and inarticulate fighters who practiced their preaching with gun and rope and knife. As I found their stories and tried to make sense of them, the chamber of horrors they had created was disturbing almost beyond comprehension. But for me the most disheartening individuals were the few well-educated, traditionally religious Christians who fought this war of all against all with clearly articulated, utterly righteous religious purpose. As it happens, both the examples I use here were on the Union side, but I am not playing the blame game here, not suggesting one side was more or less victimized or morally justified than the other.

Sergeant and later Lieutenant Sherman Bodwell, of the Eleventh Kansas Cavalry, who kept an unusually reflective diary, was a deeply religious Connecticut Congregationalist and abolitionist who moved to Topeka in 1856 to join the antislavery forces fighting Missouri slaveholders over the future of the new territory. Unlike almost any of the other men in his regiment during the Civil War, whom he characterized as "negro haters," Bodwell was a racial liberal. Indeed, during the summer of 1862, when his unit was stationed in Jackson County fighting many of the most ruthless guerrilla bands, Bodwell ran a Sunday school for little black children. "Am so sorry we are liable to be ordered away from here," he recorded at the time. "We have the best of opportunities for doing good Christian work among the colored population here." On July 4, Bodwell's unit were offered a fine dinner by the African-American Union "friends of Independence. . . . A better table, with more variety or abundance [than] I have ever seen. The colored people seem very intelligent, and glad to do us such a kindness." Bodwell extended his warmth and support to Union people of all races and ethnic backgrounds, including German Americans, widely despised recent immigrants to the Western border.

As for his lurking, vicious guerrilla enemies, Bodwell felt nothing but hatred. One dark October day in 1863, Bodwell's platoon happened into a guerrilla camp, deep in the woods, where they cut down the body of a Union soldier swinging from a tree at the end of a rope. When they left, the guerrillas had pinned a paper to the corpse's back that read: "This man was hung last evening, in revenge for the death of Ab Haller. He says that his name is Thomas and that he belongs to the Kansas 7th." Caught up in the cyclical spirit of revenge killing, Bodwell described with loathing the putrid, feral savagery of his enemies. "There seems to be something of the deathlike brooding over these camps. Always hidden . . . in heavy timber and creek timber and creek bottoms, offal lying about, cooking utensils, cast off clothing . . . the very air seems thick with the clime with which so lately they seethed."

Bodwell's diary is replete with full descriptions of the furious and thrilling catharsis he experienced when his unit chased down such subhuman fiends. Far from censoring his reporting of the murderousness of his unit's mode of warfare as did most diarists and letter writers, Bodwell concludes several entries with proud accounts of his unit killing wounded prisoners with a bullet in the face. In his fullest depiction, Bodwell put this atrocity in a Christian framework. One October day in 1863, his company flushed out two Bushwhackers, one of whom, when attempting to escape on foot, was, in Bodwell's words, "brought down" by his major. As the rest of the company remounted and rode off, Lieutenant Reese of Bodwell's platoon asked the major if he was "through with him," and after his commanding officer nodded assent, while Bodwell stood nearby, Reese "aimed and fired, a revolver ball striking just back of the eye & he was with his judge with all his imperfections on his head." As he relived this execution later on in his writing, there was something about it that remained incomplete. He regretted that he had not looked at the monster's face at the moment of death. "Lt. stood between us so I did not see his face." So Bodwell went up to Reese that night in camp and asked him about that moment. "Lt. says he intentionally raised his hand to protect himself and that an ashy paleness overspread his face, as when a cloud passes over the sun." Clearly Bodwell wanted confirmation that this beast's damned soul had flown straight down to hell. He wanted this moment of vengeance to contain clear Christian judgment that the avenging Union angels of light indeed had sent the enemy of darkness to eternal damnation as the fitting conclusion to their holy hunt.

On the day his unit was mustered out of the army in September 1865, Bodwell gave thanks to the Holy Spirit who had stood by him during his war for Christian virtue, national salvation, and racial liberation. "So ends my service, in all three and a half years filled with tokens of loving kindness of Him who granted me the privilege of standing in my lot . . . on every march and in every engagement. [For] the loving, comforting, strengthening of the Holy Spirit, even when I have been most . . . forgetful of my Christian obligation, I can never, I feel, be grateful enough."

Had the simultaneously cold-blooded and pleasure-filled moments of execution been occasions of forgetfulness of Christian obligation for which the Holy Spirit had forgiven him? Or did he remain prideful for having served the Holy Sprit when he judged and killed a lethal enemy that had sworn to judge and kill him and his brothers in arms? In either case Bodwell's Christian faith armed him to participate fully and effectively in the war of all against all. Nothing in his diary or his later life gives any evidence of regret or traumatic postcombat stress disorder. Indeed he was unconflicted in his war-revised version of Christian practice—he had no doubt he was serving God and destroying the Devil. He killed without compunction. After the war was over, I have no doubt that he reverted to the Christian God of Love, and behaved with fellow feeling and loving-kindness when he could to aid those in distress. The more absolute his faith, the more completely could he cleanse his conscience and put his past behind him.[8] He returned to Topeka and served as the well-respected sheriff of Shawnee

County, only to be killed when a drunken horseman ran him down in the street on September 12, 1871.

When he read his Bible, as he surely did every day of his life, Sherman Bodwell could have chosen reinforcing holy texts from which to derive both peace and war as the ultimate values of his faith. In the Sermon on the Mount as related in the Gospel of Matthew, he would have found the most eloquent expression of the God of love and peace. "Blessed are the peacemakers: for they shall be called the children of God," Jesus taught the multitudes. "Ye shall have heard that it hath been said, an eye for an eye, and a tooth for a tooth: But I say unto you, that ye resist not evil: but whosoever shall smite thee on thy right cheek, turn to him the other also."[9] Just as much as holy war, Christian nonresistance has a long and stirring history, from the Anabaptists of the sixteenth century and their Mennonite descendents, and the Quakers and other quietist Protestant congregations of our day, to the Hindu Mahatma Gandhi (a man who directed his nonresistance to a Christian audience who understood him from their religious perspective), to A. J. Muste and Dr. Martin Luther King. In a world wracked by repeated wars and great social injustice, this demanding implementation of the commandment not to kill has always remained a minority Christian practice. At the ethical center of Christianity, Jesus restated the Golden Rule, that admonition to fellow feeling that is at the root of all the major faiths, including Judaism and Islam. Jesus preached that the highest human good was not merely toleration but active mutuality and peacekeeping.

And yet, a Christian making war could also find moral affirmation and justification just five chapters later in the Gospel of Matthew. "Think not that I am come to send peace," Jesus commanded his disciples as he sent them forth to preach in the land of Israel. "I came not to send peace, but a sword. For I am come to set a man at variance" against his family. "He that loveth [his family] more than me is not worthy of me. . . . And he that taketh not his cross and followeth after me, is not worthy of me."[10] This is the militant Jesus calling his followers to arms, a Jesus who lived in this world as surely as did the Prince of Peace. "The Kingdom of heaven suffereth violence, and the violent take it by force," Jesus preached.[11] Sherman Bodwell marched behind that cross, as had the crusaders and the long line of Christian warriors, into lethal battle against disbelievers. When the urgent needs arise, all ideologies, Christianity included, need pliability in order to sustain equally compelling alternative interpretations. Perhaps

Matthew's conquering Gospel had been necessary to motivate a small sectarian group to contest a hostile world. But later, when used by rulers, authorities, and military leaders, this militant language takes on whole new dimensions of lethal intention.

Religious doctrine often justifies marching orders for true believers on the path of conquest. Right at the inception, embedded in the Puritan origins of America, John Winthrop preached to the very first settlers of New England on the ship bearing them to the New World that their expedition was the vanguard of the Chosen People, come to found a City on the Hill, a light unto the nations. This was to be a holy mission, not merely a material venture. They and the Indians who were already there made both peace and war, but most impressively a sporadic but protracted war to the hilt. Even Roger Williams, a Christian nonresistant who wanted to live with the Indians in peace, when aroused by deadly attacks from his erstwhile native friends, preached at them, "God has prospered us so that wee had driven [you] out of his Countrie, and had destroyed Multitudes of [Indians] in Fighting and Flying, in Hunger and Cold . . . and God would help us to Consume them."[12] The Puritan fathers sailed across the sea as colonial emissaries of the revolutionary English Protestantism of Oliver Cromwell: they carried out their attack on the Indians in the same Holy Spirit Cromwell used when he massacred the Irish. This was the language of ethnic cleansing and slaughter, of a Christian and tribal war that served as an almost eerie predecessor to the border war during the American Civil War. The beliefs and the language had not changed all that much over the ensuing two centuries—during dire times this fully armed Christian faith, articulated through the powerful metaphorical language of the King James Version of holy text, could be searched out for moral reinforcement. When the lust for vengeance overwhelmed the desire to live in peace with one's neighbors, when the Children of Light fought the Children of Darkness, moral dualism overwhelmed the oneness of God and the brotherhood of man.

Although my focus today is the Christian War God in the hearts and minds and arms of Civil War combatants in Missouri and Kansas, grounded in a centuries-long tradition of holy war, the same corpus of beliefs was turned to other uses after that war ended. Indeed, white Christian warriors destroyed Reconstruction—the northern attempt to enact biracial political and legal equality in the conquered Confederate States—deploying many of the same means and values that had been enacted along the border during the war. Well-armed paramilitary units, acting in coordination with politicians, overthrew Reconstruction in the Deep South, creating effective campaigns of organized violence against blacks and their white supporters. Not accidently, they called themselves Redeemers as they rallied the white community with endless intimidation tied to communal pageantry celebrating white blood while spilling that of blacks until they stripped their hated enemies of any political role. They believed they were routing Satan, purifying their homeland— that far from being regrettable, violence proved the depths of their faith.[13]

After ten years, northern Republicans in national power abandoned Reconstruction. In part the Redeemers had just worn them down, in part they were more interested in rapid economic development, but the Republicans also were faced with enormous masses of threatening alien immigrants, working in huge belching factories, and living in seething and corrupt new cities, all created by the full-tilt industrialization the Republican party sponsored. Much like blacks in the southern countryside, these workers were brawn at the bottom of the social scale, indispensible in good times, expendable in bad, always suspect, often despised. And some of them responded in kind, politicizing their anger at being treated as subhumans, striking out at those they believed to be their oppressors. To native-born Americans, those who spoke out this way seemed to be emissaries of European communism of a sort that had nearly destroyed Paris in 1871. When early communist workers seized power and formed a commune after France collapsed during a Prussian invasion, the French army rallied and destroyed them, killing perhaps as many as 50,000 communards, and this event struck long-lasting fear into middle- and upper-class Americans.

In the decades after the Civil War, thousands of European workers brought their radical beliefs with them into their New World proletarian experience. On May 4, 1886, during the depths of a terrible depression, at a rally of the International Working People's Association in the Haymarket in Chicago, when the police were dispersing the workingmen with their truncheons, someone from the crowd threw a dynamite bomb, and the police then opened fire. Seven policemen and an uncounted number of workers were killed in the melee.[14]

No one ever identified the bomb-thrower—it may well have been a member of the IWPA, some of whom worshipped the killing potential of dynamite—but it also may have been one of the many agents provocateurs the Chicago police employed to discredit the enemy.

In either event, the IWPA, about 80 percent German immigrants using a European revolutionary socialist analysis, had long defied and terrified the authorities in Chicago, and recently their marches and rallies, behind their banner, "No God, No Law, No Master," had begun to attract a huge new following. In their newspapers, broadsides, and speeches the IWPA expressed their rejection of all authority. Proudly atheist, they even knew how to turn the Christian values of their oppressors against them. If one searches the ever-replete Bible, one can abstract a communist version of the Judeo-Christian ethic. Albert Parsons, the Texas-born, Sunday-school-educated, English-speaking leader among the IWPA, delighted in using the Bible as his cudgel. For example on Thanksgiving Day, 1884, he spoke to 3,000 men at the Haymarket, attacking the rich capitalists "enjoying today the feast of Belshazzar . . . wrung from the blood of our wives and children." Parsons turned sacred text against his class enemies, particularly quoting his favorite verses from the Gospel of St. James: "Go to now, ye rich men, weep and howl for your miseries that shall come upon you. Your gold and silver is cankered . . . and shall eat your flesh as it were fire. . . . Behold the hire of laborers who have reaped down your fields, which is of you kept back by fraud."[15] At times Parsons was invited to speak at the leading Protestant churches of Chicago, where he repeated this news with glee to the very people he hated.

Imagine the gnawing fear of the better-off as the economic crisis in Chicago deepened and their enemies grew in confidence and defiance. After the bomb exploded, the police and politicians in Chicago burst out in hysterical demands for vengeance. This was the period of the first great American Red Scare. The revolution seemed to have begun, and those in power believed that all means to kill it had to be used. Newspapers and pulpits across the nation cried out for revenge. The *St. Louis Globe-Democrat* declared, "There are no good anarchists except dead anarchists. . . . Let us whip these Slavic wolves back to their European dens from which they issue, or . . . exterminate them." And the *New York Times* added that the remedy for "an acute outbreak of anarchy [was] the Gatling Gun," and that subsequently "hemp, in judicious doses," would admirably check the "spread of the disease." Instructed by the state's attorney to "make the raids first and look up the law afterward," the police swept the boarding houses and meeting rooms of the IWPA and arrested over 400 men, soon bringing seven to trial before a packed jury, and with nearly every voice in the nation calling out for mortal revenge, hanged four. The courts did not find the bomb thrower, but convicted the leaders on the grounds that their words had encouraged those unknown men who did the deed.[16]

On May 9, 1886, five days after the explosion, when public fury was at its peak, David A. Noble, pastor of the New Jerusalem Congregational Church preached a sermon entitled "Christianity and the Red Flag," taking his text from Isaiah: "Their feet run to evil, and they make haste to shed innocent blood . . . wasting and destruction are in their paths. The way of peace they know not." As had been the case for both sides during the Civil War along the border, Noble read the anarchists out of the human race. These were "fiends . . . fresh from European jails . . . miscreants [acting out of] cool, calculating and satanic maliciousness." They "must be made to feel the crushing weight of the authority they have outraged and defiled." Paraphrasing Isaiah, Noble urged holy retribution for the sins of these evildoers. "They have rolled their garments in blood. . . . Let them drain the dregs of the cup of their own spilling." Referring to the Red Terror during the French Revolution as well as the fate of the Commune, Noble thundered, "They have said that heads must fall; heads have fallen. . . . Let these men now have the privilege of furnishing a few heads for the basket." Mocking his enemies, Noble continued, "I know of no cause more in need of martyrs. Let them have a few as speedily as possible." And he proudly pointed behind him on the pulpit: "The Old Flag has been bathed in blood over and over again, that it might mean liberty."[17]

Ironically, during their trial, the anarchist leaders employed the rhetorical tradition of Christian martyrdom at the hands of the modern Rome and the legacy of the minutemen of the American Revolution in an effort to sway public opinion to their side. For their part, Republicans continued to wave the bloody flag of the Civil War, conveniently adapted to a new enemy. Both sides used the dominant moral beliefs that their countrymen would understand, but the state had far more power to impose its version.

Later generations of anticommunist warriors have continued to use this vision of the Christian God of War against their heathen enemies, as have many of those sponsoring wars abroad during the long-term War on Terror, those who portray their enemy as Islamic fascists. This vision of bathing the old flag in the blood of liberty conjoined to righteous vengeance remains the fundamental American language of just war.

To return to the Missouri heartland, during the nightmarish Civil War, the only alternative to combat was flight, and those who remained in the maelstrom reconstructed their worldview into light against darkness, repeatedly reaffirming their beliefs with murderous action. Even then, the ambiguity that makes us human could reemerge almost at random, leading to granting clemency here while visiting destruction there. But the essential lesson of this wartime experience was to kill them before they could kill you. It was nearly impossible to sort out some greater meaning when you were living this hell, and, on the whole, after the war was over, most combatants, just wanting to try to forget what happened, refused to discuss it.

Post–Civil War grand narrators of victimhood and justice at first sought to insist after the fact that God and justice had been all on our side and against theirs, but as the decades passed the urge for national reconciliation demanded the rebuilding of the Civil War in memory as a glorious battle between noble Americans both Blue and Gray (but not black).[18] Not surprisingly, the war of all against all was simply written out of this nationalist narrative—nothing about it could fit the notion of a redeemed and reunified nation. Even now, despite the rich and growing historiography to which my colleagues in this volume all are contributing, many other historians remain eager to consign the border war, and guerrilla war more generally, to some distant place, to serve as what they call "sideshows" to the real event—all those sublime battles and that glorious victory for human liberty the just war brought. Places like Missouri and Kansas, these historians insist, had been exceptions to the rule of civility with which most Civil War soldiers fought their war. Even more importantly for them, the ends of freedom had justified the means of war, and really that war had been a demonstration of courage and sacrifice and loyalty and manly virtue. Such assumptions may reassure us, but they are grounded in a refusal to look into the abyss that is actual war.[19]

Let me conclude, however, with an exception to this erasure of hideous memories, the deeply reflective 1886 lecture (the year of the Haymarket) given to the Minnesota Historical Society by John B. Sanborn, who had been Union commander of the five counties in the District of Southwest Missouri during the last two years of the war. Born in New Hampshire, trained as a lawyer, Sanborn moved to St. Paul in 1855, and immediately entered Republican politics. A talented volunteer officer, Sanborn rose to division commander in the army of Ulysses S. Grant during the Vicksburg campaign, after which he had been transferred into a nearly pulverized portion of Missouri. Though he rebuilt a life in politics and the law over the ensuing twenty years back in Minnesota, Sanborn remained haunted by the border war he had fought.

Prior to his assuming command, Sanborn told his audience, "during one week a Confederate force would pass through the country for a hundred miles or more and burn the houses and destroy the property of every loyal man, and before my arrival, the Federal forces would soon go over the same section of the country and destroy the houses and property of all the dis-loyal." Sanborn believed that these ferocious sweeps had reduced the population of this district from around 35,000 to about 1,500. Though he told his audience that he had put a stop to the Union side of this endless reprisal raiding, he failed to mention that on January 1, 1865, he had issued an order that banished 147 families (26 headed by women), and 97 individual women from his district, in other words around 25 percent of the remaining civilian population. He must have composed his list almost entirely from hearsay evidence, and one can assume that the houses and barns of the exiles were burned to the ground. Under enormous pressure when governing his corner of a divided nation, he too took measures he later realized were draconian and morally damaged.

During his address, Sanborn looked deeply into the heart of darkness in the sector he had experienced. "If there is anything of value to a future age to be learned" from the guerrilla war along the Kansas-Missouri border, he told his listeners—and us—"it is that there exists in the breasts of people of educated and christian communities wild and ferocious passions, which in a day of peace are dormant and slumbering, but which may be aroused and kindled by . . . war and injustice, and become more cruel and destructive than any that live in the breasts of savage and barbarous nations." At the center of the moral structure of these educated Christians, "elements of justice [were] implanted in their bosoms." During the war, the cardinal violation of this code of justice had been "the putting to death of innocent men for the offense of another man [even when] authorized by . . . government," that is to say, by the side he was serving. "Human nature itself" had burst forth "in open opposition to such an exercise of tyranny," and this had led to the "introduction of the reign of chaos."

Very clearly, Sanborn had reconsidered the humanity not only of his enemies, but of his own side as well. He dismissed none as savage aliens, but considered all of the participants, men and women alike, Northerners and Southerners, to have been educated and Christian, people much like himself, who had gone entirely wrong, reworking their essential morality in the name of the Prince of Darkness, destroying peace, creating a regime of utter destructiveness. He looked as honestly as he could into his own role and that of other Union and Confederate commanders like himself when he searched for the underlying injustice that had caused this border war to cycle downward into mutual obliteration. Authority had collapsed, peace-time morality had evaporated, chaos had reigned, Sanborn concluded his speech, when leaders had forgotten the injunction of King David, that "He that ruleth over men must be just, ruling in the fear of God."[20]

Part I

Slavery and the Politics of Law and Order
along the Border

Chapter 2

Before the Border War: Slavery and the Settlement of the Western Frontier, 1825–1845

Kristen K. Epps

In April 1843 Samuel Ralston, a slaveholder from North Carolina who had just recently settled in Independence, Missouri, penned a letter to his brother-in-law. "Missouri, at this time has more inducements for emigration than any state in the Union," he wrote. "Her soil [is] well adapted to the cultivation of the best products of the Country, and full of the richest minerals, her climate pure and healthy."[1] Ralston constantly advertised the land's great benefits, urging his family to "become a citizen of this State, and suffer me to request that you will use every exertion in your power to induce our friends in Carolina to do likewise."[2] The two enslaved adult women on Ralston's farm likely worked as domestic servants, while the three enslaved men labored in the fields, caring for the corn and hemp crops.[3] This household was only one of many to settle in western Missouri, illustrating that even from an early date, slavery was a visible part of life on what would become the Kansas-Missouri border.[4] Slaveholding Southerners looked westward, and as they settled into their new lives they transplanted the slave system into previously unknown territory, making slavery an integral part of this frontier narrative.[5] The establishment of a distinct Old South slaveholding culture among grounded elites may have encouraged putting down roots, but the narrative of Southern slaveholding was also defined by a constant push westward as slaveholders sought untainted land that held the promise of a bountiful harvest.

Slaveholding emigrants and their non-slaveholding allies who left the South in the 1820s, 1830s, and 1840s, clearly supported the expansion of the slave system into the West; the doctrine of popular sovereignty did not affect this region until 1854, but that did not mean that proslavery Southerners were ambivalent to the spread of the peculiar institution. Missourians were vehemently opposed to any stipulation that "involuntary servitude" be restricted. As one historian described it, "the Missouri position on slavery was never in doubt," for a variety of interconnected reasons.[6] Slaves contributed to the white family's well-being, financial success, and happiness by alleviating labor burdens, which was particularly important to families living on the western stretches of white settlement. Thus, slave labor carried with it tangible, material benefits to a slaveholding family. Slaveholding on the border, as in other Southern states, was also an outward sign of wealth; with this wealth came power, often in the form of political and legal authority as well as social standing. It was not uncommon for the leading men in the county—judges, mayors, sheriffs, and businessmen—to be slaveholders. Slavery also maintained a racial order that granted all whites, regardless of whether or not they owned slaves, a privileged status in the community based on their race. In the eyes of Southern whites, then, human property and the attendant social mores were essential to the success of their new ventures in the West. Of course, the enslaved members of the household, who usually had no say in the matter, relocated alongside the white family and carried with them their own culture. Unfortunately there are very few records of early slavery in western Missouri that come from the African American perspective, and there are virtually no extant records that record slaves' experiences in northern Indian Territory (what is now eastern Kansas), but a variety of public records and sources created by white individuals do show that the settlement of western Missouri and eastern Kansas included African American slaves. Their emigration signaled the beginning of a slaveholding culture.[7] The intimate lives of these enslaved individuals may lie in shadow, but the vast number of slaveholders who emigrated (including many who held prominent positions in border communities) nevertheless illustrates the existence of this labor system.

Of course, slavery on the Kansas-Missouri border would never rival the expansive plantations of the Deep South, but a small-scale system existed nonetheless. Small-scale slaveholding—which generally included a prevalence of abroad marriages, diverse forms of employment, close contact between slaves and slaveholders, and an active hiring market—was the dominant form of slavery in this region.[8] In fact, Missouri had "a larger percentage of slaves living on small holdings than any other state in the South" with the exception of Delaware.[9] According to the 1850 and 1860 censuses, which were the first to record the sizes of slaveholdings, approximately 86 percent of Missouri slaves lived in households with fewer than twenty bonds-people.[10] Although detailed census data for northern Indian Territory does not exist, it was sparsely populated and therefore consisted of small-scale slaveholdings as well.[11] Many of the earliest inhabitants in this region came from slaveowning states, particularly those in the Upper South (which includes Virginia, Tennessee, Kentucky, Missouri, North Carolina, and Maryland) where small-scale slavery had been well established for decades. As Diane Mutti Burke has concluded, these men and women "were demo-graphically prevalent and, therefore, ultimately had the greatest influence on the development of the new land."[12] The slaveholding culture of the Upper South, and its concomitant willingness to embrace bonded labor as a centerpiece of society, played a profound role in shaping life on the bor-der, even if not all emigrants were slaveowners themselves.[13] Indeed, as his-torian William Foley notes, "the cultural homogeneity of the incoming immigrants facilitated the perpetuation of emerging upper-south cultural traditions," and one such tradition was the use of bonded labor in small-scale enterprises.[14] Slaveholdings may have been small, but slavery was still a note-worthy component in this story of the Kansas-Missouri border.

Although slavery on the border first took root in the 1820s, at roughly the same time as Missouri's statehood, slavery's existence elsewhere in Mis-souri pre-dated any American settlement in the region. The slave system had existed in Missouri since the early 1700s, although the institution's reach did not yet extend westward to what would become the Kansas-Missouri border. French miners digging for silver and lead in southeast Mis-souri first used black slaves as early as 1719 or 1720. The scarcity of labor in this region made some French settlers contemplate the use of native slaves, but by the 1750s the French settlements along the Mississippi River (including new towns such as Ste. Genevieve) were generally committed to African slavery.[15] To regulate this growing labor force, French colonists instituted a "Black Code," or Code Noir. This code supported the philo-sophical and legal concept of chattel slavery, but nevertheless insisted that slaveowners treat their slaves as human property. The Code Noir stipulated that slaveholders must not separate families and "prepubescent" children on the auction block, nor work their slaves on holidays or the Sabbath, nor torture or kill their slaves. There were serious punishments in place, how-ever, for slaves who assaulted or stole from their master or mistress, making clear that the slaveholding community would not tolerate such defiance. Like other slave codes of the era, the Code Noir may have been the legitimate authority on such matters, but in day-to-day life slaveholders developed their own idiosyncratic practices and implemented the *Code Noir* as they saw fit.[16] Regardless of the potential flaws of implementation, this code illustrates that slavery did exist in Missouri while the region fell under French rule.

Likewise the Spanish, who gained control of the region in 1763 after the French and Indian War, continued to use slave labor. Unlike the French, who used slave labor to work in mines, slaves under Spanish control primarily worked in agriculture. Spanish rule came to an end, however, with Napoleon's invasion of Spain and his insistence that they return Louisiana Territory (which included the border region) to the French. Napoleon clung tightly to this last hope for an empire on the North American continent until the Haitian revolution of 1791 convinced him otherwise. With a violent slave uprising consuming his time, in 1803 Napoleon agreed to sell Louisiana to the United States for $15 million. President Thomas Jefferson, eager to gain control of New Orleans and the Mississippi River, happily obliged. In one fell swoop, the United States had doubled in size and now had control over what would become Missouri and Kansas.[17]

After the Louisiana Purchase of 1803, most of present-day Missouri shifted from French and Indian control into white American hands. Americans who had already put down roots along the Missouri and Mississippi Rivers grew concerned over the transfer of power, fearing that slavery might be outlawed. While Congress had allowed slavery's existence in the Territory of Orleans (the southern part of the Louisiana Purchase), the federal government had not dictated whether or not the peculiar institution would be sanctioned throughout the rest of the territory acquired from France (what was known as Upper Louisiana).[18] This was of particular concern because in 1800, blacks comprised 18 percent of the total population in Upper Louisiana.[19] Eventually the United States assuaged these doubts by instituting a slave code in 1804 that was actually stricter than the laws that had existed under French or Spanish rule. Thus, by 1805 when Upper Louisiana established its own territorial government, slaveholders in what would become Missouri had only grown more confident in their right to hold human property.[20]

The steady influx of new settlers into Missouri necessarily dictated discussion over when the territory might become eligible for statehood. On January 8, 1818, the Speaker of the House of Representatives presented the first petition for Missouri statehood. The ensuing debate over slavery's extension and Missouri's place in the Union would continue unabated for more than two years. In 1820 Congress finally approved the passage of the Missouri Compromise, which ensured that slavery would safely exist in Missouri. As a result, slaveholders throughout the Upper South continued to emigrate, bringing their slave property alongside the white members of the household.[21] Missouri's population grew dramatically in the ten years following statehood, rising from a total population of only 66,586 in 1820 to 140,455 in 1830.[22]

Meanwhile, slaveholders began reaching farther west, outside the major business centers of Ste. Genevieve and St. Louis on the Mississippi River, moving to small hamlets scattered throughout the Missouri river basin that ran through the center of the state. In 1808, William Clark (of Lewis and Clark fame) went farther west and built Fort Osage to establish American sovereignty in the region after negotiating treaties with the Osage bands that occupied western Missouri. The fort quickly attracted traders, military men, and other businessmen, and although it fell into decline immediately after statehood in 1821, the area became a favorite spot for slaveholders to settle.[23] This was the beginning of border slavery.

At roughly the same time as Missouri's statehood, French trade dynasties (like the Chouteaus) established fur warehouses located near the modern Kansas-Missouri border, where they employed slave labor. The governor of Spanish Louisiana had granted Pierre Chouteau and his brother, Auguste Chouteau, exclusive trading rights with the Osage, who lived in the border region. Pierre's son Francois grew up learning the fur business and established his own posts on the Kansas and Missouri Rivers. After he married Berenice Menard, also of French descent and a slaveowner herself, the young couple and at least one slave settled near Francois's primary fur warehouse, where the Missouri and Kansas rivers meet in the West Bottoms of modern-day Kansas City. They acquired other slaves during their time out West; Berenice purchased a slave girl named Nancy in 1837 as a playmate and personal attendant for her young daughter, Mary Brigitte. Presumably Nancy would also help out around the house, doing domestic chores contributing to the family's well-being in a concrete way, as well as a psychological one, since Berenice was often left alone when Francois traveled on business.[24]

The Chouteaus were the first to use slave labor at this location.[25] Chouteau's booming fur business made it necessary for at least one of his male slaves to assist at the warehouse. These warehouses were typically quite large, storing not only the pelts brought east from the Rockies, but also trade goods such as blankets, guns, coffee, beads, and other trinkets that could be traded for fine pelts. These warehouses were abuzz during the spring and summer, when local Native Americans, French trappers, and white locals congregated to do business. After an incoming shipment was unloaded from the canoe or wagon and negotiations for pay had concluded, Chouteau and his workers (including both enslaved and paid employees) would inspect, sort, and press the pelts and skins before wrapping them into packages.[26] His slaves and employees were responsible for keeping an accurate inventory of the European goods in addition to helping with other essential elements of the commercial enterprise.

Slaves owned by the Chouteau family, living at a busy crossroads where trappers, government officials, and local citizens congregated, had regular contact with other enslaved people. These posts and warehouses were popular meeting places; many of these visitors were slaveholders who likely brought slaves with them as they conducted business. For example, in 1832 a Methodist minister from Tennessee, James Porter, came out West to aid in the ongoing missionary efforts to emigrant Indian tribes located across the border in Indian Territory (present-day Kansas). He left his family, livestock, and thirty slaves at Chouteau's trading post while he procured land and a residence, finally settling in the Westport area on the Missouri side of the border.[27] No sources created by the Chouteau slaves have survived, but this example illustrates that they had some contact with other slaves living in the region, creating a sense of kinship that laid the framework for the vibrant black community that came after the decline of French influence.

The Chouteaus may have been the first to settle in present-day Kansas City, but after Francois's death in 1838, the small French settlement no longer served as a staging ground for the fur trade. Originally called the Town of Kansas, thanks to its location on the Kansas River, the town itself grew slowly in the 1840s, primarily because members of the town company could not agree on how to promote development. Although it played a key role in outfitting those traveling on the overland trails, it eventually became a regional center of business, banking, and real estate. In its early years it played second fiddle to more established communities like Westport and Independence, but during and after the Civil War it eclipsed its older neighbors and became a major center of regional commerce.[28]

The other significant settlement in the area (which today includes a number of modern suburbs of Kansas City) was Independence, Missouri. This major hub was officially founded in 1827, although a number of white settlers had lived in the area for decades at what was then called the Big Springs campsite. Daniel Morgan Boone, son of the famous Kentucky frontiersman, came to the area in 1825 when he became the agricultural agent at the Kaw Indian agency. James Shepherd, a slaveowner and cousin of William Clark, brought a group of emigrants out in 1821. In a letter to his cousin, Clark had described the area favorably, noting that "this is a beautiful land with fine soil, all the timber you would need for generations, high-growing grass for your cattle. Time is running short and settlers are pouring in and I beg you to come early."[29] Among these early families were future pillars of the Independence community, some of whom owned slaves. In fact, Shepherd himself was a slaveowner, and the enslaved men on his farm built both a temporary log house and a more permanent brick structure, in addition to their work at the Shepherd and Maxwell warehouse, a business that Shepherd began with his cousin Lucien Maxwell. Here slaves sold yokes, harnesses, and other equipment procured in St. Louis, as well as handmade rawhide whips that Shepherd had trained the slaves to make from leather received in the Indian trade. Other leaders in the Independence community were slaveowners as well, including many who had moved to town from nearby settlements like Sibley and Fort Osage. The Hudspeth, Hambright, and Chiles families had all emigrated from Kentucky, and members of each became leading figures in local government. Likewise Richard Fristoe, one of the first justices in the Jackson County Court and later a member of the state legislature, had moved to the Kansas-Missouri border in 1818 with his family and slaves.[30]

As white settlement in the region increased, especially after the Oregon and Santa Fe Trails opened, travelers began to use Independence as a starting point for their journey westward. Slaves were often at the center of the booming business of outfitting pack trains, assisting families in their covered wagons, and providing other services for the crowds of men, women, and children that flooded these towns. Both Samuel Owens, one of the most established traders on the Santa Fe route, and his associate Josiah Gregg were slaveholders who owned several trading centers in the vicinity of modern-day Kansas City and Independence. Robert Weston's shop in Independence had several outbuildings, including a wagon shop and plow factory, with much of the work there being conducted by slaves. Independence also had an iron foundry that used slave labor to forge nec-

essary items such as stoves, kettles, yokes, and agricultural implements.[31] By
the late 1840s Independence had declined as an outfitting center for overland travel, and Westport and Kansas City began to take its former place
of prominence.[32] However, Independence remained the county seat of Jackson County and would play a pivotal role in the Bleeding Kansas conflict
and the Civil War, having gained a reputation as a center of proslavery sentiment.

Neighboring Westport, another center for the overland trade, was
founded in 1833 at a site only a few miles west of Independence. As was
the case with Independence, there was a great demand for skilled wheel-
wrights and blacksmiths, and in some cases slaves were the ones who provided this service. These trading establishments provided a variety of
services, including wagon repairs, horse trading, and general merchandise.[33]
According to a later reminiscence, "in its heyday, Westport was a town to
be reckoned with. . . . Historians have estimated that no less than 40,000
westbound immigrants bought their final supplies and equipment here in
the years 1848, 1849, and 1850."[34] Leading members of the Westport community, including the McCoy and Chick families, were slaveowners who
promoted slavery's existence and made clear that slave labor was a boon to
the local economy. The town was not officially incorporated until 1857, at
which point it boasted at least 5,000 residents.[35]

In addition to those near Kansas City, other towns cropped up throughout the region, with many of these being founded by slaveholders. The site
of St. Joseph, Missouri, located in Buchanan County, was first settled in
1826, when Joseph Robidoux, a slaveholder and agent of the American Fur
Company, established a trading post. Most of these early settlers were
French-speaking traders from St. Louis, where Robidoux had been born and
where his father wielded influence in the fur business. The small settlement
primarily had contact with local natives, trappers, and traders, since this
land belonged to the Iowa and Sac and Fox tribes, and it was not part of
Missouri when it applied for statehood in 1819. In 1836, commissioners
signed treaties with these tribes to cede more land along the Missouri River,
a central waterway that was pivotal to transportation throughout the West.
This region became the Platte Purchase and included the current counties
of Nodaway, Holt, Buchanan, Andrew, Atchison, and Platte. When the
Platte Purchase officially became part of Missouri state, this area came more
clearly under American control and more emigrants moved to St. Joseph, a
promising spot for the overland trade that lay adjacent to rich farmland and

plentiful timber.[36] Rudolph Kurz, a Swiss artist who traveled throughout the American West, recorded the following description in his diary in 1848:

> St. Joseph, once the trading post of Joseph Robidoux, is situated at the foot of the Black Snake Hills on the left bank of the Missouri. Though the town was founded only six years ago there are evidences already of a rapidly expanding and flourishing city. . . . Upon my arrival the principal streets were much enlivened by fur traders and immigrants on their way to regions, as yet little known, in Oregon and California.[37]

Like other settlements on the future Kansas-Missouri border, St. Joseph was a thriving town in its early years.

Many of these early settlers in western Missouri were from Upper South states such as Tennessee and Kentucky, and while not all were slaveholders themselves, many residents supported the slave system. Slave labor was common, particularly in agricultural pursuits like the cultivation of hemp. According to one early history of Buchanan County, "many of the early settlers of the county, who brought their slaves with them, came from districts of Kentucky and Virginia, where hemp was a staple product. The first attempt to introduce the culture of this crop, which was soon to become the great staple of Buchanan, in common with other counties of the state, proved an unqualified success."[38] These white emigrants worked with Robidoux to found the city of St. Joseph in 1843, and slavery remained a part of city life until the Civil War. In 1846, there were approximately 967 residents of the city, and seventy of these were slaves.[39] The city continued to grow throughout the 1840s and 1850s, and after the discovery of gold in California in 1848, it soon became a central departure point for migrants traveling west.

North of present-day Kansas City there were other key settlements, including Weston in Platte County. The first settler to arrive in Weston was an army officer from Fort Leavenworth named Joseph Moore, who settled on the current site in 1837. Like its neighbors a few miles south, Weston was a station for emigrants and traders heading west. It also lay on the Missouri River and functioned as a key point on steamboat routes. According to a later reminiscence by local historian George Remsburg, "it had a splendid wharf, with big warehouses, where hemp and other products were stored and eventually shipped in great cargoes to St. Louis."[40] From its earliest days Weston was a proslavery town, and that reputation would follow it into the Bleeding Kansas period, when the town began to fall into decline.

The county seat of Clay County was Liberty, officially founded in 1822. Settlers had come to the area a few years earlier, drawn by the abundance of timber, clean water, and promising farmland. As one chronicler noted, "by far the greater portion of these settlers were from Virginia, Kentucky, Tennessee, North and South Carolina."[41] Because Liberty was not located on the river, much of the commercial business was conducted at Liberty Landing, about three and a half miles south of town.[42] Nevertheless, the town continued to grow. By 1846, there were three taverns, three blacksmiths, two milliners, five physicians, three saddlers, one rope factory, and a variety of other businesses and public institutions. Some of the leading merchants, like Robert and James Aull, were slaveholders, as were some of the county's first mill owners, William and Joel Estes, and Leonard Searcy, who owned a popular tavern.[43] Given the diversity of these businesses, it is likely that these slaves carried out a variety of tasks, including domestic duties and hospitality work.

Although agricultural work was certainly the lot for many slaves throughout the region, Clay County and Platte County were particularly known for their fertile soil and potential for unparalleled productivity. Staple crops such as corn, wheat, and oats were popular because they could feed one's family and livestock, or they could be bartered for goods at the local general store. But as emigrants continued their trek into the Missouri River valley in the late 1820s, farmers turned to two crops cultivated solely for profit: hemp and tobacco. Unlike cotton, hemp was well suited to the local climate and, more importantly, it was commonly grown in Upper South states such as Virginia and Kentucky, the very same states that contributed greatly to the population of Missouri. According to historian R. Douglas Hurt, in the early years of hemp cultivation the crop could sell for as much as $170 per ton in Baltimore and $225 in New York; as long as prices remained over $100 per ton, hemp was immensely profitable for Missouri farmers, even when considering the cost of transportation.[44] Prior to the mechanization of farming, most of this work was done by hand, and slaveholders called upon their slaves to furnish that labor. Slaves sowed seed; thinned out the seedlings; gathered seed needed for the next season; and plowed, hoed, and maintained the fields until August. During the fall harvest, on average each slave could complete one acre per day, using a scythe to cut down hemp stalks that ranged from six to eight feet tall.

Through the rest of autumn and into the winter, slaves gathered hemp into stacks to dry and then spread it again on the ground so the woody stems could rot and allow easier access to the fibers within.[45] In order to extract those fibers, slaves often used a device called a hemp brake, which had flat wooden boards that pounded the hemp until the fibers separated from the stalks. Hemp breaking was extremely difficult and taxing work, providing yet another incentive for planters to use slave labor.[46] When a slave exhibited a special knack for breaking hemp, it was a considerable asset.

Hemp cultivation bolstered the fledgling economy on the border, becoming a profitable enterprise for many Missouri farmers. Special commission houses cropped up throughout Missouri, including one in Liberty, and each of these facilitated an easier transfer of product to market. Furthermore, commission houses in St. Louis frequently posted advertisements in western counties such as Clay and Jackson, promising "to pay the strictest regard to the interests of those favoring him with their Business."[47] For farmers hoping to cash in on the rising demand for hemp, slaves (whether purchased or hired) were seen as a much-needed investment.

Tobacco also came to the Kansas-Missouri border alongside Southern emigrants who had previous experience with tobacco cultivation and processing. Like hemp, tobacco cultivation in Upper South states—especially states such as Virginia and Maryland—had been tied closely to the use of slave labor from a very early date. The New Orleans trade routes extended into the border region, where eager buyers encouraged farmers to raise tobacco that could be sailed down the Mississippi River and sold on the international market. Provided that the tobacco was carefully processed, it could sell for between $3.50 and $5.50 per hundred pounds in the antebellum period. Having been reared in that tradition, Missouri farmers maintained that slave labor was essential to the tobacco farm's economic well-being, with one slave potentially bringing in nearly $50 per acre.[48] One newspaper article from Clay County stated that "if the Farmers of Clay would go into the raising of Tobacco extensively it would induce 'Stemmers' to locate among us. Glasgow [Chariton County] and Camden [Ray County] are reaping great advantages from their Tobacco Manufactories."[49] By all estimations, tobacco was simply good for business. Tobacco cultivation increased throughout this period and would become central to the establishment of slavery in western Missouri.

As for the area west of Missouri—present-day Kansas—there were very few white or enslaved individuals living there at the time of Missouri statehood. This would change in 1830. In that year, Congress passed the Indian Removal Act, which moved Native American tribes from the eastern United States into a newly designated Indian Territory. Per the language in the act, the "United States will forever secure and guaranty to them, and their heirs or successors, the country so exchanged with them," a promise that would go unfulfilled.[50] A total of forty-five tribes, coming from lands reaching from the Great Lakes to the Gulf of Mexico, fell under the jurisdiction of this act, and at least twenty-five of those tribes were given land in what is today eastern Kansas, then known as northern Indian Territory.[51] These tribes included the Delaware, Shawnee, Wyandot, and Ottawa (among others), while tribes from the southeast such as the Five Civilized Tribes ended up resettling in southern Indian Territory, which is present-day Oklahoma.[52]

The sometimes-painful adjustments that were part and parcel of the "civilization" process—the process by which the U.S. government sought to destroy native culture and convert indigenous groups to white ways—meant that native peoples often developed a set of cultural values that blended Native American social practices with white concepts of racial difference. A few of these emigrant tribes had adopted white understandings of slavery, partly because of the civilization program's emphasis on assimilation, but also thanks to the influence of mixed-race tribal members, who bore the cultural heritage of both white Americans and indigenous peoples.[53] For native slaveholders, like their white counterparts, slavery became a sign of material wealth and privilege; as historian Annie Abel argued, "the acquisition of slaves enabled Native peoples to distance themselves from African-Americans in an increasingly racist white society."[54]

While it is difficult to track down the exact numbers, at least two prominent native leaders—William Walker of the Wyandot and Joseph Parks of the Shawnee—were part of the slaveholding class. Both men were of mixed-race ancestry and were prime examples of the "civilization" process, having embraced agriculture, animal husbandry, and English education for their children.[55] Parks led the Hog Creek band of the Shawnee to Kansas from Ohio in 1833.[56] According to one of Francis Parkman's travelogues, Parks owned a trading establishment in Westport, in addition to his large farm and "a considerable number of slaves."[57] By sometime in 1843 he had purchased his first slave, a sixteen-year-old man who worked as a blacksmith.[58] Henry Harvey described Parks as "a sensible, intelligent man who had long been engaged in public business. . . . His house has been the resort of all classes and the sums he bestowed on his people constituted a fortune, yet he remained a wealthy man."[59] Parks's role as chief required that he handle relations between the Shawnee and the U.S. government; he worked as an interpreter and also traveled to Washington, D.C., to negotiate more benefits for his tribe. His experience garnered him a great deal of influence and respect within Westport and surrounding communities.

William Walker and his fellow Wyandot came to the eastern border of Indian Territory toward the end of the removal process, in 1843.[60] Walker was of English, French, and native descent. His father, William Walker Sr., had been captured by the Delaware and taken from his home in Virginia while a small child, and later he was adopted into the Wyandot tribe. William Walker Sr. then married Catherine Rankin, a well-educated and refined woman of French and Indian ancestry. William Walker Jr. acted as a chief of the Wyandot and later as provisional governor of Nebraska Territory.[61] Like Parks, Walker "led the ideal life of a gentleman of ample means," which included a reliance on slave labor.[62]

In addition to the resettlement of Indian nations like the Wyandot and Shawnee, the Indian Removal Act ushered in a new emigration of white Americans, including Indian agents, military officers, traders, and Christian missionaries to the emigrant tribes. Although some white trappers, teamsters, military officers, and adventurers had set foot on Kansas soil before the act's passage, this new influx included not only whites, but also their bondspeople. Unlike the political environment present during Bleeding Kansas, these slaveholders brought slaves as a convenience to themselves and their families; popular sovereignty would not be in force until 1854, and at this point it was as yet unclear whether or not Indian Territory would indeed pass away to make room for further white settlement.

The earliest white settlement in the territory was Fort Leavenworth, which is in present-day Leavenworth County on a bluff overlooking the Missouri River.[63] The American fort was founded in 1827, but as early as 1744 the French had seen the advantages of this location and established an outpost called Fort de Cavagnial that existed for approximately twenty years; when the Lewis and Clark expedition passed through in 1801, they noted the ruins' coordinates. In 1827, thanks to the lobbying efforts of Missouri senator Thomas Hart Benton, the government established a new fort at the site to protect the overland trade. It was named after its founder, Colonel Henry Leavenworth.[64] According to Colonel George Croghan, who visited the site in 1829, "a good hospital has been erected, and four houses, originally intended to quarter one company each (though now occupied by officers), have been put up and very nearly completed, but there yet remains to be provided for officers' quarters, store houses, guard house, magazine, etc., etc."[65] As more military families arrived, a civilian settlement cropped up alongside the stockade.[66] Gradually, thanks partly to the Indian Removal Act and partly to its prime spot on the Missouri River, Leavenworth attracted visitors and residents from throughout the United States and foreign countries. By 1854, when the Kansas-Nebraska Act was passed, it was one of the most productive settlements in what would become Kansas.

Leavenworth's reputation as a proslavery town was cemented during the crisis of the territorial period, but prior to 1854 some of the leading figures at the fort were slaveholders. A central figure in the Fort Leavenworth community, if not the entire region, was a slaveholding Indian agent named John Dougherty, a Kentuckian who came to Fort Leavenworth in 1828. Indian agents who served as liaisons with the government thus shared in the fledgling establishment of slavery in Indian Territory and neighboring Missouri. Over the course of the next ten years, Dougherty tended to Indian business at Fort Leavenworth in addition to his work in St. Louis, headquarters of the western division of the Bureau of Indian Affairs. He later moved across the river to Clay County, Missouri. Dougherty was intimately involved with settling emigrant tribes on their new lands, mitigating land disputes, cracking down on alcohol trafficking, distributing annuity payments, and corresponding with the superintendent of Indian affairs, William Clark (of Lewis and Clark fame). According to a reminiscence recorded by Lewis Dougherty, John Dougherty "had a great influence with the Indian Tribes from the Missouri [River] to the Columbia [River] and assisted the United States in making many treaties. His Indian name in English was Controller of Fire Water, among his agency Indians."[67] In a land dominated by the Native American presence, Indian agents wielded measurable power.

Dougherty was not the only slaveowner to live at Fort Leavenworth in its early years. One prominent figure at the fort—Colonel Hiram Rich, the post sutler—owned slaves. Hiram Rich moved from Liberty to Fort Leavenworth in 1841 and later acted as a leader of the proslavery party during Kansas' territorial crisis.[68] Sutlers, who were responsible for supplying general goods to the military and civilians living at the fort, were "king over all territory tributary to a military post."[69] He was a particular favorite with

soldiers, since the back room of his store had beer and whiskey readily available for any man needing to drown his sorrows.[70] According to a newspaper article in the *Leavenworth Times*, "Few men, if any, in the west, were
better known than Colonel Hiram Rich, Fort Leavenworth's sutler. . . . He
knew everybody in the Platte Purchase and every Missourian who came to
this side never failed to call on the Colonel. The latch string was always
out, for those who were 'sound on the goose' in particular."[71] Rich served
the fort's inhabitants in this capacity until his death in 1862.[72] As sutler,
Rich controlled the flow of material goods into the fort and was a crucial
element in the fort's success.

According to some accounts, there were also army officers at Fort Leavenworth (although their names are not preserved in the records) who hired
slaves from neighboring Missouri.[73] Generally in these contracts, which
might be drawn up formally or scribbled on a scrap of paper, the slaveholder
rented their slave for a set period of time (usually a year) in return for a fee,
and the hiring party agreed to provide the hired slave with clothes, medical care, and adequate food and shelter. Hired slaves at Fort Leavenworth
likely worked in domestic roles if they were female, such as washing, cooking, and caring for the soldiers' homes, while male slaves may have worked
in the stables. Slave hiring, a business transaction that exchanged labor,
was prominent in the region, and thus was not confined to Fort Leavenworth.[74] According to historians Clement Eaton and Sarah Hughes, slave
hiring could allow greater flexibility within the slave system; it also allowed
those settlers who could not afford to purchase slaves an opportunity to
temporarily enter the slaveholding class and gain access to the benefits of
slave labor.[75] Slave hiring was so prevalent throughout the Upper South
that the chances of being hired out were three to five times greater than
the chance of being sold, and on the Kansas-Missouri border, the hiring of
both men and women occurred with some regularity, especially in the later
years of white settlement.[76]

One of the other early white American settlements in Indian Territory
was Fort Scott, located on the Fort Leavenworth–Fort Gibson military road,
which had been established in 1842 to preserve peace in the territory. Its
establishment was the culmination of almost a decade-long discussion about
how to address the increasingly volatile situation brewing on the Great
Plains. Not only were there conflicts between white settlers and indigenous
Indian tribes, but the arrival of new emigrant tribes also did not sit well
with native groups like the Osage who had previously controlled that ter-

ritory. At its founding, the post included three companies of dragoons to patrol the military road and supervise trade. The fort itself was abandoned in 1853, but as was the case with many military installations, a civilian settlement (this one populated primarily by proslavery supporters) had grown up alongside it.[77]

Hiero T. Wilson, a slaveholder from Kentucky, was one of the earliest and most prominent settlers at Fort Scott, having moved from Fort Gibson (in the southern part of Indian Territory, which is now Oklahoma), and opened up a sutler business with John Bugg in 1843. In 1844, shortly after this business venture began, Wilson hired an enslaved man named Louis (who was a slave of Samuel Moore), presumably to assist in the store, and about six months later he hired Nancy, a slave of Lieutenant R. E. Cochran. His store was a multistory structure located near the present-day intersection of National Avenue and Market Street. Thanks to his large inventory, Wilson catered to civilians and natives in addition to military personnel.[78] After about five or six years Bugg moved to California, and Wilson became the sole sutler in addition to serving as U.S. postmaster.[79] He also had significant contact with both the local emigrant tribes and those tribes who were native to the Missouri-Kansas border. In fact, during the fort's early period, from roughly 1843 to 1852, most of his business was conducted with tribes such as the Osage, who called him "Big White Chief."[80] After the fort was decommissioned, Wilson stayed on as a civilian, purchasing a former government building on the main plaza.[81] His influence was further recognized after the passage of the Kansas-Nebraska Act, when he served as one of the first officers for the county and as a trustee of the town of Fort Scott.[82]

One of the few surviving stories left by an enslaved person who lived in northern Indian Territory is that of Anne Shatteo, who worked as a hired slave for Hiero Wilson and then for Samuel Lewis, a trader who operated a post on the Neosho River. Her 1875 reminiscence notes that in 1847 her owner, John Crisp, gave her permission to hire out her own time. She worked at various trading posts, likely being responsible for business transactions as well as traditionally feminine tasks such as housekeeping, cooking, and childcare. Prior to her time in the territory, she had been enslaved in the household of George Douglas, who operated a farm and had a large family, making it likely that Shatteo had previous experience as a farm hand. Shatteo would eventually acquire her freedom in 1849.[83]

Although there was no official name for the settlement, a collection of proslavery settlers had also gathered at the location of the Shawnee

Methodist Mission, in present-day Johnson County, beginning in the 1830s. From 1832 to 1869, there were twenty-seven operating Protestant missions; with the exception of two missions, all of these were founded when Kansas was Indian country. The most well known of these missionaries was Thomas Johnson, a Virginian who set up the first Methodist mission to the Shawnee in 1830. In 1839, Johnson moved the mission to its present location (in present-day Johnson County, Kansas) and enlarged its ministry to include a manual labor school for Indian children that would form the basis of a thriving community. In a letter written in 1848, a young schoolteacher named Ann Archbold described the mission and its environs, explaining that the Johnson family, in addition to teachers and other necessary personnel, lived in "stately" brick houses. She continued, writing that "we have 70 cows belonging to the mission. A steam mill too where we get as beautiful flour as I ever saw. So you will see I am still in the land of plenty—yes to profusion. . . . I never had better accommodation anywhere. My washing is done in the best style by a black girl hired on purpose to wash for the Teachers and Preachers of the Institution."[84] After the Kansas-Nebraska Act, Johnson continued to promote slavery's expansion; by this point Johnson had at least six slaves, according to the territorial census taken in November 1854.[85]

A well-respected Indian agent named Richard Cummins lived on a farm adjacent to the Shawnee Indian Manual Labor School and employed at least a dozen slaves.[86] Cummins was officially the agent of the Shawnee tribe, although later he was placed in charge of all the Indian agents in the territory, and according to a reminiscence left by W. R. Bernard, Cummins's "large experience, tact, and influence with the Indians often made his services invaluable to the government."[87] As Indian agent, Cummins assisted missionary Thomas Johnson in establishing the Shawnee Methodist Mission. Cummins also supported the "civilization" process, which demanded that native tribes abandon their traditional ways and embrace white, European cultural mores. For some Indians—including those in Kansas and other tribes farther south, such as the Five Civilized Tribes—becoming fully assimilated into white culture entailed becoming an active part of the slave system, and it is quite plausible that as a slaveholder himself, Cummins supported natives' efforts to acquire human property.[88]

In summary, then, slaveholders played a pivotal role in settling the Kansas-Missouri border region, since during this early period slaveowners brought their entire household—slave and freeborn—and transplanted their native Southern culture onto the frontier. Not every emigrant was a slaveholder, but even non-slaveholding Southerners wanted to perpetuate this system. Establishing a white American presence in the region was no small task; slave labor was crucial to the success of the enterprise, whether it be a trading post, a farm, or a tavern. As a sparsely settled frontier, this region would become a paramount example of small-scale slaveholding, which often allowed for some flexibility within the system when it came to slaves' employment. Even with a paucity of sources from the African American perspective, there is no doubt that slaves helped build these frontier communities, both literally and figuratively. Progress was the leitmotif that bound white Americans, of all stripes, to the West, and for white Southerners, slavery's spread was part and parcel of that progressive spirit. The border region offers an excellent window into how small-scale slaveholding and Southern migration coalesced to influence the development of this frontier society, and thus lay the groundwork for the heated political and social strife of Bleeding Kansas and the Civil War. In these early years, where Southerners dominated the settlement process, slavery's place in the border region was a given. How quickly things would change.

Chapter 3

The Goose Question: The Proslavery Party in Territorial Kansas and the "Crisis in Law and Order"

Nicole Etcheson

Appeals to law and order suffused the secession crisis. Abraham Lincoln repeatedly invoked the law in his first inaugural address, promising to support the Fugitive Slave Law and insisting that he understood he had no "lawful right" to interfere with slavery in the Southern states. But he also insisted that "no State, upon its own mere motion, can lawfully get out of the Union." He specifically mentioned that the "resolves and ordinances" of secession were "legally void."[1]

But the very secession resolutions Lincoln condemned demonstrated the Southern sense that law and order had been violated for quite a long time by the North. South Carolina's declaration of the causes for secession accused the Northern states of having "deliberately refused, for years past, to fulfill their constitutional obligations." Northern states had passed laws in conflict with the Constitution, "the supreme law of the land." Northerners' alleged failure to abide by the Fugitive Slave Law was a principal grievance in all the secession resolutions, but Republican policy on the territories also was mentioned. Georgia's and Mississippi's documents condemned Northerners for hostility to slavery expansion, essentially "outlaw[ing]" Southern property in slaves. Texas specified that "infamous combinations of incendiaries and outlaws have been permitted in [the Northern] States and the common territory of Kansas to trample upon the federal laws, to war upon the lives and property of Southern citizens in that territory, and finally, by violence and mob law, to usurp the possession of the same as exclusively the property of the Northern States."[2]

As the Texans recognized, the Kansas issue had long exacerbated Southerners' sense that Northerners' antislavery activities defied the law. While

47

Southerners sometimes invoked "law and order" in the territories for political advantage, they became sincerely frustrated over the course of the Kansas controversy, with free-state defiance of the legal territorial government and Northern support for that intransigence. Michael W. Flamm, in his history of the law and order rhetoric of the 1960s, argues that such rhetoric certainly served partisan political purposes. But law and order appealed to voters precisely because crime was a growing problem.[3] Just so, Southerners by 1860 were not just finding excuses for secession but explicating a real grievance that events in Kansas had exacerbated. The proslavery party in Kansas Territory had seen itself as the upholder of "law and order" in the territory. Phillip S. Paludan, in a seminal article on the Civil War, argued that the North saw secession as a violation of law and order that had to be resisted. More recently, Russell McClintock has reiterated that Northerners' "passionate commitment to law and order" shaped their reaction to Fort Sumter.[4] This essay argues that the proslavery party in Kansas likewise saw free-soil actions as a "crisis in law and order" that had to be resisted. Although often depicted as flagrantly contemptuous of the law, the proslavery party actually sought to use the law as a tool to secure Kansas for slavery.

The law that organized Kansas Territory opened that territory to slavery under the formula of popular sovereignty, allowing the settlers to vote on whether to have slavery. Kansas and Nebraska territories were formed out of the northern part of the Louisiana Purchase, which had been closed to slavery under the Missouri Compromise of 1820. For that reason, Southern politicians had no interest in helping organize territories that would become free states. Missouri senator David Atchison made it clear that no territorial bill would pass unless it suited the South. In revising the Kansas-Nebraska Act, Illinois senator Stephen A. Douglas, chairman of the committee on territories, borrowed the popular sovereignty formula that had been used to organize Utah and New Mexico territories in 1850.[5]

Popular sovereignty meant that there would be none of what Missourian Claiborne F. Jackson called "infernal restrictions" on slavery in Kansas Territory. "If we can't all go there on the same [s]tring, with all our property of every kind, I say let the Indians have it *forever*," Jackson wrote. "They are better neighbors than the abolitionists, *by a damn sight*. If this is to become 'free nigger' territory, Missouri must become so too, for we can hardly keep our negroes here now."[6] Senator Robert Toombs of Georgia argued, in fact, that Northerners had not even lived up to the Missouri Compromise, having refused to apply it to territory taken from Mexico. According to Toombs, Northerners had acted in bad faith, claiming all the benefits of the Missouri Compromise and allowing none to the South.[7]

One powerful Missourian famously dissented from Kansas-Nebraska. While acknowledging that the Missouri Compromise was a law and therefore could be repealed, Thomas Hart Benton argued that to "statesmen" it was more than a law: it was a measure that had kept the peace for thirty years. Benton opposed the Kansas-Nebraska Act not only because it repealed the Missouri Compromise, but also because he did not believe popular sovereignty to be applicable to the territories at all. Benton saw the territories as minors, properly treated as wards of the government, and unready for self-government.[8]

Despite this dissent, Kansas-Nebraska passed with overwhelming Southern support. Only three of twenty-eight Southern senators voted against the bill, as did nine of eighty-four Southern congressmen. Most of the Southerners who opposed the bill either disliked the principle of popular sovereignty or feared stimulating sectional agitation.[9] Many of those who supported the bill were not enthusiastic about popular sovereignty, but saw Kansas-Nebraska as a gain for the South. While many Southern politicians would have preferred guarantees for slavery in the territory, popular sovereignty was at least better than prohibition, for prohibition implied that slavery was somehow unworthy of a place in the territories. Thus popular sovereignty removed the "stigma" the Missouri Compromise imposed on slavery.[10] However, Southern frustration would grow because, despite following the rules laid out by the Kansas-Nebraska Act, Southerners were denied the victory of a slave Kansas.

Popular sovereignty meant that the people—not Congress—would decide whether to have slavery. A Missourian might ask a newcomer if he was "sound on the goose," meaning did he support having slavery in Kansas? The "goose question" was a staple of local politics where regulating the noisy animals was a constant concern. Even before the Kansas-Nebraska Act, newspapers and cartoons had associated "the goose question" with the constantly recurring political debate over slavery. To be "sound on the goose" was to be proslavery.[11] One Missourian wrote, "Kansas is peculiarly fitted for slave labor—was intended for a Slave State, as [sic] will be so unless the South sleeps on its rights, and neglects its duty."[12] Given Kansas' geographic location, just west of slaveowning Missouri, Missourians naturally expected to dominate Kansas.

Significant migration from Northern states surprised the Missourians. In a famous story, David Atchison was on the wharf in Kansas City when a craft carrying a steam engine passed. Atchison asked his companions what it was and was told "a steam-engine and a steam-boiler." "You are all a pack of —— fools," Atchison replied, "that is a Yankee city going to Kansas, and by ——! In six months it will cast one hundred Abolition votes!"[13] Although organized emigration from New England gained notoriety, most of the settlers came from the Midwest. The first territorial census, which was completed in February 1855, showed that 46.5 percent of the territory's inhabitants were Missourians, 6.7 percent came from other Southern states, 27.4 percent were Midwestern and Mid-Atlantic state migrants, and 4.3 percent were New Englanders. The remainder had emigrated from abroad or were children born in the territory.[14] These census figures indicate that Missourians had a strong, but not unchallenged, position in the territory.

The Missourians' assumption, however, that popular sovereignty had delivered Kansas to them provoked them to overplay their very strong hand in the first Kansas elections. In the November 1854 election for territorial delegate, the proslavery candidate received 2,258 votes, whereas the remaining candidates received a total of 669 votes. A congressional investigation, as well as later historians, found that nonresidents had cast between 1,400 and 1,700 of the ballots. The census in February showed that there were 2,905 voters in Kansas Territory, yet proslavery candidates for the territorial lower house received over 6,000 votes. Again, a congressional investigation ruled at least 5,000 of those votes to be fraudulent.[15]

Although Missourians undoubtedly engaged in voter fraud, there were many excuses for Missouri voting. First, many Missourians who crossed to vote really did expect to become permanent settlers in Kansas. The census failed to count them because they wintered in Missouri, expecting to move onto their claims in the territory in the spring.[16] L. A. McLean recalled in 1857 that he had voted in the first territorial elections although he still lived in Missouri at that time. He intended to move to Kansas when the territory opened but did not do so until after the election. He crossed the border to vote, "being naturally anxious to have a voice in moulding the institutions under which I designed to live."[17] By 1857, he had lived two years in Kansas and had no regrets about that early vote. Secondly, as Kenneth Winkle has shown, residency and other requirements for voting were quite loose in the migratory society of the early nineteenth century. Newly

Border Ruffians invading Kansas. *The proslavery party was usually described as western "Border Ruffians" who were well armed, drunken, and invading Kansas Territory en masse to force slavery on its law-abiding inhabitants. Proslavery men, however, saw themselves as the upholders of law and order in the Territory. From William Cullen Bryant,* A Popular History of the United States, *1880 edition. Courtesy of the Kansas Historical Society*

arrived New Englanders voted as well, a fact Missourians were quick to point out.[18]

It is possible that cultural differences affected perceptions of the elections. Although election irregularities, including fraud and violence, were common throughout the country, they seem to have been more common in the South and West. In testimony before the congressional investigation, Missourians freely admitted that they had displayed bowie knives and guns aplenty on the day of the election. But they frequently denied that there had been violence. The more fastidious Easterners apparently found display sufficient. In many cases, free-soil judges and voters simply turned away from the polls rather than face armed—and often "well corned"—Missourians.[19] Missourian George H. Keller admitted, "There was some excitement during the election [on Nov. 29, 1854, for a territorial delegate], but nothing very serious—but a little knock-down—some of our old Kentucky election fights."[20] The Missourians apparently did not consider that interference with an election. Free-soil voters, especially New Englanders, did. Some free-soil voters testified that they simply left the polls, and saw others leaving the polls, because of discomfort with the election proceedings. Free-soil politician John A. Wakefield recalled that three Missourians offered to protect him; though personally secure from violence, he was still angered by the hostility toward free-soil voters.[21]

Some Missouri leaders such as Atchison felt that the threat to slavery was so severe that it justified bending a few rules. If a "set of fanatics and demagogues" who lived a thousand miles away could send people to Kansas, Atchison told a Missouri audience, "When you reside in one day's journey of the Territory, *and when your peace, your quiet and your property depend upon your action, you can, without an exertion, send five hundred of your young men who will vote in favor of your institutions.*"[22] Amos Rees, from Platte County, Missouri, helped organize voting parties before moving to Leavenworth himself. Rees described for congressional investigators how Missourians thought about voting in Kansas. According to Rees, after the passage of the Kansas-Nebraska Act, Missourians "always acted under the idea that slavery existed in the Territory." News that the New England emigrant movement was intended "to carry and control the elections upon the subject of slavery" caused "excitement" among Missourians: "It was looked upon as an intermeddling with our own business by foreigners." Public meetings in Missouri debated what to do. It was too late for many to emigrate and establish residence before the election. "Then it was finally determined upon, in view of the fact that large masses of men were reported to be on their way to the Territory in time for the March election, to send over our own men and meet them in their own way."[23]

Some Missourians, however, felt justified in voting because they thought Northerners were breaking the law and wanted to beat them at their own game. Missourians suspected that many free-soil voters had been "imported" by emigrant aid companies solely to vote and did not intend to remain permanently in Kansas.[24] John H. Stringfellow testified to the congressional committee that the organization of voters had been done specifically to counter the New England emigration societies. Voters came from

Missouri "to prevent or counteract illegal voting on the part of hired voters from the east and other free States."[25] After enumerating the ways that
Northern men violated the law by aiding fugitive slaves, one Missourian
argued that Southerners might be justified in bending a few rules themselves. Nonetheless, he insisted, "By the Nebraska Bill every man who happened to inhabit the territory at the time of the election was a qualified
voter. No man was ever sworn that he would not go away. There our men
stood behind the law."[26] A handbill entitled "Kansas Election!" similarly
interpreted the statute, arguing that one need not have property in the territory to be a voter: "By the Kansas act, every man in the Territory on the
day of the election is a legal voter, if he have not fixed a day for his return
to some other home."[27] Ultimately, Missourians argued they were true to
the law's letter and spirit.

Despite these justifications, it's clear that Missourians did engage in
election fraud of various kinds. They voted repeatedly, sometimes by chang-
ing hats and getting back in line. Judges of election altered the required
oaths for themselves and the voters or omitted oaths altogether.[28] Missourians did threaten free-soil voters. J. N. Mace was dragged from the
polling window by men yelling, "Kill the damned nigger-thief." Although
he survived the incident, he was struck with a club and threatened with a
knife and revolver.[29] But Mace was the exception. Most free soilers recalled
that they had desisted from voting or resigned as election judges because of
threats and intimidation. They had not let it come to a fight. Rev. Henry
B. Burgess resigned as an election judge at Tecumseh because he thought
the crowd outside was turning ugly at his insistence that voters swear the
required oath. Harrison Burson resigned as election judge at Bloomington
because Samuel J. Jones (later sheriff) gave the judges five minutes to resign
or be killed. Jones and the voters were unhappy that the judges planned to
administer the oath. The judges resigned. James B. Abbott resigned as election judge at Lawrence because he was consistently outvoted by the other
two judges as to the qualifications of voters.[30] N. B. Blanton didn't even
wait for election day to get scared. Proslavery voters told him the day before
the election that if he required the oath "their men would get enraged, and
maybe hang me; and that I had better resign."[31] The territorial governor set
aside the results in six election districts. In four of those districts, the governor specifically found problems with the administration of the oath to
the voters. Only one election was set aside largely for illegal voting. Despite
the governor's actions, the territorial legislature was overwhelmingly

proslavery. And despite the free staters' complaints, that legislature was the legally recognized body for the territory.[32]

Once it began business, the proslavery-dominated legislature proceeded to pass a slave code for Kansas Territory. Missourian Benjamin F. Stringfellow famously boasted, "They have now laws more efficient to protect slave property than any State in the Union."[33] These laws included the death penalty for inciting a slave rebellion, death or imprisonment at hard labor for helping a slave to escape, and imprisonment at hard labor for speaking or writing against slaveowning in the territory. Officeholders and attorneys were required to swear an oath to support the Fugitive Slave Law, as well as the Constitution and the Kansas-Nebraska Act, and antislavery jurors could not hear cases involving slaves.[34] Although they had bent the rules to gain control of these offices, once in control, the proslavery party in Kansas required strict observance of the law from free soilers.

The free soilers responded to the territorial legislature's election by forming an opposition movement, called the Topeka government. Arguing that the elections had been fraudulent, they declared the territorial legislature "bogus" and refused to acknowledge its authority as legitimate. Instead they held a convention at Topeka, wrote a constitution for a free state, ratified it in a popular election, and asked for admission to the Union. It was not granted, but for the next few years the Topeka movement would act as an extra-legal state government, electing a governor and legislature.[35]

It was this free-state movement that elicited strong calls of "law and order" from the proslavery party in Kansas. Spurred by the "crisis" caused by open defiance of the territorial legislature, the Law and Order Party organized in October 1855. Its resolutions called the Topeka movement "at variance with all law and entirely subversive of good order, is practical nullification, rebellious and treasonous."[36] Territorial politician John Calhoun argued at the Law and Order convention, "If the laws are unconstitutional they must be repealed at the proper tribunal. Until they are repealed they are the law of the land, and should be enforced." But, in the same speech, Calhoun and his listeners made it clear which kinds of laws he would find most congenial: "Shall abolitionists rule you? (No! Never! &c.) Give them all they demand, and abolitionism becomes the law of the Government. You yield, and you will have the most infernal Government that ever cursed a land. I would rather be a painted slave over in the State of Missouri, or a serf to the Czar of Russia, than have the abolitionists in power. (Deafening Cheers.)"[37] Governor Wilson Shannon called the free-state movement an "armed organization to resist the laws."[38] In late November, some citizens of Leavenworth planned to organize a less proslavery version of Law and Order, but their efforts were overtaken by the events of the Wakarusa War and such a milder Law and Order movement never emerged. Eventually, at a convention in January 1857, the Law and Order Party changed its name to the National Democratic Party and excluded all but proslavery men. When the Democratic territorial convention met that summer, it reiterated that Democrats were the "Law and Order party."[39]

It should be pointed out that territorial governor Wilson Shannon's participation in the Law and Order movement was no accident. Shannon was an Ohio Democrat and presidential appointee. Proslavery legitimacy in the territory derived in part from the fact that national officials, starting with presidents Franklin Pierce and James Buchanan, agreed that the proslavery forces were those of "law and order." Pierce immediately dubbed the territorial legislature elected in March 1855 as "legitimate" and the Topeka movement as "revolutionary" and potentially "treasonable."[40] During the guerrilla fighting of the summer of 1856, Kansas territorial officials identified the split in the territory as between "Law & Order men" or "law abiding men who . . . support the laws, and respect the constituted authorities of the land" and those who did not, the free staters.[41] Secretary of War Jefferson Davis agreed, instructing the army, "The only distinction of parties which, in a military point of view, it is necessary to note, is that which distinguishes those who respect and maintain the laws and organized government from those who combine for revolutionary resistance to the constituted authorities and laws of the land."[42] A later territorial governor, John Geary, pointed out that only proslavery men belonged to the Law and Order movement, but those men denounced Geary for not understanding that the free-state men were "outlaws" and their opponents were the upholders of law. When Geary seemed confused on this point, a proslavery newspaper called him no longer a friend of the law. Some settlers advocated a move towards a "Peace and Order" movement in response to the anarchy of the summer of 1856. Geary's successor, Robert J. Walker, invoked the phrase in a letter to the Buchanan administration. But the two sides were too polarized to compromise.[43]

Proslavery Kansans and their allies vilified the free-state movement as revolutionary and treasonous. A Missouri newspaper called the members of the Topeka legislature "outlaw leaders."[44] South Carolina senator A. P. Butler promised to make a speech to "vindicate the Border Ruffians," as

Missourians who crossed into Kansas Territory were called. Butler planned to cite house burning and violence by the "Abolitionists" as evidence of their "treason."[45] A Leavenworth man wrote that there was "no middle ground" between "the friends of the Constitution and laws" and "the enemies of the Constitution and laws."[46]

Throughout the era of Bleeding Kansas, the proslavery party insisted that the fact that they followed the rules gave proslavery victories in Kansas legitimacy. The proslavery side held to this even as it became increasingly clear that the free staters were a substantial number. If popular sovereignty was to reflect the will of the people, how could the proslavery party ignore the free staters? Because the free staters did not acknowledge the authority of the territorial government, the proslavery party deemed them lawless and unworthy of representation. The Pierce and Buchanan administrations supported the proslavery party in this interpretation. One historian has noted Pierce's insistence on enforcing even unpopular laws such as the Fugitive Slave Act. Certainly, Pierce asserted that he would use his powers "to support public order in the Territory; to vindicate its laws, whether Federal or local, against all attempts of organized resistance." Problems with the Mormons in Utah Territory convinced President Buchanan that lawlessness in the territories was a serious concern. In his first annual message, Buchanan announced his intention "to restore the supremacy of the Constitution and laws" in Utah. The historian David Grimsted accuses Democrats of relying on a "veneer of legality" to justify their suppression of the free staters, but for Southerners and national officials, Kansas was a part of a larger pattern of disregard for the law and the government's authority.[47]

The most serious collisions in territorial Kansas—the Wakarusa War and the Sack of Lawrence—arose out of efforts by the Law and Order Party to enforce the territorial government's authority on defiant free staters. The Wakarusa War occurred when a settler was murdered in a quarrel over a land claim. The murderer was a Missourian and the victim loosely affiliated with free-state men. Free-state militia took vigilante action against local Missouri settlers. When Sheriff Samuel J. Jones attempted to arrest Jacob Branson, with whom the murder victim had lived, for disturbing the peace, a free-state mob liberated Branson. Jones called upon the territorial governor for help.[48]

Throughout the Wakarusa War, Governor Wilson Shannon acted in the name of the law. He informed the president of the threat posed by large bodies of armed men organized for "resistance to the laws by force." After describing how Jones had lost his prisoner, Shannon linked the incident to the larger Topeka movement. "The time has come when this armed band of men, who are seeking to subvert and render powerless the existing government, have to be met and the laws enforced against them, or submit to their lawless dominion." If "Southern men" (whom Shannon equated with "the law-and-order party of the Territory") were not assured that they were protected "against the lawless acts of this armed association," they would react with force as well and the territory would spiral out of control. "[W]e are standing on a volcano," Shannon said. Shannon called upon the people of the territory to aid in suppressing the lawless free staters, called out the territorial militia, asked the army for help, and reassured Sheriff Jones that aid was on the way.[49]

Shannon was indeed right that Missourians were outraged. George W. Clarke appealed to Shannon, on behalf of the "law-abiding men," to disarm the free staters whose weapons were used "for the special purpose of resisting the laws."[50] In his diary, Missouri lawyer William Barclay Napton called the Wakarusa War "a serious collision" between the free-state and proslavery parties. The free staters had "refused obedience to the territorial laws and the Governor has called out a military force to enforce them."[51] A Lexington, Missouri, man who objected to the "rash and unwise [proslavery] legislation in Kansas," nonetheless felt that laws once passed should be obeyed. He thought the Missourians were right to go into Kansas to help restore the law.[52]

Missourians reacted so enthusiastically that Shannon and the territorial militia officers had trouble controlling the army that massed around Lawrence, Kansas, in late 1855. After negotiations with the free-state leaders, Shannon sought to disperse the force. Again, he appealed to law and order. Shannon notified the militia commanders and Sheriff Jones that there would be no further resistance to the laws.[53] Thus satisfied, and shivering in their camps during a cold spell, the Missourians left and the Wakarusa War ended.

In the spring of 1856, the proslavery party again felt that it had a legal basis on which to move against the free staters at Lawrence. Sheriff Jones still had outstanding warrants against those who had rescued Branson from his posse. When Jones came to Lawrence in April 1856, he found that free staters there resisted arrests. Soldiers had to be brought in to aid the sheriff in his duties. Members of Jones's posse recalled that when Lawrence citizens had asked for Jones's authority, his reply was the "laws of Kansas Territory." The crowd insisted that they did not recognize such laws. While Jones camped in his tent outside town, someone shot him.[54] "Continued Resistance to Our Laws!!" was the headline accompanying news of the attack on Jones in a proslavery newspaper.[55] The posse that Jones had summoned, excited by the resistance to their authority and the assassination attempt, then carried out the "Sack" of Lawrence in which the town's hotel and newspapers were destroyed.[56]

That did not end the effort to impose law and order on the free staters. In the summer of 1856, a grand jury indicted the free-state government officials for treason. Charles Robinson, one of the leaders of the free-state Topeka movement, was arrested while traveling through Missouri en route to the East. Former territorial governor Andrew H. Reeder, a convert to the free-state cause, escaped arrest and went on a lecture tour in the East, although proslavery men fumed that he should be arrested. For a time it appeared that the treason cases would be dropped, but in the summer of 1857, Charles Robinson was tried. Robinson had been elected state governor of Kansas by the free-state Topeka movement and was accused of usurping office. The defense argued that since Robinson had never claimed to be governor of Kansas territory, and as the prosecution itself claimed there was no state of Kansas, Robinson had usurped nothing. How could he be guilty of usurping that which the prosecution admitted did not exist? The jury apparently couldn't figure that out either and voted to acquit. The failure to convict Robinson ended the treason trials.[57]

Although treason prosecutions failed as a weapon against the free-state movement, the *Dred Scott* decision seemed to further buttress the South's legal position. Southerners "took this decision to mean that the property guarantee of the fifth amendment automatically extended the shield of federal protection over slavery in all national territories."[58] The *Richmond Enquirer* noted that the *Dred Scott* decision meant "the territory of Kansas belongs alike to the man of Massachusetts and to the citizens of Louisiana or Virginia. It is the common domain of all the United States, and, as such, the people of each and every State have an irrefutable right to transfer themselves and their *property* into it."[59] Even as late as 1858, when it was clear the settlers in Kansas would never accept slavery, a proslavery newspaper in the territory urged that the *Dred Scott* decision made it impossible for the territorial legislature to abolish slavery.[60]

It was the Lecompton crisis of 1857–1858 that revealed the contortions "law and order" required of the proslavery party. In the summer of 1857, a constitutional convention met at Lecompton. Free-state voters, alleging they feared more fraud at the elections, had boycotted the selection of the convention delegates. The Lecompton convention was thus heavily proslavery. The constitution they wrote provided for Kansas to be a slave state. But the Lecompton delegates were under heavy political pressure. Free staters captured control of the territorial legislature in elections held while the convention was sitting. Some observers speculated that the convention might then concede defeat for slavery in Kansas. Instead, the proslavery delegates' intransigence increased: they viewed the Lecompton Constitution as the last chance to ensure slavery in Kansas. Meanwhile, the Buchanan administration had promised that any constitution would be submitted to the voters, and a new territorial governor, Robert J. Walker, was heavily lobbying for that to happen. As a result, the Lecompton delegates submitted the constitution to the voters for ratification. But the constitutional convention did not allow voters to accept or reject the constitution in its entirety; voters could only choose between Lecompton "with slavery" or "without slavery." Lecompton "with slavery" meant that Kansas would be a slave state. Lecompton "without slavery" meant that future slave importations into Kansas would be barred, but that slave property already in the territory could legally remain.[61]

Free staters argued that the submission formula denied them a chance to totally reject Lecompton. They boycotted the ratification election, which passed Lecompton "with slavery" with over 8,000 votes, compared to less than 1,000 votes for Lecompton "without slavery." Free staters held a separate ratification election, allowing voters to accept or reject Lecompton in its entirety, in which the constitution was voted down by over 10,000 votes.[62]

The Buchanan administration, however, was under intense pressure from Southern Democrats to endorse Lecompton. President Buchanan would do so, arguing that Lecompton was the result of a legal process, and ignoring the free-state referendum. Buchanan submitted the constitution, "with slavery," to Congress, saying that the Lecompton convention was "legally constituted."[63] Attorney General Jeremiah Black said Lecompton "was the lawful work of a lawful body."[64]

Southerners agreed: Lecompton was legal. Although Northerners called Lecompton a "fraud," Southerners pointed out that the decision whether to submit the constitution at all properly belonged to the convention. Technically, Lecompton was perfectly legal. Senator Robert Toombs argued that Lecompton was a legal constitution whereas Topeka was not. Senator William King Sebastian of Arkansas similarly endorsed the convention's independence and repeated that the proslavery party in Kansas was the law and order party. Congressman F. K. Zollicoffer of Tennessee called the Lecompton proceedings, which he reviewed at length, "regular." Again, he contrasted them to the free-state movement's "revolutionary" and "traitorous" proceedings. Congressman John W. Stevenson of Kentucky argued that the Lecompton constitutional convention had been perfectly fair to the free staters.[65]

Famously, it was during the Lecompton debates that Stephen Douglas broke with the Buchanan administration. Until 1857, the author of the Kansas-Nebraska bill would have agreed that Kansas' problems resulted more from the "revolutionary movements" of the free staters than from the misdeeds of the proslavery party.[66] In the spring of 1856, Douglas described the free-state actions as constituting "an act of rebellion against the Constitution and laws of the country."[67] But he could not accept Lecompton. Douglas insisted that the document perverted popular sovereignty by attempting to circumvent the people's will and force "an obnoxious Constitution" on Kansans.[68] He argued that unless the entire constitution was submitted to territorial voters, it was not legal.[69] The Democratic Territorial Convention in Kansas followed Douglas, resolving that the refusal to submit the constitution violated the Democratic principle of the " right of the people to self-government." They called for another constitutional convention.[70]

Congress resolved the political crisis Lecompton caused by resubmitting the constitution to Kansas voters. The pretext for resubmission was a change in the land grant Kansas was to receive, but in reality Kansas voters were being given a chance to reject Lecompton. To induce them to vote in favor of Lecompton, voters were told that if they defeated Lecompton, they would lose the promised land grant and not be able to apply for admission to the Union until the territory had a population equal to that needed for a member of Congress. The wait this stricture would impose was estimated to be two years. Congressman Alexander Stephens of Georgia masterminded this formula, but it took the name of Indiana congressman William English in order to appeal to the crucial bloc of Northern Democratic congressmen.[71]

The English bill put Southerners in a bind. It was clear that if the Lecompton Constitution was resubmitted, Kansans would vote it down.

For that reason, many Southerners were initially firm against resubmission. Stephens lobbied his colleagues heavily. But there were pressures to preserve the Democratic Party and alleviate the tensions in the country. Congressman Guy M. Bryan of Texas felt compelled to list his objections to the English bill, but then said he would suppress those objections and vote for the bill in the name of Southern unity. His colleague from Alabama, Eli S. Shorter, said pretty much the same thing. Senator Toombs was less reserved and "heartily" endorsed the bill as necessary because of the issues raised by the land ordinance.[72] Georgia governor Joseph E. Brown wrote that he was happy with the resolution of the Lecompton issue: "[The] South has lost nothing of principle" with the English bill.[73] After the bill's passage, crowds serenaded the White House and heard speeches from Senators Robert Toombs of Georgia and William Gwin of California and Congressmen James B. Clay and John W. Stevenson of Kentucky and John Letcher of Virginia.[74]

Basically the English bill was a face-saving way for the South to back down after its insistence on the Lecompton Constitution. Although rejecting Lecompton meant indefinitely postponing statehood, the referendum resulting from the English bill soundly defeated Lecompton by a vote of 11,300 to 1,788. Free staters now had control of the territorial legislature and, paying no attention to the *Dred Scott* decision, set about abolishing slavery in the territory. When Democrats met in convention in 1859, they abandoned the law-and-order proslavery agenda. Instead, they resolved that Kansas would come in as a free state and that they would not distinguish between free-state and proslavery men.[75] One Kansas Democrat reported that the key to the party's future in the territory was to welcome the free-state Democrats despite the wishes of "the original democrats,—(particularly the proslavery wing)."[76]

Missourian John H. Stringfellow was the rare proslavery man who admitted defeat openly. During the Lecompton controversy, Stringfellow wrote President Buchanan to express his opposition to the proslavery constitution. He did not believe that Lecompton represented the people of Kansas—he blamed that on the failure of Southern men to move to the territory with their slaves—and feared that the effort to impose it would threaten the Union. But he located free-state success in their resistance to the laws: "The Free State men declared they would nullify all our laws, *and they did*, and resisted even to the Shedding of Blood."[77] In 1859, a Missouri newspaper noted that Kansas was ready to apply for admission with a constitution (its fourth) that should be acceptable to Congress. The editorialist favored admission and espoused a "let bygones be bygones" philosophy.[78]

Throughout the territorial crisis, Southerners feared that in one sense the free staters did obey the law: the higher law. In debates over the 1850 compromise, New York senator William H. Seward had insisted that "there is a higher law than the Constitution" in arguing against slavery extension in the territories. "Higher law" became a catchphrase among white Southerners capturing their sense that Northerners often followed their consciences rather than legal statutes and constitutional rulings concerning slavery. In a campaign speech in 1856, Senator R. M. T. Hunter of Virginia pointed out that the free-state movement had no sanction from Congress or the territorial legislature. If accepted, it would sanction the "higher law" doctrine and allow the subversion of existing governments. Speaking in Poughkeepsie, New York, Hunter pointed out that such a doctrine was as dangerous to the peace of the North as to that of the Southern states.[79]

John Brown's raid on Harpers Ferry, Virginia, was just such an example of the dangers of the higher law. Speaking after John Brown's execution, the abolitionist Wendell Phillips explicitly rejected "law and order" as "a base motto," preferring "God and Justice."[80] After the raid, William Bigler of Pennsylvania told his friend James Buchanan that "it was for traitors like he that you were asked to permit the laws to be trampled underfoot."[81] In Bigler's mind, Brown was associated with lawlessness in the territory. The majority report of the congressional committee that investigated Harpers Ferry (called the Mason report after Virginia senator James M. Mason, the committee's chairman) noted that Brown "was extensively connected with many of the lawless military expeditions" in Kansas Territory.[82] For Southerners, of course, what made Brown's lawlessness so frightening was the latent potential violence of the slave revolt he tried to instigate.[83]

Ironically, the lawless free staters of Kansas were admitted to the Union during the secession crisis that, as Paludan noted, seemed to Northerners lawless. Some Southerners were still quibbling about the technicalities of the free-state Wyandotte Constitution Kansans submitted in the winter of 1860–1861. But when Southerners left Congress as their states seceded, Kansas was easily voted in. President Buchanan had the honor of signing the bill for Kansas statehood on January 29, 1861.[84]

Statehood made the free-state movement, long accused of revolution, the legal government of Kansas. Charles Robinson, once the defendant in a treason trial, became Kansas' first state governor. Kansas statehood coincided with what Northerners saw as the lawlessness of secession. William W. Freehling argues that the South's combination of republicanism for whites and racial domination of blacks could not coexist with true majority rule. Preserving white supremacy would always require Southern whites to balk at majority rule, if that majority threatened slavery. Freehling details both the decades-long effort of fire-eaters to persuade other Southerners that slavery was not safe in a Union that tolerated antislavery sentiment as well as the successful plotting of the secessionists during the winter of 1860–1861. Freehling acknowledges the frustration white Southerners felt at being denied a slave Kansas.[85] Southerners had followed the law in Kansas Territory. They had moved there when the territory opened, voted in its elections, had their victories certified by the territorial officials, and faced defiance by the losers that continued throughout the territorial period. The Kansas-Nebraska Act had not brought the South additional territory, but a frustrated sense that Northern lawlessness would block slavery at every turn.

Chapter 4

"Nigger-Worshipping Fanatics" and "Villain[s] of the Blackest Dye": Racialized Manhoods and the Sectional Debates

Kristen Tegtmeier Oertel

On the afternoon of May 22, 1856, Massachusetts senator Charles Sumner sat at his desk on the floor of the Senate, busily affixing stamps to copies of his speech, "The Crime against Kansas," which he had delivered three days before to his colleagues. In this controversial speech, Sumner used sexually explicit metaphors to depict the depredations committed in Kansas by proslavery settlers. He singled out South Carolinians in particular, and used Senator Andrew Butler as an example to prove his point. He argued:

> The Senator from South Carolina has read many books of chivalry, and believes himself a chivalrous knight, with sentiments of honor and courage. Of course he has chosen a mistress to whom he has made his vows, and who, though ugly to others, is always lovely to him; though polluted in the sight of the world, is chaste in his sight. I mean the harlot, Slavery. For her, his tongue is always profuse in words. Let her be impeached in character, or any proposition made to shut her out from the extension of her wantonness, and no extravagance of manner or hardihood of assertion is then too great for this Senator.[1]

Sumner implied that Senator Butler engaged in illicit sexual activity, both extramarital and interracial, by representing slavery as his "black mistress." Butler, an old man and a reputed drunk, was not present to hear Sumner's acerbic comments, but his cousin and comrade from South Carolina, Representative Preston Brooks was. Brooks took it upon himself to avenge the personal assault on Butler's character, and he walked up to Sumner at his desk that afternoon in May, addressed the senator briefly, and then proceeded to bludgeon him with his gutta-percha cane until Sumner stumbled, bleeding and half-conscious, into the center aisle, where he collapsed and was finally rescued by several bystanders.

The fallout from the caning bombshell quickly spread across the country, and reports of the event stoked the fires of sectionalism, embers that needed little fuel in the spring of 1856 after news of Bleeding Kansas punctuated the already tense political atmosphere. The newspapers immediately lauded their respective heroes: Southern papers praised Brooks for preserving his state's honor, and Southerners across the region endorsed his violent attack by sending him dozens of gilded canes to replace the one that had broken on Sumner's head. Northerners, on the other hand, expressed outrage at the incivility of such an attack and questioned Brooks's so-called honor and his manhood. The *Boston Courier* claimed, "There is no chivalry in a brute. There is no manliness in a scoundrel."[2]

The divergent responses to Sumner's caning and to the events surrounding Bleeding Kansas reveal two opposing definitions of manhood at midcentury. Most Southerners embraced a martial manhood, one that touted violence as a suitable, indeed a necessary, tool used by honorable men to settle disputes; many Northerners, however, advocated a more restrained manliness, one that controlled the inner brute and sought conflict resolution through civilized debate rather than fisticuffs. But the reports of Sumner's caning also reveal a common thread that tied these two variant manhoods together. Just as Sumner maligned Butler by linking him with the "harlot," slavery, Northern and Southern men attempted to degrade each other's masculinity by literally and metaphorically blackening it. White men, North and South, jealously guarded their whiteness and viewed any threat to their racial identity as an attendant threat to their gender.[3]

The scholarship on gender and men has ballooned since Anthony Rotundo published his path-breaking study *American Manhood* in 1993. Rotundo charts the evolution of manliness from its communal roots in the colonial era, to "self-made manhood" in the Revolutionary period, to a "passionate manhood" that arose in the late nineteenth and early twentieth centuries. The individualistic and self-made man who emerged from the smoke of the Revolution gradually gave way to a more violent, "primitive" manliness by the dawn of the twentieth century. Rotundo and scholars such as Gail Bederman have argued that this call for a regeneration of man's inner savage was in response to the feminization of society in the nineteenth century; women, with their newly minted powers of civilization and their high-minded morality, had used their feminine talents to begin reforming society's ills and also to force their men to repress their competitive, aggressive spirits. Men like Teddy Roosevelt rebelled against this "moral governorship" and rode roughly across places like San Juan Hill in Cuba to assert their distinctly masculine, hard-hitting manhood.[4] While Bederman's and Rotundo's analyses of manhood provide useful models to help scholars begin to understand the complex historical forces that impacted gender roles, they fall short in two ways: first, their evidence stems largely from Northern, middle-class sources, which causes them to locate the rise of "passionate masculinity" in the late nineteenth century when in fact it existed in the South and West much earlier; and two, Rotundo in particular ignores the existence of African American men and the issue of race. These oversights beg the questions: How did black manhood impact white men's understanding of their gender identities? How did the sectional debate over slavery challenge white manhood? How did white men use racism to attack each other's manliness?

As Northern and Southern men battled over slavery in the West and as newspaper editors and public citizens debated the meaning of Sumner's infamous caning, they carefully crafted a manhood that was civilized, assertive, and virile without being either too brutish or too effete. To be brutish and animalistic was to be like the savage slave or the actual savage, the black and red men who peopled the plains and plantations and who had to be civilized or mastered by white men. But a manhood that was too restrained risked being defined as feminine, weak, and passive, adjectives more often affixed to women and black Sambos, not white men. The sectional debates at midcentury reveal how both Northern and Southern white men manipulated popular anxiety about the racial Other to fight the battles over slavery's expansion—to raise the fearful specter that blackness and/or redness was overpowering whiteness.[5]

Now let us return to Senator Sumner, who lay bleeding and permanently crippled in his Washington, D.C., home, and who came to symbolize all abolitionist men and many Northern men during that spring in 1856. Some Southerners initially doubted the severity of Sumner's injuries, claiming that the senator was "playing possum." A paper in Richmond, Virginia, did not believe that

the well-deserved *gutta-perching* [Sumner] received was of so severe a character as to detain him in confinement for more than a week. But we believe it is a miserable Abolition trick from beginning to end—resorted to keep alive and diffuse and strengthen the sympathy awakened for him among his confederates at the North. Nigger-worshipping fanatics of the male gender, and weak-minded women and silly children, are horribly affected at the thought of blood oozing out from a pin-scratch.[6]

Some reports, however, acknowledged the damage done to Sumner and gleefully highlighted Sumner's inability to defend himself from Brooks's cane. The *Charleston Mercury* concluded that "Sumner was well and elegantly whipped, and he richly deserved it. . . . [He] is much the largest and most athletic man, and, had he resisted, might have defended himself."[7]

Southern papers accused the "Black Republicans" of falsely recasting the event as a cowardly attack on a helpless, innocent man and insisted that Sumner's outrageous speech provoked a violent response. In fact, Brooks himself argued that the speech was so egregious that it did not merit the "honorable" response of a duel. The *Richmond* (Virginia) *Whig* noted that "the brave and honorable man, who, hedged about with privileges, insults an individual, will make reparation . . . according to the usages of gentlemen; but the blackguard, who does the same thing, being insensible to the dictates of honor, can only be reached by the cowhide or bludgeon."[8] Sumner, a blackguard and a card-carrying, "nigger-worshipping" Black Republican, did not possess honor or the right kind of manhood—instead, his gender identity was equated with blackness, a manhood that could be controlled only by using a "cowhide or bludgeon." Sumner was being mastered just as Southerners mastered black men.

Recent scholarship on black masculinity and plantation patriarchy helps us understand why and how Southern white men attempted to spin the Sumner caning as a proper manly response to abolitionist attack. Darlene Clark Hine and Earnestine Jenkins label black manhood as a "resistant masculinity," one that spoke to "an evolving black male consciousness that linked freedom to black men's radical resistance."[9] The essays in Clark Hine and Jenkins's reader illustrate the numerous ways black men consistently resisted white attempts to emasculate them and to deprive them of their rights as men: to protect and provide for their families and to defend their homes. One of the most obvious examples of resistant masculinity in the border region was the runaway slave. Napoleon Simpson, a Missouri slave, escaped from his Jackson County plantation and fled through Kansas to

Iowa, only to return six months later to retrieve his wife and children. But as he returned to his old plantation, the local slave patrol caught wind of his intentions and attempted to capture him. Simpson illustrated his bold resistance by using a Sharps rifle to violently defend himself and shot one of the slave catchers; his quest for his family's freedom ultimately failed, however, after one of his pursuers shot and killed him.[10]

As enslaved men like Simpson worked to free their families from bondage and endured the violence and injustice of slavery, free blacks like Dr. John Rock identified the resilience and strength exhibited by black men and weighed these against the less powerful "biological" features of white men: "When I contrast the fine tough muscular system, the beautiful rich color, the full broad features, and the gracefully frizzled hair of the Negro, with the delicate physical organization, wan color, sharp features and lank hair of the Caucasian, I am inclined to believe that when the white man was created, nature was pretty well exhausted."[11] Similarly, David Walker in his famous *Appeal* claimed "that one good black can put to death six white men," and called upon his enslaved brothers to violently overthrow the institution of slavery.[12] Clearly black men refused to allow slavery and racism to wholly emasculate them and used violence and aggression to maintain their status as men.

In response to the "resistant masculinity" exhibited by men like Walker and Simpson, white men created an elaborate patriarchal structure designed to control not only slaves, but all social subordinates, including free blacks, women, and children. In Lorri Glover's study of elite white manhood in the early nineteenth century, she claims that Southern men's "transition to manhood played out against a backdrop of bondage; they became men in part by personifying the antithesis of their slaves and became southern by protecting that institution." When black men exercised their resistant masculinity, by fighting back when threatened with a whipping or risking life and limb in order to protect their wives or daughters from sexual molestation, they upended patriarchal control and challenged a core foundation of white Southern manhood. Glover concludes that Southern men came "to understand how thoroughly their identity as men depended on dominion over slaves."[13]

Linda Frost makes a related assessment of Confederate identity during the war, as expressed by the white male press, and argues that Southerners grounded white identity and morality in the institution of slavery. The editors of the *Southern Literary Messenger* claimed, "Morally, slavery is essential to the highest development of both races. Destroy it, and the slave sinks to savage life; and the master loses those great qualities which have so marked the men of the South in all our history."[14] Reinforcing stereotypes of slaves as either savage or childlike, unable to function without white (male) oversight, the paper warned against abolition because of its threat to the black race. But the paper also implied that if abolition occurred, Southern manhood would become unglued, as its connection to "those great qualities which have so marked the men of the South"—mastery, chivalry, and whiteness—dissolved. A degradation of black manhood accompanied the assertion of Southern white manhood; white men could be masters of only savages and children.

As Southern men defended the institution of slavery with paternalist myths, they also cemented their claims to masculinity by degrading Northern manhood and linking it with blackness and racial Others. The most frequent and well-known method of racializing Northern men was, of course, by constantly referring to them as Black Republicans in the press. For example, the editors of the *Charleston Mercury* ran a story in 1856 entitled, "The Black Republican Balderdash," in which they challenged the politicized reports of Bleeding Kansas that highlighted the "nefarious designs of the South upon Kansas and the North. . . . We entreat respectable men who allow their nerves to be shaken by this rhodomontade, to understand that it is all mere gabble, uttered in order to keep the black republicans together until after election."[15] Southern men need not be alarmed by the news coming in from territorial Kansas because they could be reassured that it was only "mere gabble" (akin to female gossip?) spewed forth by "black republicans," lesser men who weren't "respectable" like the Southern men of Charleston.

Similarly, the *Mississippian*, based in Jackson, alerted its readers to the "Black Republican Notion of Negro Equality," which the paper ironically identified as hypocritical in a story about a free black man in Michigan who filed suit against a steamboat operator who refused to allow him to ride in the white cabin. The case went all the way to the state Supreme Court, which "consisted exclusively of Black Republicans!" but was ultimately decided in favor of the steamboat company. The paper concluded that the decision confirmed the "moral inferiority of the black man," but the author also implicitly endorsed the benefits of paternalism for blacks in his criticism of the decision: "These [Black Republicans] fondly flatter the negro with abstractions of equality and fraternity; but in practice they never fail to treat him with contumely and aversion."[16] Southern masters, one can assume, would never consider blacks as their equals, but they would treat them kindly as slaves. The critique effectively questioned Northern manhood by reminding the reader that Black Republicans professed "negro equality," but only Southern masters walked their talk, wrapping notions of black inferiority in a swathe of white paternalism.

Black Republicans not only were degraded because of their affiliation with abolition and "negro equality," they were also deemed fanatical by the Southern press. After William Seward delivered his infamous "irrepressible conflict" speech in the fall of 1858, a Raleigh, North Carolina, paper claimed that Seward, "by that speech, has placed himself on a level with Garrison and his fanatical crew, and at an immeasurable distance in mischief of purpose ahead of those who have been designated as 'Black Republicans.'"[17] Here Seward's reputation suffered a fate worse than other "Black Republicans" and officially attained the status of malevolent fanatic according to Southern readers.

Similarly, Missouri slaveholder William B. Napton referred to his new Kansas neighbors as abolitionist "fanatics" and racialized them by conflating their behavior with Indians: "A horde of our western savages, with avowed purposes of destruction to the white race, would be less formidable neighbors." Another Missourian worried that thousands of "Hessian band[s] of mercenaries [would be] sent here as hired servants, to do the will of others, to pol[l]ute our fair land, to dictate to us a government, to preach Abolitionism and dig underground Rail Roads."[18] These Southern men cast Northern emigrants to Kansas as foreign invaders, "negro lovers" who would soon become "negro stealers," hell bent on destroying the institution of slavery and, as Napton feared, the white race itself.

The "negro stealer" who instilled the most fear in Southern men was, of course, John Brown, and reports of his actions in Kansas and Harpers Ferry often classify him as a "bloody savage" and racialize his manhood. John Doyle, whose father and brother were murdered by Brown and who testified during the congressional investigation of the Pottawatomie massacre, described Brown as "dark complected" [sic] and claimed the other men who rode with Brown "were of sandy complexion." Doyle's mother, Mahala, remembered that Brown gave a "wild whoop" after committing the bloody deeds, and a picture of dark-skinned savages emerges from her testimony, not a group of civilized white men.[19] After the Harpers Ferry attack three years later, Brown was repeatedly called a savage. In a letter to the *New York Journal of Commerce*, "Southern Law Judge" called Brown a "ferocious and bloody savage" and wondered, "was the Magna Charta devised for wild beasts, or those in human form who are worse, those who are *hostes humani generis?*" The "southern law judge" further argued that Brown's execution was justified and bristled that the "Lynch code" would take care of other abolitionists who, "worse than the [Rocky Mountain] bear," attacked Southern homes and institutions.[20]

In an attempt to control these abolitionist savages, Southern men turned to lynch law and violence, components that undergirded their Southern male honor. The *Richmond Enquirer* suggested that "negro loving" men, like hysterical women and children, simply deserved a good whipping. The *Enquirer* first racialized Republican men by connecting them with "Negros" and Jews; then the paper challenged Republicans' arguments against the extension of slavery in the West by characterizing them as overly emotional, even feminine. Claiming that Republican men harbored an "intense affection for the negro [that] is like that of a Virginian for his daughter," they highlighted how this "love" for "the negro" had disabled them from rationally and logically debating the topic of slavery's extension. Refusing to engage Republicans in this debate "until the philanthropists have recovered their temper and their speech, (for now they fume and stammer worse than Hotspur, and talk thicker than Moses or a young Dutchman)," they then suggested why Republicans should embrace slavery's growth.

The *Enquirer* argued that Northerners would benefit from slavery in the West because it would allow the North to continue to increase industrial production by using the South's raw materials. They emphasized the two sections' harmonious economic relationship, but they simultaneously feminized Northerners and bolstered the South's rugged masculinity by, ironically, attaching it to slavery: "[Expansion] will enable the North to confine herself chiefly to light, easy, in-door work, and to skillful occupations, which pay well, whilst the slaves, on more fertile soils, are producing by hard out-door work (which best suits them), increased quantities of grain and raw materials to exchange with her for merchandise and manufactures of all kinds."[21] The *Enquirer* corralled the feminized North quite literally inside a domestic sphere, implicitly linking its "light, easy" industrial work with women's work, while placing the South in the public sphere, working outdoors with its slaves producing raw materials for northern factories. The

Enquirer attacked Northern manhood on two levels, by racializing and feminizing it, but their critique rested on the backs of their slaves and perhaps even on the "resistant masculinity" that black men projected.[22]

But like all rebellious slaves and children who opposed their masters, Northern men deserved and in fact needed a proper flogging. The *Enquirer* ended its story by issuing an offer of reconciliation with Republicans, but only after the Northern fanatical children had come to their senses:

> When the isms get through with their hysteric fits, sardonic grins and spasmodic convulsions, and are quite restored to speech and hearing, we would like to have a little quiet talk with them on the various topics which we have but touched. Like spoilt children, they will see that they have been crying for poison instead of candy, and that both the refusal and the flogging, which we gave them, "was all for their own good."[23]

Once Northern men regained control of their white, masculine identities by ceasing their "hysteric fits" and by speaking in English rather than in "thick" ethnic tones, then civilized Southern men would be happy to engage them in political conversation. But first, of course, they had to be whipped.

Senator Sumner could personally attest to Southerners' willingness to wield the whip in defense of their ideas. In response to Sumner's caning and to critiques of his manhood, Northern men launched retaliatory attacks at the Southern plantation system and at Southern manhood itself. But they did so by also manipulating common fears of blackness and otherness, equating Southerners with their slaves, and constructing Southern men as savage brutes and passionate, uncivilized primitives. The *Boston* (Massachusetts) *Bee* reported on Sumner's beating using the most incendiary language:

> Hon. Chas. Sumner . . . of this city, was ferociously and brutally assaulted in the National Senate Chamber yesterday, by a cowardly scoundrel named Brooks. . . . This bully Brooks who has disgraced the name of *man*, ought to be branded as a villain of the blackest dye, and then mercilessly kicked from one end of the continent to the other. The black mark of Cain will stand out on his brow to the last moment of his disgraced life.[24]

The *Bee*'s report stripped Brooks of his manhood and blackened his character and indeed, his skin, as the "black mark of Cain" cast a dark shadow on his face. His barbarism qualified him as an uncivilized brute, and savages had dark skin in the nineteenth-century mind's eye.

Similarly, the *Pittsburgh Gazette* argued that "barbarians and savages would not be guilty of such unmanliness" and noted that the punishment meted out by Brooks surpassed the commonly accepted dose of "39 lashes" used in corporal punishment statutes and slave codes. The *Gazette* expressed outrage that "fifty blows [were] inflicted upon an unresisting victim, until the weapon of attack was used up, and not one hand raised among the bystanders to stay the fury of the perfidious wretch."[25] According to the *Gazette*, Brooks's behavior exceeded the bounds of civilized manhood, and he used his cane as he might have used a whip to punish his slaves.

In fact, some Northerners worried that Southerners' ultimate goal was to enslave the North by pushing slavery across the northern and western borders and thus forcing Northern men to submit to Southern designs for slavery's expansion. The *New York Tribune* articulated these fears in the wake of Bleeding Sumner and Bleeding Kansas:

> The South has taken the oligarchic ground that Slavery ought to exist, irrespective of color—that there must be a governing class and a class governed . . . we must expect that Northern men in Washington, whether members or not, will be assaulted, wounded or killed, as the case may be, so long as the North will bear it . . . whether the common ground where the national representatives meet is to be turned into a slave plantation where Northern members act under the lash, the bowie-knife and the pistol, is a question to be settled.[26]

Fears of slavery "irrespective of color" proliferated in the spring and summer of 1856, as reports of the Sack of Lawrence warned Northerners of the "border ruffian" code that stripped free staters of their rights and freedoms. In a Fourth of July speech, William Lloyd Garrison claimed that slaveholders made no distinction between the subjugation of "the Negro" and of the white man: "Her [the South's] . . . border ruffian leagues; her yokes, and fetters, and whips, and thumbscrews; . . . her suppression of free speech and her bloody enactments; . . . her invasions of Kansas, and sacking of its villages and subjugation of its population; her ten thousand thousand [*sic*] crimes and horrors are all, all necessary, if she would perpetuate her terrible system of chattel servitude." Garrison equated Southerners' violent control of their slaves with their conquest of Kansas, and he cited the Kansas Territorial slave codes, which threatened physical punishment for both rebellious blacks and abolitionist whites, as further evidence of Southerners' insatiable desire to enslave anyone who questioned their right to expand slavery. White free-state men could find themselves literally in chains and sentenced to two years of hard labor if they dared to express their antislavery opinions. Garrison manipulated white anxiety over slavery, in this case white slavery, to argue for the abolition of black slavery. He even warned, "The Southern organs now proclaim the right to enslave all laboring people without regard to complexional distinctions!"[27]

Indeed the news from Kansas confirmed Northerners' worst fears about Southern designs on their freedom. H. Miles Moore, who lived in Leavenworth in 1855, recorded an incident involving a mock slave auction of an abolitionist by a group of proslavery men. Moore wrote, "They took [the abolitionist] . . . in a warehouse, stripped him to the waist, tarred and feathered him and brought him up into town, [where they] mounted him on a rail. . . . Dr. Ransom's old darkey, Joe, auctioned him off and bid him in at one cent."[28] Not only did the proslavery settlers literally blacken him by tarring his skin, but they symbolically enslaved him by selling him at auction. Southern men would assert their mastery at any cost it seemed, but to do so they had to emasculate and blacken their opponents by treating them like slaves.

Northern men were not immune from using similar tactics, however, as they accused South Carolina's Brooks of savagery and characterized Southern men in general as animalistic and uncivilized. Referring to the events in Bleeding Kansas as a "reign of terror" instigated by proslavery men, the *Boston Daily Atlas* called Brooks a ruffian and surmised that "the mouths of the representatives of the North are to be closed by the use of bowie-knives, bludgeons and revolvers."[29] The prospect of civil debate waned as Northerners cast Southern men as violent and brutish, incapable of exhibiting the civilized behavior so common among restrained Northern men. Ruffians like Brooks and his western counterparts in Missouri were, quite simply, more like animals than men. On the eve of the Sack of Lawrence, free-state settler Marc Parrott wrote to his brother from Lawrence and reported, "The border ruffians are <u>sure</u> of their prey this time. The Lawrence party are <u>defeated</u>." Painting an ominous picture of ruffians perched on a bluff ready to pounce on a helpless Lawrence, Parrott depicted the proslavery forces as animals, eager to seize their "prey." Julia Louisa Lovejoy, another antislavery settler, reinforced the idea that Southern men were closer in species to animals than men. She wrote, "The Free State men, are shot down by pro-slavery villains, as beasts of prey . . . the dogs of war, are let loose." She worried that "unless heaven interpose, we shall be swept away, by an overwhelming army, led on by the whiskey-demon."[30]

Other reports from the field in Kansas also likened Southerners to savage beings. James Manning Winchell emigrated to the Kansas Territory in the 1850s and described his Missouri neighbors in ways that cast doubt on their manhood and aligned them with racial Others. Winchell wrote:

> We had seen specimens of the native Missourian all the way up the river, but here [in Kansas City] they were abundant, and mingled with other varieties . . . with the semi-civilized Indian, the dirty greaser, the Spanish Mexican . . . and the "puke," native to the soil and ready to make money out of all. These latter were generally great, slouching figures, fond of tobacco and whiskey, and very limited in their range of culture.[31]

Similar to the "dirty greaser," Missouri "pukes" were lesser men, and like the local Indians, they were "native to the soil," and addicted to tobacco and alcohol. The "pukes," as historian Michael Fellman introduced them over two decades ago, not only lacked whiteness but even lacked human qualities. Another account, recorded by a free-state emigrant from Pennsylvania, described the Missourians who threatened her homestead as a "herd of border ruffians," linking them more to buffalo than to men.[32]

While local settlers wrote about "ruffians" from their posts in Kansas and Missouri, a group of Baptist ministers from Massachusetts agreed with their assessments, calling the attack on Sumner a "brutal, murderous, and cowardly assault," and reporting that the "simultaneous violence on the plains of Kansas" was "*seldom paralleled among savages,*—all being the evident workings of the same spirit of slavery,—serve to show the appalling depravity generated by the slave system, the bold and determined character of the Slave Power."[33] Similarly, the Bunker Hill Republican Club issued several resolutions in response to Bleeding Sumner and Bleeding Kansas, and warned that "when Slavery thus 'posts' itself and its desperate wickedness, in red letters, in one of the highest places of the nation, it behoves [sic] every man with a spark of patriotism in his soul . . . to read the frightful lesson." The "B.H. Republicans" argued that Brooks and the Border Ruf-

LIBERTY. THE FAIR MAID OF KANSAS_IN THE HANDS OF THE "BORDER RUFFIANS".

John L. Magee, Liberty, the Fair Maid of Kansas, in the Hands of the "Border Ruffians," 1856. *This political cartoon shows the "Fair Maid of Kansas" begging for mercy from Democrats like James Buchanan, Franklin Pierce, and Stephen Douglas. They laugh and belittle her request to "Spare Me Gentlemen," and instead threaten to kill her as they scalp free soilers and burn the town of Lawrence, Kansas, in the background. Courtesy of the Library of Congress, Rare Book and Special Collections Division, Alfred Whital Stern Collection of Lincolniana*

fians acted "in the manner of savages" in their violent response to Northerners' attempts to exercise their constitutional rights; these rights were "being 'crushed out' in flame and blood" by "the Border Ruffian and Central Ruffian Democracy," and the B.H. Republicans implied that the same savage behavior exhibited by the Missourians in Kansas was being exercised and condoned by the chief ruffian in the White House, President Pierce.[34]

In addition to hyperbolized reports from and about Kansas, the Northern press also used images to reinforce the idea that Southern "border ruffians" approximated Indian savages. In one famous political cartoon published in 1856, Democrats James Buchanan, Franklin Pierce, Lewis Cass, and Stephen Douglas are all depicted as rapacious, villainous savages who deprive "Liberty, the fair maid of Kansas" of hearth and home. Scenes of burning free-state communities linger in the background as a drunken Franklin Pierce steps on "Liberty's" flag, the U.S. flag, while Stephen Douglas scalps a helpless free-state man lying next to her. The message was clear: a white, feminized, innocent Kansas suffered at the hands of slimy, uncivilized Southern men, who were all deemed border ruffians, although none of them resided in the region at the time or hailed from Missouri, except Cass. Southern men scalped their victims, just like their Indian neighbors on the plains.

Republicans constructed proslavery men as savage Others, a quasi-racial connotation that repeatedly equated Southerners with Indians and barbarism. Linda Frost finds a similar trend during the Civil War, when the Northern press racialized and demonized the Confederacy. A cartoon published in *Frank Leslie's Illustrated Newspaper* accused the Rebels, including "Rebel Ladies," of using Yankee skulls to decorate their homes, and the caption compares Confederate war practices with "savage tribes":

> The outrages upon the dead will revive the recollections of the cruelties to which savage tribes subject their prisoners. They were buried in many cases naked, with their faces downward. They were left to decay in the open air, their bones being carried off as trophies, sometimes, as the testimony proves, to be used as personal adornments, and one witness deliberately avers that the head of one of our most gallant officers was cut off by a Secessionist, to be turned into a drinking-cup on the occasion of his marriage.

Readers of *Leslie's Illustrated* were titillated and horrified by the thought of Yankee corpses being molested and defiled, soldiers' bones made into souvenirs. *Harper's Weekly* provided yet more evidence of "Secesh Industry" by printing an engraving that included a "Goblet—made from a Yankee's skull" and a "Necklace of Yankee teeth."[35] Based on testimony from Union soldiers, the papers confirmed what many Northerners already believed: that Southern men were savage animals, not chivalrous knights.

Perhaps one of the most intriguing attempts at racializing Southern men and indeed, the institution of slavery itself, can be found in William Henry Seward's "Irrepressible Conflict" speech, delivered in October of 1858. Seward painted the differences between the free labor and slave systems, and by extension between Northerners and Southerners, in stark terms. He identified the roots of these differences in the history and biology of colonization, arguing that slavery was introduced in America "as an engine of conquest, and for the establishment of monarchical power, by the Portuguese and the Spaniards. . . . Its legitimate fruits are seen in the poverty, imbecility, and anarchy which now pervade all Portuguese and Spanish America." The free-labor system, on the other hand, "is of German extraction, and it was established in our country by emigrants from Sweden, Holland, Germany, Great Britain, and Ireland." Aligning slavery with the swarthy, southern European monarchies that supposedly promoted "mestizaje" and intermarriage with Indians and slaves in America, Seward constructed a racialized hierarchy of labor systems, privileging northern, white Europeans and their free-labor societies north of the Mason-Dixon line. He attributed the "strength, wealth, greatness, intelligence, and freedom" that characterized Americans, especially non-slaveholding Americans, to this history of northern European colonization, and conversely, characterized all slaveholding societies as despotisms. Furthermore, he cautioned that despots, that is, slaveholders, will stop at nothing to acquire the means by which they can maintain their control over their underlings. As he neared the close of his incendiary speech, Seward claimed, "This dark record shows you, fellow-citizens . . . that of the whole nefarious schedule of slaveholding designs which I have submitted to you, the Democratic party has left only one yet to be consummated—the abrogation of the law which forbids the African slave-trade."[36] Using the threat of the Atlantic slave trade, which would open the floodgates for the forced immigration of thousands of nonwhites and non-Europeans to the United States, Seward capitalized on his Northern audience's fears of the racial, uncivilized Other to argue against the slave power.

Like Seward, William Lloyd Garrison raised the specter of blackness and slavery overwhelming the nation, and added insult to injury by not only racializing Southern men but also feminizing them and the peculiar institution they protected. Referring to the South repeatedly as "she," Garrison fumed, "She can neither be honest nor pure, neither merciful nor magnanimous, neither enlightened nor civilized. Her fertile soil must gradually turn to ashes." The South was savage, clothed in darkness and impurity, and slavery made "her" infertile. Furthermore, Garrison worried that the South would "plunge [herself] deeper and deeper in barbarity and guilt" as slavery expanded westward. Framing the South as feminine and uncivilized, Garrison ultimately castigated his fellow Northerners for "our alliance and union with such a *race of tyrants and barbarians!*"[37] He classified Southerners as racial Others, a race that could not change and was inherently savage, and asked his audience to join him in calling for disunion.

Barbarians, pukes, border ruffians, and Black Republicans paraded across the public's consciousness in the late 1850s as sectionalism exploded into civil war. The players in Bleeding Kansas and Bleeding Sumner used these terms not only to question their opponents' racial origins but also to demean their manhoods. Both Northern and Southern men feared losing their whiteness because as their racial identity became destabilized, their masculinity also teetered on the brink of uncertainty. Quite simply, to be a man was to be civilized, white, and free in the nineteenth century. The rhetorical battle over slavery's extension that prefaced the outbreak of full-scale violence in 1861 reveals that white men made earnest attempts to define themselves as white and free—and often in the process, they blackened their opponents, comparing them to racial Others or slaves and trying desperately to assert their mastery.

Senator Sumner never recovered from the injuries he suffered from Brooks's cane. And critics of the brand of manhood Sumner had embodied called upon Northern men to step up to the plate and be masters themselves or risk becoming slaves. The editors of the *New York Tribune* said it best when they argued, "If, indeed, we go on quietly to submit to such outrages, we deserve to have our names flattened, our skins blacked, and to be placed at work under task-masters; for we have lost the noblest attributes of freemen, and are virtually slaves."[38]

Chapter 5

"The Noise of Democracy": The Lecompton Constitution in Congress and Kansas

Pearl T. Ponce

At the end of 1857, President James Buchanan stood at a crossroads. Although he had supported the Lecompton Constitution in his annual address, he had done so before Kansans voted on the question. But regard-less of residents' views, he believed the territory had "occupied too much of the public attention," which could be better devoted to more significant issues. With or without slavery, admission was critical as it would allow the new state to "for the first time, be left . . . to manage her own affairs in her own way."[1] Presented with such a negative vote, however, it was unclear how Buchanan would respond. After two successive governors advised him that the constitution was flawed, would the president consider whether these men discerned a reality imperceptible from distant Washington? Would he listen to a growing outcry against the constitution evident in both Kansas and Congress? Ultimately, Buchanan would not reassess his plans for the territory. Driven by party concerns in advance of the 1860 presidential election and a genuine belief that the ongoing Kansas conflict endangered the Union, Buchanan insisted that apprehensions about the constitution's legitimacy and whether the people's will was being respected simply were not as important as seizing the opportunity the Lecompton Constitution represented. Ultimately, the combination of an overly invested president and a dutiful but reluctant governor shaped the consti-tution's fate.

With Kansas' Governor Robert Walker and Secretary Frederick Stan-ton absent from their posts (the former had resigned, the latter had been removed), the administration needed a loyal emissary, and Buchanan tapped former congressman James Denver. As one antislavery advocate recounted, his appointment came as proslavery forces were losing. "Seven Governors—all, all sent as messengers to plant slavery on Kansas soil—had been thwarted, and failed."[2] Denver's selection to succeed where others had faltered came as a surprise, most of all to Denver himself. Yet he was a logical choice given his frontier experience in California, where he had served on a relief committee to protect immigrants in 1850 before being elected to Congress in 1855. After one term, he joined the Indian Bureau. On December 10, while touring Kansas as commissioner of Indian affairs, Denver learned Buchanan had appointed him territorial secretary. Informed that the legislature was due to convene and he was needed to represent the government, he accepted, but Denver insisted on being replaced after the session ended because he was loath to leave the Bureau.[3] Eleven days later, however, he was named acting governor and after two months, promoted once more. Denver became acting governor on December 21, the same day residents would vote on the Lecompton Constitution. In addressing the territory, he expressed confidence that Kansas had "enough of the conservative element remaining to uphold and enforce the laws" and listen to "the voice of reason." He reminded free-state men that "abandoning the elective franchise" could be perceived as indifference to the question.[4] Although this election passed without incident, rumors abounded that the next one would be disrupted. On January 4, Kansans would select state officers under the Lecompton Constitution, while the free-state faction had scheduled a separate referendum to vote on the constitution itself. Denver dispatched troops to protect the polls and addressed the long-standing electoral issue of who was a bona fide Kansas settler. The governor warned that "mere presence" alone was insufficient to warrant a right to vote and those attempting to vote illegally would be arrested.[5]

A conscientious executive, Denver's greatest challenge was his utter lack of interest in the position. Barely two weeks after his initial appointment, he complained that Kansas had "been cursed of God and man. Providence gave them no crops last year, scarcely, and now it requires all the powers conferred on me by the President to prevent them from cutting each other's throats."[6] Thus, his immediate focus was extricating himself from the territory. By January 11, he had already reported to the administration that not all of its goals were viable. Although most Democrats wanted a slave Kansas, many would be satisfied with a free state so long as the party remained dominant. Denver had a plan to "localize the Kansas question, heal all breaches in the Democratic party on that subject, and effectually stop abolition clamor." But first, the Lecompton Constitution would have been set aside. If the administration would do so, Congress could enable a new convention and order the territory to send the constitution directly to Buchanan, who would then proclaim Kansas admitted. However straightforward, Denver's plan was unfeasible because bypassing the legislative branch, which had authority over the territories, would be unconstitutional.[7] Moreover, Buchanan had no interest in abandoning the Lecompton Constitution. As Secretary of the Interior Jacob Thompson promptly told Denver, they had to stay on course or suffer criticism from both sections.[8]

Thompson further advised the governor to control local politicians, but the free-state legislature proved as aggressive and intransigent as its proslavery predecessor. For instance, the legislature passed an act authorizing another constitutional convention, to Denver's displeasure. "I concluded that we had constitutions enough," he explained. "We had then pending before Congress the Lecompton Constitution, which was a pretty ugly-looking affair all around. We had the Topeka Constitution, which was objected to on the other side just as much; and then we had the Territorial Government established by act of Congress, and I thought we had about as much government as one little Territory could very well live under." Denver resolved to pocket-veto the bill, but the legislature endorsed it as if he had returned it; thus, when the bill reappeared, he burned it. However, the legislators persevered, and on March 9, they declared the burned bill legal and moved forward with convention plans.[9]

In Washington, Buchanan pressed the Lecompton process forward undeterred by results from the January 4 election. The more than 10,000 votes Kansans had cast against the constitution seemingly did not register as he assured a friend that same month that "the Kansas question, from present appearances, will not be one of much difficulty." He believed the territory would become a slave state because congressmen who rejected the constitution risked being ousted in that year's midterm elections. He was confident these men understood that "their safety consists in their firmness & fidelity"[10] and declared passage "vital to his administration."[11] Buchanan was not alone in discounting the free-state vote, for as one Washington newspaper wrote, the referendum was unauthorized and "can in no way affect the legal character and obligations of the instrument."[12] A convention's decision on how or if to submit a constitution to a popular vote did not affect its validity.[13]

On February 2, Buchanan urged Congress to accept the constitution because it reflected the Democratic principle of nonintervention while removing the slavery question from that body.[14] He reminded them that "a great delusion seems to pervade the public mind" due to propaganda that gave the impression that Kansas had two parties divided by the slavery question. That was not true. Instead, Kansans were divided by their adherence to the law. There were those in Kansas "loyal to this government and those who have endeavored to destroy its existence by force and by usurpation—between those who sustain and those who have done all in their power to overthrow the territorial government established by Congress." Moreover, the free-state faction continued to cling "with such treasonable tenacity" to their revolutionary course.[15] Buchanan emphasized the Lecompton convention's legality, dismissing free-state protests because they had opted out of the process. He would have preferred a popular vote, of course, but he deferred to the convention's right to make that decision. Most important, to repudiate this constitution in favor of "the disaffected" would only increase agitation, while accepting it would allow local questions to be decided at local ballot boxes. But if Kansas was admitted, the "dark and ominous clouds" hovering over the Union would, Buchanan concluded, "be dissipated with honor."[16]

But anti-Lecompton forces were resolute. Even if Congress accepted the constitution, Kansans would not: "*Civil war first,*" one Kansas antislavery advocate insisted.[17] Proslavery proponents were equally angered by the possibility that a legal constitution would be rejected. Many Southerners believed Congress was obligated to accept it on principle, to acknowledge Southern rights. "We want no more compromise," the *Charleston Mercury* stated.[18] Alabama's *Spirit of the South* concurred, arguing that to turn Kansas away solely because of slavery "adds the insult of supposing we can be amused by the trick" of saying that a state can be admitted, but rejecting it when it presents a slave constitution.[19]

On February 6, Senator Stephen Douglas of Illinois issued a letter to John Forney, the organizer of an anti-Lecompton rally in Philadelphia, which argued that the convention had erred: it had only been authorized to determine Kansans' views on admission, not to write a constitution. As such, Democrats who believed in "the doctrine of self-government and popular sovereignty" should repudiate it.[20] Kansas' most recent executive team joined Douglas in dissent. Both Walker and Stanton condemned the constitution before various large demonstrations against it; Stanton alone spoke in Columbus, Albany, Philadelphia, and New York.[21] Removed for calling a special legislative session for Kansas' newly elected free-state legislators,

Stanton expressed little regret, claiming instead to be gratified that he had allowed the people's "real will" to be expressed. Now that they had done so, the Democratic Party should "defend the true principles of constitutional liberty," which would bring Kansas peace if only Congress would listen.[22] Walker's speeches emphasized that he had accepted the governorship only because he and Buchanan both believed the constitution would be submitted to a popular vote. Although he denied charging the president with "willful deception," Walker's speeches did just that. He decried Buchanan's annual message where the president focused solely on the slavery clause of the constitution as evidence of duplicity. Had he known that the president harbored such opinions, Walker would have refused the assignment. Instead, to his "surprise and astonishment," Buchanan had developed a new theory of submission.[23] Combined with the wide dissemination of Walker's resignation letter, such speeches rallied anti-Lecompton forces.

To parry this attack, Buchanan carefully cited Walker's letters, then before the Senate, to demonstrate the Topeka government's illegality.[24] It posed so great a threat that he could not justify the time needed to elect delegates, hold a convention, and frame a new constitution.[25] Other northern Democrats, like New York congressman William Maclay, agreed that there was no need to repudiate Lecompton. Like Douglas, Maclay referred to the party's popular sovereignty and nonintervention doctrines, but cited them in arguing that the best way to ensure peace in Kansas was to insulate the convention from national pressure. Furthermore, Congress could not be charged with forcing a constitution on an unwilling territory because a legally convened body of Kansans had written it.[26] However, Democrats like Buchanan and Maclay were no match for the Douglas-Walker-Stanton trifecta.

Douglas hoped the Senate's Committee on Territories would report an acceptable bill, but there was "no hope of an amicable adjustment of the Kansas question."[27] Instead, on February 18, the committee issued three reports: a majority report supporting the Lecompton Constitution; a minority report charging that Kansas' admission under it would "give success to fraud and encouragement to iniquity"; and a second minority report, written by Douglas, urging rejection on the grounds that it did not reflect the will of the people.[28] These reports prompted a flurry of speeches, with Democrat James Hammond of South Carolina refuting Douglas's conception of the "will of the people" and arguing that a convention could not be dismissed as a mere "creature of the Territory Legislature." Compared to a convention, the territorial legislature was a "petty corporation, appointed and paid by the Congress of the United States, without a particle of sovereign power." Because of rapid population growth, conventions represent the people when called; allowing legislatures to subsequently annul their decisions would engender an endless cycle of revisions and amendments, and place elected officials over the will of "the people." Like many Southerners, Hammond believed opposition to Lecompton masked a sectional bias.[29]

On the other side of the aisle Republican Lafayette Foster of Connecticut argued that the president had not provided a "statesmanlike reason" to accept the constitution—instead, Buchanan was merely a party man wanting to institute slavery in Kansas.[30] But despite such views and Douglas's active dissent, with thirty-nine Democrats in the Senate, the bill was safe. A number of amendments did indicate how senators were attempting to manage the controversy. Robert Toombs of Georgia, for instance, wanted to clarify that residents could amend the constitution.[31] Samuel Houston of Texas suggested submitting both the Topeka and Lecompton Constitutions to a popular vote and enabling a new convention if neither was accepted.[32] James Green of Missouri proposed linking Kansas' admission with that of Minnesota.[33] John Crittenden of Kentucky wanted to return the constitution for a popular vote: if accepted, it would become a state without further debate. But all amendments were defeated, and on March 23, the Senate accepted the Lecompton Constitution 33 to 25.[34]

Warily watching these proceedings, Buchanan was convinced that Crittenden's proposal would be disastrous and intensified his campaign when the House resurrected it. First, he reached out to Denver, flattering the governor by commenting that had he been sent to Kansas "instead of Walker, the territory would have been in a much more quiet condition than it is at present." Buchanan believed the bill would pass because its defeat would be so costly: not only would it lead to a decline in property values and foreign trade, but the American people would worry about the Union's stability. Another constitution could not be framed in time; unless the Lecompton Constitution was accepted, the territory would "be the sport and the capital of the Black Republicans in the Presidential election of 1860."[35] But despite administration pressure, the Lecompton Constitution immediately faltered in the House when it was referred to a special committee chaired by Thomas Harris of Illinois instead of being sent to the Committee on Territories. Harris was a friend of Douglas, and his feelings were well known; in early February, he had sent a supportive letter to a protest meeting against the Lecompton Constitution arguing that the people could not yield their rights to a convention and that despite being "stigmatized and abused," its opponents would persevere. While Harris appreciated "firmness in an Executive," Buchanan was unlike former president Andrew Jackson, who always "went with the masses of the people, never against them."[36]

The House opposition rejected the president's pleas and attacked the constitution's legitimacy. For instance, Kansas delegate Marcus J. Parrott asserted that the Topeka and Lecompton Constitutions were vastly different. The first was born of the people as a result of their rights being violated; the second was "the evil spawn of usurpation" which, without popular support, slinked along "like a convicted felon." Parrott acknowledged that the free-state men had not participated in the constitutional process, but insisted they had been "lulled into indifference or deluded into inaction" by both Buchanan's and Walker's pledges that they would later be able to vote on the constitution.[37] The administration's friends stressed the process's legality. James Dowdell of Alabama pointed out that many state constitutions used the phrase "we, the people" but had not been subject to popular suffrage. Moreover, conventions were "*the people* in an *organized* capacity." The real violation would be to dismiss the convention's work. Rejecting the constitution in favor of another vote "to ascertain whether the voice spoken by her convention is the truly expressed will of the people" would be "to exercise arbitrary power." Dowdell also ominously mentioned that his state legislature, like that of Georgia, stood ready to "resist aggression" should Lecompton be rejected.[38]

But while Congress had not required previous territories to submit their constitutions to a popular vote, Kansas was so divided that doing so seemed prudent. "When the voice of the people is ambiguous, or in doubt, or against the constitution," Samuel Cox of Ohio argued, "it is clear Congress should require a popular verdict before it should pass judgment."[39] Because of such views, a version of the rejected Crittenden resolution gained favor in the lower chamber as William Montgomery of Pennsylvania proposed returning the constitution to Kansas, where a new constitutional convention could amend the document before submission to a popular vote.[40] But accepting the Lecompton Constitution by relying on future amendments was, as Daniel W. Gooch of Massachusetts stated, tantamount to inviting civil war in the territory. "If ever there was a people of the globe, that needed a constitution, which should not be touched or altered for years to come, that people are to be found in Kansas."[41] Nonetheless, despite such concerns, the amended bill passed the House on March 31 by a vote of 120 to 112.[42] The House's refusal to accept Lecompton outright occasioned a large celebration in Leavenworth, where more than 3,000 people gathered to "celebrate the downfall of the Lecompton swindle" and offer cheers for the "120 who defended our cause in the House of Representatives."[43]

The Senate refused the substitution, and a conference committee, which included Senators William Seward of New York, James S. Green of Missouri, and Robert Hunter of Virginia and Congressmen William English of Indiana, Alexander Stephens of Georgia, and William Howard of Michigan, was formed to propose a bill acceptable to both chambers. They embraced English's plan to return the constitution for a popular vote, stipulating that rejection would delay statehood until Kansas met population requirements for a representative (93,420); if accepted, the new state would receive a generous land grant.[44] The compromise allowed Democrats like Cox to soothe their consciences: it gave the people an opportunity "to kill it if they did not like it" while giving congressmen like him the ability to insist that "at no time did I ever give in my adhesion to the Lecompton Constitution."[45]

The conference bill passed Congress on April 30: 30 to 22 in the Senate and 112 to 103 in the House.[46] Buchanan greatly preferred the Senate bill, but was pleased with the compromise for Kansans would "decide their own destiny." Whatever the outcome, he believed "the Kansas question as a national question is at an end."[47] But Buchanan was overly optimistic. On the night after passage, Senator William Gwin of California spoke before a victory celebration at the White House and baldly stated, to applause, the consequences of the territory's rejection of the compromise: "If she rejects it . . . then let Kansas shriek and let her bleed, for she shall never come in until she has sufficient population."[48]

The United States Democratic Review was as confident as Buchanan that the English bill had settled the Kansas question, but "whether Kansas will reopen the question remains to be seen."[49] The Democratic party line emphasized that Congress had passed judgment and left Kansas' future to its residents. However as the January vote ought to have warned, there was considerable antipathy toward the constitution, and the compromise bill's provisions were unlikely to help, especially given the controversy over the land grant. While its size was not at issue, the bill's unprecedented conditions led opponents to derisively call it the "English Swindle" or "Lecompton, Jr." The *Freedom's Champion* claimed that Congress insulted them by "attempting to *buy* their manhood, and *bribe* them" while threatening to deny them statehood should they refuse.[50] Most worrisome was the bill's failure to describe a future land grant if Kansans repudiated the English bill. However, the government believed these provisions were appropriate; in fact, the other grants Kansans cited were "too extensive and beyond former precedents in similar cases." Instead, they were being asked to support a grant similar in size to that of Minnesota, and the matter was appropriately referred to voters.[51]

The land grant issue also reanimated a long-standing debate over land sales. In late December 1856, then Kansas governor John Geary had urged the government to delay sales, arguing that peace was worth more than the "the entire value of the lands."[52] Since the Northwest Ordinances, land policy had been evolving to ease settlement and encourage development. Historian Paul Gates asserts that by mid-century "settlers had been granted the right to buy land at low prices, the right to enter upon and select the public land before speculative monopolists could anticipate them, and the right to have at least a year of residence and development before they had to pay for their tracts."[53] However, under Pierce and Buchanan, land was offered to individuals for sale rather than converting it beforehand to public domain and subjecting it to public-land laws; this led to rampant speculation, which, when combined with administration efforts to increase revenue from land sales, alienated settlers from the party.[54]

When Buchanan commenced land sales while simultaneously encouraging support for the English bill, the situation worsened. Although he might not have intended to link the two, residents viewed his timing with suspicion. Because few surveys had been completed, many settlers thought they would have years before payment was demanded. Moreover, these funds were not desperately needed—in comparison with the total income of the federal government, land sales contributed 12 percent in 1856; 5 percent in 1857; and between 4 and 7 percent in 1858.[55] John Everett was one of many residents infuriated by Buchanan's new policies. "The approaching land sales are being used as a screw to force the poor settlers to vote for the Lecompton Constitution," he wrote. If they voted yes, sales would be postponed; if they voted no, they would continue. Everett complained that money was scarce and that residents thought he had ordered land sales to "exert the power of the creditor which the President possesses to force the poor debtor to vote according to his will. A new illustration of popular sovereignty truly!"[56] Like Geary before him, Denver had wanted to delay land sales until the following spring but was overruled; sales started on November 1 and damaged the administration's standing in Kansas.[57]

Voters in southern Kansas, however, were distracted by ongoing disturbances, which had started in mid-December 1857 when the sheriff of Bourbon County requested federal troops because he could not fulfill his responsibilities without them.[58] During skirmishes between local officials and a militia company led by James Montgomery, a federal soldier was killed. Most disturbing, Denver reported to Secretary of State Lewis Cass, was that the county's free-state men seemingly supported these activities.[59] Some residents had been driven from the territory by force, others by fear. One party, commanded by Charles Hamilton, returned in May and killed five free-state men and wounded four others. As far as Denver could determine, none of the victims had been implicated in the earlier events. At most, these men had "sympathized with Montgomery and his band so far that they took no steps to protect their neighbors, who differed with them in political opinions, from their depredations."[60]

Denver sent Lieutenant J. P. Jones to investigate. He reported that Missourians wanted their stolen property returned and Montgomery arrested; if he was not stopped, they would not hinder Hamilton in his goal "to take Montgomery, dead or alive." The situation remained volatile, and Jones recommended troops be dispatched to prevent Missourians from interfering in southern Kansas.[61] In late May, Denver headed to Fort Leavenworth, where he was "greatly astonished" to find he had only foot soldiers at his disposal. Without the cavalry, he had to rely upon often complicit local citizens, free-state men who might have "preserved the peace had they been so disposed," Denver complained, but whose "fanaticism and bitter political feelings induced them to allow the robbers to plunder the pro-slavery people first, and next the free-state democrats and conservative men generally, without restraint."[62] In June, he cited renewed depredations after troops were reassigned to Utah to further his argument that Kansas needed these troops. In their absence, he was dependent on partisan territorial courts to keep the peace, which amounted "almost to a denial of justice."[63]

Next, Denver traveled to Fort Scott after hearing reports that Montgomery had tried to burn it down. "Had such an act been done by savages," the governor commented, "it would have produced a thrill of horror throughout the whole country," but many free-state men supported Montgomery. When he arrived on June 11, "the people seemed to have forgotten that they had a civil governor," but he soon had the people more disposed to uphold civil authority. Town residents accepted a series a resolutions including agreeing to avoid land quarrels; stop frivolous arrests and prosecutions; restore peace; and enforce the laws, while Denver pledged to withdraw troops once he was convinced the community was at peace.[64]

Although the Fort Scott agreement settled the immediate problem, the military continued to trouble Denver. On June 28, T. W. Sherman, the commanding officer of Fort Leavenworth, informed Denver that the Department of the West had ordered the second infantry from Fort Scott. Denver protested, cited his authority to use federal troops to keep the peace, and expressed his concern that "any new and unexpected movement of the troops among a people greatly alarmed and very suspicious cannot but be very prejudicial and the results of which I will not be answerable."[65] Sherman again asked permission on July 6, but was again refused. Despite Denver's orders and his own agreement to remain, Sherman left for Fort Leavenworth only to have to turn back after 100 miles when direct orders from the War Department for him to stay put arrived. In doing so, Sherman thus effected precisely what Denver wished to avoid—marching back and forth through a still uneasy region in what might be perceived as a show of force rather than a relocation—leading the governor to insist on his removal.[66]

These troubles in the southern counties were not directly relevant to the English bill, but demonstrate how easily partisan fighting could erupt and destabilize the territory. Missouri's governor had warned Denver in early August that he might post armed guards to protect the border to avoid a conflict that would damage the nation.[67] Over the summer, then, Denver tried to ensure a fair election on the constitution while juggling troubles in the south, a recalcitrant commanding officer at Fort Scott, and financial worries, as his predecessor had spent a year's budget in a quarter. But he found little sympathy—when Denver complained in June, Thompson reminded him that a "true soldier will endure without a murmur the hardships of a long march."[68]

Throughout, the governor pursued his favorite project—trying to persuade Washington to allow him to resign, but Buchanan would not relent. Although Denver disagreed with the administration's Kansas policy, he proved his loyalty by keeping his feelings private. But the administration's tendency toward linkage extended to the governor as well: Thompson tied Denver's release to Kansas' acceptance of the English bill. "Should the people accept, you can be early relieved, and your work is done; if they reject, your influence will be needed to keep peace, and prevent an effort to come here with a new and another constitution." More important, Kansas could not be allowed to affect the election of 1860 as it had that of 1856.[69] Denver had scant hopes the English bill would be accepted, and without it, he would be stuck as governor until after the presidential election. Although he withdrew his resignation after this June letter, he would find his backbone shortly thereafter.

Before he could leave, Denver had to oversee the election. On August 2, Kansans overwhelmingly rejected the English bill: 1,788 for and 11,300 against. As always, a few observers clung stubbornly to their hopes. In September, for instance, the *Richmond South* declared that they had achieved a "respite, in which, with proper effort, we might yet establish slavery in Kansas."[70] However, the territory's rejection clearly signaled that Kansas was lost both to the Democratic Party and slavery. As the *New Orleans Daily Picayune* reported, the vote revealed that Kansas would not become a slave state; "it is finally and irrevocably a free-state, as it has for a long time been perfectly evident that it could not be permanently anything else."[71]

After this vote, Denver reported that "peace now reigns where but lately all was confusion" and, so, on September 1, he resigned effective October 10. He proudly noted that he was able "to withdraw United States troops entirely from Kansas affairs" and that civil authority was "everywhere respected; that the laws are everywhere enforced; that our citizens are now as well protected in their persons and property as in any other new country."[72] The administration accepted his resignation reluctantly—even on the day it took effect, Thompson sent Denver a pointed letter emphasizing Buchanan's desire to retain him as larger goals were still at stake.

> You see that the administration is bound to resist the admission of Kansas till she has the requisite population. You have influence with those people and you can prevent Kansas from making an application this winter and by another year she will probably have the necessary population. The Democratic party is to be awfully split up in the event Kansas comes in before she has a Representative population. We think you can prevent this, and if you do, you have done an essential service to the Administration and to the party.[73]

Despite such pressure, Denver was resolute.

In his final address, the governor told residents that although he had quieted the territory, it was up to them to keep the peace. Federal intervention was "a stigma on the American people who boast of their voluntary obedience to the laws and their ability to govern themselves." Although he appreciated the regrets expressed after his resignation, Denver advised Kansans that the executive made "but little difference" so long as "the people are true to themselves and true to American institutions."[74] Now that the latest controversy had ended, it was time for Kansans to behave in an orderly manner.

Denver's popularity was probably due to an attitude uncommon among his predecessors. "I did not belong to the Territory," he recalled. "I was not here as a citizen of the Territory; I was here as a representative of the Federal Government. I therefore took no part in the local affairs of the Territory, only so far as was necessary to represent the Federal Government. While I had my own views as to the great question that agitated the country . . . I did not propose to mix with it."[75] As Thompson had remarked, Denver proved among the more popular territorial governors. Indeed, both free-state and proslavery factions attended his farewell banquet.[76]

Although former governor Wilson Shannon dismissed Denver's accomplishments—"If I were a Governor again," he groused, "I would do as Denver does—sit in my chair and do nothing"—he had the smoothest administration of Kansas' territorial governors, perhaps because he was the least invested.[77] All appointed were ambitious, but his ambitions were well satisfied as commissioner of Indian affairs. Moreover, unlike those who began their terms by spouting neutrality but soon revealed marked preferences, Denver remained apolitical in his public persona. A loyal Democrat, his letters reveal considerable antipathy for free-state legislators, but although impatient to return to normal life, he remained professional. And while the administration's goals were not achieved, Denver left Kansas in far better shape than he found it—whether from a sense that such behavior would no longer be tolerated or from sheer exhaustion from years of turmoil, there would be "no more 'Kansas troubles.'"[78] Indeed, his successor Samuel Medary reported "a different population there from what I expected, a population that was disposed to listen to what was said to them, who were disposed for peace."[79]

Within the territory, the two factions evolved into more typical party rivals. On November 25, Democrats called a convention at Leavenworth and stated that slavery would not be an issue. Among the resolutions they passed was one acknowledging that "the causes which have hitherto divided and estranged the people of Kansas no longer exist." However, they remained suspicious of Republicans for their "negro-equality tendencies" and favored excluding free blacks from Kansas.[80] Similarly, the original free-state party, a fragile organization due to its overreliance on personality, was finally replaced by an official Republican party.

Kansas' subsequent path to statehood was far quieter than many expected. Despite Denver's exhortations against more constitutions, the territory submitted a free-state constitution to Congress on January 6, 1859. As it was still underpopulated, no action was taken. Two months later, residents voted to begin the process anew that summer in Wyandotte, where the most pressing question before the convention was whether a new state had to absorb territorial debts and pay for damages inflicted by previous skirmishes.[81] On October 4, Kansans accepted this constitution 10,421 to 5,530.[82] Free-state activists saw the vote as the final defeat for slavery in Kansas. "We heard the booming of cannon along the river," Julia Lovejoy reported, "that told us that free principles were triumphing, and pro-slavery subserviency was breathing its last gasp in Kansas."[83] The Wyandotte constitution passed the House on April 11, 1860, but the Senate delayed action until after the presidential election.[84] During debate on the bill, from December 11, 1860, to January 21, 1861, six southern senators withdrew and returned home.[85]

Despite Buchanan's disappointment with the territory's rejection of the English bill, he believed he had diverted territorial attention "from fighting to voting, a most salutary change."[86] In the spring, one newspaper had warned that the English bill would have unintended consequences: "They proclaim that the Democracy have *settled* the Kansas question. They are only mistaken a little in the terms," the *Freedom Champion* editorialized. "Instead of the Democracy *settling* the Kansas question, the *Kansas question* has most effectually *settled* the *Democracy*."[87] But although the party was hurt in midterm elections, the English bill was not entirely to blame as economic conditions and long-standing party divisions in key states played a part.[88] Even though the party was hurt in Pennsylvania, its native son was sanguine about the rebuke and reassured his niece that Democrats would nonetheless succeed in the upcoming congressional session. "Poor bleeding Kansas is quiet and behaving herself in an orderly manner; but her wrongs have melted the hearts of sympathetic Pennsylvanians or rather Philadelphians."[89]

Because of his identification with such a widely despised bill, Buchanan was forced to justify his support of the constitution. "In the course of my long public life," the president wrote in his second annual message on December 6, "I have never performed any official act which, in the retrospect, has afforded me more heartfelt satisfaction. Its admission could have inflicted no possible injury on any human being, whilst it would, within a brief period, have restored peace to Kansas and harmony to the Union." Buchanan admitted that while he had advocated a popular vote on the constitution, he had had to defer to the convention's decision. Nonetheless, he was implacable in his conviction that his position was just, and neither the election results nor the bluster of prestigious critics could budge him.[90] In truth, the English bill's defeat had settled the Kansas question—the territory was not admitted, but, unlike earlier rejections, the terms for admission were clear; without the requisite population, Kansas would not become a state. However, if by the elusive peace and harmony he mourned in his speech Buchanan meant that the Kansas issue would continue to haunt the Democratic Party in national elections, then he was correct.

Buchanan recognized that the Kansas conflict meant that the national administration had to reassess its relationship to its territories, and he urged Congress to impose regulations to avoid a repeat of a debacle that was fueled, in part, by ambition. "It is surely no hardship for embryo governors, senators, and members of Congress, to wait until the number of inhabitants shall equal those of a single congressional district," the president reasoned. "They surely ought not to be permitted to rush into the Union with a population less than one-half of several of the large counties in the interior of some of the states."[91] This was sensible, but myopic nonetheless as Buchanan had tried to usher Kansas into the Union under precisely these circumstances.

In his memoir, a defensive Buchanan argued that civil war would not have arisen had Kansas residents respected the *Dred Scott* decision. Seeing this Supreme Court decision supporting their rights rejected by Republicans had swung many Southerners into "the hands of disunion agitators."[92] However, Buchanan did not adequately address the more important defection from within his own party—"the Douglas Democracy."[93] The carving off of support from both sides left Buchanan standing alone on a very narrow plank, propped up by only the most vehement slavery proponents. Not surprisingly, Buchanan found criticism of his conduct unfair as he was convinced that, once he became president, he could not favor a political plat-form above a Supreme Court decision.[94] However, Buchanan wanted and helped produce this decision, so his actions were not as objective and man-ifest as he preferred to remember. Moreover, the issues the *Dred Scott* deci-sion was to have settled were not relevant in Kansas, where voter fraud and the inability of the populace to vote on the Lecompton Constitution, not the status of slavery in the territory, were the critical issues.

When Buchanan returned from England on April 23, 1856, a great New York crowd had greeted his steamer. Gratified by his reception, Buchanan told the crowd that he had "been for years abroad in a foreign land, and I like the noise of democracy." When Buchanan was selected soon after as the Democratic Party's presidential nominee, he was hailed as "the consis-tent statesman, the pure patriot, and the honest man." He was described as a man having a "progressive view of public questions," but who had "that healthful degree of conservatism which checks excesses, guides events within the bounds of reason, and in fact sustains that healthful progress of society which is equally removed from rashness as from the dead calm of inactivity."[95] Buchanan must have been shocked that merely two years into his presidency the enchanting "noise of democracy" had transformed itself into a deafening roar of disapproval and dissent.

Part II

Making the Border Bleed

Chapter 6

The Illusion of Security: The Governments' Response to the Jayhawker Threat of Late 1860

Tony R. Mullis

The fearful consequences liable to result to the nation from any conflict of arms between citizens of the State of Missouri, and those of the Territory of Kansas, even though resulting from an effort to maintain the law and to shield the innocent from harm, cannot now be estimated, owing to the fact, that exaggerated reposts of any such occurrences are very certain to be circulated, and the minds of the people to become unduly excited.

Robert Stewart to James Denver, August 7, 1858

By late 1860, Bleeding Kansas no longer dominated the national media as it had during the brutal summer months of 1856 or with the Lecompton Constitution debate that followed from 1857 to 1858. The large-scale assaults by proslavery Missourians, whom many had characterized as "border ruffians," had ceased after the 1856 elections. In response to the border ruffian threat, many free-state supporters formed defensive associations to protect their communities against these attacks. Once these threats dissipated, several of these groups went on the offensive. These Jayhawker bands freed slaves in western Missouri, aided fugitive slaves, and hoped to abolish the evil institution through violent means.[1] Not all Jayhawkers were ideologically motivated; some simply sought revenge against those who had committed depredations against them. With the exodus of the most virulent proslavery zealots from the territory by 1860, Kansas appeared to have transitioned to a peaceful era where rule of law would dominate.

The relative calm that characterized the territory in late 1860, however, was illusory. Underneath the territory's fractured veneer were significant centripetal and centrifugal forces converging to disrupt that tenuous façade of peace. Like a fault zone between tectonic plates exerting tremendous pressure on each other beneath the earth's surface, Kansas appeared relatively secure to the contemporary citizen, but just under the surface, it was on the verge of disaster. The southeast Kansas and southwest Missouri regions served as the virtual epicenter of a potential catastrophe. From a national perspective, the *Dred Scott* decision and the defeat of the Lecompton Constitution had not eliminated the vitriolic debate over the expansion of slavery. The election of Abraham Lincoln in November and the subsequent secession convention in South Carolina set the nation on course for an enormous rupture. At the local level, ongoing vigilante activities targeting proslavery advocates, free-state supporters, and abolitionists continued without much national interest until November 1860, when Jayhawker activity in and around the town of Fort Scott and the Kansas-Missouri border escalated. A closer examination of the federal government's and the state of Missouri's response to the Jayhawker guerrilla campaign of late 1860 offers insight into the nature and character of the larger conflict that erupted in 1861.

The convergence of these external and internal forces along the Kansas-Missouri border in late 1860 could have been cataclysmic. Missourians trembled in fear of alleged or reported Jayhawker invasions, while the deployment of Missouri militia along the unstable border alarmed Kansans. The incidents, reports, and rumors that led to the so-called Southwest Expedition proved far less menacing than what the media or local citizens envisioned. Nonetheless, the deployment of the United States Army to the region, the positioning of Missouri militia along the border to prevent invasion, and the believable threats of Jayhawker raids challenged the Missouri, Kansas territorial, and federal governments' ability to respond to the perceived crisis. Ultimately, the federal, state, and local governments were powerless to restore the rule of law and to secure permanent political order. The Jayhawkers achieved their limited objectives in the face of state-sanctioned coercive power. But how did they achieve their objectives without precipitating a larger crisis or civil war? Traditional fears associated with a standing army, the sophistication of the Jayhawkers' operations, and the structural limitations of the federal system to respond effectively to local ideologically motivated criminal activity with national implications explain why the Jayhawkers succeeded. The best the federal and state governments could do was to maintain the illusion of peace as the tremors associated with the irrepressible conflict increased in magnitude.

Charles "Doc" Jennison's Jayhawkers triggered the crisis when his band

Charles Ransford "Doc" Jennison.
*Along with fellow abolitionist James
Montgomery, Charles Ransford Jennison
(1814–1871) led armed raids against the
proslavery settlers and forces on both sides
of the Kansas-Missouri border. During the
Civil War his Seventh Kansas Cavalry
Regiment were widely known as
"Jennison's Jayhawkers." Courtesy of the
Kansas Historical Society*

captured and executed at least three "Pro-slavery" individuals in November 1860. The victims' alleged crimes ranged from aiding in the recovery of fugitive slaves to simply talking "too conservative."[2] Jennison's vigilante actions coupled with a Jayhawker raid on the town of Fort Scott on November 19 necessitated a response from both federal and state authorities.[3] The Fort Scott raid had forced the Third District judge, Joseph Williams, and the majority of his staff to flee to Missouri. The executions and dispersal were clearly illegal, but no one on the Kansas side seemed able or willing to arrest the perpetrators. Revenge, plunder, and violent protest against the Fugitive Slave Law motivated the Jayhawkers. They hoped to render the Fugitive Slave Law obsolete by targeting those who supported slavery while liberating slaves from bondage. But there were significant obstacles to the Jayhawkers' political agenda. Federal and local law enforcement, the United States Army, territorial and state militia, and other vigilante groups offered potentially lethal responses to Jayhawker activities. Yet, the key Jayhawker leaders, Jennison and James Montgomery, managed to elude capture and continued to achieve their goals in the face of over-whelming numbers and capabilities.

The federal government and the state of Missouri had few practical options to restore order as long as the Jayhawkers practiced effective guerrilla tactics and maintained a reliable sanctuary in southeastern Kansas. Previous governors, army commanders, and local law enforcement officials had tried, but their successes were limited. One option previous territorial governors had used was the army. As a national, disciplined, and theoretically impartial force, the army could normally compel order and promote security. Unfortunately, there were limits to its employment in domestic civil disorders. Most of these earlier territorial governors were reluctant to use the army, but there was no other competent force available. When these governors used regular troops, they were always under the command of a civilian authority in accordance with the principles and guidelines associated with posse comitatus and War Department restrictions.[4] The other option was martial law. Although this was theoretically feasible, no federal or state official used it. A martial law declaration could be just as dangerous to the region's peace and order as uncontrolled Jayhawker or other vigilante activity.

Neither option offered a satisfactory solution. The eventual response, a more aggressive use of the army, went beyond the civilian control normally associated with posse comitatus, but fell short of martial law. By all contemporary measures of success, this hybrid solution worked. By the middle of December, the various Jayhawker bands had dispersed, the vigilante executions had ceased, and the threat of invasion to Missouri evaporated. That apparent success, however, was illusory. A more in-depth analysis of the Southwest Expedition and an assessment of the major factors that limited the use of the army suggest a different conclusion.

The War Department's understanding of the border crisis was manifest in its orders to Brigadier General William S. Harney. Because the Jayhawker raid on the town of Fort Scott had dispersed the United States District Court, forced Judge Williams to flee to Missouri, and indicated intent to invade Missouri, Harney was to go to Fort Scott and take appropriate "steps to break up the lawless band." Colonel Samuel Cooper, the War Department's adjutant, informed Harney that "as soon as legal process shall issue for the arrest of those Robbers . . . you will proceed at once to break up the band & capture the offenders without any regard to consequences."[5] Harney's instructions clearly reflected the federal government's intent to respond to the threat and to the security concerns associated with a possible invasion.

Secretary of War John Floyd had no qualms about placing the army under civilian authority to enforce law and order in Kansas and simultaneously provide for the security of Missouri. The caveat of "without any regard to consequences" in Harney's instructions was particularly noteworthy. All prior guidance stressed caution in the army's dealings with local populations. Restraint and nonviolent conflict resolution guided army involvement in domestic affairs. This more aggressive use of federal force revealed a heretofore-absent determination to use the full power of the federal government to enforce federal law, eliminate the Jayhawkers, and restore order.

The lame duck administration of James Buchanan was now willing to risk the potentially negative consequences of unleashing the army against the elusive Jayhawkers. "It is hoped that the eight companies of U.S. troops at your command will be ample force to break up [James] Montgomery's band," Cooper commented; "if not you are fully authorized to call to your aid any additional U.S. troops within the limits of your department."[6] Clearly, the Buchanan administration was deadly serious in its objective to resolve the border difficulties. The army, however, simply did not have the necessary resources. With or without the assistance of the Kansas and Missouri militias and law enforcement officials, the army was again in a precarious and potentially lethal situation. If the federal government used coercive or lethal force against American citizens, regardless of their political views or the nature of the associated criminal activity, what would the consequences of those actions be?

As Harney proceeded to Fort Leavenworth to gather what troops he could, Governor Robert Stewart ordered his Missouri militia to the border. The Missouri legislature had authorized the tremendous sum of $30,000 for the governor to use as he saw fit to resolve border troubles.[7] With this funding, Stewart could support state-sponsored military action for about a month. Brigadier General Daniel Frost, the Southwest Expedition commander, led the force. As Stewart directed, Frost informed Harney of his orders and his force's capabilities. Frost reported that he was en route to the border "with orders . . . to repel any invasion of the State." "My command," Frost stressed, "is well organized and properly armed, and will be as serviceable as any regular I have ever seen by the time I reach the border."[8]

Frost's command numbered up to 1,000 troops by the time it reached the state line. In the spirit of cooperation, Frost informed Harney that the governor's instructions allowed him "to respond to <u>any</u> call you may make upon me or my Command and it will afford me great pleasure to place myself under your orders to go to such [points] and perform such duties as you may require of me." "My only object," Frost emphasized, was "to maintain the dignity and laws of the United States as well as the State of Missouri." Frost's men were "sworn regularly into the service of the State" and were required "to sustain the Constitution and Laws of the United States as well."[9]

Cooperation with the army was one matter, but the Southwest Expedition also needed the cooperation and tacit support of the local citizenry. Unfortunately, the Missouri militia was not always able to gain that collaboration. "I found that orderly, industrious, and peaceable citizens have been warned to leave," Frost commented, "or that they would be robbed and hung. Many have deserted their homes." Most significantly, from a military perspective, "[m]any [citizens] along our route have failed to treat us with ordinary civility for fear of incurring the displeasure of these Kansas outlaws and marauders."[10] The local population was vital to any successful military or policing operation. Whether protecting Missouri from invasion or capturing outlaws, without civilian cooperation there was limited intelligence to plan for and react to Jayhawker activities. The obvious effects of the Jayhawkers' terror campaign inhibited the militia's ability to conduct its mission. Without the people's cooperation and support, no amount of military presence could stop Montgomery's Jayhawkers.

Nonetheless, the Missouri militia proceeded to the border in good order. Harney never called upon Frost or his troops. He was probably correct in avoiding any association with the Missouri militia. The integration of the militia with United States regulars could have triggered a far more serious situation. Despite the benefits of additional troops and resources, the animosity and distrust that usually existed between state and regular forces could have complicated Harney's operations. The perception of army regulars and Missouri militia acting as a police force in Kansas could have been too much for the locals to bear in 1860. Kansas too had its own territorial militia, but any thought of combining with the army to pursue the Jayhawkers into Missouri could have been equally disastrous. The army's mission was to restore law and order, not create circumstances that could lead to civil war. Augustus Wattles, a staunch Kansas abolitionist, voiced those concerns. He questioned Missouri's motives for deploying so many troops along the border. "The old cry of insurrection. When they [proslavery advocates] are defeated is familiar to all." Wattles further lamented, "How can Kansas be in insurrection against Mo.?" Interesting question, but Wattles explained that "the story is intended to rain an excitement to blind the country to the great outrage against the settlers in selling their farms at the present Land Sale."[11]

Wattles also downplayed the alleged Jayhawker threat to Missouri. "Montgomery has no 1000 men nor 500 men nor any number of men from [xxx]." He believed that Judge Williams and the like exaggerated numbers in order to exacerbate border tensions. Mongomery's followers were no more than a group of settlers who came together "to protect their property against speculators." Wattles concluded, this "is formidable only to those who are intending wrong."[12] The last comment appears to be a criticism of proslavery territorial officials who Wattles believed were conspiring to create yet another slave territory by controlling land sales and using the army to remove free-state settlers from existing claims on various Cherokee tracts.

Wattles believed that land sales and protection of local claims were greater concerns to free-state locals than invading Missouri. The "settlers cannot pay for their claims and the President, as I understood, advised them to combine for their mutual protection. They have done so." Wattles revealed what he believed were the real reasons for the crisis. Regarding the federal and state attempts to eliminate the Jayhawkers, Wattles assessed, "But as this breaks up the plan of ridding Southern Kansas of free State settlers it is called an insurrection and Capt. Montgomery & others are charged with crime, and Gen. Har[n]ey is sent with the U.S. army to arrest them." From Wattles's perspective, "all this (federal and Missouri military activity) is to cripple the free State by depriving the settlers of their home & thus removing one great obstacle to the making of a new Slave State out of Southern Kansas & the Cherokee Country."[13] As farfetched as Wattles's explanation may seem, it undoubtedly resonated with some.

James Montgomery, however, had a far different assessment. In a letter to George Stearns, he mentioned "the flight of Judge Williams and the Marshal from Fort Scott. So great was the Stampede from the Fort," Montgomery observed, "that the place was almost instantly deserted. The only federal official to remain at Fort Scott was the land receiver." Montgomery praised the land receiver's actions because they proved that he "possesses a good conscience; and they [presumably Fort Scott residents] now listen with confidence to what he tells them."[14] This implies that if the land office and the upcoming land sales were not specific targets, then the Jayhawker visit did at least separate those who feared them from those who were tolerant or supportive of their cause.

Days after the Fort Scott raid, the territorial secretary, George Beebe, visited Montgomery. Beebe was acting governor while Samuel Medary was absent. Montgomery claimed that Beebe "had heard strange rumors of our doings, and like a sensible man as he appears to be, came in person to ascertain the truth in regard to affairs." Montgomery concluded that Beebe "found where the wrong lay." If Montgomery was correct, Beebe left believing the Jayhawkers acted "calmly and dispassionately, on well established precedents." Allegedly, Beebe promised to do all he could to protect Jayhawker rights, but he recommended that they resolve their differences in the federal court. The assumption was that Beebe would "reform abuses in that department."[15]

If Montgomery accurately portrayed Beebe's sentiments, then it appears that the Jayhawkers could co-opt the territorial government. Beebe's emphasis on a judicial resolution reflected a traditional American approach to conflict resolution. Of course, Montgomery did not trust the federal courts, especially the Third District Court. After all, Judge Williams had issued an indictment against Montgomery for the murder of former deputy marshal John Little during the rescue of Ben Rice at Fort Scott in December 1858.[16] The implication was clear. If Beebe could have a "friendly" judge appointed to the district court in lieu of the departed Williams, then the Jayhawkers might be willing to comply with accepted judicial proceedings. A new judge might allay Jayhawker threats to law and order in Kansas, but it did not eliminate the threat of an invasion of Missouri.

Before the Jayhawkers could plan or execute any sort of operation in Missouri, they had to respond to the army's presence in Kansas. "Our people are very destitute," Montgomery explained, "and if they let the troops loose upon us, we may be chased all over Kansas; and possibly into Arkansas, and we will need all the help we can get, for in that case we will have no time to work for anything." Harney was clearly a concern. But Montgomery had outfoxed and outmaneuvered the army before. Montgomery used the army's presence to support his operations. "All that is needed here," Montgomery explained, "to make the times interesting is the presence of United States Troops." The Jayhawker leader played on traditional American fears of a standing army by telling Medary that the army's presence in southeast Kansas "would be considered insulting to our dignity as free-born American citizens."[17]

Montgomery's interpretation of why the Buchanan administration sent the army to capture him is intriguing. "You are aware," he informed George Stearns, "that Uncle Sam is making some big splurges out this way, he has let 'Old Harney loose,' but for all that he is likely to effect, he might as well have been kept at home." The army's response was not based on "the hanging of a few scoundrels." Montgomery believed the army was after him because there was a "nigger in the woodpile." "The 'nigger' is here," he admitted, "but Uncle Sam can't get him." This incriminating but insightful comment suggests that Montgomery saw all governmental responses to his actions through the prism of the Fugitive Slave Law. "Nothing short of stationing a Regiment in every county will prevent us from keeping him [fugitive slaves] here," Montgomery proudly exclaimed, "and, when that is done, we will pass him [fugitive slaves] on somewhere else. The Government has taken great pains to make the country believe that 'Montgomery and his band' do not belong to the people."[18]

Displaying another characteristic of guerrilla warfare, Montgomery justified his actions as those approved by and for the "people." "The action of Montgomery and his band, was not only endorsed, but declared to be 'the act of the people.' The men composing the 'Executive Committee' are obliged to keep out of the way, at present, but can have a home among the people; and our darkies too are welcome wherever we go." In a subsequent letter, Montgomery stated that his band was "a myth. Montgomery's men are the people, and Montgomery himself is one of them."[19] Montgomery's language exemplified future insurgent leaders' understanding of this kind of war.

Normally, most vigilante or self-protection associations had refrained from engaging the army. The army was one of the few largely neutral entities in Kansas, and all sides recognized its impartiality. To Montgomery, however, the army was nothing more than the government's coercive tool to enforce immoral laws or to support proslavery government officials. He normally avoided lethal confrontations with better-armed, -trained, and -equipped entities. But he was also willing to fight if the circumstances were favorable. Again, Montgomery understood the basic tenets of guerrilla warfare and never risked his force unless the odds favored him.

Even when he was outmanned, Montgomery displayed an impressive understanding of how to manipulate the government's response to Jayhawker actions in his favor. "Our late experience in the 'war of extreme ferocity,' has been decidedly rich," Montgomery informed F. B. Sanborn. In his astute analysis of the challenge Harney faced in countering Jayhawker operations, Montgomery concluded, "Harney was powerless, here, and, of that, no one was more sensible than himself. Had he proclaimed Martial Law, as we supposed he would do, He would have got himself ingloriously whipped." No one knows for sure if this would have occurred, but Montgomery's backhanded compliment to Harney was quite revealing. "We did not wish to fight, but we would not have held still to be murdered. We had only to mount a small active force and play off. The scarcity of food would have compelled the troops to keep close to their wagons."[20]

His Jayhawkers' limited numbers coupled with their inherent mobility and lethality frustrated the army's attempts to capture them. Moreover, the army's reliance on its own organic sustainment capability and its usual lack of cavalry to match the Jayhawkers' mobility reflected a perennial operational constraint. All Harney could muster from Fort Leavenworth and Fort Riley was two artillery companies, one dragoon element, and one infantry company.[21] Without the means to match the Jayhawkers' operational advantages, the army could not be used effectively. "By shifting frequently," Montgomery stressed, "we elude the troops, and this is thought better, under the circumstances, than fighting them."[22] The bottom line in Montgomery's tactical approach was that "large forces would have moved too slow, and small forces could not have taken us."[23]

The army's presence did hinder Montgomery's operations. Montgomery lamented that he might have "to stay away from my family all winter." Certainly, this was a difficult decision, but his commitment to his cause and the support available made these types of sacrifices a minor inconvenience. While evading the army, Montgomery planned to continue his mission. By "extending our 'Wide Awake' Organization, and in taking care of our fugitives," Montgomery continued his crusade while on the run.[24] He could do so because he had the knowledge and faith that he had the necessary local and external support to continue Jayhawking until the Fugitive Slave Law was obsolete. "This is an interesting experiment," Montgomery confided to Stearns, "and must not be allowed to fail. If we are able to maintain our position, and of this I have no doubt, the Fugitive Slave Law is dead; and slavery will quickly disappear from Missouri, Arkansas, and the Cherokee Country."[25]

Faith in his cause alone was not sufficient to eradicate the Fugitive

Slave Law. Montgomery also possessed other distinctive advantages. "With our knowledge of the country and the favorable disposition of the inhabitants, One Hundred Thousand men could not have done what Harney was ordered to do." Current counterinsurgency doctrine validates Montgomery's assertion. FM 3-24, *Counterinsurgency*, suggests, "maintaining security in an unstable area requires vast resources." Few would have disagreed with this claim. "In contrast, a small number of highly motivated insurgents with simple weapons, good operations security, and even limited mobility can undermine security over a large area."[26] Montgomery's Jayhawkers certainly met these criteria. While there is no way to prove Montgomery's declaration, the army's inability to use all available means suggests that Montgomery understood the limits of any counterinsurgency operation. As a measure of success, the Jayhawker leader boasted that the army did "not even compel us to send away our fugitives, of whom we had ten of different ages and sexes."[27]

While Montgomery could generally co-opt local and territorial officials and outrun or outfox the army, he was somewhat perplexed by Governor Stewart's deployment of state militia. Contrary to what many Missourians assumed, Montgomery was not interested in invading Missouri. "I am not in favor of invading the slave states so long as they keep themselves at home. But if they cross the line to interfere with us as Missouri is now threatening to do," Montgomery stressed, "then I would consider the war begun."[28] Montgomery claimed he was unaware of Stewart's purpose for sending the militia. "The rank and file threaten to come over," he reported, "but that will be as the leaders say." It is difficult to believe that Montgomery would be clueless about the militia's stated purpose to repel Montgomery's anticipated invasion. From the Kansas side, one could easily conclude that an invasion was imminent if one was unaware or uninformed of Stewart's intent and orders. Even if Montgomery knew of Stewart's plan, it is likely that he would see it as a ruse to hide Missouri's true intentions.

In reality, Governor Stewart had severely restricted his militia's operations. The militia went to the frontier for purely defensive purposes. At no time were they authorized to cross into Kansas. Stewart fully understood the consequences of a state force operating in a federal jurisdiction. In his restrictive guidelines, the governor authorized Colonel J. F. Snyder to "use all available means at [his] command in repelling the invasion and inflicting condign punishment upon the invaders of our peace." Most importantly, the militia must "be cautious not to infringe upon the Constitutional laws of the Federal Government by following the invaders over the State line into Kansas Territory."[29]

Stewart was consistent in his guidance. In response to threatened violence and criminal activity in April 1859, Stewart provided clear but restrictive instructions. Neither G. A. Parsons, adjutant general of the Missouri militia, nor his troops were authorized to "cross the line into Kansas Territory, either in the effort to expel marauders from the State, or to arrest them; nor to do any overt act tending justly to engender strife between the citizens of Kansas Territory and of this State." Parsons's only object was to adopt "whatever measures are necessary for the preservation of the lives of our citizens and the protection of their property." He was also "to provide for the instant assistance of the civil authorities in their efforts to arrest and bring to justice any marauding bandits found in the said district of country south in the State, liable to suffer from their incursions."[30] Clearly, there was no implied or stated intent to invade Kansas.

Stewart's guidance demonstrated a sensible understanding of the complexities of meeting his official obligations. He had to defend and protect his citizens; it would have been politically unacceptable to do otherwise. At the same time, he needed to prevent a larger conflict. His challenge, like that of Medary in Kansas, was to keep the local citizenry out of the security and law enforcement business. Given the ubiquity of vigilante committees, self-protective societies, and normal criminal activity of the region, that objective was a tall order.

In the end, there was no invasion of Missouri, and law and order concerns around Fort Scott lessened. The Southwest Expedition was reduced following the Jayhawker dispersal. A reduced element was left behind to defend the border. The smaller Southwest Battalion eventually faded away as the nation moved closer to civil war. The army left two companies behind to keep the peace, but it too would soon reorient its focus from the western border to the growing conflict in the East.[31]

Kansas became a state on January 29, 1861. The change in status altered the formal relationship between Kansas and Missouri, but it did not lessen the border tensions. Just weeks prior to statehood, Montgomery made a somewhat prophetic observation. "A vote is soon to be taken to determine whether Missouri will secede or not. If she goes out, she will soon be a free state. She will certainly attack us, here, and we will, as certainly, fight her." On that account, Montgomery was correct, as Jim Lane's raid on Osceola revealed in September 1861 and William Quantrill's retaliatory raid on

Lawrence confirmed in August 1863. "This will make warm work for a time, but a short war is preferable to a continuance of the present state of affairs."[32] Perhaps a short war would have been preferable, but it took four long, bloody years to resolve that ordeal.

Given the actions and reactions of the major players associated with the last political killings in Kansas and the Fort Scott raid, what best explains the apparent failure of Missouri, the Kansas Territory, and the United States Army to eliminate the Jayhawker threat? Alternatively, perhaps it is better to ask why the Southwest Expedition has received minimal attention. Most interpretations conclude that Harney's arrival forced the Jayhawkers to disperse, or in other words—"mission accomplished."

A closer examination of Montgomery's motives and actions provides a different conclusion. The army's presence in and around Fort Scott in December 1860 and the Missouri militia's deployment to the border did appear to accomplish the collective governments' objectives. The Jayhawkers did disperse before any anticipated invasion of Missouri occurred. The vigilante executions ceased, at least temporarily. The combined effects of establishing a defensive force along the border, plus the use of the army as an active law enforcement capability, were rational and feasible governmental responses. But were those actions really successful?

The evidence suggests that these indicators of success were illusory; the army's apparent triumph was nothing more than a veneer that masked the reality of a Jayhawker victory. Montgomery and his band were in no way defeated, discouraged, or permanently dispersed. The army was unable to arrest or eliminate a single Jayhawker. The movement did not wither and die. The decentralized Jayhawkers merely used traditional insurgent tactics and dispersed because they were at a tactical disadvantage. Their ability to blend in with the local population and the active and passive acceptance of their activities made it virtually impossible for the army to find, let alone eradicate, the Jayhawkers short of measures that were more draconian. General Order 11 would be representative of the harsher measures the federal government employed to eradicate guerrilla activity in four western Missouri counties in August 1863.

Because Montgomery understood that the army could use its inherent force and coercive power only to a certain point, he used those constraints in his favor. Montgomery continued his crusade against the Fugitive Slave Law despite the army's presence and the Missouri militia's deployment along the border. He effectively challenged the government to up the ante by declaring martial law. Although some recommended such a declaration, levelheaded thinking on Medary's part prevented that option.[33]

A *New York Times* article captured the essence of Medary's dilemma. It asked a fundamental question—were Lykins (now Miami), Linn, and Bourbon Counties truly in insurrection? If not, was there an inherent danger in declaring martial law? "Should such a fatal policy be adopted," the reporter warned, "there is no predicting the end." Moreover, Medary adamantly opposed Missouri forces crossing the border "under any circumstances." The article predicted, "bedlam will run loose here from that moment. Gen. Harney is known to be unscrupulous in these matters, and therefore Gov. Medary feels that he needs 'holding in.'"[34]

The Kansas governor understood the severe implications and consequences of declaring martial law. The presence of United States regulars, Kansas forces, multiple local law enforcement officials as well as the Missouri state militia could have triggered a national civil war had he declared martial law. Many of the locals undoubtedly wanted an end to the violence and suffering. But they were also suspicious and concerned about the use of the army and other forms of state-sanctioned coercion to resolve the problem. These fears explain why it was so difficult for the army to restore law and order.

There were at least four reasons why the army failed. The first was the long-standing historical fear of using the army to enforce the law. Using military force to achieve security and order is always a delicate operation in a democratic society because, unless that force is restrained, it can be used for oppression and tyranny. From the Boston Massacre to the use of federal militia in response to the Whiskey Rebellion to Bleeding Kansas, the use of the regular military to enforce law generated a great deal of fear and skepticism. One of the biggest fears was the use of the army beyond posse comitatus in order to implement martial law. During the Fort Scott incident, the *New York Times* reported that "Gen. Harney and some of the territorial appointees" had made "a strong effort" for Medary to "proclaim martial law in these lower counties, but that the Governor [was] very punctilious in his refusal." The reporter reinforced traditional American concerns when he concluded that the empowerment of the military in a martial law situation would set an unfortunate precedent and could prove catastrophic. "On all former occasions," the reporter observed, "the civil authority in Kansas has been superior to the military, and it is liable to prove a great calamity, if that great principle does not hold good now."[35]

Should Harney be let loose, as Medary feared, the renowned Indian fighter might resolve the border situation through the application of lethal force to compel the adversary to abide by his will.[36]

Previous Kansas governors dealt with similar circumstances, and each tended to resist using the army unless it was necessary. For example, Governor James Denver had requested and received army detachments for the Fort Scott area on several occasions before and after the Marais des Cygnes Massacre of May 1858. By August, he felt he could withdraw the regulars, but left a contingent of volunteers under the command of Captain A. J. Weaver. The captain's force was also insufficient and generated its own concerns. Weaver too was uncomfortable using military force to police the area. After Weaver reported that all was quiet, he expressed his and others' hopes that "every semblance of Military power may soon be withdrawn from civil affairs."[37]

The militias themselves were also problematic. In Missouri, J. F. Snyder was "thoroughly satisfied that military force is absolutely necessary to enforce the laws and restore peace to this locality, but I am also convinced that it would be highly imprudent to call out the militia of this County." Snyder recommended that Governor Stewart "order out one of the St. Louis independent companies, or give me power to call out a company from my county or the adjoining counties, to equip them immediately and place them here on active service as Rangers."[38] The danger of using local militia in 1860 was the same as it had been during the earlier years of Bleeding Kansas. Impassioned and angry locals tended to lose any sense of perspective, objectivity, and restraint when it came to their own homes and their own security. Disciplined, impartial army soldiers and more distant state militia would mitigate the emotions and limit the potentiality of a larger conflict.

The second reason why apparent success was illusory was political. No politician or political appointee wanted to be responsible for more death and destruction, but they did not want anarchy either. Perhaps Governor Medary summed up the challenge best. "When the evil-doer is covered with the mantle of party politics, and wrested from the hands of justice as a partisan measure," Medary observed, "the axe is laid at the root of our free institutions, and the cruelest of Despotisms will rise up, a monument to infamy, to mark their place."[39] Governor Stewart, even though a lame duck, had no motive to use his role as commander-in-chief to widen the conflict. He consistently restricted the militia's operations and provided clear and restrictive rules of engagement. The president, also a lame duck, had nothing to lose politically, and he upped the stakes by sending Harney to resolve the problem at the risk of generating a greater conflict. Fortunately, Montgomery and most Jayhawkers understood their limits as well. They had no desire to use lethal force unless the army used it first. As Montgomery surmised, "We did not wish to fight, but we would not have held still to be murdered."[40]

Third, traditional operational concerns also hampered the army's capability to stabilize the border region. These constraints ranged from restrictive rules of engagement to resource limitations to operational security concerns. Perhaps the greatest limitation was resource constraints; the army simply had too few soldiers to stabilize the region effectively. Federal and state decision makers were either uncertain about the number of forces required or unwilling to expend the necessary resources to fully pacify and secure the Kansas-Missouri border. No one in authority was willing to provide the required level of effort to subdue fellow citizens or to capture marauding outlaws. Moreover, the political leadership did not consider more radical solutions such as those General Thomas Ewing pursued following Quantrill's Raid on Lawrence in August 1863. The effects of a General Order No. 11 initiative in 1860 might have achieved positive results, or it could have triggered a larger conflict.[41] The thought of depopulating entire counties of known or suspected guerrillas was unpalatable. Given these constraints, the army could do little to pacify or arrest Montgomery and his followers. The Jayhawkers' motivation, superior armaments, and superb operational security virtually guaranteed success against the government's counterguerrilla forces.

Operational security was an especially intriguing Jayhawker advantage. Jayhawkers knew the region's human and physical terrain since they were local residents. They also developed secret protocols to identify fellow members.[42] They were, as Montgomery boasted, "of the people" and those that were against them were usually intimidated to the point that they were neutralized. Most along the border were probably passive bystanders who opted out of any tangle with the Jayhawkers or the government. The federal and state government forces, however, were not so fortunate. The people expected to know what their army or what their respective militias were doing. Following the May 1858 Marais des Cygnes Massacre, one of Stewart's supporters was shocked to discover that Stewart's instructions to a militia commander in Independence were not published in the local paper. Some feared that without widespread knowledge and dissemination of the governor's intent in employing the state militia, Stewart's actions might "be misconstrued."[43] This was only one example of the governments' requirement to keep the public informed, but it also kept the Jayhawkers informed of the governments' intent and the militia's movement.

Another concern was the fundamental nature of the operations. Posse comitatus was designed to aid civil law enforcement in the execution of laws; it did not lend itself well to traditional security operations where the military had the lead. The Jayhawkers committed criminal acts, but Missourians saw them more as a security concern. The former would normally necessitate a law enforcement response, while the latter was a public safety issue. The army or the state militia would normally respond to security threats. But under the resource-constrained circumstances of 1860, they could not secure the area and arrest all the outlaws without a massive and continuous presence. As Governor Denver concluded in 1858, the "contiguity of the States of Missouri and Arkansas to the territory of Kansas affords so many facilities for persons committing offences against the laws of one to escape to the others and thus escape punishment." "These offenders," Denver surmised, "can always keep beyond the reach of any military force, and they can be exterminated only by the active and energetic exertions of the people themselves. In fact, it is better at all times that the people should be taught to rely on themselves for protection against such offenders and in the maintenance of the laws."[44] Denver was not alone in his emphasis on the people as the solution. Ironically, the same people Denver encouraged to resolve the law and order challenges were the ones Montgomery considered his supporters.

The last obstacle to an effective governmental response was structural. The federal system simply lacked an acceptable means to resolve cross-jurisdictional conflicts. The army was readily available to assist civilian authorities in times of crisis, but the state had to request federal assistance unless federal property was involved. Kansas was a federal entity, and the governor generally had authority to use federal troops, with certain restrictions, to help enforce the law.

By late 1860, the federal, territorial, and state leadership was in transition. Medary had decided to resign his office as early as November 1860; Stewart's term ended in January 1861, and Abraham Lincoln was awaiting inauguration. Moreover, there was no one entity in the federal system that could resolve the multijurisdictional problem without declaring martial law and using the army. There was neither a national gendarmerie nor a Royal

Canadian Mounted Police equivalent that could provide a national response. No other organization possessed the trained personnel and adequate resources to address the border crisis of late 1860. The danger of combining federal, state, and local capabilities to meet those challenges was potentially worse than the actual Jayhawker threat. At its very core, the Fort Scott incident was a local law enforcement and security problem with national implications, but there were no national means to resolve this challenge. A national police force may not have resolved the border situation, but it could have offered the possibility of an impartial, unified response without risking real or perceived military control.

In the shadow of the Civil War, the relatively bloodless Jayhawker raid on Fort Scott in November 1860 and the subsequent response from the federal and state governments pales in comparison. Historians have tended to ignore or minimize the significance of this event, and that is understandable given the limited impact it had.[45] But if one digs deeper and views the incident from a law enforcement, insurgency, and security prism, it is representative of an American approach toward domestic order and security. From Montgomery's nuanced and sophisticated use of terror and force to eradicate the Fugitive Slave Law to the various governmental responses to stop him, it reveals an American society that was skeptical if not fearful of the use of state-sanctioned force to resolve political or criminal crises and a society that was ill-structured to respond to them.

Americans should be skeptical of the use of regular army or militia forces in domestic situations. That does not mean that there is no role for their use, but that the circumstances should be rare and justified by the exigency. Without a robust national law enforcement capability to address large-scale multijurisdictional crises, there is no other institution that can address the law-enforcement challenges that the border crisis of 1860 represented. Even then, a highly motivated, armed, sufficiently funded, and well-led organization such as the Jayhawkers proved they could use righteous violence to achieve their aims with minimal threat to their existence. Fear of a standing army will always characterize an American society cognizant of its civil rights and individual liberties. There may be times, however, when that army is needed to protect those cherished liberties through the maintenance of political and societal order. The tension between liberty and order will always remain below the surface of American society.

In a larger context, the Southwest Expedition showed that all sides involved in the border crisis understood the limits regarding those "fearful consequences" Governor Stewart warned Governor Denver about in 1858. Maintaining the status quo along the border, despite its periodic violence and disorder, was certainly preferable to all-out conflict. On the one hand, excessive or lethal force on the federal, state, or territorial government's part could have fatally severed the weak cords that held the Union together. Anything less than complete annihilation of the Jayhawker threat, on the other hand, kept the border tensions regarding slavery and its expansion alive. For their part, the Jayhawkers' limited albeit controversial assault on the peculiar institution kept them below the threshold of civil war. All involved seemed to know their limits, and they stayed within them in hopes of preventing national suicide. Perhaps those federal, territorial, and state officials so often maligned for incompetence did the best anyone could have done given the inadequate resources and inflamed tensions of the antebellum era. The Civil War may have been inevitable, but the federal, state, and Jayhawker leadership in November and December 1860 demonstrated that national unity, however weakened, could be maintained through a measured and rational response. Yet, without the power or capability to maintain or to enforce order and unity on the entire nation, it was only a matter of time before secession, the bombardment of Fort Sumter, and President Lincoln's call for 75,000 volunteers forced the issue of civil war.

Once the Civil War began in 1861, the guerrilla tactics Charles Jennison's and James Montgomery's Jayhawkers employed in late 1860 became less constrained and more lethal as the war for the Union unleashed the baser instincts of Kansans and Missourians. The Union army responded to the internecine violence along the border with greater force and conviction that was lacking when the federal government saw the border troubles as a law enforcement challenge. The concerted efforts most Kansans, Missourians, and the federal government made to prevent civil war in late 1860 were admirable, but ultimately they could not contain nor prevent the various forces that collided along the Kansas-Missouri border from erupting into the greatest crisis the republic had ever faced.

Chapter 7

"If I Went West, I Think I Would Go to Kansas": Abraham Lincoln, the Sunflower State, and the Election of 1860

Jonathan Earle

When the new Republican Party held a presidential rally in Pittsburgh in 1856, just two years after the Kansas-Nebraska Act brought the slavery issue to the forefront of American politics, Pennsylvanian Walter Whitehead proudly hoisted aloft a U.S. flag with a large star urging the admission of Kansas to the Union as a free state. The rally was part of the presidential campaign of that year, when Republican John C. Frémont challenged (and lost) to Pennsylvania's own James Buchanan. Four years later, after moving to Kansas, Whitehead carried the same flag in numerous rallies in support of the second Republican candidate for president, Abraham Lincoln.[1]

Whitehead hoped to cast a Republican ballot in the 1860 election, as he had four years earlier. Yet the votes of Southerners and Democrats in Congress ensured that Kansas would not enter the Union before six Southern states had seceded, and Whitehead was thus prevented from voting in the election that made his hero the sixteenth president of the United States. The support of Republicans like Whitehead, however, on the border and especially in Kansas, figured largely in Lincoln's political life. To put it bluntly, without Kansas, Abraham Lincoln would never have been president of the United States. Moreover, if it were not for Kansas, Lincoln would not just have lost the 1860 presidential election—he wouldn't even have been a candidate. Or a national political figure. Without Kansas, Abraham Lincoln would have, in all likelihood, remained a crackerjack lawyer, a leading citizen of Springfield, Illinois, and a caring family man. He would have pointed to a single term in Congress as the high point of his political life—a term in which he did not distinguish himself in any significant way.[2]

Certainly Lincoln was no failure. But "one-term congressman" and "wealthy and able railroad lawyer" are hardly equal to the nearly universal praise now heaped on Lincoln, the president who regularly tops the lists of our most effective chief executives.[3] Exactly what role did the Sunflower State—and the Kansas-Missouri border—play in the life and career of Abraham Lincoln? How did Kansas, both as a real place and as a metaphor (or a symbol) change the course of this man's trajectory, and that of our nation? And why should residents of this particular manmade geographic entity feel a special connection with Lincoln?

Abraham Lincoln visited Kansas, the place, just once, for a week in the late fall of 1859. It was not an insignificant visit: over the course of the trip, Lincoln made important contacts, tried out new ideas, honed an impressive speech, and saw firsthand the place that had captured his (and the nation's) imagination and hijacked its politics. But when Lincoln made his sojourn to Kansas, he did so as yet another politician seeking the support of the state's Republicans in an upcoming campaign. His speech did not even merit a single line in the *Leavenworth Freedom's Champion*—the leading newspaper in the thriving town where he gave it. And in the end he had to capture the Republican nomination in 1860 without the votes of the Kansas delegation, which stuck with New York senator William H. Seward.

Still, when asked if he would advise someone to "go West" in the months after his territorial foray, Lincoln replied: "If I went West, I think I would go to Kansas—to Leavenworth or Atchison. Both of them are, and will continue to be, fine growing places."[4] Clearly something about Kansas connected—in a powerful way—with the all-but-declared candidate. And if it wasn't his Kansas journey, which took place during a brutally cold week in early December 1859, what was it?

Plainly stated, Kansas (the idea this time, as well as the actual place) offered Abraham Lincoln the "road back" to national political prominence, after a five-and-a-half-year period in the political desert of central Illinois. It did so in a way that allowed the former conservative Whig to highlight, in new, historically grounded, and moral language exactly why slavery had to be stopped at Kansas' front door. In other words, the controversy over Kansas gave Lincoln specifically (just as it had Republicans generally) an ideal case study from which to proceed in his personal antislavery journey.

Flag with Kansas State Star, 1856. *Walter Whitehead first carried this hand-crafted flag urging the admission of Kansas to the Union as a free state at a Republican campaign rally for John C. Frémont in Pittsburgh, Pennsylvania, in 1856. Four years later it was used at a rally for Lincoln in Kansas Territory. The flag currently is on display in the main gallery of the Kansas Museum of History. Courtesy of the Kansas Museum of History*

Finally, Lincoln's thinking on Kansas also showcased a politician who had, in the previous half-decade, metamorphosed from a rather typical (even "low-road") office seeker and holder into the rhetorically gifted statesman we celebrate today. The debate (and then fight) over Kansas was the issue that created the Republican Party and rescued the career of its first president.

Lincoln's Kansas-centric period began after his rather ignominious departure from national politics. Lincoln had promised during his campaign for Congress in 1846 that he would serve only one term, and his friends and backers in Illinois were all too happy to accept his self-imposed term limit. Thing is, Lincoln really wanted to stay. Increasingly at home in Washington, Lincoln wrote to his law partner that "if it should so happen that nobody else wishes to be elected, I could not refuse the people the right of sending me again." The people decided otherwise, and in 1848 voters in Lincoln's district elected a Democrat.[5] As a lame-duck congressman being succeeded by a member of the opposing party, Lincoln had very little clout with the new administration of President Zachary Taylor, for whom he had campaigned. He applied to be commissioner of the General Land Office, but was passed over for the job. He was offered the governorship of the Oregon Territory, which he declined, saying he wished to return to Illinois and his law practice (he was also an adroit enough politician to know that Democratic Oregon, once it became a state, would never choose a Whig as governor or senator). So Lincoln dejectedly returned home, his public career apparently at an end.[6]

The following five years were ones of introspection, melancholy, and growth for Lincoln—what biographer Michael Burlingame characterized as his "mid-life crisis."[7] After continuously running for (and serving in) office for the nearly two decades after he turned twenty-three, he felt he had left public life behind. He experienced more heartache—the Lincolns' three-and-a-half-year-old son Eddie died of pulmonary tuberculosis—but joy as well when Mary gave birth to two more sons: William Wallace Lincoln in 1850 and Thomas "Tad" Lincoln in 1853. He rapidly rose, in the words of a colleague, to "the head of his profession in this state"; certainly he made a lucrative living as a lawyer for Illinois railroads including the Rock Island and Alton and Sangamon. One notices a difference in tone in Lincoln's correspondence, public speeches, and written articles. The partisan, low-road politician of his thirties (prone to ridicule opponents whom he held in low esteem and to use character assassination as a political tool) was becoming the high-minded statesman we recognize in his later writings.

Lincoln also began seriously to reflect and to brood about not living up to his expectations for himself: "How hard—Oh how hard it is to die and leave one's country no better off than if one had never lived," Lincoln's law partner William Herndon reported his lamenting in 1851.[8] And it was also a time when he contemplated, with refreshing honesty, what he saw as the shortcomings of his character. Realizing he had far less education than his congressional colleagues, he began to read deeply in Blackstone, Shakespeare, and even Euclid. He built up his law practice, and honed his ability to address a jury and impress judges. In short, during this period of "down time" he was becoming the Abraham Lincoln we know.

Then, something unusual happened that changed Lincoln's trajectory once and for all. On January 4, 1854, Democratic Illinois Senator Stephen Douglas introduced a bill to set up a government in vast parts of the old Louisiana Purchase north of present-day Oklahoma all the way up to the

Canadian border. At the time, the United States consisted of 31 states, 16 free and 15 slave, with Northern states rapidly outpacing Southern ones in population. Under the 23-year-old "Missouri Compromise," slavery was to be excluded from parts of the Louisiana Purchase north of 36°30'. Having "lost" California, which had entered the Union in 1850 as a free state, Southern Senators were determined to salvage some slave soil out of this new territory—and Douglas, as a leading aspirant for the Democratic presidential nomination, was all-too-happy to oblige. In a move to make the bill more palatable to Southerners, Douglas divided the territory in two, and the Kansas-Nebraska Act was born.

To many Northerners growing weary of domination by slaveholders in all three branches of government, this looked suspiciously like a scheme to mark out Kansas for slavery and Nebraska as free soil. Douglas himself, a believer in and originator of "popular sovereignty," famously said he could "care not" whether the settlers in new territories voted slavery up or down as long as "the tide of immigration and civilization" was permitted to roll onward.[9]

Yet thousands of Americans *did* care—they regarded the expansion of slavery as a national question, and a moral one. "Anti-Nebraska" meetings exploded across the North, uniting old Whigs, Free Soilers, and antislavery Democrats weary of carrying the South's water in national affairs. New Englanders banded together to form "emigrant aid" companies to help antislavery settlers move to Kansas. Standing in the well of the Senate, New York Senator William Seward told his Southern colleagues: "Since there is no escaping your challenge, I accept it in behalf of the cause of freedom. We will engage in competition for the virgin soil of Kansas, and God give victory to the side which is stronger in numbers as it is in right."[10]

A group of antislavery congressmen led by Ohio senator Salmon Chase published "An Appeal of Independent Democrats" and laid out the case for a new political alliance to be born in opposition to slavery's expansion. "We arraign this bill as a gross violation of a sacred privilege; as a criminal betrayal of precious rights; as part and parcel of an atrocious plot to exclude from a vast unoccupied region immigrants from the Old World and free laborers from our own states, and convert it into a dreary region of despotism, inhabited by masters and slaves."[11]

The Kansas-Nebraska Act would also be the spark that catapulted Lincoln the Illinois circuit lawyer to national political prominence (much to the later chagrin of Republicans such as Seward and Chase and, of course, the Democrat Stephen Douglas). But Lincoln spent most of the pivotal spring of 1854 in court as the old compromises were dismantled and the great Whig party disintegrated. Instead of being involved in the central issue of the day, he was arguing his most important (and certainly most profitable) case in front of the Illinois Supreme Court.

As a private citizen in 1854—neither holding nor seeking a public office—Lincoln claimed to feel no compelling reason to make a public statement on the Kansas-Nebraska bill. But once he decided to take part in what was becoming known as the "anti-Nebraska" movement, he neither hesitated nor held back. And, curiously, he did so as an old-fashioned *Whig* (and not as an abolitionist, free soiler, or even a self-described anti-Nebraska man).[12]

As soon as Congress adjourned in August of 1854, Douglas decided (against the advice of his friends) to return home to defend his legislation. He joked that he could have journeyed back to Illinois by the light of the burning effigies of himself. Waiting for him there was his old rival—for Mary Todd Lincoln's hand in marriage, for supremacy in the Illinois State House, for high political offices to come. Eager to display the fruits of his weeks of intensive historical research and rhetorical honing, Lincoln practically stalked Douglas, with friend Jesse Fell even proposing a "joint" debate. Douglas, not surprisingly, refused. But Lincoln began an effective strategy of speaking to crowds soon after Douglas had finished his own address. His central argument: that Douglas, heretofore a great champion of the Missouri Compromise of 1820, had thrown it overboard to appease slaveholders and his own political fortunes. He carried with him clippings of Douglas's original, pro-Compromise speeches. His speeches at Bloomington and, later, at the Illinois state fair in Springfield "sparkled with wisdom and wit." He made it crystal clear (this was 1854) that he intended to "MAKE and KEEP the distinction between the EXISTING institution, and the EXTENSION of it." He kept coming back, again and again, to the "sacred" Missouri Compromise, which had kept the sections at peace for more than three decades, and was the descendant of Thomas Jefferson's own Northwest Ordinance, which barred slavery from the territories that later became Ohio, Michigan, Wisconsin, Indiana, and Illinois.[13]

But at its base, Lincoln's attack on the Kansas-Nebraska Act was a moral attack on the institution of slavery. Douglas took pains to say his bill was about settling the West and advancing civilization, and not about slavery at all, and Lincoln swooped in with a powerful moral indictment. Indifference in regard to slavery, he pointed out, was impossible: "This *declared* indifference, but as I must think, covert *real* zeal for the spread of slavery, I can not but hate. I hate it because of the monstrous injustice of slavery itself. I hate it because it deprives our republican example of its just influence in the world—enables the enemies of free institutions, with plausibility, to taunt us as hypocrites."[14]

Lincoln's new, highly *moral* argument against Douglas's Kansas-Nebraska bill was far, far more compelling than his earlier attacks on Democratic policies like the tariff, internal improvements, and even the war against Mexico. It was the Kansas imbroglio that gave Lincoln the committed Whig the political push it took for him to become Lincoln the Republican.

Kansas also figured powerfully in Lincoln's next serious tangle with Douglas—the famous debates of 1858, where the two battled it out for a seat in the United States Senate. Having won the legalization of slavery in the territories with the Kansas-Nebraska Act, proslavery forces moved to ensure that it would remain legal when Kansas became a state by enshrining the institution in a new state constitution. This required some ruthless political maneuvering, since legitimate antislavery settlers vastly outnumbered proslavery ones in Kansas Territory by 1858. To make a long, complicated story short, the proslavery legislature (elected largely by fraudulent proslavery votes) called for a constitutional convention at Lecompton to prepare Kansas for statehood. But free-state voters refused to participate, claiming (correctly) that the process for selecting delegates was rigged. At the ensuing constitutional convention, a proslavery constitution was hastily approved.

The Lecompton Constitution was too much even for Stephen Douglas, who broke with administration Democrats over the issue. He said he could not "vote to force this constitution down the throats of the people of Kansas . . . in opposition to their wishes and in violation of our pledges." The constitution was defeated in Congress, but that didn't mean the state would be allowed to enter the Union as a free state any time soon.

But Lincoln wasn't about to hand Douglas a victory. At one of their famous debates at Freeport, he forced Douglas to choose between two options, either of which would seriously damage Douglas's popularity and chances of getting reelected. Lincoln asked Douglas to reconcile his doctrine of "popular sovereignty" with the Supreme Court's *Dred Scott v. Sand-*

ford decision, which essentially declared that Congress's ban on slavery in parts of the Louisiana Territory (and thus any territory) was unconstitutional. Douglas responded that the people of a territory could keep slavery out even though the Supreme Court said that the federal government had no authority to exclude slavery, simply by refusing to pass a slave code and other local legislation needed to protect slavery. Douglas grievously alienated Southerners with this "Freeport Doctrine," seriously damaging his chances of winning the presidency in 1860. As a result, Southern politicians would use their demand for a slave code for territories such as Kansas to drive a wedge between the Northern and Southern wings of the Democratic Party. In splitting what was still a national political party, in fact the only national political party in 1858—and one of the last remaining national institutions in the country—Southerners all but guaranteed the election of a Republican in the next election. If Republicans chose the right candidate, that is.

Who would that Republican candidate be? William Seward, author of the famed "Higher Law" speech, was the clear front-runner, along with Salmon Chase and St. Louis lawyer Edward Bates. Political experts gave the Illinoisian very little attention.[15] Lincoln and his close coterie of supporters knew they had to campaign hard for the nomination, and attract attention well beyond the confines of his home state. This is the predominant reason he accepted two speaking engagements in the fall of 1859: one to address New Yorkers (and the national media) at the Cooper Union and another to visit a distant relation named Mark Delahay in Kansas.[16]

Delahay, originally from Maryland, was a founder of the Kansas Republican Party and a newspaperman in Leavenworth who had married Louisiana Hanks, a distant relative of Lincoln's mother Sarah Bush Lincoln. A trip to Kansas Territory at the request of this distant relation, Lincoln reasoned, would allow him to travel to the center of the storm, help Kansas Republicans with an upcoming local election, and rough out new ideas for the bigger speech he had agreed to deliver in New York the following February.

Lincoln took the day-long train trip across Missouri on the newly completed Hannibal and St. Joseph Railroad, and crossed the Missouri River to Elwood, Kansas Territory, by ferry on December 1, 1859.[17] That night he gave a speech in the dining room of the Great Western Hotel. The candidate began by explaining how Kansas' settlers violent territorial experiences were, in fact, unique: "Your territory," he said "has a marked history—no other territory has had such a history." The rest of the short address strove for moderation and what we today would call "bipartisanship." Both parties, he said, shared responsibility for making Kansas "bleed." And John Brown—whose raid on Harpers Ferry threatened very real harm to Republican candidates in 1860—was wrong on at least two counts: for clearly violating the law and for doing absolutely nothing to eradicate his supposed enemy, slavery. Lincoln did say, however, that "John Brown has shown great courage [and] rare unselfishness, as even [Virginia] Governor Wise testifies. But no man, North or South, can approve of violence and crime."[18] The next morning, which newspapers reported as bitterly cold, Lincoln traveled to Troy, Doniphan, and finally the bustling town of Atchison. The latter had been, until 1859, a proslavery enclave and a base camp for the border ruffians who terrorized free-state towns like Lawrence and Topeka. That evening Lincoln addressed a large crowd for more than two hours—but apparently his remarks did not even merit a line in John Martin's Republican paper, *Freedom's Champion*. This had less to do with what he said and everything to do with future governor Martin's own political preference in the contest—he was a Seward man through and through and later said he "hoped to kill off" Lincoln by ignoring him in his paper.

It was in Atchison that Lincoln was told of John Brown's execution for treason in Charles Town, Virginia, and again he tried to distance himself (and his party) from Brown's actions, while still admitting admiration for his moral stand against the slave power. "Old John Brown has just been executed for treason against the state. We cannot object," he reasoned, "even though he agreed with us in thinking slavery wrong. That cannot excuse the violence, bloodshed, and treason. It could avail him nothing that he might think himself right."[19] This truly off-the-cuff comment—which came after an interruption and, thus, was an unlikely part of Lincoln's prepared remarks—offers an interesting window into the candidate's evolving answer to the Brown conundrum. Brown's methods, for Lincoln, were neither the proper way nor the Republican way to rid the world of slavery. Yet seemingly in spite of himself, Lincoln could not help but qualify his negative comments. It was here that Lincoln first used the cautionary tale of John Brown as an explicit *political* warning: should demagogue Democrats succeed in using Brown to defeat the Republican Party, antislavery sentiments would hardly dissipate. Instead, they could find a new, more dangerous channel, and many more Browns could strike. In his avoidance of a disavowal of a man willing to go to the gallows for his hatred for slavery, Lincoln happened upon a new and, dare I say, conservative argument for supporting the Republicans' gradual moderation on the slavery issue. ("Vote for us or . . . a peaceful, political solution to the issue may be blocked, for good," he seemed to say).[20]

The next day, December 3, Lincoln traveled to Leavenworth for the main event of his Kansas sojourn. This bustling town on the Missouri River was in 1859 the largest city in the American West between St. Louis and San Francisco, with a population of nearly 7,500—similar in size to Lincoln's hometown of Springfield. (Without some clever maneuvering by the smaller "Town of Kansas," 35 miles downriver, to secure the first railroad bridge across the Missouri, it could easily have been the site of future international airports, major-league baseball franchises, and maybe even "Leavenworth Jazz" and barbecue.)

By far the most significant thing about Lincoln's December 3 Leavenworth speech was that in it was the germ of another speech, one delivered in February 1860 at the Cooper Union in New York City—the candidate's official "coming out" to the national press corps.[21] In Leavenworth, Lincoln jettisoned much of the language he used in Atchison and Elwood, focusing not on the immediate elections at hand but the larger political issues of the time. Most importantly, he made the point that, with the Kansas-Nebraska Act, the Democratic Party had adopted a radical "new policy . . . based on the idea that slavery is *not* wrong"—one that abandoned the long-standing views set out by "Washington and his compeers," our Founding Fathers. This was a key rhetorical point, especially since Jacksonian Democrats had been campaigning for years as the rightful heirs of Jefferson and Madison.

Lincoln denied he was an abolitionist, intent on setting out on a path to "destroy slavery" where it already existed; he wanted only to halt its spread into new territory. This, he said, was simply and "exactly the policy of the men who made the Union. Nothing more and nothing less." This argument—that slavery should be excluded from the western territories and that this policy represented the will of the Founders (even those who themselves held slaves) was central to the Cooper Union address—a speech the *New York Tribune* cited as "one of the most happiest and most convincing political arguments ever made in this City. . . . No man ever made such an impression on his first appeal to a New-York audience."

The reporter for the Democratic *Leavenworth Weekly Herald* could not have disagreed more with the *Tribune's* Horace Greeley. "We have seldom heard [a speech] where more spurious argument, cunning sophistry, and flimsy evasions were mingled together, and made to work out all right." Two days later, the same paper reported the speech thusly: "To sum up the whole, we characterize his efforts as weak in the extreme and he himself an imbecile old fogy of one idea; and that is—nigger, nigger, nigger."[22] Rarely had a proslavery journalist more accurately shown his colors. Luckily the town of Leavenworth was big enough for two papers, and thus we also have a report from the *Leavenworth Daily Times*. According to the *Times*, Lincoln "sought to make no display, but gave home-bred truths in a home-bred style that touched the hearts of his hearers and went home to all. . . . At the close of his speech he was greeted with a cordial round of cheers which made the old hall ring."[23] Indeed, Lincoln's December 3 Leavenworth speech, and a follow-up he made in the same town two days later, was the most forceful, morally grounded, and provocative he had produced since his debates with Douglas in 1858. As one recent scholar put it, he displayed a powerful ability to "provide historically educated, logical counterarguments to Democratic positions." With intensive research over the next month into the earliest Congresses and their votes on legislation in the early republic, Lincoln made the point that the Founders supported the Republican ideal of containing slavery even more precisely in New York six weeks later.[24]

Lincoln's campaign for the presidency contained extremely few missteps. Certainly the speeches in Atchison, Doniphan and Leavenworth provided opportunities to try out new ideas and rhetoric (and show him just how much primary research he would have to do before speaking in New York's Cooper Union). But his trip neither helped the Republicans in their local elections nor won him the support of the Kansas delegation to the Republican convention in Chicago. Kansas' delegates began the convention and ended it supporting William Seward's nomination. Perhaps this is why, during his own brief sojourn to Kansas just six weeks before election day in 1860, Seward heaped praise on the territory and its antislavery zeal. "[You have] made Kansas as free as Massachusetts, and made the Federal Government, on and after the 4th of March next, the patron of Freedom—as it was at the beginning. You have made Freedom national, and Slavery sectional," Seward told a crowd of 6,000 people in Lawrence—6,000 people who couldn't cast a ballot in the election. "No other hundred thousand people in the United States have contributed so much for the cause of freedom."[25] Perhaps. But Kansas figured strongly in the histories of the new Republican Party and, during the campaign of 1860, its two leading lights.

Chapter 8

"A Question of Power Not One of Law": Federal Occupation and the Politics of Loyalty in the Western Border Slave States during the American Civil War

Christopher Phillips

In February 1862, the Missouri provisional government's new state trea-surer, George Caleb Bingham, saw a troublesome development in his already war-torn state. Garrisoning Kansas federal volunteers in the west-ern portion of Missouri were subjecting civilians "to a kind of winnowing process by which the 'tares' were to be separated from the wheat—the loyal from the disloyal portion of the inhabitants." Bingham's winnowing was in fact a reference to measures implemented by federal and state military to accomplish sharp categorizations of loyalty and disloyalty among a deeply divided populace in an ostensibly loyal slave state. Bingham went on to describe what had become widespread practice among military personnel that, despite the famed "Missouri Artist's" keen eye for detail, many others were also by then seeing clearly around them: "The statement of a single individual . . . was to be taken as conclusive [and] it was not, for a moment, deemed necessary, that any investigation, in form, should take place. . . . He drew a line, sufficiently legible, between Unionists and Secessionists, without exhibiting the latter in colors so dark as to render their redemp-tion hopeless."[1]

The wartime intersection of loyalty definitions among divided civilian populations and the rapid erosion of civil liberties—often murky and always contested—were revealed again to the American public during the past decade. In the aftermath of September 11, 2001, and during foreign con-flicts in Iraq and Afghanistan, wounds not seen in this country since the Vietnam conflict have reopened over the nature of citizens' loyalties. The

exclusionist treatment of Muslim Americans both by the federal enforcement agencies and by non-Muslim residents, especially during the years of
the George W. Bush administration, had not been seen since the Second
World War, when the federal government interred Japanese Americans and
confiscated their property. During the American Civil War, and especially
in border slave states like Missouri, similar such questions of loyalty and
the curtailment of civil liberties by both federal and state governments sur-
faced early. More, with the active assistance of locals, it emplaced harden-
ing definitions of loyalty and disloyalty onto a population with a wide array
of political stances about the war. Among these were neutralism (citizens'
personal decisions actively to support neither belligerent in wartime) and
neutrality, an official position that Kentucky's legislature voted to adopt
and that Missouri's provisional government suggested but never officially
approved. Missouri's 1861 convention, which would establish the proviso-
rial government, did approve an amendment to its request that the president withdraw federal troops from "the forts within the borders of the
seceding States where there is danger of collision between the State and
Federal troops," a clear message to the administration that coercive measures there and elsewhere ran counter to state sovereignty.[2]

In 1861 and 1862, educated citizens like Bingham—not only in Missouri but in other border slave states—saw developing around them a
dominion system, an integrated if imperfectly implemented knot of counterinsurgency measures administered by federal and state government officials and commanders and conducted by low-level post commanders, the
largest portion of whom were volunteers, assisted by civilian informants.
Included were such measures as military districting and garrisons, civilian
assessments (or levies), the imposition of martial law (or the suspension of
civil authority in favor of military rule), a provost marshal system, and trade
restrictions. By it, military leaders restricted civil liberties at the local level
as part of a broader strategy to establish control of a "chaos of incendiary
elements," as one commander referred to the local, often armed populations whose true loyalties were frequently uncertain and ephemeral. Under-
girding all of it was the contest for definitions, in this case of "loyalty" and
"disloyalty," between the federal military and civilian residents symbolized
by the oath of allegiance. The outcome of this struggle would have a direct
effect on societal harmony and authority in Missouri and all of the divided
border states virtually for the duration of the war.[3]

Administering this dominion system, which began in parts of the border states as early as 1861, required interaction between federal troops, militia or home guard, and Unionist citizens. It also placed real impositions on local populations. Garrisoning towns, especially small ones, often required the commandeering of many if not most of these communities' physical structures and private homes for the army's use. Damage or destruction often followed, as did the confiscation of private property. Once the garrisoning of local towns had been accomplished, ferreting out and suppressing perceived disloyalists—their primary task—required search patrols, small and large, whose soldiers performed professionally under the best of circumstances and overzealously, even murderously, under the worst. In either case, cavalry patrols regularly roamed the countryside on "scouts" looking for disloyalists, saboteurs, and guerrilla bands who operated strictly on their own until April 1862, when the Confederacy passed its Partisan Ranger Act, commissioning officers to organize bands of partisans that were already in operation as well as those that would later form.[4]

The long list of complications for the occupying troops was headed by the expanse of territory to control, and doing so fell heavily upon these patrols, or scouts. The nearly two-week scout of one battalion of the Second Missouri Cavalry, commanded by Lewis Merrill (and known as "Merrill's Horse") through Saline and Lafayette Counties—the heart of Missouri's slaveholding district—in December 1861 was characteristic of many such patrols. In this case, the scout was heavy. Three hundred militia horsemen under Captain George C. Marshall along with three companies of regular U.S. cavalry left Sedalia on December 3, rode "northeast through Richard Gentry's farm and encamped at Union Church, on Dr. Cartwright's farm," where they took several prisoners. The following day, they moved again northeast 15 miles to the rendezvous of a large group of guerrillas, where the advance guard took fire before an estimated sixty rebels who "then retreated into the brush." The federals found there two "kegs of powder and a quantity of parts of cavalry equipments." The force encamped on a farm nearby, where after, on December 5, the horsemen rode another 15 miles northeast, taking prisoners, horses, and mules, before encamping "on the farm of the notorious Claiborn[e] F. Jackson [Missouri's exiled secessionist governor], and raised the Stars and Stripes over the traitor's house."

The following morning, they rode northeastward again, through Arrow Rock, "where we found several kegs of powder concealed in warehouses; destroyed the ferry-boat, and while doing it our men were fired upon by a few men from across the river; the fire having been returned, the enemy ran." Moving northward along the Missouri River, at Saline City they captured some arms and more powder and encamped on a local judge's farm, before heading north again and capturing two Confederate recruiting officers. Near Glasgow a detachment of about twenty-five men engaged a force of rebels encamped near a prominent mill, taking prisoner some twenty-eight men who "were caught playing cards and others getting breakfast . . . and getting their arms, ammunition, teams, cooking utensils, &c." After encamping overnight on yet another farm, the column turned westward and rode about thirty-five miles, claiming stolen "government wagons, 5 of which we brought with us and destroyed 3, being unable to get mules or harness to bring them with us," and encamped on the farm of a local secessionist about 2 miles from Waverly. That night, rebel horsemen under the noted cavalry leader, Jo Shelby, "try to annoy us by firing at our pickets and to try to scare us by bombarding us with a 10-inch mortar loaded with mud." On the morning of December 10, the column rode into Waverly without any resistance, confiscating powder they found concealed there as they searched some of the stores, one of which was Shelby's ropewalk, where they "found nine kegs of powder and the mortar concealed under a platform," as well as destroying the carriage for a six-pound cannon that had burst a few days earlier. The federals quickly dispersed Shelby's horsemen, after which they rode southward some 60 miles over three days, reaching Sedalia on December 12. All told, the battalion rode more than 200 miles and encamped exclusively on the farms of identified or suspected secessionists. The only casualties were one soldier who broke his leg because his saddle twisted and another who accidentally shot himself.[5]

However patriotic were the motives of most soldiers and officers, many of them had arrived in the slave states from free western states with preconceived notions of their inhabitants as uniformly wealthy, proslavery, disloyal Southerners. Many feared that rebel control of these neighboring slave states posed a threat to their own homes, and the presence of secessionist sentiment along with the activities of saboteurs and armed insurgents only confirmed their prejudices. Distinctions between loyal and disloyal residents quickly evaporated in their minds, especially among those soldiers and officers hailing from the region's northernmost sections. Violence erupted nearly immediately. On the early morning of June 15, 1861, a detachment of the Second Iowa Infantry, moving westward on a rail expedition ordered by Samuel R. Curtis to secure the Hannibal and St. Joseph line in northern Missouri, debarked at Stewartsville, a sleepy rail town lying east of St.

Joseph. At several prior points, Curtis reported encountering those he called rebels, arresting some and firing upon those "several who fled." Within minutes of arriving "at the front," as one of these volunteers referred to northern Missouri, another shot to death an alleged disloyalist, nineteen-year-old Donald M. McDonald, son of an agent for the railroad, during a fracas. (Later reports alleged that a displayed secession flag was involved. In his official report, Curtis declared that the "homicide" resulted from the young man attempting to fire a revolver at his troops, a charge disputed by onlookers.) But for the fact that the killing occurred in an ostensibly loyal state and that premeditation was charged in the Missourian's death—the soldiers' intent to kill reputedly decided beforehand while in Hannibal—the event was nearly the inverse of the much publicized shooting of Illinoisian Elmer Ellsworth, a federal officer and a former law student of the president's, by a northern Virginia secessionist only two months earlier. Such charges appeared to have little troubled the detachment's commander, Lieutenant Colonel James M. Tuttle. "Perhaps I am responsible," he defiantly averred years later when confronted publicly about the incident. "If so, I have nothing to take back. Our business down there was to put down the rebel colors and of course we commenced as soon as we saw where the work commenced. . . . His flag came down and so did he."[6]

Beyond confronting secessionists in these states, many such federals evinced distrust, even disdain, for the mass of residents, and singled out slaveholders in particular. In February 1862, an elderly resident of Lincoln County, Missouri, David Bailey, believed that prejudice against slaveholders undergirded the federals' violations of his personal neutralism and what he believed was his state's neutrality. A War of 1812 veteran who had since lived in his present community, Bailey, like his "Honorable high minded Intiligent and Law abiding" neighbors, "wished to remain Nutral in this awfull Contest—and did not believe at the commencement of this Civel war that the Union could be restored by Coersion . . . not now and never was in favour of Secession but allways was and are now for the union as it was—and for the Constitution as it is." Most, like Bailey, were "Slave holders and opposed to Emancipation and do not wholley approve of all of the acts of the present Administration," but "would Like to Stay at home in peace and Strictley attend to their own Concerns—and do not wish to take up armes in any way whatever—and coud not be coaxed in to the Southern army." Bailey was now certain that "this is the class of Citizens that those in Power think proper to designate as Secessionist, disloyal Rebels and Sympathizers and treat them as Such—they have taken all their armes from them they have arrested them and taken them to headquarters, and made them take the oath and give bonds in Large amount—they impressed their Horses and their waggons and teams and Slaves just where and when they please in the most insulting manner." One Kansas volunteer officer, Wyllis C. Ransom, an abolitionist hard-liner who had moved to Kansas from Wisconsin just prior to the war's outbreak and whose Sixth Kansas Cavalry was the subject of numerous complaints of theft and wanton destruction in western Missouri, concluded that the broadest portion of the area's populace, regardless of their political stance, was disloyal. He recalled that

> at the outbreak of the war the people of the rural districts of the western part of the state of Missouri were divided into three classes—The first comprising one quarter were loyal to the United States but for the most part, of necessity, secretly so, and were soon compelled to join the Union armies or to seek the protection of Union communities. Another quarter were open in their hostility to the government, and showing their faith by their work. . . . The remaining half were secretly hostile to the United States though professedly friends, non-combatants or neutrals. It was from the last class that the cruel wars of Missouri were mostly realized.

Neither time nor the outcome of a bitter war dimmed Ransom's recollections of federal commanders' on-the-ground view of these neutralists as disloyalists. In a general order he issued in the fall of 1863, Brigadier General John McNeil, a Canadian-born St. Louis Yankee by then notorious for his role in the "Palmyra Massacre" in 1862 and now forced to suppress partisans in southwestern Missouri, made unmistakable the stern terms of qualified loyalty. "The citizen who has chosen the position of neutrality," he decreed, "and who claims or has claimed to have 'done nothing on nary side,' is not loyal."[7]

The general belief that any were disloyal, including neutralists, who did not fully support the federal government's presence in these states derived from the highest authority. On July 4, 1861, the day that patriotic Americans nervously celebrated the date of the nation's founding (one that Confederates celebrated not at all), the president unambiguously stated his views on neutrality, the stance purported by various means by many in the border slave states, including Missouri and Kentucky. He condemned the stance as outright secessionism and those who favored it as disloyal. In his message to Congress, Lincoln sneered at the posture of "the border States, so called" for "being almost *for* the Union." "'Armed neutrality,'" he averred, was "disunion completed. Figuratively speaking, it would be the building of an impassable wall along the line of separation . . . [that], under the guise of neutrality, would tie the hands of the Union men." This falsity, he argued, "recognizes no fidelity to the Constitution, no obligation to maintain the Union; and while very many who have favored it are, doubt-less, loyal citizens, it is, . . . treason in effect." Lincoln clearly approved of reordering these states by the elevation of unconditional Unionists over "*professed* Union men" who favored neutrality and who were thus latent, if not overt, secessionists. Federal commanders in these states were thus authorized to treat as such all citizens who were not avowedly loyal. "This government," he reasoned, "has no choice left but to deal with [insurrec-tion], *where* it finds it." In Lincoln's mind, by summer's end in 1861, author-ity in the border states resided with unconditional Unionist minorities within their populations and not those who affected claims of neutrality. Conditional unionism was, in the anxious president's mind, disunionism.[8]

Confronting personal disputes, feuds, slights, and political differences that lurked beneath this inside war only complicated the uncertainty of free-state troops surrounding the loyalties of these slave staters. Having fes-tered for years, old wounds were broken open by the war and its resultant societal divisions, becoming scores to be settled by accusations and arrests. War offered what one local called an "evening-up time . . . [when] many a man became a violent Unionist because the ancient enemies of his house were Southern sympathizers." In May 1862, John M. Schofield complained that the war in Missouri, indeed the border region generally, was largely "the result of old feuds, and involves very little, if at all, the question of Union or disunion." Class resentments certainly triggered many loyalty complaints against prominent landowners. One property was of particular importance—slaves. As one Missourian of moderate means later sneered, "the cry of 'disloyal' could be very easily raised against any man who hap-pened to have a superabundance of property."[9]

The home guard and state militia who supported or replaced the gar-risoning troops were as much contributors to this private war as they were caught in its crossfire. A resident of Elk Fork, Missouri, complained that his local home guard "came from all parts of the County and Some of them have little grudges at their fellow Citizens and they make use of their opportunity to avenge themselves." Lincoln himself heard similar complaints "that arrests, banishments, and assessments are made more for private malice, revenge, and pecuniary interest than for the public good." The abuses by both federals and Confederates, militia and home guard, were pronounced enough for John C. Frémont and Sterling Price, while both led "antagonist forces" in the field in Missouri in November 1861, to issue an unusual joint proclamation pledging that "future arrests or forcible interference by armed or unarmed parties of citizens within the limits of said State for the mere entertainment or expression of political opinions shall hereafter cease; . . . and that the war now progressing shall be exclusively confined to armies in the field." Six weeks later, Henry W. Halleck, recently placed in command of the Western Department with headquarters in St. Louis, pledged to disband home guard units in Missouri "as rapidly as I can supply their places" with state militia. As Halleck and his successors would find, little if any relief ensued.[10]

Local Unionists' targeting of secessionists and neutralists, especially prominent ones, figured into occupying federal troops' widespread rejection of local citizens' shaded political stances. Didacticism of this sort often put these officers at odds with local militia commanders and provost marshals who believed they better knew their home communities and states than did those from elsewhere, and thus knew better how to treat residents whose loyalties were indefinite. In December 1861, Samuel Shelton, a farmer living near New Haven in east central Missouri, found himself arrested by a squad from the Ninth Iowa Infantry, the local garrison force at Pacific, a vital junction of that railroad's main line and south branch. The volunteer regiment's commander, Francis J. Herron, ordered Shelton held as a secessionist for reputedly organizing a disloyal home guard unit the previous May, the day of the federals' capture of St. Louis's Camp Jackson. At Wilson's Creek, where Herron both "saw the elephant" and tasted defeat, he had quite possibly faced some of those in Shelton's company who had enlisted in Price's army after Nathaniel Lyon's capture of Jefferson City. The newly minted lieutenant colonel likely now spoiled for retribution when locals told him of Shelton's company. That Shelton was a sixty-nine-year-old veteran of the War of 1812 and father of twenty-three, was hard of hearing and in poor health, mattered little. "He believed that the South, was entitled to certain rights which the North had refused her, and without respect was a southern rights man." But "had he supposed that it was designed to resist the authority of the Government he would have had nothing to do with it." "The Union ought to be maintained," he proclaimed proudly. That he was unrepentant about his political beliefs about the rights of slaveholders now mattered far more.[11]

Widespread military arrests like Samuel Shelton's, often made "on the slightest and most trivial grounds" (including for simply writing to those in the Confederate army or states), occurred throughout the border slave states. Without oversight, prisoners jammed courthouse jails and other sites of confinement, "arrested without any cause, except that they were reported secessionists," as one St. Louisan reported. The historian Mark E. Neely, closely examining the federal government's arrest records during the war, has concluded that some 13,000 civilians were arrested throughout the nation, the largest portion in the border states. He finds rightly that by far the largest number of these arrests occurred in Missouri, an "extraordinary" number by his own admission. Yet Neely acknowledges that poor record keeping and fragmentary evidence likely would ratchet up even that estimate, especially in the war's first year.[12]

When the bluecoats came, with them arrived a clear rejection of distinctions between loyal and disloyal residents and of the idea that simply declaring unionism put any above suspicion. Among the complications that these free-state troops found in the states across the Mississippi and Ohio Rivers was a deep ideological division over slavery that had, by the start of the war's second year, worked its way into the enlistment process *within* the federal ranks, separating federal volunteer and state militia units into largely antislavery and proslavery camps. This separation was especially evident in Missouri. The provisional state government's organization of the Missouri State Militia (MSM) saw slaveholders and proslavery men dominate its ranks, just as they did many local home guards. Their officers boasted that they would preserve "law and order" indiscriminately, whether against rebel insurgents, fugitive slaves, or abolitionist marauders. Antislavery radicals opted for enlistment in federal regiments rather than the state militia. Although they wore the same uniform, these units were often uncooperative with one another in the field, contributing greatly to military and government leaders' efforts to eliminate home guard units in the state and to replace the MSM with a new, more reliable militia organization: the Enrolled Missouri Militia (EMM).[13]

By the spring of 1862, in response to this internecine war then gripping both states, federal forces in Kentucky and Missouri were commanded by hard-liners. In Kentucky, Jeremiah T. Boyle, a prominent unconditional Unionist and emancipationist who had actively recruited men into federal rather than merely state service and had recently led Kentucky men at Shiloh, quickly reimplemented the blanket arrest strategy his predecessor, William T. Sherman, had tried unsuccessfully to suppress. On June 1, immediately upon taking command in his home state, he issued a series of orders that required all former Confederates and Southern sympathizers to give up their firearms, take the federal oath, and give bond for future good conduct, and that authorized the arrest of those who refused as well as those who did or said "anything . . . with the intent to excite to rebellion." As in Missouri, violators faced imprisonment or execution. Boyle's self-styled "sifting" policy, which received approval from the army's judge advocate general, Kentuckian Joseph Holt, would continue "until the last Jeff. Davis sympathizer is cleared out." Baptist minister William Conrad recalled the local sheriff being instructed that "every man of able body and good mind was to take up arms against any body who was for the Sesesh [sic] and that any body who did not obey was to stay in his house and would be shot down if he left it." Temporary local jails and prisons, such as at Louisville, Lexington, Newport Barracks, and Camp Chase near Columbus, Ohio, soon brimmed again, filled with alleged "enemies in our camps." Widespread outrage caused federal officials in Louisville to order that the names of those arrested no longer be published in the city's newspapers. Women as well as men were among the names. By September, the secretary of war, Edwin M. Stanton, ordered Boyle to halt all arrests unless on the order of Kentucky's governor.[14]

Facilitating the number of these arrests in Missouri and Kentucky, especially, was the establishment of the provost system the war's first year. Commanders of the various federal and Confederate armies and military departments appointed provost marshals, often local residents who hired their own staffs, charged with preserving order by policing behind the lines. Only in the summer of 1862, when George B. McClellan assumed command of the newly formed Division of the Potomac, which included the departments of Northeast Virginia and Washington, were orders issued that described the duties of provost marshals within a wartime field army. For the duration of the war, each division, brigade, and corps of the federal army included a provost marshal. Until that time, as John M. Schofield wrote of their use in Missouri, such officers were

Issuing passes at St. Louis. *A wood engraving of federal provost marshals issuing travel passes to citizens in March 1862. From* Harper's Pictorial History of the Civil War, *ed. Alfred H. Guernsey and Henry M. Alden (Chicago: Puritan Press, 1894), 292. Courtesy of the Library of Congress*

entirely independent of all commanders except the commander of the department, and hence of necessity pretty much independent of him. The local provost-marshals are appointed by the provost-marshal-general, or by any local commander and approved by the provost-marshal-general. They get all their instructions from him if they get any at all; make all their reports to him if they make any at all, and are responsible only to him and the department commander for the manner in which their duty is discharged.

Widespread abuses and lack of uniformity in carrying out their responsibilities prompted his successor, Samuel R. Curtis, to condemn the "creation of the so-called provost-marshal [that] invented a spurious military officer which has embarrassed the service." Curtis went on to complain that "Everybody appoints provost-marshals and these officers seem to exercise plenary powers."[15]

Nearly immediately upon the original implementation of the provost system in Missouri and Kentucky, federal authorities began mandating formalized oaths of allegiance that quickly became the most ubiquitous symbols and tools of government authority. Although most in the occupied areas of the seceded states found federal oaths repugnant, nowhere were they more opposed than in the border slave states. The assumption that disloyal majorities of secessionists and neutralists were cowing loyalist minorities in the border states inverted the war-makers' still common view of the populations of the Confederate states. Even Unionists objected to being forced to take the federal oath. A soldier wrote home to his aunt when administering the oath that "It just sutes me to hear [disloyalists] grumble," but Unionists' objections surprised him. "It dont hurt a union man to take the Oath," he admitted, "but we find once in a while one that hates to take the Oath but durst not say anything Once in a grate while they are catched by some of us that over hear their conversation and then put them under an arrest." One woman spat that "every one has been required to take the oath—they are then called Loyal—What a mockery."[16]

Small wonder a number of men who objected to the prescribed oaths (especially those with legal training) recognized that they had little choice but to take them, but only if altered to conform with their personal notions of loyalty. After losing his seat on the Missouri Supreme Court for refusing to take the convention oath, William B. Napton sought to practice law to support his large family. Doing so required him to take the oath. He presented an amended version of it in St. Louis, which stated that his taking of it should not

> be understood as denying or disavowing any opinions or sympathies expressed or entertained, in reference to the past action of the federal or state governments, which opinions and sympathies I do not regard as having anything to do with one's allegiance or loyalty, and I protest against the validity of all that part of the oath which related to *past acts* as conflicting with the Constitution of the United States and the fundamental principles of all our state governments.

The court clerk allowed the amended oath. Equivocation of this sort was not always so successful. Thomas B. Gordon, a Georgia-born attorney living in Bath County, Kentucky, presented such a reworded oath to the deputy provost marshal "with that construction I would take *it* to avoid going to prison, but under no circumstances could I take the other . . . objectionable oath." After first paying a $20 fee he considered extortionary, Gordon was subsequently imprisoned and required to take the prescribed oath and to present a $3,000 bond. "I do not feel that I have forfeited any right possessed before," he wrote after his release, still troubled by his decision to submit. "I have suffered oppression of one kind rather than of another. That I have chosen the lighter, rather than suffer the more severe but certainly more honorable—The issue above will be whether I did right."[17]

Loyalty oaths, as scholar Harold M. Hyman has argued, across American history but especially during the Civil War, largely failed as an accurate measuring device. Yet as "partisan weapons," loyalty oaths were means of creating imagined communities by making them wholly politicized over the war. Those who balked implicitly rejected either the legitimacy of their state governments, whether elected or provisional, or a federal government now headed by Republicans. Residents' refusal to take either the federal or state oath thus smoked them out, as it were, especially the final words by which they swore "SO HELP ME GOD." One southeast Missourian knew well the ideological dimensions of many of his neighbors' feigned neutrality that taking the oath would unmask. "They believe this war is waged against slavery," wrote Joseph C. Maple, an Ohio-born Baptist minister who shared his neighbors' anger at the dominion system, which he condemned as "the Republican mode of carrying on war. . . . The one side is abolition and the other side proslavery, they are determined if they fight to fight for the South. Hence they do not wish to take an oath which will cut them off from giving aid to the South." The oath sharpened blurred lines, to great advantage to the government, as Barton Bates saw it. "The doubtful men, thinking they were getting to the strong side, [are] joining the rebels," he boasted to his father, "but I believe we are really better off having them avowed against us than as pretended neutrals, and the promises of vigorous action lately are bringing them out more decidedly some on our side, and some more openly in a position in which we can whip them." Indeed, those so exposed were arrested, publicly listed, and required to post bond (from a few hundred to many thousands of dollars) in order to gain their release, with Unionists as sureties to guarantee their future good behavior. In the Liberty, Missouri, district, near the Kansas border, in 1862, provost marshals required 612 persons to post bonds totaling some $840,000. The provost marshal in Palmyra, near the Mississippi River, reported taking in as much as $1 million that year.[18]

The dominion system's reliance on oaths (and lists of those who had and had not taken them) to suppress local disloyalists who were spread throughout their districts stemmed in part from vulnerability. Their small, town-based garrisons were hard-pressed to keep order, especially when they were far from the main occupying army's presence. A well-known portrait artist in Lexington, Missouri, believed that the state's militia act, which required the oath of all military-age men, "is at best but a desperate effort to make it appear that a majority of the people of [this] state are Loyalists, but it is certain to prove the contrary if it proves any thing." Moreover, local residents frequently manipulated the oath, taking it disingenuously to retain a semblance of normalcy in their daily lives. However "loyal" their taking of the oath made them officially, their true loyalties lay hidden. A Kentuckian wrote that some of the residents around him "say that they did not mind taking the oath as they did not consider it binding on them, in fact they would rather take the oath than not as it gives them protection and they can get passes to go where they please." Another argued, given that disloyalists were "doubtless willing to take the oath prescribed with a mental reservation as heretofore expressed by many to disavow its obligations," that "it is proper therefore that the State authorities should be advised of the proclivities of the applicants." As such, department commanders and provost marshals routinely required accompanying verification of letter writers' own loyalty in order to solicit a response to their claims or grievances. Mistakes occurred frequently, eliciting remonstrances that required commanders to discern whether names on lists were legitimate or not, and whether the information they had received on such individuals was accurate or politically contrived. "Sir, you have the name of Hansbrough of Downingsville on your list as a rebel," wrote C. H. McElroy to Charles Whittlesey at his headquarters in Warsaw, Kentucky. "The parties who furnished you with his name say that it is an error; that he has always been an active union man—The error probably occurred from having used his name as a reference in regard to some traitors."[19]

Unpopular though they were, oaths had an obvious practical value. Identifying known—much less unknown—secessionists was a challenge, perhaps *the* challenge for federal authorities. Putting it before residents would, if imperfectly, verify their base loyalty by their either taking or refusing it, and the lists generated were essential identification tools for federal commanders in local areas. Taking such an oath presented a crisis of both honor and conscience for many citizens, even neutralists, it being the most visible symbol of personal coercion. For many white Kentuckians and Missourians these oaths were at best superfluous, they being residents of loyal states, and at worst unconstitutional, assuming their guilt before their innocence and abrogating their first amendment rights. They resented that local commanders and provost marshals forced them on residents who did nothing more than speak out in favor of Southern rights. "There are a number of influential citizens in this vicinity of rebel proclivities," wrote one cavalry colonel in southern Kentucky, "who although they have not committed any overt act . . . in conversation they have defended the cause of the South in a very noisy and offensive manner. Some of these, I have placed under bonds and obliged them to take the Oath of Allegiance." Worse, once they had taken the oath or posted bond, or both, they would yet be marked, fearful of visits from any who were known to be disloyal that would soon bring armed federals to their door. As a bonded Missouri resident wrote in October 1862 after sending away one such visitor, "I was fearful that some of the Negroes about the house might see him. The danger was greater to us than to him. He saw that he was an unwelcome visitor, and left as abruptly as he came." Despite capricious and even corrupt determinations of loyalty and disloyalty, Lincoln left to department commanders the discretion to make such decisions, recognizing that this was the single most critical point with which to win his case in the border states. As he wrote his department commander in Missouri, assessing the loyalty of residents "must be left to you who are on the spot."[20]

Oaths also visibly divided local communities. Reprisals often followed, resulting in societal upheavals that in some cases worked to the government's advantage. Just as Unionists, government troops, and home guards used the oaths against neutralists, Southern sympathizers, and secessionists who refused to take them, Southern-sympathizing residents often chastised their like-minded neighbors who did take it, or supported it, whether feigned or not, as cowards or disloyalists to the Southern cause. Shunning was only the most benign form of retribution made against oath-takers; many others were insulted, threatened, and even attacked for their capitulation to Yankee aggression. Or worse, they were turned in to garrison commanders as disloyalists to the Union's cause. In July 1862, merchant John Scott found himself arrested by armed state militia in Miami, Missouri, with guns pointed, for disloyalty, only to learn after his bonded release that a neighbor, "one of the most violent and uncompromising secessionists, intolerant to Union men, getting ready to go to the Southern army and having [secession] flags on house and business building," had reported him following a private disagreement between them.[21]

Complaints from prominent Unionists about the occupiers' strident measures were plentiful, questioning their severity, their capriciousness, and especially their corruption. Most important, the federals' presence seemed to be fueling the insurgency in Missouri. William G. Eliot, a St. Louis Unitarian minister and unconditional Unionist who was deeply involved in the civilian costs of the war as founder of the Western Sanitary Commission, questioned the ability of the military to "assort and classify these, so as to indicate the dividing line of loyalty and disloyalty . . . is a task of great difficulty." He saw only harm to the public weal. "The bitterness of feeling," wrote the concerned clergyman, "will renew the personal hostilities which were beginning to disappear, and, thus fanned, the secession element will refuse to die."[22]

With federal authorities seeking, as one resident characterized it, to "separate the sheep from the goats," and, with soldiers from the northernmost portions of the western free states often severe in their treatment of all suspected disloyalists, the cauldron of Confederate sympathy soon boiled over. That so many of these armed and aggressive outsiders used the institution of slavery against them only deepened proslaveryites' sense of alienation, causing many to renounce their loyalty to the government that the soldiers now represented. While defending Richmond, Kentucky, against Edmund Kirby Smith's advancing Confederates during the hot summer of 1862, a southern Indiana volunteer officer was surprised at the cool reception his regiment received from residents. Frustrated, he vented to his wife, "These Kentuckians are willing we should fight for them, but they don't seem very willing to feed us." One loyal Kentucky minister, dismissed from his congregation for espousing unconditional support for the government, nevertheless found himself suspect when attending to federal soldiers convalescing in Shelbyville simply because of his Kentucky hailing. On New Year's Day in 1863, William Moody Pratt noted in his diary that he had "visited Hospital at Science Hill to preach. One of the attendants told me it was suspected that I was a secessionist and if so the men did not want to hear me. I never felt so indignant in my life. I have visited the hospital for a year, done all I could for the poor fellows, and have made every sacrifice demanded for the government. . . . I left them and dont intend to return."[23]

What spilled out from the ranks of small and non-slaveholders was a new class of Southerners—political Southerners, like Peter Collins—who turned against the war and especially the federal prosecution of it by evincing sympathy for, if perhaps not an outright allegiance to, the region that these Yankees assailed. These former Unionists no longer based their identity on abstract theories of government or liberty. The driving engine was a personalized aggrievement, a sense of victimization that many residents conjured easily after the decade-long sectional struggle over slavery previous to the war. Under such circumstances, the transition to disloyalist could be rapid. A railroad superintendent wrote soberly in August 1861 that the hard war tactics he had witnessed along his line in north Missouri "have tended greatly to weaken the Union cause, and in the State where I am acquainted there are far less Union men than two months since." Many "*for the South'* . . . know very little of the South or her institutions, and can't begin to know how to love her," scolded one Unionist Kentucky minister of angry congregants who sought to remove him in the early summer of 1862. "*Politics*," he spat, "they falsely call Patriotism and Treason and their conflict." Another Unionist Kentuckian remarked of the rapid changes he observed in his community. "This secession is a disease—a disease, Sir. It can be caught in a night. I have seen people go to bed as good Unionists as there are in the country and wake up in the morning Secessionists."[24]

What this Kentuckian termed "secessionism" was in fact a more subtle, clandestine culture of dissent emerging among border residents. Declaring oneself a rebel in an ostensibly loyal, occupied state was a dangerous position, with soldiers and Unionists together outnumbering and openly targeting known disloyalists. Many former Unionists had taken the oath of allegiance, and thus were on record as supporters of the national government, a record that federal troops (and unconditional Unionists) would use against them. These Unionists eagerly exposed disloyalists who signed affidavits attesting to their neighbors' or family members' loyalty, thus subjecting them to arrest or assessment. Opposition to the federal war effort, which often was tantamount to support for the Confederacy, was thus forced underground, replaced by a generic, and ultimately safer, Southern identification, one that was not so easily judged as being disloyal and by which gray areas, so important to former conditional Unionists, could yet exist. Privately affecting the badge of "rebel" meant for many a simple opposition to the excessive use of force by the federal occupiers. Publicly embracing the badge of either rebel or Southerner identified oneself as a citizen who, beset by an aggressive antislavery host, believed he or she bravely yet peacefully defended the nation's republican tradition by upholding slave-holders' rights *within* the nation. Although in the proclaimers' minds either term allowed dissent without treason, neither was in fact safe to proclaim, as an 1861 exchange between one Kentuckian and a squad of home guards revealed. When Thomas Parsons's Unionist home guard captured an armed secessionist party near Mount Sterling, they interrogated one of the residents they passed in their chase. Parsons, whose two brothers had enlisted (and would die fighting) in the Confederate army, asked, "What is your politics Mr. Ross?" The man replied, "Well now these are mighty squally times, but I am never afraid or ashamed to tell my politics. . . . I am a Southern man." When the man asked theirs, they replied that they too were Southern men, the "Rebel ruse" having encouraged the man to speak freely of his knowledge of the militia they had been unable to capture. ("'That is what all of us southern men think,' said someone.") Parsons then revealed that the squad was Unionist and arrested the man.[25]

For these political Southerners, the free western states and their soldiers were now indistinguishable from the North and the Yankees who had brought about the war. Even those who once hailed from these same western states proclaimed their own Southernness as the war found them. Perry H. Collins, a thirty-seven-year-old Ohio-born farmer living in Buchanan County, Missouri, was questioned by the local provost marshal in late February 1862 for claiming that he was "openly opposed to the United States and that he was a proud Southern man. He offered his horse to anyone that would take up arms against the United States but could not go himself because of convenience. He would, however, if forced, go into the field with his gun and die as a Southern man rather than live as a Northern man."[26]

Beyond such dangers, Southernness could also be used as a weapon. Linking all the free states and their soldiers to Northerners offered political Southerners an accessible and retributive stereotype of their own to throw back in soldiers' faces, by which they judged a monolithic, Northern, "Yankee" culture. An Ohio volunteer soldier, while stationed in Frankfort, Kentucky, in the fall of 1862, gained the trust of residents enough to engage several in a series of political conversations. Despite his best intentions, one impression of theirs of him quickly became clear. While many residents and families disagreed "over the old grinds, 'nigers' 'Southern rights,' etc. . . . the North is something they didn't understand." Such an association they knew most free-state westerners loathed, and these new

Southerners, especially women, laid it on gleefully. "I knew those North Western people would rather you should call them devils than Yankees," observed Kentuckian Lizzie Hardin. Indeed, when her western Kentucky relatives used the epithet for her soldier husband, referring to him as their "Yankee Cousin," southern Illinoisian Mary A. Crebs related it unhappily in her letter to him. A federal soldier stationed in Arkansas in 1862 referred selectively to his army's "Northern regiments" as those "from Wisconsin, Kansas, Minnesota, and Iowa." Native slave staters were not exempt from such abuse. "The Southern party claimed to consist of the old Kentucky families who came out of Virginia," asserted one woman, "and reproached the Unionists with being Yankees and those allied to the Yankees." Kentuckian Martha M. Jones explained that her husband's painful decision to abandon the Union and support the Confederacy (and join its army) in the spring of 1862 did not make him a traitor to the Union. It made him a Southerner, and a brave one at that. "A rebel I admit he is, from the whole abolition faction and dominion," she wrote to her Unionist father, and "he could have taken an oath of allegiance to that people, and *remained* at home. He has linked his fortunes with the southern people, from an unalterable conviction of the justice of the cause and . . . [to] bring the blessing of civil liberty once more to our bleeding country." Only once he and his brothers had made their decision to fight for the Confederacy and its cause did Kentuckian Tom Bullitt, once a self-proclaimed "western man," revel in his "Southern birth, and southern acquaintance." With the fervent faith of a latter-day convert he would write home while confined in an Ohio prison in 1864, "The South is my home—To her, My energies and my life are pledged." Of the political basis of wartime cultural identity in these border states, Cora Owens observed of those enrolled in her Louisville school: "Two girls are down from St. Louis and any stranger might judge them to be Southern, but both are Northern in politics, and one is a yankee."[27]

In early 1862, Bernard G. Farrar, Missouri's provost marshal general, huffed from his headquarters in St. Louis. "It is now purely a question of power not one of law," he wrote. At nearly the same time, that state's lieutenant governor, Willard P. Hall, spoke to conditions in his state even more laconically, if not quite accurately. "Amidst armies," he asserted, "the law is silent." In wartime, law and power were nearly indistinguishable. Farrar's and Hall's candid views of the authority of an occupying army among a growingly hostile citizenry were placed, curiously, in the context of Hall's instructions to desist in arresting civilians around the state merely on suspicion of disloyalty. But it spoke rightly to the circumstance in the border slave states where martial and civil law coexisted, at least in theory. The contest between them, waged largely over creating binary definitions of loyalty and disloyalty, would similarly recolor these states' once-shaded civilian landscapes into monochrome canvases of blue and gray.[28]

Chapter 9

"Slavery Dies Hard": Enslaved Missourians' Struggle for Freedom

Diane Mutti Burke

By his own account, the twenty-nine years that Henry Clay Bruce spent enslaved in the Upper and border South prepared him for his eventual life in freedom. Bruce, his mother, and his siblings benefited from a fairly permissive master who allowed his slaves to learn to read and granted them liberal mobility throughout their western Missouri neighborhood. Bruce spent much of his time in slavery hired out to a succession of Missouri farmers and tradesmen for whom he performed a myriad of tasks, often with little direction from his employers. While watching and waiting for his opportunity to grasp freedom, Bruce became a student of human nature, learning how to work with white men, how to lead others, and how to look out for his own needs and those of his family. He also gleaned important information about the lay of the land and the circumstances and personalities of his neighbors—both black and white—as he traversed the countryside doing the business of his employers and occasionally enjoying the company of other enslaved people. Even though he was proud of his solid work ethic, and in fact argued that he influenced his experience in slavery in positive ways because of his faithfulness, when the opportunity presented itself in the midst of the turmoil of the Civil War, Bruce, like many others, grabbed his chance, and with his fiancée in tow, made his way to freedom in neighboring Kansas. In the process, he asserted his manhood and took a powerful step toward not only achieving his personal liberty but also demonstrating his worthiness for citizenship.[1]

It is not surprising that Henry Bruce launched his bid for freedom from the border state of Missouri, given the history of slavery in the state. As Kristen Epps describes in her contribution to this collection, Missouri was settled by small-slaveholding migrants from the Upper South who were attracted by a climate in which they could replicate the patterns of diversified agriculture and small-scale slavery found in their original backcountry homes. Plantation slavery never took hold in Missouri; instead residents adapted the institution to suit the economic needs of the state's border location. Missouri farms were typically modest in size and required few workers; therefore, the vast majority of slaveholders owned fewer than ten slaves. Most enslaved people worked as general farm hands or domestic servants, and owners typically hired out underutilized laborers to their neighbors or employed them in nonagricultural business pursuits. Slaves performed the most arduous tasks on Missouri farms, but because overseers were rare, slaveholding men and women usually directly supervised and assisted this labor. The economic and emotional interdependency that existed between small slaveholders and their slaves complicated their interpersonal and work relations and provided them with extraordinary opportunities to influence one another's lives. Slaves' family and community lives were also affected by the predominance of small-scale slavery. A majority of Missouri slave couples lived on different slaveholdings, and slave-quarter communities were the exception rather than the rule.

Although the vast majority of Missourians had roots in the Upper South, a growing number of foreign- and northern-born settlers moved to the state after 1830. By the eve of the Civil War, the large number of non-slaveholding residents resulted in the enslaved population comprising less than 10 percent of the total. Even though slavery remained viable throughout the antebellum years, the demographic changes and the unique conditions of small-scale slavery set the stage for the institution's rapid disintegration during the Civil War.[2]

Missouri's geographic location had always concerned slaveholders, but they were particularly alarmed by the unobstructed border between Missouri and Kansas south of the great bend in the Missouri River, especially after Kansas Territory was opened for settlement in 1854 and free-state settlers flooded into the new land. Many Missouri slaveholders worried that Kansas abolitionists would entice their slaves to flee, although in reality few successfully escaped. The fear that Missouri's border location rendered slavery vulnerable approached hysteria for many slaveholders, and, although there was disagreement about how to best achieve this goal, most believed that the only way to protect slavery in Missouri was to guarantee that Kansas enter the Union as a slave state. One Missourian wrote from Boonville in 1854 that locally it was the "prevailing opinion" that if slavery was prohibited in Kansas Territory "slaves will almost be value[d] less in

Missouri." Highly publicized slave-stealing forays, led by Kansas abolitionists John Brown and John Doy, heightened white Missourians' concerns and ultimately led them to strengthen the slave patrol along the state's western border.[3]

The Kansas statehood controversy exposed the vulnerabilities of border slavery, but the violence that exploded during the Civil War ultimately led to its destruction. In many parts of the South, the unity of the white population in support of the war and the distance of plantations from the center of fighting kept discord under the surface for much of the war. In contrast, in Missouri, political quarrels that once simmered beneath the surface dramatically erupted during the earliest days of the conflict. The divisiveness of wartime politics fractured a white community that before the start of the war had been virtually united in support of both slavery and Union. White Missourians began to choose sides as Union forces swept through the state during the summer and fall of 1861 and a secessionist guerrilla insurgency emerged to counter what many saw as a hostile military occupation. The fabric of Missouri society was irrevocably rent by the resulting internecine bloodshed that scourged the state during the ensuing years. The ambiguities and conflicts that always had plagued the interactions between the slaveholders and slaves who lived on the state's farms were exacerbated by the unfolding uncertainty and violence. Although already compromised by the realities of life on slavery's border, enslaved Missourians' families and communities were further complicated by the deprivations and dislocations brought about by the fighting. As the war progressed, many of Missouri's nearly 115,000 slaves took advantage of the chaos and struck a blow for their own freedom.[4]

The Civil War turned Missourians' lives on end no matter which side they supported. Violence escalated after the autumn of 1861 as marauding forces from both sides roamed the countryside, pillaging, burning, and killing. Residents living near the Kansas border faced particular hardship as both Union raiders out of Kansas and Missouri secessionist guerrillas devastated the region. In the process, hundreds of Missouri homes were looted of everything from clothing to guns, and many were ultimately ransacked and burned. Lizzie Brannock described the situation in western Missouri: "Our country is desolate, indeed almost entirely a wilderness, robbery is an every day affair so long as their [sic] was anything to take our farms are all burned up, fences, gone, crops destroyed no one escapes the ravages of one party or the other."[5]

Missouri slaveholders were devastated by what the war had wrought; violence, death, and destruction touched the lives of many, and all experienced the upheaval of the prewar social order. As much as they were discouraged by the turn of events, perhaps most distressing was the realization that their long-term fears about the stability of slavery suddenly were realized. During the first years of the war, a good number of white Missourians maintained loyalty to the Union, believing that the federal government would best protect slavery. Certainly, President Abraham Lincoln had indicated that he intended to cater to the conservative Unionists who had worked so hard to keep Missouri in the Union. As the war progressed, it became apparent to many that the Union army was not adequately protecting slavery and in some cases was actually undermining it. The North's eventual turn toward emancipationist goals led some who might otherwise have remained loyal to the federal government to begin to actively promote the goals of the Confederacy instead. In August 1863, H. B. Johnson, the Union provost marshal stationed at Lexington, observed: "The Negro in this County is the all 'inspiring theme' with many of the people . . . the source of all our trouble, and the great question that divides the people[.] Hundreds of men who were it not for the negro would be union men are now very doubtful. Many of them make the preservation of the institution of slavery a 'condition precedent' to the Union thereby effectually identifying their interests with the rebellion."[6]

As hard as owners tried, it was nearly impossible to isolate slaves from the political discussions of the day. Enslaved people collected and shared information and speculated about what wartime developments meant for them. According to Henry Bruce, black Missourians had long paid attention to local and national politics but paid particularly close attention to the progress of the war, talking about it whenever they met. Bruce claimed that they "understood the war to be for their freedom solely, and prayed earnestly and often for the success of the Union cause." Literate men and women gained access to newspapers and passed the "latest news" to their neighbors, and "from mouth to ear the news was carried from farm to farm, without the knowledge of masters."[7]

The tensions and ambiguities that had always existed in the relations between Missouri owners and slaves became more pronounced during the war years as enslaved people became emboldened by the opportunities for resistance made possible by the wartime turbulence. They simply had less incentive to work hard for their owners as labor discipline eroded and as freedom appeared possible. Missouri slaveholders increasingly complained about their slaves' poor conduct and work habits. Slaveholders were concerned about the erosion of labor discipline, but they recognized that the greatest threat was that their slaves would simply leave. Enslaved Missourians capitalized on the turmoil created by the presence of the Union army and the political divisions among white Missourians and left their owners by the thousands. As they fled, they took advantage of the intricate web of social relations that they had so carefully cultivated during slavery, putting their associations and knowledge of the local geography to good use.[8]

Many white Missourians initially could not accept that their slaves were making their own decisions to flee and instead accused federal soldiers of encouraging their "loyal" servants' defection—most often blaming Kansans, whom they derisively called "Jayhawkers." In late 1861, when federal forces abandoned Springfield, Missouri, over 500 slaves joined Lane's Brigade as it marched into Kansas; in 1862, Mrs. Silliman of western Missouri claimed that her slave woman was enticed by Union soldiers to run away to Kansas; and later that year, Edward Samuel reported to President Lincoln of a "Jayhawker" raid into Clay County in order to *recruit* negroes for Genl Lanes negro Brigade" in which 40 horses and 25 slave men were taken. Samuel reasoned that "our people desire to live in peace with the people of Kansas," but that such raids made it impossible. Secessionist slaveholder Elvira Scott protested federal hypocrisy in 1862, asking: "If they do not intend to interfere with slavery why have Federal soldiers stolen thousands of slaves from their masters?"[9]

Indeed, Kansas military leaders, such as James Lane and Charles Jennison, believed that in order to effectively strike against their secessionist enemies in Missouri they must deprive them of all of their assets, including their slaves. While soldiers, such as Lane's and Jennison's Jayhawkers, did "steal" some Missouri slaves, most often slaves gladly accompanied Union soldiers, whom they recognized as harbingers of their freedom. General John C. Frémont's August 1861 emancipation proclamation was one of the first concrete suggestions to enslaved Missourians that the war would result in their liberation, and around that time they began to seek protection from nearby Union troops. Many people living along the border made their way to Kansas, where they assumed they would find friends, while those living in the state's interior flocked to the nearest Union military encampments.[10]

The federal government ultimately was forced to grapple with the question of the status of those who made their way behind Union army lines. Just as in the eastern theater of the war, there was tremendous confusion within the army regarding fugitive slaves, who were oftentimes referred to as "contrabands" because it was assumed that they had been owned by the enemy and, therefore, were considered contraband of war. Army officers at both departmental and local levels asked for clarification on the status of runaways. In August 1861, Congress weighed in on the issue, allowing the military to retain slaves who had been used in the Confederate war effort, but remaining ambiguous on the question of their freedom. At first, both Abraham Lincoln and Union commanders were concerned about maintaining the loyalty of Unionists and ordered the return of fugitive Missouri slaves to their owners. President Lincoln quickly rescinded General Frémont's 1861 emancipation order in an effort to appease loyal slaveholders, and General Henry Halleck, who became commander of the Department of the Missouri in November 1861, went so far as to issue General Order No. 3, which barred fugitive slaves from military encampments, in order to spare officers the confusion of determining their owners' status. The force of events soon rendered this policy impractical as the number of enslaved people seeking military protection multiplied; in the end, enforcement was sporadic and largely dependent on the discretion of individual soldiers and officers. Some returned runaway slaves to their owners, whereas others, many who served in units from free states, were sympathetic to the plight of the fugitives and put them to work within their camps rather than return "the slaves of traitors while the secessionists are robbing & plundering loyal men in the western part of the state."[11]

The Second Confiscation Act, passed by Congress in July 1862, stipulated that the military could seize the property—including the slaves—of those disloyal to the Union, and in December 1862, General Samuel Curtis, the new commanding officer of the Department of the Missouri, issued an order that authorized provost marshals to grant freedom papers to slaves who belonged to secessionist slaveholders and who made it to Union army camps. President Lincoln reiterated his intention to protect the property of Unionist slaveholders, however, when he specifically excluded Missouri and other areas of the South under Union military control from his January 1863 Emancipation Proclamation. In addition, in the spring of 1863, under pressure from Hamilton Gamble, Missouri's conservative Unionist governor, and his allies, Lincoln replaced General Curtis with General John

Schofield, who he believed would be more attentive to the concerns of Unionist slaveholders.[12]

It was challenging for the Union army to put the various federal slavery policies into practice, however, because it often was difficult to determine the true loyalties of Missouri slaveholders. In reality, few soldiers questioned fugitive slaves' veracity when they declared that their owners were disloyal, and, indeed, many were inclined to believe that most white Missourians—especially slaveholders—were on the wrong side of the war. Loyal Lexington slaveholders complained to Governor Gamble, "no matter what proof the master offers, the negroes say that they be long [sic] to secessionists, and the officers believe them." For their part, enslaved Missourians interpreted the various military orders as acts of emancipation and continued to run away regardless of their owners' political persuasion. In the end, in spite of Lincoln's efforts to protect the slaves of loyal owners, the situation on the ground had deteriorated to such a degree that it made his promises difficult to keep. In the summer of 1863, the pro-Union state convention reconvened, minus pro-secession delegates, and recognized the reality of the situation when they passed a compensated and gradual emancipation plan that would go into effect in 1870.[13]

As more slaves fled, Missouri slaveholders, loyal and disloyal alike, became extremely anxious about protecting and maintaining slavery. The loss of even one slave had tremendous economic consequences for small slaveholders because most owned only a few adult slaves, but the extreme emotional response of many suggests that they had a significant social stake in slavery as well. Not only did losing their slaves potentially compromise their plans for their own families' futures, but it also disrupted the social and racial hierarchy that Missouri slaveholders had worked so hard to maintain. The initial response of many Missouri slaveholders was to exhaust all options in order to bring their runaway slaves home. Loyal Missourians at least had the satisfaction of appealing to military and governmental authorities, while those who supported the Confederacy had no possibility of a hearing. Both loyal and disloyal slaveholders were dismayed by the ways in which the Union military presence and secessionist guerrilla insurgency destabilized slavery in the state, and they became increasingly distressed as the world that they had created began to slip through their fingers. Many simply directed their anger and frustration at their slaves.[14]

White Missourians—Confederates and Unionists alike—unleashed a reign of terror as they frantically tried to maintain Missouri's slavery regime.

Fugitives reported violent abuse at the hands of owners who desperately worked to control their slaves. "Nearer time for us to be freed, the owners got meaner all the time," former slave Tishey Taylor remembered. The fact that black and white Missourians lived and worked together so intimately likely made slaves' disaffection feel even more personal. The primary focus of the violent reprisals and intimidation was slaveholders' desire to keep slaves working on their farms, however. Military officials reported the efforts of secessionist guerrillas to terrorize local citizens who hired former slaves, threatening to drive both employers and employees away.[15]

Some white Missourians callously destroyed the lives of enslaved people in a desperate attempt to maintain their property or, at the least, eke out a last few dollars from the dying institution. Concerns about runaways prompted some to "refugee" their slaves south, with Texas as a favorite destination. Richard Kimmons's master feared that federal soldiers would confiscate his slaves and so he sent them to his son living in Texas, leaving his crops standing in the fields. Believing that emancipation was imminent, other Missouri owners merely cut their losses and sold their slaves in Kentucky or Texas, where they commanded higher prices. Esther Easter was taken from Jackson County south to Texas, where she was immediately sold, and Union military officials calculated that as many as a thousand Missouri slaves were sold in Lexington, Kentucky, in the autumn of 1862. The Union army patrolled the highways and railroad lines in an attempt to stop these abuses. Mark Discus's Dade County master wished to set his slaves free "when he saw how things was goin'," but the master's oldest son loaded him and "four others of the best slaves in a wagon" and took them south, where he intended to sell them. Union soldiers encountered the group close to the Texas state line and freed them. Soldiers also removed slaves from a train on the Pacific Railroad line outside Otterville in order to stop their transport out of state for sale.[16]

White Missourians increased the presence of slave patrols in an effort to maintain labor discipline and control the movement of those slaves who remained on the state's farms and plantations. Saline County slaveholder Elvira Scott observed in late 1862, "People seem apprehensive of trouble with the Negroes. The patrol is out every night." Slaveholders feared their slaves, but slaves had much greater reason to fear patrollers. Former slave William Black remembered the brutality of wartime patrollers: "If we didn't have a pass de paddyrollers would get us and kill us or take us away." Patrollers had always brutalized slaves, but on the eve of emancipation there now was less expectation of restraint because owners had little to lose if their slaves were maimed or killed. Many Civil War–era "patrollers" were indeed Confederate Bushwhackers, who attempted to intimidate local slaves into remaining with their owners, targeted white Missourians who hired former bondsmen and -women for pay, terrorized slave women through physical and sexual assault, and after 1863, brutalized slave men on their way to enlist in the Union army. Confederate soldiers and guerrillas kidnapped others and took them south, where they were sold. General Thomas Ewing, commander of the District of the Border, believed that a primary reason that western Missouri slaveholders fed and supplied guerrillas was because of their valuable service in helping to maintain slavery.[17]

Disloyal Missourians were concerned with not only those slaves who ran away, however. The possibility that the enemy potentially lived within their own households terrified them as well. Slaves frequently reported their owners' secessionist activities, which ranged from lending material aid and comfort to Bushwhackers to burning railroad bridges and riding with the guerrillas. In a reversal of decades of Missouri law that would not allow for the testimony of blacks against whites, military provost marshals used the testimony of slaves as they built cases against white Missourians accused of disloyalty. And indeed, many secessionists were arrested or retaliated against on the word of their former slaves. Some owners attempted to suppress loquacious slaves through intimidation, violence, imprisonment in local jails, or taking them south. For those who informed while still enslaved, the consequences could be dire. Fully understanding the risks of reporting, Chillicothe slave Eli Andrews asked military authorities for a pass out of the state for himself and his family in return for testimony that his master had aided Bushwhackers and burned a Hannibal and St. Joseph Railroad bridge.[18]

African Americans greatly supported the war effort through both their spying efforts and their manual labor, but the federal government initially refused to allow black men to fight. In the summer of 1862, however, a few Union army officers experimented with recruiting African American men as soldiers. As a continuation of his policy of depriving the enemy of their financial assets and in recognition that the refugees might be successfully turned into a fighting force, Senator Lane organized one of the first African American regiments, primarily made up of former Missouri slaves who had escaped into Kansas, without official consent. The First Kansas Colored Infantry engaged in the first armed military action by African American troops during the Civil War at the Battle of Island Mound, in Bates County, Missouri, just over the border from Kansas, in late October 1862. After Lincoln's January 1863 Emancipation Proclamation authorized the recruitment of African American soldiers, many other former Missouri slaves crossed over the state line into Iowa and Illinois, filling the ranks of the United States Colored Troops regiments raised in those states. Concerns about a negative response from conservative Unionists initially delayed recruitment in Missouri, but General Schofield sanctioned the enlistment of all slave men regardless of their owners' loyalties in November 1863. Missouri slave men flocked into the Union army after official recruitment began. By this point, they understood that military service would result in their immediate freedom, would allow them to assert their manhood and rights to citizenship, and might result in the liberation of their families as well.[19]

A few Unionist slaveholders encouraged enlistment because they recognized that their slave men might enroll with or without their permission, and they reasoned that, at the very least, African American soldiers would help meet the local draft quota. Missouri slaveholder William Thomas actually asked the local provost marshal to force the enlistment of his enslaved blacksmith, Anderson, who was "loafing about for the last six months rendering service to no one." In addition, Unionist slaveholders also hoped that the federal government would reimburse them for the loss of their slaves who enlisted in military service. Hundreds of self-proclaimed Unionist slaveholders filed slave compensation claims with the United States government, but in the end they were never reimbursed for the loss of their property.[20]

Many owners discouraged and even physically intimidated their slaves to keep them from enlisting, while others chose a different approach and guaranteed their slaves better conditions and even wages. Henry Bruce's master offered him "fifteen dollars per month, board and clothing" and a general pass if he would "remain with him on the farm," and Spotswood Rice's master attempted to bribe him by promising to give him land and a house if he would stay and manage his farming affairs. Some enslaved men remained a short while, but eventually many, such as Bruce and Rice, ran off to enlist or fled the state altogether. In contrast, Union military records are littered with reports of owners who attempted to thwart enlistment through violence and intimidation. Many enslaved men literally risked their lives as they journeyed to recruitment stations. Slaveholders and guerrillas patrolled the roads at night in order to apprehend men on their way to

The Skirmish at Island Mound, 1863. *The First Kansas Colored Infantry, formed by Senator James Lane in the summer of 1862, fought secessionist guerrillas at a site along the Marais des Cygnes River, just over the Kansas state line in Bates County, Missouri, in late October of that year. Island Mound was the first military engagement between African American troops and Southern forces fought during the Civil War. From Harper's Weekly, March 14, 1863. Courtesy of Ellis Library, University of Missouri–Columbia*

enlist. A Lafayette County man who attempted to enroll claimed that it was safe to travel only at night, reporting, "it was worth a negro's life, almost, to try to get away." Field officers routinely argued that the military should more actively protect potential recruits, recognizing that the continued violence would dampen future enlistment prospects.[21]

While calculating the risks of enlistment, enslaved men considered the consequences of their actions for their kin as well. Some women and children followed their husbands and fathers to army posts, but many more initially remained with their owners, where they often suffered abuse. Slaveholders expected that the work of the farm would continue even after the men left, and many women complained that they now were "made to do the work formerly performed by the men." Some slaveholders verbally and physically abused women and children, while others either callously forced them off their property to fend for themselves or shipped them out of state for sale. Union military officers feared that if the army turned a blind eye to this abuse it would result in "hundreds of able bodied men" who would be "deterred from enlistment by fears of their families being abused or sold to Kentucky." A few reasoned that it was immoral to allow the mistreatment of "the wives and children of these, Sable 'Patriots' and true 'Heroes' [sic]." Officers were unsure if the wives and children of soldiers were indeed free, and many requested clarification of their status, asking their commanders: "What are we to do with the women and children?"[22]

Formerly enslaved soldiers believed that the answer to this question was simple. They emphatically argued that their military service guaranteed the freedom and protection of their family members. They agonized over the fate of their loved ones left in bondage, pleading with Union military officials to intercede on their behalf. Some, such as Spotswood Rice, argued that their military service guaranteed the freedom and protection of their family members. In September of 1864, while stationed at Benton Barracks in St. Louis, Spotswood Rice penned two letters regarding the welfare of his children, who remained enslaved in Howard County. Rice explained to his daughters Corra and Mary that they should not despair that they had not yet gained their freedom, but instead "be assured that I will have you if it cost me my life." He expected to march to Howard with a combined Union military force of black and white soldiers and intended to use the full power of the government to liberate his children from their owners, who, he believed, were working against the laws of God in keeping them. Rice had heard that Mary's mistress, Kittey Diggs, had accused him of trying to steal his child away from her, and he proclaimed that "She is the frist Christian that I ever hard say that aman could Steal his own child especially out of human bondage." In another letter written to Diggs that same day, Rice damned his daughter's mistress to hell and threatened her: "Now you call my children your pro[per]ty not so with me my Children is my own and I expect to get them and when I get ready to come after mary I will have bout a powrer and autherity to bring hear away and to exacute vengencens on them that holds my Child." In case Diggs did not understand that the federal government would back him in his claims to his children, he assured her that "I have no fears about geting mary out of your hands this whole Government gives chear to me and you cannot help your self." In like manner, Sam Bowmen threatened the owner of his wife and children, informing him that he must allow his wife to leave if she chose because a "Soldiers wife is free."[23]

Some soldiers took matters into their own hands and liberated their family members who remained in bondage. Missouri slaveholders told stories of white soldiers who aided black soldiers as they attempted to free their wives and children. In March 1864, the assistant provost marshal stationed in Howard County reported that some newly freed men, who had recently enlisted in the army, had returned from St. Louis "with some white soldiers and [were] hauling off tobacco from their former masters and owners and taking their wives and children." And Willard Mendenhall wrote of his wife's Saline County relatives: "One of thare negroes (Bob) that ran off some time ago, went home one night last week, took a squad of white men with him and took his wife and two children away, stole two hoarses from his master at the same time." The image of white and black men, both wearing blue uniforms and working in concert to free Missouri slaves, must have been a frightening prospect for many white Missourians. These return trips were made at great risk, however, as a former Platte County slave named Sam Marshall learned when he ran afoul of local Missouri State Militia soldiers, who severely beat him as he attempted to take his children with him to Leavenworth, Kansas. Against tremendous odds, thousands of Missouri men brought about their own freedom and helped facilitate the liberation of their family members as well.[24]

In the end, more than 8,300 black Missourians, 39 percent of the state's African American men of service age, served in the five regiments of the United States Colored Troops that were recruited in the state, but many more enlisted in nearby Kansas, Illinois, and Iowa. Not all enslaved Missouri men took this route to freedom, however. Some men entered into free labor arrangements in their neighborhoods, while others flocked to nearby towns and cities or simply left the state altogether. Certainly, not all men chose to enlist—whether for family reasons or because they had struck free labor deals, but, as Henry Bruce learned, it was difficult to avoid enlistment once recruiting agents swarmed the state and fellow slave men began putting pressure on friends and neighbors to join. Bruce took to hiding during the day and sleeping in the woods at night in order to keep from being detected by enlisted men who were scouring Chariton County looking for prospective recruits under the direction of recruiting agents from Iowa. By the summer of 1864, recruiters found it difficult to locate many more men willing to enroll. Many Missouri slave men had achieved their freedom by then and were now more interested in working for wages.[25]

As the war progressed, Missouri slaves became less tolerant of slaveholders' abuse because they knew that, although the risks were great, they had the option to leave. Like many white Missourians, they believed that the federal government should safeguard their rights, and they repeatedly asked the provost marshals and other military officials for relief from abusive owners, rights of free passage, material aid, and assistance in disputes over their freedom. It was reported that the "state of their minds is such that they cannot be reduced to slavery again in the first morning of their freedom."[26]

Many enslaved Missouri men, women, and children reasoned that the best way to safeguard their freedom was to make their way to the surrounding free states. Platte County slave George Washington literally walked across the frozen Missouri River in the frigid winter of 1861–1862 to freedom in the abolitionist stronghold of Quindaro, Kansas, and in April 1863, a Kansas City, Missouri, newspaper reported that large numbers of freed slaves "are constantly streaming through our streets," presumably on their way to Kansas. A year later, Henry Bruce escaped to Leavenworth with his fiancée, eluding the men who pursued them, riding on his master's horse. The couple simply boarded a train on the Hannibal and St. Joseph Railroad line at Laclede and rode it to St. Joseph, where they crossed the Missouri River to freedom in Kansas. Given its free-soil history, enslaved Missourians believed that Kansas was a place where they might find assistance, and they actively worked to make their way there, hoping that the citizens of the new state would provide them with protection as well as gainful employment. Even General Ewing promoted Kansas in this way, observing that former slaves found "ready employment and earned comfortable livelihoods" in the state.[27]

In reality, many who hazarded running away faced an uncertain future in freedom. Women, children, and the elderly often remained in close proximity to military encampments because they feared guerrilla violence or capture by their former owners if they moved back into the countryside, while others moved to Union strongholds such as St. Louis or towns in bordering free states. The large number of refugees quickly overwhelmed these communities. As early as July 1863, Captain G. W. Murphy reported the presence of 270 women and children in Sedalia, Missouri, who were "suffering for some thing to eat." One former solider reported after a recent trip to Missouri and Kansas that he saw a number of freedpeople "all most Thread less and Shoeless without food and no home to go . . . as fur as I can see the hole Race will fall back if the U. S. Government dont pervid for them Some way or ruther." There were some private philanthropic efforts to aid refugees in urban areas, but in the countryside the task rested primarily with the army. Military officers looked for solutions to the growing refugee problem in garrison towns. Many did not have the resources to feed, clothe, and shelter the refugees, or provide them with medical aid. Some commanders requested material assistance, while others sought ways to employ those living among them. The Union commander in Independence wondered if he might be allowed to put the nearly 300 "old men, women, and children" who made his garrison their home to work on nearby "deserted farms" that had been abandoned in the wake of General Order No. 11. The military increasingly looked to transport out of state as the solution to the growing refugee problem, however. One officer reasoned, "Some of them may be sent to the western Border where they can join their friends who have escaped into Kansas."[28]

In truth, freedpeople's reception was not always cordial even in the free-state stronghold of Kansas. Refugees frequently faced a mixed reception in their new communities, where racism and white supremacy was often virulent and competition from an influx of African American workers was unwelcome by many. In early 1864, military officers from western Missouri attempted to transport newly freed women and children to Kansas, but they were stopped at the state line by Kansas troops. The refugee women, children, and elderly were stalled near the border at Little Santa Fe in Jackson County, destitute and suffering from smallpox. Henry Bruce reported a similarly hostile reception in Leavenworth where he faced discrimination from black Kansans who had been free before the war and white Kansans who cheated former slaves who had little experience with managing their own finances.[29]

On January 11, 1865, Missouri slaves were officially emancipated by a resolution of the Missouri State Constitutional Convention that was dominated by Radical Republicans, although some Missourians at the time questioned the body's authority to abrogate property rights and free slaves. This challenge to the so-called Drake Constitution was largely meaningless, however, because by this time, most enslaved Missourians—especially enlistment-age men—were already free. Missouri slaveholders had an extremely difficult time adjusting to the changes to their lives brought about by the emancipation of their slaves, and many still clung to slavery as a system of labor and racial control. At the start of the war, Missouri slaveholders never could have imagined a world in which their former slaves were emancipated and they were forced to hire them as paid laborers. Once Missouri slaves were freed, farmers often continued to employ them as general farmhands and domestic workers as they had before the war, but many found it difficult to adapt to the new management practices of free labor.[30]

Many former owners did not graciously accept the end of the labor and social system from which they had so richly benefited. "Slavery dies hard[.] I hear its expiring agonies & witness its contortions in death in every quarter of my Dist.," Brigadier General Clinton Fisk reported of the situation in central Missouri in March 1865. No longer bound by the obligations of ownership and demoralized by their wartime experiences, some owners drove their former slaves off of their land in the midst of winter, while others made it extremely difficult for them to leave by either not informing them of emancipation or attempting to coerce them to remain as wage laborers. Some chose to stay with their owners for a time after emancipation because they had few resources and because they "didn't know nothing else to do." Many people were forced to take great risks to break the bonds of their enslavement even though they already were legally free. Many freedpeople streamed into local towns or military garrisons for protection as they suffered increased violence from white Missourians as they made the difficult transition to free labor and faced the possibility of a biracial democracy. Former Boone County slaves flooded into Columbia after a series of lynchings in the countryside in the month directly after emancipation. The Union commander in Lafayette County was forced to issue an order that stipulated that anyone who threatened freedpeople would be considered in league with the Bushwhackers who were terrorizing and murdering local African Americans and would be charged as an accessory to these murders. The demographics of the Missouri countryside actually changed as a result of this postwar violence. The river counties never again could boast of African American populations as large as before the war; many people chose the relative safety of Missouri's towns and cities instead.[31]

Freedpeople's relationships with white Missourians certainly were forever altered, but they likely were more concerned about what freedom meant for their own families and communities. Their lives changed dramatically in the years following emancipation. The turbulence of wartime Missouri and men's enlistment separated many families during the course of the war, and thousands of women and children faced freedom without the support of their husbands and fathers, who frequently died in the Union army. The large number of Missouri women who filed widows' and orphans' pension claims attests to appallingly high death rates among African American soldiers and to the struggles faced by their families after their deaths.[32]

The end of slavery also created opportunities, however, as many of the families that had been separated during slavery by estate divisions, sales, and abroad unions, as well as wartime dislocation, were reunited under the same roof, sometimes for the first time. Freedpeople worked to reconstitute their households after the war, but, as was the case during slavery, not all of them sheltered nuclear families. It was common for extended kin, and even neighbors, to live and work with one another in common purpose. Assembling a household of individuals who could work together as an economic unit was the primary goal, but expanding the definition of "family" to include extended kin and those permanently separated from blood relatives was a priority as well.[33]

Aware of the ongoing violence and skeptical that economic opportunities existed in Missouri, many freed Missourians remained in Kansas, Iowa, or Illinois, where they had fled during the war. Henry Bruce and his wife, Pauline, were two of the more than 17,000 African American residents of Kansas in 1870. Bruce did not return to Missouri, but instead opened a business in Leavenworth, and when it failed he gained employment as the doorkeeper at the Kansas statehouse through the patronage of the state's Republican Party. In 1881, he moved to Washington, D.C., where for the rest of his life he worked at federal jobs secured for him by his wealthy and influential brother, the former western Missouri slave turned Mississippi senator, Blanche K. Bruce. This fortuitous connection to his kinsman allowed Henry Bruce to prosper in postwar society.[34]

Other formerly enslaved Missourians continued to face discrimination and poverty. The years ahead would prove to be difficult for both black and white Missourians as they forged a new relationship in freedom, but Missouri freedmen and -women continued to work toward a future in which they could manage their own families and communities, acquire an education, negotiate the terms of their labor, and assert their rights as American citizens.

Chapter 10

The Guerrilla Shirt: A Labor of Love and the Style of Rebellion in Civil War Missouri*

Joseph M. Beilein Jr.

On the afternoon of October 27, 1864, Union soldiers wheeled the dead body of the infamous rebel guerrilla "Bloody" Bill Anderson into the town of Richmond, Missouri. They stuck his wild-haired corpse in a chair and propped him up in front of the courthouse—where a roistering crowd of townspeople, including a dentist who part-timed as the local photographer, gathered to yawp and gape. Here, dead, was the man who over the previous summer had killed untold numbers of Union men; here, cold, was the man—some said murderer—who since June had mutilated soldiers and waylaid civilians too. At some point that afternoon the crowd parted shoulders and elbows long enough for Dr. Robert Kice, Richmond's aforementioned dentist-photographer, to take a famous image. Anderson's likeness is as macabre today as the corpse must have been for the gawking villagers then: bearded, bucktoothed, arch-eyebrowed, and wide-eared, a crazy mane obscuring the two bullet holes in his head, there he is, propped up with a revolver across his stomach, gripping it at his belt, posed but poised to maim again.[1]

And there he is: killed, in his guerrilla shirt. The shirt is homemade, and garish for being homemade, hand-stitched in flowers of all shapes and sizes and colors. It is an oddly bedazzling garment for any man to wear, let alone a man of notorious repute for mayhem.[2]

The objectification of Anderson's body points to a conflict deeper than the political dispute between Southern-sympathizing Missourians and the Union. This was a clash of divergent concepts of manhood. For the Union men who killed Anderson, stripped his body down to his colorful shirt, and displayed his corpse, he was a different type of man. He was a guerrilla. Demonstrated through his warfare, the guerrilla's nature was woefully out of step with that of "civilized" men. In fact, Union officers, who saw themselves as the enlightened sons of civilization trying to wage a conventional war for their country, described the guerrillas as they did Native Americans during the Indian Wars. The guerrillas were "cowards," "fiends," and "savages," labels that were only confirmed by their exotic and unusual appearance. Yet, for the men who were guerrillas, their seemingly irregular look signified important components of a distinctive manhood born of their slaveholding society west of the Mississippi. Through an analysis of the guerrilla's appearance this article will not only reveal that the guerrillas possessed a distinctive form of masculinity but will also show that their vision of manhood was a guiding force in their particular brand of warfare.[3]

Several works have suggested the importance of gender in the guerrilla conflict. The most influential work on guerrilla warfare in the Civil War, Michael Fellman's *Inside War*, is the first work to enter into a discussion of masculinity when discussing the men involved in the guerrilla war. In his chapter "Brother Killers: Guerrillas and Union Troops," Fellman grounds his discussion of men in male-male relationships and sees these men in terms of a Freudian metaphor. Reading the experience of these men at war through the "language of oedipal rebellion," he posits that the experience of the guerrillas in this conflict was one of rebellious sons. These sons resisted the authority of their symbolic fathers in the form of the Union government, only to be forced to submit to their fathers once again when captured or killed. Keeping with the familial theme, Fellman tweaks the metaphor to describe the period of time in which these rebellious youngsters were running roughshod over the countryside. At a certain point, when both the guerrillas and the Union troopers were caught in the whirlwind of violence that was guerrilla warfare, Fellman sees both groups of men as virtually the same and both teetering dangerously close to outright nihilism. They were all "brother killers."[4]

In examining the role of women and the guerrilla war, Fellman again leads the way. His chapter "Women as Victims and Participants" is a demonstration of guerrilla war spilling over boundaries that formal war, at least in an ideal sense, typically respected. He concludes that regardless of their respective loyalties, the relationships between men and women were utterly destroyed by the war. This take on male-female relationships has been challenged in recent years by scholars of gender who see the nature

Death Photo of "Bloody" Bill Anderson, 1864. *One of the posthumous images of "Bloody" Bill Anderson in his homemade guerrilla shirt, generated by Dr. Robert Kice at Richmond, Missouri, on October 27, 1864. Note the bullet holes. Courtesy of the State Historical Society of Missouri*

of the relationship between women and men in the guerrilla war in a very different light. Kristen Streater's essay, "'She Rebels' on the Supply Line," sees some order in the chaos. She demonstrates that instead of the formal army supply line that might otherwise provide men with materiel, a domestic supply line was operated exclusively by Southern-sympathizing women for their men. This cooperative effort between women and men became the logistical backbone for guerrilla warfare. Building on this line of argument, LeeAnn Whites's article, "Forty Shirts and a Wagon Load of Wheat," contends that despite the ambivalent treatment of women by historians of the guerrilla war, "women, like men, played a critical, systematic part in the waging of that conflict." She returns them to the center of the action in Missouri as actors in the guerrilla war, not simply the war's victims.[5]

This essay builds on the coupling of the concepts put forth by Streater and Whites on the one hand, and the literature on manhood during the antebellum period and the Civil War on the other. When looking across the field, it is evident that the work on manhood asserts that there were distinctive constructions of manhood in the North and South and even within the sections themselves. I place the guerrillas in the context of Southern manhood. Though guerrilla manhood would take on several subforms of Southern manhood during the war—the self-reliant and independent backwoodsman, the Indian fighter, and the hunter, all who led the way in previous conflicts—at their core the guerrillas, who were the products of Southern lineage and who had a strong interest in the survival of the institution of slavery, saw themselves as Southern men. In *All That Makes a Man*, Stephen Berry contends that the belief by white men of the planter class that the fulfillment of their manhood required both love and immortality best articulates the connection between the relationships maintained by rebellious women and men and the violence undertaken by men like Anderson. Berry cites James Henry Hammond, the prolific Southern diarist who said to achieve immortality was "to fill a niche in History to the end of time," and the Civil War offered the guerrillas just such an opportunity to achieve this kind of immortality. Love could mean "friendship— the love of male for male—but primarily it meant the romantic love of man and woman." Love and immortality were "each beholden to the other. The woman, once acquired, would sustain and bear witness to the male becoming; the male would in turn reconceive his becoming as a tribute to her love." Though perhaps the guerrillas did not articulate their ideas in such a romantic or overblown manner as Hammond, we will see that threads of love and of immortality were interwoven into the identity of these men and, indeed, their shirts.[6]

The geographic location of this guerrilla war was an important factor in the centrality of women to the war effort as well as the style of clothing with which they outfitted their men. When young men left their homes along the western border of Missouri to protect their neighborhoods from "jayhawking" Kansans in the late 1850s and the first year of the 1860s, they did so with whatever clothes their women had made for them. As the border war became the Civil War in 1861, the Confederate army and its affiliate, the Missouri State Guard, were unable to provide a substantial defense of the border. In the formal army's stead, young men remained at home to protect their vulnerable communities, and their women began to make shirts for their men that were especially suited for the extended duty outdoors. It is unclear exactly who made the first guerrilla shirt, or who wore it, but it quickly became popular among the men in Quantrill's band. Andrew Walker, who initially rode with William Clarke Quantrill but later joined George Todd's band and would have fought alongside Anderson at different points in the war, offered insight into the guerrillas' style throughout his memoir. He recalled that by the spring of 1862, the guerrillas "affected but one garment that might be distinctive; a handsome, embroidered overshirt . . . was worn at nearly all times, by each and all of us."[7]

Rebel women responsible for creating guerrilla clothing designed a shirt unlike any other military garb of the day. William E. Connelley offered the first historical description of the guerrilla shirt. He described it as "cut low in front, the slit narrowing to a point above the belt and ending in a ruffle-bunch or rosette. This slit was usually bound or faced with some fabric of light weight and brilliant color, as were the pockets and sometimes the tail." The pockets were "of generous capacity—one on each breast." The shirt was "made from any cloth of sufficient weight," and its design allowed for a "variety in cut, and in color [that] ranged from the brilliant scarlet of red flannel to the somber, subdued, and discouraging hues of the homespun butternut." The shirts "were usually made for the guerrillas by their wives or sweethearts" and "were elaborately ornamented with fine needlework."[8]

The shirts were emblematic of the guerrillas' style more generally, the greatest influence on which was the look of the frontier hunters who had straddled the fringes of the white and Indian worlds since very early in the European settlement of the Americas. Some of these white hunters had so merged the two styles that they were derided by other European Americans as "white Indians." In his biography of the consummate American hunter, Daniel Boone, John Mack Faragher says, "Hunters from both cultures dressed in a composite of European and Indian style." He writes, "The hunting shirt was a loose frock that reached halfway down the thighs. . . . In the front folds of the shirt hunters kept small rations of provisions." The general appearance of the hunters was also influenced by the cultural exchange. For instance, according to Faragher, "Like Indian men, American hunters let their hair grow long and dressed it with bear grease, plaiting it into braids or knots." Just as Indian hunters painted their bodies and attached ornaments to their hair, "American backwoodsmen heading into battle frequently adopted a similar style of ornamentation."[9]

Like the wives of those backwoodsmen who outfitted them during the frontier wars, when the Civil War swept onto the border, women became the quartermasters of the guerrilla war effort, with their domestic skills becoming highly valued military tools. Before the war in Missouri, women produced clothing for themselves, their men, and their children. When their brothers were learning how to use firearms and ride horses, girls were learning how to spin, weave, and sew. In mastering their skills, women used every possible material to clothe their families. They made clothing from wool shorn from sheep raised on their farms, small amounts of homegrown flax and cotton, and whatever textiles could be purchased or otherwise procured from local marketplaces. When their clothes wore out or were lost, the guerrillas returned to their women for replacements. The climate of Missouri, prone to rapid fluctuations on the thermometer and barometer, took its toll on clothing. In addition to natural deterioration, the nature of combat in guerrilla warfare, typically in the form of an ambush or a running fight, often forced guerrillas to flee their hideouts and their supporters' homes in such haste that they left pieces of clothing behind.[10]

To communicate the beauty of the connection between themselves and their men, rebel women attempted to recreate the most beautiful things they knew—flowers. These women were aware of the great symbolic value of flowers and that a language of flowers existed, each type of flower standing for a different idea or emotion. For instance, daisies symbolized innocence; violets, faithfulness; pansies, thought and remembrance; and red roses, love. Using this language, women spoke to their men and spoke about their men to anyone who laid eyes on their shirts. They used green thread to stitch long vines of garland that looped around deep-cut collars and across large pockets. Along the garland, rebel women used red, blue, yellow, purple, and white thread to stitch roses, bluebells, daisies, violets, and dogwood blossoms. Each shirt cost those women who did not have access to homegrown wool between fifteen and twenty dollars. This was a hefty cost—a hefty cost unless, of course, its message was priceless.[11]

Of the shirts that appear in surviving photographs, no other is as intricate as the one worn by Anderson on the day he died. Flowers of varying sizes and colors created a border around its collar, covered its pockets, and even decorated its sleeves' cuffs. The flowers stand out not only because they appear in such a great quantity but because the black material from which the shirt was made offers an outstanding backdrop for their bright colors, not unlike real flowers springing out of freshly tilled earth. These stitched flowers may have been strung together by a vine of garland, but the black-and-white quality of the photograph prevents us from knowing for sure. What is evident, however, is that whoever made the shirt for Anderson had hands that were both talented and industrious.[12]

Itself a labor of love, the guerrilla shirt worn by Anderson offers a starting point for understanding the connection between his deep affection for his women and his quest for immortality, the two components of guerrilla masculinity. Few guerrillas left written evidence of the significance of immortality in their lives. However, the wartime ritual of having one's picture taken shows not only that the concept of immortality was present in the minds of the men serving in the guerrilla ranks, but that immortality was inextricably entangled with feminine love. Sitting for a moment or two while the lens registered their likenesses, the guerrillas created what words could not, indelible images of themselves at an important time in their lives. The practice of having one's picture made shows these men wished to be remembered as soldiers, and in giving the image to a sweetheart or female relative, they wished to be remembered by the women they loved. One of these men might have had the morbid fantasy that someday his sweetheart would take in the frozen image of her man, dressed in the clothes she had made for him and holding the weapons he used to bloody the men who threatened her. Once his likeness was made, the guerrilla need not worry about his legacy. He would be remembered as a man.[13]

While romantic love was important as an expectation and goal, female love for Anderson came first from his sisters. While we do not know if he ever gave one of his sisters a photograph of himself, it is quite possible that one of his sisters was responsible for the beautiful shirt he wore on the day he died. Having lost both parents just before the war, the Anderson children were reliant upon each other. When both Bill and his younger brother, Jim, left home to fight in the brush, Mary Ellen, Josephine, and Jane must have been deeply affected. In 1860, the girls were only fourteen, eleven, and eight. Not only were their brothers putting their own lives at risk, but their absence made their sisters that much more vulnerable. The mutual reliance, the emotions brought on by missing their older brothers, and the general stress of war could easily have inspired the creation of the ornate guerrilla shirt Anderson wore.[14]

During the summer of 1863, the Union general Thomas Ewing went after rebel women like the Anderson sisters because they were the source of logistical support for the guerrillas. Ewing, as shrewd an observer of the guerrilla system of warfare as any Union officer, saw that material support traveled along highly gendered lines of blood, affection, and friendship. He would later articulate this observation in the short-lived General Order No. 10, in which he declared, "The wives and children of known guerrillas, and also women who are heads of families and willfully engaged in aiding guerrillas, will be notified . . . to remove out of the district and out of the State." With this logic in mind, Ewing arrested the Anderson girls, Charity McCorkle Kerr, Nannie Harris McCorkle, Susan Crawford Vandever, Armenia Crawford Selvey, Susan Munday, Martha Munday, Mrs. Lou Munday Gray, and Mollie Grandstaff. He put these women—the sisters, cousins, wives, and sweethearts of a few notable guerrillas—in a makeshift prison in the Kansas City neighborhood of McGee's Addition.[15]

Given what we know about their gender relations, guerrillas undoubtedly interpreted Union counterinsurgency measures through the lens of manhood. Their reactions to these measures were further exacerbated when an accident seemingly undermined the very foundation of guerrilla masculinity. On August 13, the makeshift prison for women collapsed, killing four women outright and seriously injuring many others. Josephine Anderson, fourteen at the time, was killed. As a result of the collapse, sixteen-year-old Mary Ellen Anderson was crippled for the rest of her life. The fall broke both of Jane Anderson's legs, injured her back, and cut up her face. She was only ten years old. John McCorkle, who had a sister killed and a sister-in-law seriously hurt, expressed the sentiments of many of his guerrilla brethren when he said the recent tragedy was "the direct cause of the famous raid on Lawrence." Years later, he claimed that the guerrillas had plenty of reasons for going to Lawrence. Men from Kansas had burned down their homes, killed their fathers, and stolen their families' property—all things they would later inflict on the residents of Lawrence. However, for McCorkle and no doubt Anderson as well, the cause that outweighed all others was that their "innocent and beautiful girls had been murdered."[16]

News of broken and lifeless female bodies set off an alarm in the minds of the guerrillas, not unlike the ones that had been triggered in men generation after generation up and down the American frontier as it crept westward. The guerrillas seem to have adopted not only the frontier hunter's style but his warfare as well. The guerrillas envisioned themselves as the rangers who rode across the landscape unfettered by anything save their homes and families, which they were protecting either through the direct defense of the settlements or in their strikes against Indian villages and European outposts. This type of warfare was not limited to battlefields but was taken into the very household of the enemy. Dwellings were burnt. Food was taken and eaten or destroyed. Enemy men, simply because they were men, were by definition combatants and were often killed whether they were armed or not. Attacks were not limited to men but extended to women and children. Though guerrilla warfare was influenced by this model of frontier warfare from the outset of the Civil War, it had held closer to the limits of nineteenth-century conventional warfare in respect to the treatment of women. Now, with the knife taken to their women, these men viewed themselves differently as men, and with this, the shape of the guerrilla conflict would change as well.[17]

Like white frontiersmen reacting to Indian attacks on their homesteads or Indians reacting to attacks on their villages, the guerrillas determined to take the war to the closest enemy settlement and destroy it. On August 21, a large body of guerrillas under Quantrill raided Lawrence, Kansas, during which Anderson demonstrated that he had begun to see himself in the same vein as the frontiersmen who likewise had been unfettered by the regimentation of the regular army. Armed or not, Union men were a threat to Southern women and had to be killed. The guerrillas killed somewhere between 150 and 180 men, most of them unarmed. There is really no way of knowing how many men each guerrilla killed, because most guerrillas did not offer details on the raid, even if they contended that their actions were justified. According to one account, Anderson told two Lawrence women, probably recently widowed, that his "two sisters, with three other ladies, were crushed to death," in a prison collapse. Another account claims that Anderson said to an onlooker, "I'm here for revenge and I have got it." Popular accounts of the raid state that Anderson was personally responsible for the deaths of fourteen men.[18]

Just months after he did more than his share of widow-making at Lawrence, Anderson took a bride. Over the winter of 1863–1864, he met a woman in Texas and fell in love. Her name was Bush Smith, and she could have easily been the seamstress behind the creation of the shirt that appears in the 1864 posthumous photograph. Besides her name and her relationship with Anderson, little is known about this woman; she is the subject of many historical rumors, for lack of a better phrase. With scant evidence, historians assert that Smith was a prostitute who worked in a saloon in Sherman, Texas, a town close to the guerrillas' camp. The saloon in question was owned by Jim Crow Chiles, a man from Jackson County who not only was known to the guerrillas but likely had relatives among Quantrill's men. Regardless of Smith's occupation or historical reputation, however, there is enough evidence that she and Anderson formed a strong relationship. They were wed in the spring of 1864, before the guerrillas returned to Missouri.[19]

A guerrilla wedding like the Anderson-Smith nuptials would see women turning out in fancy dresses and men also dressing in their finest clothes. The groom may have worn an outfit like the one he wore on his death day: a white hat with a large black ostrich plume, a guerrilla shirt, a blue waistcoat, and a well-tailored, dun-colored frock coat. Standing beside Anderson, his fellow dandies would have been decked out in fine jackets, coats, and hats, each man accentuating his individuality. Walker remembered that such fine clothing was not simply worn at weddings but that the guerrillas "always, unless in exceptional straits, wore the best of clothes," such as "a rather large slouch hat . . . and boots, with spurs." While women made much of their clothing, the guerrillas had to purchase or steal these accessories from local merchants. Occasionally women purchased items for the guerrillas. The Spencer women of Johnson County, for example, bought "seven pairs of boots and three or four hats" for a group of male relatives out in the brush. The most conspicuous of these things, fine hats with feathers, were much sought after. The guerrilla Joseph Bailey made sure to note in his memoir that after a skirmish, he took from a man he killed a hat decorated with an ostrich plume. He wore this prized trophy for a brief time until he left it behind when fleeing the home of his sweetheart.[20]

Clothing was important for the guerrillas in conveying their individuality when they faced members of their own community. However, when Anderson and his warrior-groomsmen turned toward their enemy, clothing became a weapon. Nearly as quickly as the war began and the Union army conformed in blue uniforms, the guerrillas began to wear blue jackets and coats stolen from their enemies or taken off the bodies of the Union soldiers killed in combat. Walker attested to this addition of the blue uniform to the guerrilla wardrobe, saying that while they never wore Confederate uniforms, they "very often wore plain citizen's clothes, more often Federal uniforms." He went on to say that even though the guerrilla shirt "was worn at nearly all times," "a Federal cavalry coat was worn over it."[21]

Wearing their blue coats out in the brush, the guerrillas easily tricked Union patrols. Walker recalled one instance early in the war in which Union troopers surprised the guerrillas and gained the upper hand, only to be confused and deceived by their disguises. Immediately following their initial volley toward the guerrillas, the Union patrol rode closer and, as Walker said, "Seeing so many of us with blue uniforms, it occurred to them that we must be another of the several Federal scouting parties that were out after us." In the moment that the patrol hesitated, the guerrillas opened up on them. Walker remembered, "The captain shouted excitedly: 'Don't shoot here, don't shoot here.'" Todd, who was leading the guerrilla band, yelled back, "'Who are you?'" The Union captain replied that he was a Union officer. The guerrillas fired again. Clearly confused, the Union captain shouted out again, exclaiming, "'I am not Captain Todd, the bushwhacker, neither am I Captain Gregg.'" According to Walker, when the fighting was done, nineteen of the fifty-two Union troopers lay dead, without the loss of a single guerrilla.[22]

The blue uniform, an important part of guerrilla strategy, was also a trophy. Following the skirmish with Union troopers, Todd's guerrillas probably scoured the corpses of the nineteen dead troopers for things of value, while the few men without blue jackets almost certainly wrestled uniforms from the unwieldy and mortified bodies. After losing his own clothes in a close escape from Union troopers who beset his winter hideout, Walker procured his Union garb in just this way. Following another fight with Union troops, a group of guerrillas that included Walker came up to the body of a dead Union soldier. The dead man was, according to Walker, "just my size and well dressed. I traded clothes with him on the spot; and I looked like a soldier I can assure you, with his brand new uniform, cavalry boots, blouse, and overcoat." This man's clothes were not just a useful disguise.

He clearly admired them; perhaps this reflected how he viewed the now dead soldier. Furthermore, just as a hunter wearing a buffalo coat conveyed a certain message to other hunters, by wearing a blue jacket, a guerrilla was boasting to all who saw him that he had bagged a Union trooper.[23]

In addition to their admiration for their enemy's wardrobe, a few other aspects of the guerrillas' appearance were distinctive and therefore worth pointing out. Guerrillas were known for their long hair and penchant for facial hair, making them conscious of these aspects of personal style in others. In their portraits, we see that some of the men were too young to grow proper beards, but all who could grow facial hair did so, and most of the men had long hair, although it was sometimes covered by a hat. Walker described the guerrillas' and especially Quantrill's use of facial hair. He said, "In order to escape recognition by day, the guerrillas changed their personal appearances . . . especially by changes of the style of beard." Walker observed that "Quantrill's beard grew faster than that of any other man I ever knew, and he remodeled it often. I do not remember ever to have seen him without a mustache . . . and he seldom wore chin whiskers, but made the most of the fruitful possibilities of sideburns."[24]

McCorkle described the guerrillas' personal style in contrast to that of regular Confederate soldiers. As the guerrillas headed south during the late fall of 1862, they came into contact with regular Confederate forces in Arkansas, where McCorkle bumped into an old friend, a Missourian named Henry Brookins. According to McCorkle, "Brookins and I had agreed not to have our hair trimmed nor to shave until the war was over. I had kept my promise and when I saw Brookins, he had his hair nicely trimmed and cleanly shaved except a long mustache." Upon seeing his conservatively groomed friend, McCorkle said, "With my long hair which was then below my shoulders and with my flowing beard, I walked up to him, caught him by the mustache and said, 'Henry, you lied to me. Where is your hair?'" Brookins told McCorkle, "They would not let us wear long hair in the South; if we would not have it trimmed they would throw us down and cut it off for us."[25]

If the regular army style reflected the stability of the formal system of war, then it would seem that the guerrillas were wearing, modeling, and performing the instabilities of their theater of war. In the photograph for which Anderson sat while he was among the living, his long, black, curly hair is like a woman's, but his beard is of the piratical sort. On the upturned brim of his black hat is a silver star, denoting military rank, while the hint of a plume more befitting the hat of an eighteenth-century macaroni can be seen peaking out just above his hat. Anderson's posture is somewhere between those of a general and of a barroom card shark, with one hand firmly gripping his lapel while the other is relaxed, resting over the edge of a nearby chair back and revealing a gold ring on his pinky finger. He wears the black or blue velvet coat of a gentlemen farmer, the type of wealthy agrarian who needs the brace of revolvers around Anderson's waist. In short, he is a fop, but deadly.

This picture of violent burlesque was only accentuated by the gory trophies displayed by the guerrillas. A quintessential image of their bloody pageantry was on display October 11, 1864, when Anderson and his men rode into Boonville to meet the ragtag invasion force of "butternuts" led by Confederate general Sterling Price. Price's army was far from uniform, but aside from the occasional involvement of the Cherokee forces in Confederate operations in the western theater, a more striking disparity in two parties of Southern-sympathizing troops was likely not seen during the war. The general, a Missourian, Mexican War hero, and former governor of the state, planned his invasion with the idea that if he could capture St. Louis, the North would lose its taste for war and vote Lincoln out of office. Without the resources to achieve his goals, the invasion was ill-fated, and by the time Price reached Boonville, he had given up hope of capturing St. Louis. When the guerrillas came to meet him, they were not dressed in the humble, monotone clothes of other Southern soldiers but "in black or dark suits, and had their hats fantastically decorated with ribbons." Seemingly in contrast with the flowing rainbow of ribbons, the saddles and bridles of the guerrillas' mounts were decorated with human scalps that twisted and bounced to the rhythm of the horses' canter.[26]

In the months leading up to this moment, trophy-taking of this kind became a more prevalent part of the war for the guerrillas, signaling the full evolution of guerrilla manhood into something more akin to the model of masculinity embraced by the generations of hunters and woodsmen that preceded these men. A July 7 open letter from Anderson to two Lexington newspaper editors and several Union army officers, considered even then to be "a curiosity and specimen," offers a rare chance to get into the head of the guerrilla captain. The epistle demonstrates that Anderson's war—his reasons for fighting, his actions, and his ends—was not just a thoughtless exercise in nihilism but rather an experience to which he had devoted much thought. As alien as the thoughts in this missive may be to us, a com-

mon theme runs throughout the letter that demonstrates a particular reason and logic for Anderson's actions, based on his time and place in the
world. From beginning to end, the letter places conceptions of manhood
and masculine prowess front and center in the minds of the guerrillas.[27]

In the middle of this long letter is a short message to a Union officer
named Burris; this is the key to understanding the entire document and the
mindset of the man who reeled it off. In a few lines set off by themselves,
Anderson said, "Burris, I love you; come and see me. Good-by boy; don't
get discouraged. I glory in your spunk, but damn your judgment." Such a
goad can be seen as evidence of an arrogant and heretofore successful guerrilla. However, I think such an observation overly simplifies Anderson's letter, especially this particular portion, reading it only for its tone and nothing
more. Under the surface of this taunt, Anderson was saying that his foe was
formidable. He was a man. Anderson could only glory in his opposition if
his opponent was worthy, and, embodied here in Captain Burris, Union
officers were worthy. But by damning his judgment, Anderson was saying
that this Burris had made choices he could never make. Furthermore, in
critiquing Burris's choices, Anderson, perhaps in a moment of reflection,
must have known that his own actions likely confounded Union officers.
He knew that while they both were men, they were not the same. And they
certainly were not brothers.[28]

Anderson articulated that it was attacks against Southern women—
women just like his sisters and his wife—that were at the root of this difference. In fact, he told the newspaper editors that he became a guerrilla
because "the Yankees sought my life, but failed to get me. Revenged themselves by murdering my father, destroying all my property, and have since
that time murdered one of my sisters and kept the other two in jail twelve
months." Anderson addressed a later portion of the same letter to General
E. B. Brown, the commander of Union forces stationed in Lafayette
County, where the general had ordered the arrest of a number of rebel
women. Anderson scolded Brown, saying that he believed him "to be a man
of too much honor as to stoop so low as to incarcerate women for the deeds
of men." To Anderson and his fellow guerrillas, for Brown, Burris, the other
Union officers, and the whole Union army "to stoop so low" was to move
away from the most important tenet of the guerrillas' understanding of manhood. These two groups of men were sliding further away from each other
on the spectrum of manhood.[29]

In the wake of his sisters' arrest; the prison collapse; General Orders

Nos. 10 and 11—which both targeted women; and the continued arrest, confinement, and banishment of rebel women throughout the state, Anderson's concern for the fate of Southern women was well founded. This attack on the very heart of the rebel community was an indication of what some Union officers had in mind for Missouri's Southern-sympathizing community. In an August 15, 1864, letter to Major General William Rosecrans, the commander of the Department of the Missouri, General Clinton Fisk discussed his counterinsurgency strategy: "I am now at this end of the district to do all I can by my personal presence to organize a sufficient force to <u>exterminate</u> the fiends." Fisk was articulating what a great many Union officers must have thought, that this war could be won only if those rebels, those fiends, were wiped off the face of the Earth. He went on to say, "Nothing short of holding the bushwhacker aiders and abettors responsible with their lives and property for these barbarous acts will ever drive out the murdering villains." These terms were not unfamiliar in the lexicon of nineteenth-century U.S. military officers, being reminiscent of the way they talked about dealing with the Indians, that other group of people whose fighting style perpetuated stereotypes and cultural misinterpretations among many army officers.[30]

Fittingly, the guerrillas only embraced frontier-style warfare more as their opponents sought to eradicate them for doing so. At the one-sided Battle of Centralia, which took place on September 27, 1864, a large body of guerrillas, which included Anderson and his men, marked the bodies of some 125 Union troopers they killed, nearly the entire federal command in that battle. The day after the battle, a Union colonel, Edward A. Kutzner, arrived at the scene. He reported that in a field three miles outside of Centralia, the guerrillas with "great superiority of numbers and arms broke through the line, completely surrounding the troops, giving no quarter and mutilating bodies." A Lieutenant Clarke recounted the details of the mutilation. He reported, "Ears were cut off, and all commissioned officers were scalped . . . [and] the privates were cut from one wounded soldier while living and thrust in his mouth." All signs point to the targeting and assaulting of rebel women as the source of this ghastly bloodletting.[31]

Bloody scenes like that of Centralia were rare, but scalping had a well-defined place in American warfare for hundreds of years preceding the Civil War. Among Native Americans, scalping originally had a meaning that was both sacred and social. When a scalp was taken, there was a transfer of power by which the warrior who took the scalp became the master of the scalped person's living spirit. Scalps were treated with the same respect as any living being. In fact, bringing home a scalp from battle was the equivalent of taking a living captive who then became a dependent member of the warrior's household. While they may not have fully believed that a scalp was a living spirit, whites surely understood that scalp taking was proof of one's valor on the battlefield. With every scalp that a warrior took came recognition of his increased prowess by his community. While the white settlers attempted to transform this native practice into a business, promising a bounty for the scalps of hostile Indians, scalp taking still retained much of its original meaning. It remained among all of its practitioners a transfer of one person's power to another and a symbol of martial prowess.[32]

The original meaning of scalping seemed to hold sway with the guerrillas. Anderson and his men were notorious for taking scalps; most notable of these was Arch Clement, Anderson's second in command. In one well-documented instance, in July 1864 outside Huntsville, Missouri, Clement scalped two Union soldiers whom Anderson's band had just killed in an ambush. On the body of one of the dead men, Anderson or one of his men left a note. In broken spelling it read, "You come to hunt bush whackers. Now you are skelpt. Clemyent skept you. Wm. Anderson." Based on the poor grammar of the note, it would seem that this note and Anderson's longer letter had different authors, but both were clearly written with Anderson's permission. In leaving a note that could no longer be read by its recipient, the guerrillas were leaving a calling card, telling whoever found the bodies that Clement and Anderson now possessed the scalps of these men. They had become masters of these men and were more accomplished warriors for having done so.[33]

On October 11, these scalps and those pieces of men taken at Centralia dangled from the bridles of the guerrillas' mounts and ribbons fluttered about their heads—the picture of guerrilla manhood at its most extreme. The eyes of one Boonville observer, an outsider to the rebel community, were drawn to the bloody scalps and saw the guerrillas on parade not as staunchly independent men or highly accomplished warriors but as a group of savages, one indistinguishable from another. He was seeing evidence of only one-half of guerrilla manhood, the trophies taken. Those ribbons fluttering so close to the scalps created such a grotesque juxtaposition that it must have seemed the guerrillas were making light of their bloodletting, it was merely a joke, all of which only heightened the observer's focus on the scalps. Though he could not comprehend them, if he had, he would have seen that those streamers of colored thread suggested another kind of prize, a trophy given. Those ribbons dancing so whimsically in the air were like flags announcing the presence of trophies hidden from view, prizes representing the other half of guerrilla manhood.[34]

Inside their clothes and close to their persons, the guerrillas held onto warped inversions of the ribbons and scalps: locks of their women's hair bound together by ribbons and twine. These tokens, tucked away in the pockets of their colorful shirts, another guerrilla trophy, escaped the eye of that man at Boonville. Some guerrillas, notably Anderson, seemed reticent to expose their shirts, symbols of intimacy that they were, to the world outside their community. Like the dainty locks of hair, the shirts were gifts from and pieces of their women. And like the love infused in them, the shirts marked the powerful but vulnerable part of their war, the part that had to be protected from ill-willed outsiders.[35]

To see the guerrillas as they saw themselves and as seen by their female kin—independent men eternally bound to their women—we must weave together two seemingly dichotomous lines of thought: ribbons and bloody flesh, Southern-sympathizing women's hair and Union men's scalps, feminized shirts and jackets of dead men, trophies given and trophies taken, things hidden and things brazenly displayed, the invisible and the visible, love and immortality. We need not ignore the complexity of these men and their appearance. Seen by an outsider, they might have appeared patched-together, out-of-focus, out-of-fashion, shape-shifting, liminal men; murderous, walking send-ups of dandies, each with an Indian eye for style. Yet it is important to remember that when these men saw each other out in the brush or their women laid eyes on them as they trotted up the road to their homes, they saw each man, each guerrilla as he saw himself. They were Bill, Jim, Arch, and Jesse. They were brothers, sons, sweethearts, and husbands. Most of all, they were men.[36]

When Anderson tumbled from his horse on October 27, he had a scalp hanging from the bridle of his horse and in his pocket a lock of hair from his wife and another from a sister. His killers found these bits of feminine hair when they stripped him down to his guerrilla shirt, a sort of unmasking by which his true identity was revealed. In their final act as the creators of his shirt, Anderson's women had marked him not only as a guerrilla and a man but also as a trophy. He was the trophy of all trophies taken by Union soldiers in Missouri. Because such a trophy had to be shared, he was photographed and his death image was passed around the Union army, then, generations later, passed down to historians. The continued relevance of this haunting image suggests that Anderson achieved immortality, at least by Hammond's standards. His killers knew many would see this picture, for many years to come, but they had hoped that Anderson's strange appearance would guarantee that he would be remembered only as a savage, a hope that has been realized. However, in revealing his shirt and photographing it, those Union troops unwittingly tied one strand of guerrilla manhood to the other, thus completing the fabric of masculinity. Not only does the surviving image deepen and color Anderson's place in the history books, but it plainly shows that he wore his heart on his sleeve.[37]

Part III

The Border War Reconstructed and Remembered

Chapter 11

The Lexington Weekly Caucasian: *White Supremacist Discourse in Post–Civil War Western Missouri*

Aaron Astor

"We are Caucasian in blood, in birth, and in prejudice, and do not expect to labor to place above us, in the scale of civilization, in morality, in use-fulness, in religion, in the arts and sciences, in mechanics, either the Mongolian, the Indian, or the Negro."[1] So announced western Missouri's newest weekly journal's public salutation in April 1866. If this introduction did not suffice to outline the explicitly racial appeal of the state's newest voice of "the Democratic, and Conservative parties," surely the sheet's analysis of the current debate over the Civil Rights Bill made the editors' intentions clear. "The bill to dissolve the Union, debase the white man, enfranchise the negro, and perpetuate the Radical party in power *ad infinitum*, commonly called the Civil Rights Bill . . . ," the *Caucasian* lamented, "has been carried, as it is claimed, by the Constitutional majority over the President's objections."[2] As each subsequent edition of the fiery newspaper would attest, Radical Reconstruction offered an unprecedented and tyran-nical affront to white supremacy, white liberty, and white-controlled gov-ernment.

The *Lexington Weekly Caucasian* quickly established itself as one of the leading papers west of St. Louis and acquired a national reputation for vitu-peration, sarcasm, and militancy. While it would eventually be surpassed by journals in the fast growing metropolis of Kansas City such as the *Times* of John Edwards, the *Lexington Caucasian* clearly served as a leading voice of opposition to Missouri's Radical Republican regime led by Governors Thomas Fletcher and Joseph McClurg in the years following the Civil War.

Unsettling as the journal's style may be to modern ears, the *Caucasian* only marginally surpassed in vitriol the typical white supremacist discourse

189

of widely circulated Democratic papers such as the *Chicago Times* or *Cincinnati Enquirer*, or the unapologetically pro-Confederate *Memphis Avalanche*. The paper's roots lay in the rough and tumble late antebellum world of Missouri's sectional politics. William G. Musgrove, born in Lexington, Missouri, in 1843 and one of the first editors of the *Caucasian*, met his future partners Ethan Allen and J. M. Julian before the war. After publishing the *Carrollton Democrat*, Musgrove briefly stewarded a pro-Confederate newspaper in Lexington that was suppressed by Union military authorities. Musgrove and Allen then joined forces with the Confederate army campaigning through western Missouri in late summer 1861. They printed the reports of Confederate General Sterling Price as well as other officers during the Siege of Lexington in September 1861. Musgrove sold his interest in the paper to Peter Donan in 1868, but continued in the newspaper business as a Democrat and, in the 1890s, as a Populist.[3] But the tone of the *Caucasian* hardly wavered as editorship passed in 1868 from Musgrove, Julian, and Allen to the Mississippi-born Donan, who would later found the equally bombastic *St. Joseph Vindicator*.

At times the editors resorted to deliberate shock value to draw attention and readership, as when the *Caucasian* heralded the impending Fifteenth Amendment in 1870 with the headline: "Nigger Equality. The Fifteenth Bedamnedment Certain to be 'Ratified.' Hell Just Ahead. The Only Way of Salvation: Rub in the Nigger! Official Equality the Watchword. Black the Winning Color for Congressmen and All Federal Officers."[4] Appearing above this incendiary pronouncement was the affirmation: "State Sovereignty! White Supremacy! And Repudiation! This is Liberty!"

The enclosed commentary set a new standard for vitriol the likes of which were likely never surpassed in mainstream American print journalism—even in the tumultuous years of Reconstruction. "Yes, the work is done! Shuffle your jay-bird heels; pat 'Juba'; and shout with barbaric delight, ye lousy, devil worshipping chattels of Carolina rice-plantations!" the *Caucasian* proclaimed in mock celebration. "Screech your beastly exultation, ye man-eating savages of Dahomey and Loango! Howl your ecstacy, ye vermin swarming, filth-reeking Hottentots! You're all citizens—voters—sovereigns—of the glorious 'American Republic'—While five hundred thousand WHITE MEN are disfranchised aliens!"[5] The references to "Hottentots" and "man-eating savages of Dahomey and Loango" suggest a deeper level of racial anxiety than presented in most conservative newspapers of the day. This was, after all, the moment when European powers began to eye the African interior and its resources for colonization. Constructing the peoples of sub-Saharan Africa as subhuman was hardly a new rhetorical move in the late 1860s, but the contrast with the supposed advancements in white civilization on the world stage added a global context for this white supremacist discourse. Western Missouri stood, in the white imagination, on the literal frontier of white civilization. As Kristen Tegtmeier Oertel has shown, the Kansas wars of the 1850s reshaped both the geographic and demographic borders of the American republic, with Native Americans, whites, and blacks negotiating a Western space at the edge of the white civilizational imagination.[6] For Peter Donan, then, the triumph of black suffrage literally reversed the march of white civilization in the West and symbolically inverted white Missourians into colonized Africans.

The reference to "five hundred thousand WHITE MEN" as "disfranchised aliens" confirms this cultural inversion. White Missourians' masculinity was so undermined by the Fifteenth Amendment that they had become aliens in their own land. What emasculated white Missourians more than anything else, according to the *Caucasian*, was the underhanded way in which Radical Republicans passed the Fifteenth Amendment. Instead of winning it squarely on the battlefield, the *Caucasian* regularly complained, the Radicals pushed black suffrage through devious means and fraud. Even paramilitary gangs like the Ku Klux Klan or the various and assorted detritus of the Bushwhackers could not overcome the Unionist militia on their own. Unable to resist this outrage directly, white Missourians were forced to resort to subterfuge—"playing possum"—to regain white supremacy.

When Peter Donan took full editorial control of the *Caucasian* in 1868, the paper served as a leading national voice in the fight against Radical Reconstruction. Donan directly tied the struggle of local white conservatives—both ex-Confederate and Unionist—to the national resistance movement then pushed by the Ku Klux Klan and the Democratic Party across the South. Donan's commentary on political strategy was particularly acute, calling for rogue voter registration rolls that would challenge the legitimacy of the state's new Radical Republican process. As early as 1866 the *Caucasian* encouraged ex-rebels to vote in defiance of the state's Radical registration system and proffered specific instructions for how to do so:

1. Be registered; demand it as a fight; and let registrars reject you if they will. But if rejected sue registrar, commissioner and whoever else gets between you and your right of suffrage.

2. Offer your vote at the polls. If rejected, keep the proof of the fact and sue every mother's son of the judges.
3. Take the oath, as you would take anything else forced upon you—a man's life in self-defence.
4. If you are still refused, establish polls of your own, outside of the radical graveyard, appoint judges, take the votes in regular order, and according to law, and let the poll books be held in judgment against the party in power. They will not always be in power.[7]

Missouri conservatives in the postwar period thus set out to cast the new radical voting system as illegitimate and undemocratic. One critical component to what nearly all border state whites considered legitimate democracy was the restriction of suffrage rights to white men. Not surprisingly, conservative Democrats portrayed their Radical opponents as supporters of Negro suffrage and, consequently, defilers of the American democratic tradition—despite the fact that Missouri Radicals had refused, so far at least, to extend voting rights to blacks. The symbolism of this rogue registration strategy is striking for its critique of Radical violations of nineteenth-century white-based democracy, and its employment of the discourse of legitimacy to undermine the new order. The reference to the "radical graveyard," for example, suggests that the new and illegitimate claimants of power had effectively murdered the American democratic tradition. But this "death" was temporary as the Radicals would surely "not always be in power."

More striking is the reference to "law," as if the new Missouri constitution was both illegal and irregular. "Appoint judges, take the votes in regular order, and according to law," the *Caucasian* had suggested, "and let the poll books be held in judgment against the party in power." The insistence that "regular order" and "law" would bear eternal witness to the claims of white supremacist anti-Radicals resonated strongly not only in Missouri but across the entire ex-Confederacy. A year later, when Congress would establish military Reconstruction over the entire former Confederacy outside Tennessee, ex-rebels would employ similar tactics to delegitimize the new process. To the *Caucasian* and its later acolytes, the Radical Reconstruction process was lawless and temporary, to be treated, ironically, with the same kind of utter contempt that anticolonialists across the world treated their European imperial occupiers. The juxtaposition is striking: just as the *Caucasian* castigated the new voters as "man-eating savages from Dahomey and Loango," then under the process of European colonization, the paper encouraged the very sort of nonviolent (for the time being, at least), counter-hegemonic resistance to its own Radical imperial overseers.

The *Caucasian* carried on its political advice in the same vein for the next several years: a mixture of symbolic resistance, imbued with explicit white supremacist discourse, and unsubtle support for paramilitary violence against black and white backers of Radical Republicanism in Missouri and across the nation. In 1870, for example, the *Caucasian* encouraged Missouri voters to "play possum" and support the Liberal Republicans of B. Gratz Brown and Carl Schurz only because their election would be certain to result in removal of the Confederate disfranchisement provisions.[8] As predicted, the Liberals gave way quickly to the real Democrats who would dominate Missouri politics for a century. Donan was so inspired by this homegrown strategy that he managed to convince the national Democratic Party in 1872 not to nominate a candidate, and simply rally to the standard of Horace Greeley and the Liberal Republicans. This proved much less successful in the end, but it does show how influential the *Caucasian* was as a political organ on the national stage.

In the months following passage of the Fifteenth Amendment, the *Caucasian* showed a political deftness that must have shocked its core readers. Accepting black suffrage as law, the *Caucasian* then hoped—as did other Southern Democratic papers—that it could appeal to black conservative voters by celebrating the "surprisingly civil" manner in which black Missourians had celebrated the amendment's passage. "The negro has behaved himself far better than we had any right to expect him under the circumstances through which he has passed. Far better. The love of liberty is inborn, in the black as well as white, and can scarcely be eradicated or lessened."[9] The *Caucasian* reiterated its rejection of the amendment and heaped scorn upon white Radicals who "forced upon the negro a privilege he never had or desired." But it stoically accepted the "fact that blacks are to vote, and will vote despite any captious opposition to it."[10] And it placed partisan hatred of Radicalism over white supremacist unity by declaring conservative intentions to "vote for the negro whenever and wherever he is opposed by a radical alone, believing him to be more honest, if not more capable, than any of the radical tribe."[11] The *Caucasian* clearly believed that by praising the "behavior" of the African American community, and acquiescing in the permanence of black suffrage, it could woo black voters into the Democratic, or at least the Liberal, camp.

Still, the *Caucasian* distinguished itself not by its cynical mastery of partisan politics, but by the forceful racial rhetoric that it applied to the most mundane of political matters. The *Caucasian* regularly mocked the role black soldiers played during the Civil War, employed casual racism in its description of matters seemingly unrelated to race at all, and playfully taunted western Missouri's black population after each act of public racial violence.[12]

Predictably, the *Caucasian* also attacked the Freedmen's Bureau on a regular basis, for both its purported mission and its "wasteful" cost. Its diatribes against the bureau suggest an appeal to working white men's sense of racial entitlement. In a scathing comment titled "Cost of the Nigger," the *Caucasian* reports that the "bill reported to Congress, a short time ago, by Thad Stevens, proposed appropriating the following amounts to keep Mr. Nigger & Co. in ease and comfort." After outlining various administrative costs of the bureau totaling over $9 million, the piece concludes, "That will do pretty well for Sambo, especially when the tax is laid upon those who were forced to loose his money value in the war."[13] The juxtaposition between "honest" property holders and ex-slave recipients of aid living in "ease and comfort" stoked the resentment of both the former slaveholding class and the non–slaveholding white population in Missouri.

But the appeal to the white working class was made explicit in a commentary in the same issue on a labor dispute in Massachusetts in which "Forty white men have been discharged by the Cambridge, Mass. Horse railroad company and forty negroes hired in their place." As the Massachusetts newspaper explained—and quoted approvingly by the *Caucasian*— "The whites refused to work with the blacks, and of course wherever the radicals can have control they will give the negroes the preference over honest white labor." The *Caucasian* editorialized in typically sarcastic style, "Well, why should they not do so? They hold there is no difference between the one and the other." Alas, Radical Republican plans for political equality for African Americans would inevitably lead to the replacement of "honest white labor" with cheaper, black workers.

The *Caucasian* was particularly incendiary when discussing racial violence against African Americans, characterizing it as a form of justified resistance to "Nigger misrule."[14] The paper celebrated the white assailants during the infamous Memphis and New Orleans riots in 1866. But in reaction to Radical Republican concern in the "Nigger papers" about white paramilitary violence in Missouri itself, the *Caucasian* mocked the "Whine

About Arming" by resorting to the call for protection of "the conservative people of this state." Even more, the *Caucasian* justified white violence by implicating the "insults and impudence" of African Americans in freedom. Violence was, thus, self-defense as the *Caucasian's* editors insisted upon their peaceful intentions. "We want no one killed. Democrats and conservatives wish no more blood shed. We have had enough of it. But they are not ready and we hope they never will be to allow these woolly heads to slip up on them in the dark, and kill them merely because they are unprepared." In a paean to revenge, the *Caucasian* concluded, "They are not willing that Kansas red legs and jay hawkers should visit them at midnight." Despite use of the third-person plural "they" to distance itself from the subject under discussion, the *Caucasian* was clearly referring to its own readers and supporters willing to avenge the "crimes" of the Radicals.

There were limits to the *Caucasian's* celebration of racial violence—especially if the perpetrators could be easily described as disorderly ruffians of no political persuasion. A "shootout" in Saline County revealed the *Caucasian's* attempt at evenhandedness. After consuming several bottles of liquor, three brothers named Elson entered Miami, Missouri, and announced to all present that they planned to "kill a nigger." Shortly afterward, they shot a black man randomly. After the black man ran into a hotel for protection, the brothers shot at the white hotel keeper. Perhaps because of the second transgression—attempting to murder a prominent white businessman—a white mob retaliated and shot the Elson brothers. Though drunk, the Elsons apparently felt they could murder at will any African American they chose. The random nature of the attacks undoubtedly contributed to a generalized fear among the black community in central Missouri. But the account from the *Saline Progress*—copied approvingly and in full by the *Caucasian*—describes the Elsons as attacking "an unoffending colored man who happened to pass along near them," though never mentioning any community outrage at the attempted murder of the black man.[15] Because the Elsons had entered the town in a "most riotous and disgraceful manner," the *Caucasian* felt that this particular incident was unjustified and even dishonorable.

Still, the *Lexington Weekly Caucasian* was as incendiary a journal as the name suggests—even by the standards of the day. Alas, the most intriguing question to emerge is a matter of place. Why did such an explicitly white supremacist newspaper appear in Lexington, Missouri, of all locales? The timing of the *Caucasian's* arrival is easy enough to appreciate, given the racially charged nature of Reconstruction and the national struggle over the transition from slavery to freedom. This was, after all, a time when the national Democratic Party couched its appeal for the "Union as it is, the Constitution as it was" under the common masthead "This is a White Man's Government." But the place requires some explanation, especially given the peculiarities of Civil War era politics in western Missouri. Much of the Reconstruction struggle across the former Confederacy took on an explicitly racial character. As historian Steven Hahn reminds us, white Southern fear of black political power was very real.[16] And considering the revolutionary changes at the local level in the plantation districts of the lower South, ex-Confederates had reason to worry about genuine threats to traditional white supremacy.

But western Missouri was not the lower South. The racial and ethnic demographics were different in Missouri. The agricultural crop mix was different in Missouri compared to the plantation monoculture of the cotton South.[17] The primacy of industry—especially in St. Louis—gave Missouri's economy a different character than in the lower South.[18] The nature of warfare was different, with guerrilla struggle, atrocities, and civilian expulsions defining life in Civil War western Missouri. Even the chronology of events was vastly different, with the war effectively beginning six years prior to hostilities across the rest of the South.

In fact, western Missouri would seem, at first blush, to be the *last* place in which unreconstructed rebels would resort to explicit calls for white supremacy given the intraracial character of Reconstruction politics there. Indeed, while much of the postwar South's core support for Radicalism could be found mostly—and at times entirely—among the ex-slave population, Missouri offered a striking exception. A home-grown, white-based Radical movement took hold in the latter years of the Civil War, fueled by anger over guerrilla atrocities and a desire to remake Missouri into a Northern-style, free-labor state.[19] A coalition of St. Louis merchants and industrialists, Ozark Unionists, German immigrants, and newer settlers from the Midwest provided a solid foundation for Radical Republicanism after 1865. It was never enough to constitute a majority, so the architects of the new constitution incorporated a series of disfranchisement provisions to maintain power, including a registration system sure to be dominated by Radical Republican governors in perpetuity. The state's ex-slave population served more as an afterthought in the minds of Missouri's Radicals than a source of mobilization. In fact, Missouri Radical Republicans were unique in refusing to enfranchise their state's black population, failing to coalesce behind a statewide black suffrage referendum in 1868. If the ex-Confederates and their conservative allies were to paint an honest portrait of their political enemies, they would find a population looking—racially, at least—much like themselves.

Moreover, the labor battles that pitted freed men and women against their former masters across the former Confederacy found little analogue in western Missouri. Unlike in the cotton belt, Missouri's slave-produced hemp crop effectively collapsed after 1865, largely forestalling the demand of landowners to return their former slaves to the fields.[20] In fact, slavery's collapse in Missouri's Little Dixie region along the Missouri River portended much less mayhem than in the cotton belt of the lower South as farm owners simply converted their fields to the less labor intensive production of wheat.

And yet, it was here that one of the most explicitly white supremacist journals in American history appeared and thrived. Historians delving into the social and political world of post–Civil War western Missouri have long noted the iconic *Caucasian*. The final chapter of Michael Fellman's *Inside War* references it, as does T. J. Stiles's more recent biography of Jesse James.[21] Both Fellman and Stiles cite the *Caucasian* as evidence of continued bitterness among the former slaveholding class in the aftermath of guerrilla war and emancipation. James S. Hughes's study of slavery and emancipation in Lafayette County highlights the sarcastic tone of the newspaper, its willingness to publish Ku Klux Klan advertisements, and its support for the expulsion of Missouri's—and America's—black population.[22] And Lewis Saum's analysis of *Caucasian* editor Peter Donan's national influence underscores just how powerful the fiery Mississippi-born editor's rhetoric could be and the extent to which conservative Democrats across the country looked to the newspaper for inspiration and guidance.

But nobody has, to this point, satisfactorily situated the visceral racism of the *Caucasian* in either its regional or its national political context. The *Lexington Weekly Caucasian* served as a critically important border state voice of both actual ex-Confederatism and a more potent kind of belated Confederatism among very conservative white Unionists horrified at the radical turn of the Civil War. Grassroots—and elite—white conservative outrage at Radical Republican dominance in Jefferson City—and in Washington—fused with racial anger over the subversion of the traditional racial and social order in the pages of the *Caucasian*. In an era known for its shocking racial politics, the *Caucasian* would play a leading role in the political and cultural "redemption" of the white South and, importantly, white America as a whole. Its white supremacist discourse must be seen as a response to very real revolutionary pressures emanating from within western Missouri's unique Civil War and emancipation experience, and in a national context whose currency already traded in competing notions of white liberty and republicanism.

To understand the appearance of this oddly named newspaper we need to examine the nature of slavery's demise in western Missouri, including the role of racial violence in the midst of the well-chronicled guerrilla war that decimated much of western Missouri. Slavery showed signs of serious weakness by the end of 1861, especially after Confederate troops abandoned Lexington following a successful siege of the town in September of that year. As regular Confederate troops, many of them enlisted from the western and central Missouri River counties, departed for Arkansas, they left behind a chaotic scene dominated by roving bands of pro-Confederate Bushwhackers, invading Kansas Jayhawkers, and an ever-changing mélange of Unionist militia and regular Union army officers tasked with keeping order.

But one police power that did not remain intact was the antebellum slave patrol, which had long protected the peculiar institution both along slavery's border and within the Southern heartland. With the patrollers now off in the Confederate (and occasionally Union) army or in competing militia and guerrilla bands, the slaves of the Missouri River valley sensed a unique opportunity to run for freedom. Though many patrollers hoped to return fugitive slaves to their masters while in the bush, most found that task impossible in the face of an increasingly potent counterinsurgency campaign. A well-organized slave patrol system simply could not survive a guerrilla war, and the first to discover that breach were slaves probing the policing system that long had held their ambitions for freedom in check.

Henry Clay Bruce, a former slave in nearby Chariton County, Missouri, chronicled this remarkable process, as slaves passed news about safe routes to Kansas or reliable and sympathetic Union militia.[23] Considering the proslavery conservatism of the state's provisional Union government under Governor Hamilton Gamble, and the deeply conservative nature of most Unionists in the area, this sort of intelligence regarding militia attitudes toward slavery was of immense importance.

Slavery largely collapsed by 1863, as slave prices fell to a fraction of their prewar value, and even many skeptical Unionists started to sound the death knell of the institution. At that point the debate centered on how fast and under what terms slavery would die, not whether it would survive intact. Unlike fellow border state Kentucky, where Unionists insisted even after the Civil War ended that slavery could survive, Missouri Unionists concluded by early 1863 that the days of chattel slavery were numbered. The exemption of Missouri from the Emancipation Proclamation did little to assuage the fears of Missouri slaveholders.

The final death knell came with the enlistment of slaves in the Union army, a process that unfolded with remarkable alacrity in 1864. What made this process so revolutionary in Missouri was the speed and scope of the enlistment process, and the ways in which slaves themselves employed the enlistment experience to advance a radical notion of a biracial republic no longer based on the principle of white supremacy. As for the suddenness of enlistment, the numbers and anecdotes tell the story clearly. A local provost martial remarked to General Schofield of a "stampede of negroes" to enlistment centers in December 1863. By January 15, 1864, dozens of slaves enlisted in central Missouri's slave-rich Howard County alone. By the end of February more than 3,700 African Americans enlisted in Missouri, with central and western Missouri's Little Dixie producing a significant portion of the total. Many slaves traveled to recruitment sites on their own, while others joined as a group. Seven of John R. White's slaves—William, Adam, Alfred, Sam, Andy, Preston, and Jacob—all enlisted together at the Fayette provost marshal post in the first weeks of January 1864.[24] White was one of Missouri's largest slaveholders; the seven who joined represented a mere tenth of White's total holdings, though it signified a dangerously collective action on the part of a portion of his slaves.[25] At Fayette, where John White's slaves enlisted, 174 African Americans joined the service in the first two months of the year. In Brunswick, just up the Missouri River from Fayette, another 128 slaves joined in the same period. Perhaps the most impressive recruitment site in central Missouri was Boonville, where Lieutenant C. S. Swamp presided over the enrollment of 436 African Americans—nearly all of them slaves—into the Union army.

But it was the political message of rapid-scale enlistment that so shook the Missouri countryside. Many slaveholders had pledged loyalty to the Union from the very beginning, including some of the state's most respected leaders such as William Switzler, James Rollins, and Odon Guitar. Local Lexington Unionist Richard C. Vaughan vowed to destroy the rebel army and its backers, but had insisted that emancipation and racial equality were out of the question. Yet, slaves would not be deterred by the conservative warning from Unionists not to interfere in a "white man's war." As Bruce wrote, "Slaves believed, deep down in their souls, that the government was fighting for their freedom, and it was useless for masters to tell them differently."[26]

The final indignity to white conservatives came not just with passage of the so-called Drake Constitution of 1865, which proscribed so many Lafayette Countians from the voting process, but with the placement of black troops on guard over the new postwar order. In Lexington, avowed and committed Unionist Richard C. Vaughan expressed shock and outrage over the use of black troops to arrest two pro-Confederate judges for refusing to abdicate their offices in accordance with the new constitution.[27] The same story repeated itself throughout western Missouri, with uniformed former slaves posting sentinel over public buildings, policing a social order that until so recently had regarded them as mere property. In an age when citizenship and military service went hand in hand, black participation in the postwar militia confirmed for Missouri's white conservative population that emancipation would be used as a first step toward equal citizenship rights in a new Missouri. In other words, black men would now become full citizens just as ex-Confederates would lose citizenship rights—to vote, hold office, or even maintain professional positions like teaching, preaching, or practicing law.

It was that challenge to the traditional order that provoked a response from the *Caucasian*. The first reaction to this threat to white supremacy, however, came from the hands of Bushwhackers themselves. Though many Bushwhackers ignored the collapsing slave system around them, some took out their frustrations on ex-slaves more fiercely than they did on rival white Unionists. No guerrilla exemplified this more than Jim Jackson, who roved the central and western Missouri countryside in 1864 and 1865, threatening to kill every black person he saw—regardless of age or gender. This was especially the case after the state's emancipation of slavery in January 1865. As most guerrillas wintered in Texas, Jackson and his band remained in Missouri. What makes Jackson's actions unique among the Bushwhackers, however, were the motives. In the lower South roving paramilitary bands threatened slaves with violence if they refused to return to the plantations and labor for their former masters. In western Missouri, however, gangs like Jackson's hoped to eliminate the black population entirely, often threatening whole communities with mass slaughter in the event of failure to leave.[28] With the final collapse of the hemp industry, and the transformation of Missouri farming toward cereal production and cattle raising after the Civil War, farm owners did not feel the need for a pliable labor force as in the lower South. Small-scale slaveholders accustomed to extra slave support in the household likewise learned to adjust to family and hired wage labor. The ex-slaves, many of them armed and bearing federal insignia, were seen as nothing more than a nuisance and a painful reminder of how far in status the slaveholding class had fallen. The combined demographic result of Jackson's gang of murderers and the economic shift away from the old staples of hemp and tobacco was staggering. In 1860, Lafayette County boasted the largest slave—and black—population of any county in Missouri. By 1870, the black population in Lafayette County actually dropped by over 36 percent, even as the overall population grew in size.[29] Most likely, Lafayette County's former slaves simply left, voluntarily or not, for Kansas, Kansas City, or St. Louis. Lafayette County, like much of Missouri's Little Dixie region, had become significantly whiter in the years following the Civil War. Many of Lafayette County's slaveholders left as well for Texas, as did many other Southern sympathizers after the war's conclusion. Replacing them were legions of new farmers from the Midwest and from Germany.

So that gets us back to the *Caucasian*. After all, the *Caucasian* was more than a voice of Democratic resistance against the policies of Missouri's Radical Republican Party, its voter registration process, and its very legitimacy. It was also a leading national voice for the return of white supremacy in all matters of political, economic, and cultural life. And its appearance is a result of a paradox in postwar Missouri life: resistance to white Radical rule gained currency by imputing the racial implications of Radical control, even as the black population literally dissipated in the small towns of central and western Missouri. Alas, black political power proved so threatening precisely where it was so easily circumscribed by white Radical party machinery, and by simple demographics.

But as we have seen, the threat from African Americans in western Missouri to white supremacy came less from their numbers than from their motives. White Radicals could be castigated as vengeful Jayhawking thugs. And some of them—particularly the newcomers arriving in the late 1860s—envisioned a more Northern-style industrial capitalist system than the old small-slave yeomanry. But rarely, if ever, did white Radicals honestly espouse racial equality in any meaningful sense. When the Unionist-only electorate rejected black suffrage in a statewide referendum in 1868, it demonstrated the white basis of Radical Republicanism in Missouri, and the unwillingness of these supposed champions of racial equality to challenge the tenets of white supremacy. If anything, white Radicals were profoundly ambivalent about black civil and political rights, having supported basic civil rights and education for African Americans in 1865 but doing nothing beyond that. Malign neglect would, in the end, convince many African Americans that the Radical Republican party was not the "friend of the colored race." In the critical years of 1870 to 1872, when the Radical regime collapsed, African Americans were deeply divided between Radical and Liberal factions, thus helping to herald the return of the White Man's Democracy.

With little fervent black support, white Radicals found themselves in a position of ideological weakness, having conceded to conservatives the basic assumptions about race shared across the spectrum. Both conservatives and white Radicals agreed that Missouri must continue to be run by whites and for whites, the only question being which white subgroup and through what means. African Americans, by largely emancipating themselves through military service, directly challenged both ex-Confederates and conservative ex-Unionists. An explicitly white supremacist discourse advanced by the *Lexington Weekly Caucasian* served the purpose of uniting whites of all political stripes against the Radical Republican Party, even as the Radicals refused (until it was far too late) to avail themselves of the black electorate that supported it. To defenders of the old social order, the conservative case could be made more forcefully by identifying the Radical opposition not with vindictiveness and proscription, but with the explosive charge of racial treachery.

As Nicole Etcheson has pointed out, the 1850s border war between Kansas and Missouri centered on competing white notions of liberty.[30] I would argue that this held true in the postwar years as well, though it took on a very different character. Prior to 1861 pro-slavery whites could argue, as Christopher Phillips has laid out, that slavery *was* democracy,[31] even as Kansas free soilers could proclaim their liberty from both slavery and a black population. By 1865, however—and especially by 1870—former Confederates and white Unionists would argue that the greatest threat to liberty in Missouri came not from the return of ex-Confederates to power, but from black social revolutionaries who would overturn all of Western civilization if allowed free rein. And so, despite the absurdity of this fear in a place like western Missouri, the *Lexington Weekly Caucasian* worked assiduously to unite all ex-Confederates with the newly arriving pro-Union migrants from the Midwest and from Germany under the banner of the Democratic Party.

Accentuating the *Caucasian's* message was the simple passage of time. The "bloody shirt," which did so much to rally Unionists to the Radical standard in the latter years of the war, gradually lost appeal by the end of the 1860s. In its place emerged the newly formed Liberal Republican movement, which insisted that enfranchising African Americans before restoring voting rights to ex-Confederates violated commonly accepted principles of white, Midwestern republicanism. In other words, white Radicals could accept black suffrage only if all whites could vote as well. Because this position was based on the primacy of race over loyalty—why, after all, should loyal African Americans, many of them ex-Union soldiers, have to wait until the infamous Bushwhackers of old got their rights back—the *Weekly Caucasian* was uniquely positioned and designed to exploit that opening. By making the argument about race, first and foremost, the *Caucasian* lent a discourse of racial solidarity that could overwhelm any residual bitterness over competing loyalties or wartime atrocities.

The significance of the *Caucasian* was paramount, both for Missouri and for the nation as a whole. As much racial violence as there was in the immediate post–Civil War era, no other cultural phenomenon linked race, politics, violence, and citizenship so early on as the *Weekly Caucasion*. As historian Elaine Parsons has discovered regarding Tennessee, a state whose Radical Reconstruction timeline roughly corresponds to that of Missouri— with Radicals taking control of state government in early 1865—the nascent Ku Klux Klan would not develop a similar kind of racial invective until mid-1867 at the earliest.[32]

As such, the *Weekly Caucasian* is critical because it served as the vanguard of an explicitly racial anti-Reconstruction strategy, several months before other editors and paramilitary organizations would take their cue. A whole year before passage of congressional Radical Reconstruction, the *Weekly Caucasian* offered an early rubric of resistance based on white racial solidarity that would be quickly copied throughout the Confederate South. In the end, it is impossible to understand the regional politics of postwar western Missouri or the national struggle over Reconstruction without coming to grips with the appearance of the *Lexington Weekly Caucasian*.

Chapter 12

"We Promise to Use the Ballot as We Did the Bayonet": Black Suffrage Activism and the Limits of Loyalty in Reconstruction Missouri

John W. McKerley

On November 11, 1870, the editor of the *Missouri State Times* surveyed the results of the recent statewide elections from his desk in Jefferson City. Only a few days before, Radical Republicans, who had captured the state's government during the Civil War, had been decisively defeated at the polls. The outcome had been precipitated by a split in the Republican ranks over suffrage restrictions. In 1865, Radical leaders had placed provisions in the state's new constitution disfranchising wartime "disloyalists" and non-whites.[1] Over the next five years, these provisions sparked diverse opposition movements as well as a failed 1868 referendum on black suffrage. By 1870, opponents had gained enough support within the Missouri general assembly to pass amendments removing restrictions on voting and office-holding based on race or wartime loyalty. When Radical leaders failed to commit the party to the amendments, opponents of disfranchisement bolted and nominated former United States senator Benjamin Gratz Brown for governor on a Liberal Republican ticket. Democrats took advantage of the split, supporting Brown for governor and focusing on electing Democrats in other races. After a bitter campaign, Brown bested the Radicals' sitting governor, Joseph W. McClurg, by over 40,000 votes; the amendments were ratified by overwhelming majorities; and Democrats gained control of the Missouri general assembly, four congressional seats, and almost three-fourths of elected countywide offices.[2]

The *Missouri State Times* had sided with the Liberals, and the paper's editor, Horace Wilcox, paused after the election to reflect on the struggle that had torn apart the state's Republican Party and catapulted Democrats back into power for the first time since the opening of the secession crisis.

"Now that the smoke of battle has cleared away, and the Liberal Republican—or the Bolting, if you please—banner is seen emerging bullet-riddled but crowned with victory from the conflict," Wilcox wrote, "it is well to recur to a phase of the contest that *must be remembered.*" The phase to which he referred was the role played by the state's black men, who had been enfranchised earlier that year by the ratification of the Fifteenth Amendment. Like many white Liberals, Wilcox had been an early white supporter of black men's voting *rights* but had become increasingly disappointed with the results of black men's short-lived voting *records*. Rather than exhibiting a manly independence, Wilcox argued, black voters had instead followed the instructions of James Milton Turner, a prominent black politician aligned with McClurg's faction. For Wilcox, this alleged lack of independence was not only a slight against the longtime white supporters of black voting rights but evidence that black men were as potentially dangerous to good government as opponents of black suffrage had always claimed:

> It was urged that [the black voter] would prove neither an intelligent nor an independent voter—that he would prove only so much material for reckless demagogues to operate on. And here, in the first experiment—in the first essay to make use of the privilege—we find the negro voter swayed as one man who had power over them saw fit, and against the white class conspicuous for what they had done to secure to the negro the privilege! The negro voter has been like clay in the hands of the potter, in the hands of J. Milton Turner![3]

Wilcox's reflections are important because they direct our attention to a comparatively little studied aspect of the history of Reconstruction: the efforts of black people in the border South to gain the vote for black men and then to use it effectively in their individual and collective interests. As Aaron Astor has demonstrated, while the border war focused attention on Missouri's western frontier, the experience of emancipation also connected the state to the larger drama of the transition from slavery to freedom. Not surprisingly, the narrative of black struggle for and over the vote in the immediate post-emancipation period has been dominated by events in the former Confederacy, where the vast majority of former slaves lived and where black men obtained the vote through the Military Reconstruction Acts of 1867.[4] Black men's votes transformed black southerners' self-

James Milton Turner. *After the Civil War, James Milton Turner (c. 1840–1915) worked for the Missouri Department of Education, establishing over thirty new schools in the state for African Americans and providing support for Lincoln Institute. In 1871, President Ulysses S. Grant appointed Turner United States minister to Liberia, the first African American to hold that position. After his return, Turner organized the Colored Emigration Aid Association to provide assistance to blacks migrating from the South. He also fought to secure equal tribal rights for blacks formerly enslaved by the Cherokee Indians. Courtesy of Lincoln University, Jefferson City, Missouri, and the State Historical Society of Missouri*

organization and biracial coalitions into successful Republican parties across the region. Although black southerners were never able to turn these parties into uncontested vehicles for black interests—or, for that matter, agree on what those interests were—they revolutionized the political life of the former Confederacy through the election of hundreds of black officials.[5]

Black political activism around enfranchisement took a different path in the border South. Excluded from the Reconstruction Acts, the loyal governments of Missouri, Kentucky, West Virginia, Maryland, and Delaware failed to enact provisions enfranchising black men before the ratification of the Fifteenth Amendment. In three of these states—Missouri, West Virginia, and Maryland—Republican dominance had been based on white not black votes, and relatively small black populations meant comparatively little opportunity for black political power. In Kentucky and Delaware, where slaveholders and their interests were stronger, Democrats rejected not only black suffrage but all the postwar federal amendments in a show of defiance against congressional Republicans and their interference in what had hitherto been state prerogatives.[6] In the border South as a whole, white resistance to black political participation was so widespread that historian Eric Foner found only one black person—Missouri's James Milton Turner—among his survey of black officeholders during Reconstruction. While Foner missed some officeholders (as this essay demonstrates), his count also points to the importance of the Reconstruction Acts (which went above and beyond enfranchisement through military intervention) for black political empowerment.[7]

Yet, as significant as the differences were between Reconstruction in the border South and the former Confederacy, they should not be allowed to obscure either black border Southerners' activism in support of the vote or the impact of voting rights on the states' communities of black activists. Like their counterparts elsewhere in the former slave South, black Missourians engaged in a wave of popular political organizing in the wake of emancipation. Frustrated with the 1865 constitution's limitations, black men and women united across lines of class, color, culture, and generation to demand manhood suffrage. They framed their demands within a nonracial vision of republican manhood, but they also expressed grave doubts about the influence of "traitors" and "rebels" at the ballot box, calling for a biracial, loyalist alliance. As the Republican Party split, however, so did the postwar coalition of black activists. For most black Missourians, at least initially, frustration and disappointment at the hands of white Republicans remained less dangerous than the immediate re-enfranchisement of white disloyalists, and they sided with McClurg and his Radical regulars. A significant minority, however, including many leaders of the postwar suffrage movement, abandoned their previous support for disfranchisement, instead forging an alliance with the Liberals. Still others eschewed the Republicans altogether in favor of negotiating the most advantageous terms possible with resurgent Democrats. Far from the voting chattel imagined by Wilcox, black Missourians helped to shape the political debate over enfranchisement and struggled to advance their individual and collective interests within their own political context.

In January 1865, delegates to an all-white state convention adopted ordinances emancipating "all persons held to service or labor as slaves" and restricting the apprenticeship of freedpeople. A later ordinance reorganized the Missouri militia along nonracial lines.[8] Delegates followed these ordinances with a new constitution that not only removed racial restrictions on testimony and the acquisition, holding, and transmittal of property, but also provided for black Missourians' equality before the law in regard to punishment, unrestricted exercise of religious worship, and acquisition of education.[9]

Although Missouri's new constitution was arguably the most progressive in the former slave states in the period before the Reconstruction Acts, it failed to address many of the needs of black people. The constitution had declared that black people were not to be "hindered in acquiring education," but white Missourians, including white loyalists, burned black schools and challenged the spending of public funds to support black education.[10] White Missourians contracted with black men and women for labor but refused to pay for the services performed. Local authorities blocked relief to black migrants, white judges refused to accept black testimony, and former slaveholders continued to hold black children in bondage as apprentices without their parents' consent. "Many Colored parents complain that Slave-holders still retain their children contrary to law," reported the Freedmen's Bureau superintendent at Cape Girardeau in July 1865.

> In some cases to evade the law they tell those whom they hold in bondage, that they are free but keep them in Such terror that they fear to express a wish to leave their owners. Other Masters claim that they

retain those children legally, because they were bound out to them, though relatives were not consulted in Such transactions nor do they wish such a relation continued. All this amounts to practical Slavery and keeps those families broken up and scattered.[11]

Contributing to and compounding these problems were laws excluding black people from jury service, officeholding, and the vote.[12] Even before the constitution's ratification, black Missourians had begun to organize in support of black men's enfranchisement. In a petition of January 31, 1865, over ninety "colored citizens of the city of St. Louis" appealed to the state's constitutional convention "to extend to them the elective 'franchise.'" They supported their petition with several arguments based in gendered conceptions of universal suffrage and the obligations of citizenship. First and foremost, they argued that voting was an "inalienable" right and that black men had "been too long, deprived of its exercise." But beyond the rightness of their cause, they believed, was their clear proof of loyalty and fulfillment of the obligations of manhood and citizenship. As "the only true representatives" of Missouri's black troops, the petitioners claimed that black men had demonstrated their "patriotism" and undeniable "loyalty" to the state and federal government through their military service and eligibility for the draft. They also appealed as taxpayers, drawing on the Revolutionary logic that "taxation and representation are inseparable." Finally, they petitioned as men educated enough to read the United States and Missouri constitutions and to write their names.[13] Despite these arguments, however, the convention was unmoved. Although some delegates supported the notion of nonracial voting in the abstract, they refused to include black suffrage out of fear that the state's white loyalists would reject the constitution (and its crucial provisions disfranchising disloyalists) when it came time for ratification.[14]

Over the next several months, as the federal presence in the state declined and the limits of the new constitution became clear, black Missourians worked to transform their initial postwar petition movement into a more permanent organization. The most important institutional outgrowth of this organizing was the Missouri state affiliate of the National Equal Rights League, a black federation established during the war to promote emancipation, legal equality, and suffrage rights.[15] On October 2, the Missouri league was founded in St. Louis at a mass meeting of black men and women. They elected Preston G. Wells as chairman and Blanche K.

Bruce as secretary.[16] Wells, a free black man from Kentucky, owned a successful barbering and hairdressing business. In his late fifties or early sixties at the time of his election, Wells was among the eldest of the league's leaders.[17] Bruce was a twenty-four-year-old former slave from Virginia who had learned the printing trade after being brought to Missouri by his master in the 1850s.[18]

In addition to Wells and Bruce, the meeting elected an executive committee to "[provide] for a series of mass meetings, to procure speakers of our own color, and to prepare an address to our people throughout the State, and to take such other steps as shall be in their judgment necessary to aid in securing those rights and franchises that belong to us as American citizens."[19] The committee's chairman was Henry McGee Alexander, a businessman in his late forties, who had prospered supplying provisions to steamboats. At least four of the committee's original seven members had been free before the war (Alexander, Francis Roberson, Samuel Helms, and Moses Dickson), and most of them (Roberson, Helms, Dickson, and George Wedley) had worked as barbers, a skilled trade common among postwar black politicians. One, G. P. Downing, was a physician. At least four of the men (Alexander, Roberson, Helms, and Downing) were among the signers of the petition of January 31, and two (Alexander and Dickson) were prominent black Masons. The committee later added a secretary, James Milton Turner. In his mid-twenties, Turner was the son of a free black "horse doctor" and an enslaved woman. He later claimed that his father purchased him and his mother out of slavery, but the details of his emancipation are unclear. Once free, however, Turner received an early education in a clandestine school located in the basement of St. Louis's African Baptist Church and later studied at Oberlin College in Ohio.[20]

Despite their relative success, none of these men was an uncontested representative of St. Louis's "colored aristocracy." Indeed, while several of the men appeared in the 1858 description of that aristocracy penned by one of its members, Cyprian Clamorgan, none received his unconditional approval. Clamorgan praised Alexander as "a good business man" but added that rumors of his wife's impropriety had meant that he was "not admitted into the first circles, and consequently lives somewhat retired."[21] Likewise, Roberson, whom Clamorgan described as "one of the talking barbers" who could "rattle out more nonsense in ten minutes than any sensible man would believe in a week," was "not in the best standing."[22] Wells, however, stood out as a target of Clamorgan's calumny. "As a faithful historian,"

Clamorgan wrote, "it is our unpleasant duty to speak of the vile and unworthy, as well as the good and virtuous," adding "nothing but this sense of duty could induce us to mention in this connection a character so far below the common level of humanity as P. G. Wells."

> He has been here about twenty years, and in all that time has led the life of a spy and a dog. At one time he earned a precarious liv[e]lihood as an informer against his own race. He is a tall, pompous black man—a great braggart, and says more in one minute than he will stand to in a week. He is not only treacherous and deceitful to his own color, but has deceived and cheated every white man who has trusted in his promises.

According to Clamorgan, Wells owed what standing he had to his wife, "a tall yellow woman" with "natural sense and a sound judgment," who owned a lucrative boardinghouse.[23]

These men's election in the fall of 1865 revealed that the relative wealth and education that characterized members of the state's antebellum free black minority—only 3 percent of the state's 118,000 black people were free in 1860—remained factors in determining post-emancipation leadership opportunities. But it also suggested the importance of wartime and postwar service.[24] Whatever the basis for Clamorgan's allegations against Wells, the "tall, pompous black man" had distinguished himself during the war as a delegate to the 1864 convention that had created the National Equal Rights League.[25] Bruce, after fleeing slavery during the war, had established schools for black people in Kansas and Missouri.[26] Dickson had been an antislavery activist in the Midwest since the 1840s, settling in St. Louis in 1859. He had not served in the Union army but later claimed to have participated in several battles as an "independent fighter."[27] Turner, although not holding an elected position in the league, also owed his entrée into postwar politics to his wartime service. During the war, he had been employed as a body servant to a Union officer, Colonel Madison Miller of St. Louis. When Miller was thought dead after the battle of Shiloh, Turner conveyed the colonel's effects (including a substantial amount of money) to his grateful wife, the sister of Republican Thomas Fletcher, Missouri's first postwar governor.[28] Such wartime service—especially actions promoting slavery's destruction and assisting freedpeople—likely endeared these men to a rank and file that included numerous wartime migrants from the countryside and representatives of the over 8,000 black Missourians who had served in the Union military.[29]

Led by the league's executive committee, black Missourians articulated their own vision of political reform in the state. At the meeting of October 2, they adopted a series of resolutions reflecting their frustrations with the constitution's failure to make good on the promise of equality before the law. They drew on a broad rhetoric of nonracial republican manhood "without distinction of class or color" to support black voting rights. But they also asserted that black men's access to the suffrage was justified by their new status as "freedmen" and by their demonstration of loyalty through armed service, distinguishing themselves from people disfranchised on account of failures of "patriotism," "valor," and "heroism."[30] These resolutions formed the basis for a petition submitted to the Missouri general assembly that called for "*efficient free common schools*" and the removal of whiteness as a qualification for voting rights.[31]

The executive committee elaborated on these themes in an address to the "friends of equal rights." In the address, the committee at once argued for a vision of "universal suffrage" based in republican manhood and a particularistic and pragmatic approach to voting rights. At the heart of the address was an appeal to a broad-based republicanism founded in a "citizenship based upon a principle so broad and solid that upon it black men, white men, and every American born can equally, safely, and eternally stand."[32] The committee called for universal suffrage, but it also made clear that its vision of republicanism emphasized men's fulfillment of the obligations of citizenship, especially the obligation to defend the nation against treason. While not evoking disloyalist disfranchisement per se, the committee argued that black men could help to maintain Republican supremacy through a biracial alliance of loyal men. At the same time that the committee's members claimed the "privilege which is now given to the very poorest and meanest of white men who come to the ballot-box," they demanded black suffrage "as those who have been true and loyal to our Government from its foundation to the present, and who have never deserted its interests while even in the midst of treason and under subjection to its most violent enemies."[33] Appropriating the words of President Andrew Johnson, they asked "that the 'two streams of loyal blood which it took to conquer one, mad with treason,' shall not be separated at the ballot-box," and they called for the right to vote to aid in "the maintenance of authority over the disorganizing elements which attend a returning peace."[34]

Anticipating white fears of private association flowing from such an alliance of loyal white and black men, the committee denied any interest in "social equality."[35] It also acknowledged distinctions of class, color, and culture between black Missourians. Its members qualified the broad appeals put forth at the mass meeting with a list of acceptable—if not ideal—substitutions for universal suffrage, including restrictions based on "wealth" and "intelligence," arguing "that the entire ignorance and stupidity of the people should not by any presumption be wholly charged to the account of ourselves."[36]

Moving from rhetoric to action, the Missouri league expanded its campaign over the next year. After hiring Turner and distributing the address "throughout the State and through many portions of the East," they sought out "distinguished speakers" to "awaken our people" to the league's work. In late November 1865, they enlisted the assistance of the president of the national league, James Mercer Langston, who toured the state. Langston's tour—which took him to Hannibal, Macon, Chillicothe, St. Joseph, Kansas City, Sedalia, and Jefferson City—was capped by a speech delivered before the Missouri general assembly and a packed crowd of segregated onlookers on January 9, 1866. The committee published Langston's speech together with the address and distributed and sold the combined work to defray expenses.[37] Later in January, the Missouri league led a parade in St. Louis to celebrate the anniversary of emancipation and to highlight their continued demands for equality before the law. The parade's participants revealed the rich associational life that undergirded the suffrage movement in the city and the degree to which the league's leadership was supported by a broader social base. In addition to the executive committee, the parade included black members of the Missouri State Militia (including part of a regiment led by Francis Roberson, now a colonel), the Colored Masonic Fraternity, Colored Ladies' Union Society, Sunday School groups, and the Colored Mechanics Association. "Probably there was never before so large a turn-out of the dusky element in Missouri," the St. Louis Daily Missouri Democrat reported.[38] Over the next several months, the league's local affiliates passed out petitions calling for school and suffrage reform (ultimately garnering almost four thousand signatures), and Turner traveled outside St. Louis to distribute the address and advance the league's program.[39]

Black Missourians' initial postwar activism spurred white Republicans to address some of their demands, but these efforts fell far short of producing the reforms black Missourians had envisioned. In late 1865 and early

1866, Republicans in the general assembly introduced at least four bills to extend voting rights to black men. While some measures called for immediate enfranchisement, others proposed substituting racial restrictions for various forms of education and literacy tests. Regardless of the formula, however, all such measures failed.[40] As the Missouri league reported to its members in January 1867, "no appeals were able to move that body from its purpose to continue unjust discriminations in its organic laws against those who were and ever have been brave friends and loyal to the very principles which that body claimed to represent," adding "your committee would earnestly recommend that this honorable body be also addressed by petitions and appeals for equal justice towards all who are loyal to the State and government, without respect to the *color of the loyalists' skin*."[41] Black Missourians were most successful in their calls for education reform, but here too Republicans fell short of black expectations. For example, while legislators reorganized the state's public schools to authorize and require boards of education to establish segregated schools for black children out of a common school fund, they provided for the closing of black public schools in cases in which the average number of children fell below twenty.[42]

Although black suffrage and education found supporters among Missouri's white Republicans, the party's leaders still feared that white voters (even limited by disloyalist disfranchisement) would reject a biracial alliance. In particular, Republican leaders suspected that white loyalists would be persuaded by Democratic claims that extending voting rights to black men in Missouri would undermine white supremacy and make the state attractive to black migration. When Congress defused the potential for massive black in-migration by extending voting rights to black men in the former Confederacy, Missouri Republicans quickly approved an amendment to remove whiteness as a qualification for voting and submitted it for popular ratification.[43]

This sudden shift in policy briefly caught black Missourians in the midst of a leadership vacuum. The Missouri league appears to have dissolved sometime in early 1867 (perhaps due to financial pressures), and members of the executive committee went on to pursue a number of related agendas, especially the advancement of black education. One league activist, Blanche K. Bruce, followed the promise of military Reconstruction to Mississippi, where he eventually became a U.S. senator.[44] Back in St. Louis, the absence of statewide leadership was filled in July 1868 by the Colored Men's

Central Impartial Suffrage Club, formed "for the specific object of agitating the question of 'impartial suffrage' . . . [and] to co-operate with the Radical Republican party of the State of Missouri." Black Missourians also advanced their suffrage agenda at a state convention called to consider sending delegates to a meeting of black border Southerners, their "disfranchised brethren," to be held in Baltimore. On July 17, the convention (with Preston G. Wells as its president) elected four delegates, including William P. Brooks, a minister, and Charlton H. Tandy, a former carriage driver and Missouri militiaman.[45] The convention ordered that "a public demonstration" take place later that month and adopted a resolution endorsing the new St. Louis club.[46]

As the ratification vote neared, black Missourians engaged in the furious debate over black suffrage raging in the state's newspapers. "What the colored man wants is the same political right that is but justly given to all citizens of this country, the right of representation," Moses Dickson told the readers of the *Democrat*. Much as the league had done in 1865, Dickson appealed to white Republicans to support black men's voting rights as a means by which to forge a biracial coalition of loyalists. "We stood shoulder to shoulder with the loyal white man and aided to put down the great rebellion," he wrote. "For this we have incurred the lasting enmity of the rebel Democracy. They will not forget us, but will oppose us in everything that tends to elevate and enlighten. Will the loyal white men come to our aid now, and give us the ballot to protect us against this same rebel Democracy? We promise to use the ballot as we did the bayonet, to uphold the honor and dignity of our common country." He likewise qualified his appeal to speak to the racial and class ideologies of white loyalists, decrying any interest in social equality and asking "Can any person tell when and where the ballot made the levee rats, gutter snipes, sneak thieves and bloated loafers the *social equals* of the refined gentleman?"[47]

Despite such carefully qualified appeals, however, the amendment went down to defeat at the same time that Republicans extended their control over the state's government. The Democratic presidential candidate lost the state to Republican Ulysses S. Grant by over 25,000 votes. Likewise, almost 20,000 voters carried Republican gubernatorial candidate Joseph W. McClurg to victory over his Democratic opponent, John S. Phelps, and Republicans stood to dominate both chambers of the general assembly. The amendment, however, received only around 55,000 (or 43 percent) of approximately 129,000 votes cast. Republican leaders had largely accepted black suffrage, but they failed to convince a majority of the state's white loyalists to support a measure that would have enfranchised black men while leaving some 30,000 to 50,000 white men disfranchised.[48]

Indeed, after 1868, an increasing number of white Republicans shifted their emphasis from black suffrage to resolving the problem of disloyalist disfranchisement. A vocal minority within the party had been growing in opposition to such disfranchisement almost since its inception. Centered in St. Louis and drawing significant support from Missouri's German immigrant communities, these dissident Republicans regarded disfranchisement as unsustainable for a range of political and ideological reasons. For most dissidents, disfranchisement had been a necessary wartime measure that had outlived its usefulness. Slavery had been the source of the rebellion, and without the peculiar institution to support, disloyalists could be safely integrated into the state's free-labor future. For others, maintaining disfranchisement was not only a violation of the principles of republican governance but also a threat to postwar economic development and internal peace. Dissidents, and Germans in particular, regarded disfranchisement as encouraging despotism and corruption, both of which they associated with the suffrage provisions' prime architect, Charles D. Drake, a St. Louis lawyer and inveterate nativist.[49]

For most dissident Republicans, black suffrage and the re-enfranchisement of white disloyalists were necessary and inseparable preconditions for the success of Reconstruction in Missouri. In linking the two, however, many white dissidents reflexively conflated black political interests with their own, crafting a vision of the public good that could resolve the state's racial, class, and cultural tensions through the leadership of its "best men." In January 1870, the *Democrat* (which had become the state's premier dissident paper in the English language) published an editorial that claimed to support black men's right to dispose of their political rights as they saw fit but that also set forth what the paper believed to be the proper limits of such political independence. While it advised black voters "to watch their own interests," the paper suggested that such interests were identical to those of the party (at least the dissident faction it represented) and the state's white majority. Having determined that removing restrictions on white disloyalists was the only way to ensure postwar peace and prosperity, the paper advised black voters to advance the public good by casting their ballots against disloyalist disfranchisement and its supporters. In words that suggested paternalistic condescension and even a veiled threat, the *Demo-*

crat assured its readers that black Missourians would come to recognize where their true interests lay: "They have the good sense to know, we trust, that measures which keep alive the flames of civil strife are most injurious to them, the newly enfranchised citizens, and that they need above all things, peace, and the spirit of peace."[50]

With the ratification of the Fifteenth Amendment, dissidents (now increasingly calling themselves "Liberals") demanded the abolition of disloyalist disfranchisement, and black Missourians were increasingly forced to choose sides. The consequences of this split in the Republican ranks became clear during the municipal elections of 1870, which took place in the spring, shortly after the Fifteenth Amendment's ratification. Tensions between black voters and Republican Liberals were particularly high in Springfield, where Liberals joined with Democrats in nominating a "Citizen's Ticket" that the Democratic *Springfield Leader* described as constituting the city's "best men." By contrast, the paper described the ticket's opponents as "party hacks—blood suckers on the body politic" who had "conceived the idea that with the assistance of the negroes they could carry the city and run it in their own interest."[51] The city's black residents, however, actively sought to turn black men's newfound access to the ballot to the advantage of themselves and their community. When Radicals called a convention at the county courthouse to nominate candidates for municipal offices, black Missourians turned out in force. In the words of the *Leader*, "The south side of the [court] house was jammed with negroes, interspersed with white Radicals, which made the scene unique and grotesque." After a relatively peaceful meeting, the convention nominated Julius H. Rector, a schoolteacher of mixed race, for the office of councilman in the city's second ward. On Election Day, the city's black men repeated their show of strength, casting enough ballots to ensure an overwhelming Radical victory in the city and electing Rector by the single largest margin of any single councilman. Even as the *Leader* denounced the results as fraud, it had no choice but to recognize black voters' decisive role in the election. According to the paper: "A new epoch dawned on the political history of our country last Tuesday." "Legally or illegally—right or wrong—the negroes voted and decided the contest."[52]

As it became clear that McClurg would face challengers from within his own party, the question of black men's representation came to a head during the state executive committee's efforts to craft a method for selecting delegates to the party's upcoming convention. The first proposal ignored race and followed precedent, providing each county with delegates based on the vote cast for the Republican candidate in the last presidential election. After considerable lobbying from Turner, however, the committeemen added an additional delegate for every 150 black men or fraction thereof. When it became clear that Radical regulars on the committee intended for counties with less than 150 black residents to have at least one black delegate, Liberals objected on the grounds that such a scheme would allow delegates to be elected in counties with very small black populations and thus potentially overrepresent Radical strongholds in the countryside. The final plan favored the Radicals, providing for the election of 797 total seats at the convention, 180 of which would be reserved for black Missourians.[53]

Settling the apportionment question, however, only shifted the center of the debate to local contests for the election of delegates across the state. The election of delegates was particularly contentious in St. Louis, where German immigrants bolstered Liberal ranks and black residents were increasingly divided. In the tenth ward, the *Democrat* reported that a "dense column of colored folks" constituted nearly half of the Republicans gathered. After a struggle for control of the meeting, party members "moved that only those who could write should be allowed to vote, and that each voter should himself write the names of the candidates of his choice." The measure failed, but when it appeared that one (presumably white) Republican was coordinating black voters, a "German gentleman . . . jumped up excitedly, and bellowed out . . . 'Are those colored men all your slaves!'"[54] But perhaps the most dramatic conflict took place at King's Saloon in the city's eighth ward. According to the *Democrat*, approximately half of the people who came to watch and participate in the vote were black, with the street in front of the saloon "filled with colored men, who were unable to squeeze into the room." When it became clear that Liberals had control of the meeting's agenda, Radical regulars, led by Turner and a white Republican, challenged the legitimacy of the process and attempted to stall the election of delegates. The Liberals, strengthened by a contingent of black supporters, ultimately regained control of the meeting and elected Brown delegates "by a considerable majority." They included three black delegates: William P. Brooks, George Wedley, and Preston G. Wells.[55] A crowd of white and black Liberals then forcibly ejected Turner and his supporters from the saloon, producing a melee in which Turner "[had been] in danger of losing his life."[56]

Battles like that at King's Saloon reflected the degree to which Liberalism appealed to many black leaders and a significant minority of the rank and file (at least in St. Louis). Although we have little evidence with which to reconstruct their motivations, black Liberals like Wedley, Wells, Brooks, and their supporters (including Dickson and Tandy) appear to have come to the conclusion that disloyalist disfranchisement was counterproductive and even dangerous in the context of the Republican split. Support for Radicals had produced relatively few gains for black Missourians since 1865, and advocating a policy in which black men could claim the vote while tens of thousands of white men remained disfranchised seemed sure to antagonize the white majority. Of course, their support for Liberalism may have been prompted as well by local patronage networks and a desire to advance their own careers (although it might be noted that Wells, who had been appointed notary public by McClurg, was risking his own position, at least in the short term).[57] St. Louis was a Liberal stronghold, and it is not surprising that the city's white Liberals would turn to local black leaders with statewide connections for support. Likewise, class may have played a role, at least among the leadership. While black Liberals like Wells and Wedley may have believed that accommodating the return of white disloyalists was best for freedpeople as well as themselves, their relative wealth, skill, and political connections would have made them better able to prosper in the context of white Liberalism's "colorblind" policies. In a speech before a Liberal audience in St. Louis on September 10, Wedley, instead of returning to the league's policy of a biracial alliance of loyal men, asserted that "the time had come when the public safety permits the enfranchisement of those heretofore disfranchised." "The colored had always been liberal people," he maintained, asking "shall we now appear before the world as illiberal and narrow-minded?"[58]

Black Radicals were led by Turner, who had risen from serving as the league's secretary to become the most prominent black orator in the state. As with black Liberals, Turner's loyalty to the Radicals likely resulted from a complicated sense of personal and community interest. After the league's dissolution, Turner migrated to Kansas City, where he taught school. He later served throughout the state as an investigator for the Freedmen's Bureau and the Missouri superintendent of public schools.[59] These experiences taught him the benefits of patronage, but they also brought him into greater contact with recently freed slaves than many of his peers. While Turner may have calculated that loyalty to Missouri Radicals would stand him in good stead with their allies in the Grant administration (indeed, he later requested and received the position of minister to Liberia), his willingness to risk life and limb for a cause that was increasingly unpopular among the black elite—but not among Missouri's freed majority—suggests genuine concern for the broader consequences of disloyalist disfranchisement.[60]

In January 1870, Turner had claimed that he would support the repeal of disloyalist disfranchisement after the Fifteenth Amendment's ratification, but he had changed his mind by April, arguing that the state's white majority would defeat attempts to extend any rights to black Missourians that were not already explicitly guaranteed under the terms of the amendments (in particular jury service). Thus, he counseled black men to "look well to their interests" and vote against the amendments to the state constitution at the general election.[61] Turner was not blinded by the Radicals' self-serving appeals for black support; rather he appeared to remain convinced that the league's approach—a biracial coalition against the forces of treason and unalloyed white supremacy—was the best means by which to advance black interests in the state. In his response to the veiled threat posed by the *Democrat*, Turner outlined his own conditions by which black Missourians might bolt the party. "I believe I can safely say," he declared, "that colored men of this State and of the United States will vote as integral parts of the great Republican party, *so long as it adheres to its great cardinal principles.*"[62]

As the election approached, each side resorted to a variety of tactics to realign and reshape the electorate. In October, the editor of the *Democrat* and an accomplice offered Turner a bribe if he would support Brown and the amendments. Turner refused and caused the paper considerable embarrassment by making the offer public.[63] In Springfield, the group of Liberals and Democrats that had earlier combined to oppose Rector threatened black men with indictments for illegal registration and indicated that they would be barred from the polls if they refused to support the Liberal ticket.[64] In Clay County, Democrats pursued a campaign to buy or coerce black votes for the party's candidates and their allies. In addition to holding lavish celebrations for black Missourians in the run-up to the election, they spread rumors that McClurg's administration was going to levy a tax on adult black men and that failure to pay such tax would result in imprisonment.[65] But the electioneering of most importance to black Missourians arguably came from their erstwhile Radical allies. In late September, McClurg issued a letter to registrars that instructed them to act in a "spirit of liberality" toward prospective black voters as well as white disloyalists.[66] In a last-ditch effort to defeat Liberal Republicans at any cost, the secretary of the Radical state central committee instructed party members to support Democrats over Liberals in close local races if Democrats would agree to cast their votes for McClurg.[67]

Such tactics left black Radicals like Turner with few options. Indeed, in the end, it was McClurg and not the Liberals who compelled Turner to rescind his opposition to disloyalist re-enfranchisement. Shortly after McClurg announced his shift in position, Turner admitted that "the position from which colored men opposed the amendments is no longer a tenable one," and he recommended that black Missourians support them. Although Turner made speeches favoring the amendments, he concluded the campaign by declaring his own candidacy for Congress in St. Louis's Second District in a final, if only symbolic, attempt to advance his own vision of black political empowerment.[68]

Although we cannot accurately estimate black Missourians' voting behavior because of their relatively small numbers (no more than 10 percent of approximately 200,000 registered voters), we can make some generalizations based on anecdotal evidence.[69] On the one hand, it seems very likely that most black Missourians supported McClurg. Wilcox claimed a black majority for McClurg in Jefferson City, and the *Louisiana Journal* reported a similar result. Both cities had become centers of black life during the war, as recently freed slaves fled to urban areas in search of freedom and safety. Black support for the amendments is less clear, but it was likely concentrated in St. Louis. While the *Democrat* claimed that "a large proportion" of black St. Louisans supported Brown and the amendments, the paper also reported that several hundred black residents reacted with dismay to Turner's advocacy of the amendments at a Radical meeting in late October.[70] "Mr. Turner's speech was very handsomely turned," it wrote, "but it was coldly received by his colored hearers." "It elicited no applause, and a good many left the hall in [disgust]."[71] At the level of county and local offices, the results are even less clear. Wilcox argued that most of Cole County's black voters (who had been decisive in the success of the entire Radical ticket in Jefferson City the previous April) followed McClurg's directive (through Turner) and supported Democratic candidates in local races.[72] Regarding Missouri as a whole, however, the state's premier Democratic paper in the English language, the *St. Louis Missouri Republican*, emphasized the failure of new black voters to carry Radical candidates over direct support for Democrats, observing that Democrats had "no reason to regard [black suffrage] with special disfavor" because "[it] has proved too insignificant to do them any harm, and in some places it has even given them a little aid."[73]

Regardless of whom black voters supported, the Republican split and the Democratic resurgence following the 1870 election spelled the end of Missouri's experiment with Reconstruction. In the wake of the 1870 election and the abolition of disloyalist disfranchisement, Democrats quickly reasserted their dominance. In 1872, Democrats regained the governor's office, and three years later they succeeded in revising and replacing the hated constitution of 1865. The new constitution emphasized restrictions on state power while simultaneously placing limits on those local and individual activities that Democrats and their allies deemed dangerous to "the good of the whole." While their experience with suffrage restriction undermined support for poll taxes, they provided for the disfranchisement of those men who had become dependents of the state, including paupers and convicts.[74] After the constitution's ratification, Democrats maintained harsher disfranchisement penalties for men convicted of crimes against property, and they shifted the crime of miscegenation from a misdemeanor to a felony in 1877.[75] Although the state's white Republicans (even when united) had often proved to be unreliable allies for black Missourians, the period after 1870 saw a precipitous decline in black people's ability to influence what remained of the party. Missouri law no longer prevented black men from registering, voting, or holding office on the basis of race alone, but few white Republicans were willing to press black demands or place black candidates in positions of power and influence, especially over whites. In 1872, Turner made an unsuccessful bid for a seat in the Missouri House, and Republicans refused to nominate him as a candidate for Congress in 1878.[76] By 1880, he had joined with other black Missourians (including former Liberals) to appeal to Republican president Rutherford B. Hayes to "elevate a colored man to a responsible official position in Missouri . . . [to] reunite the colored people, who are now disaffected on account of having to carry the burdens of the party without charge or emoluments."[77]

On the whole, black Missourians' suffrage activism in the immediate postwar years reveals the importance of paying close attention to the complex interactions between local, state, and national politics when examining the timing and trajectory of black political activism during Reconstruction. Much as historians of emancipation have demonstrated how the process of slavery's destruction was influenced by the interplay of local, state, and federal actors, so too local politics and state policy combined with federal laws to shape the opportunities and limitations of black organizing in the war's aftermath. In Missouri, we see that the state's 1865 constitution—long regarded as the key to the state's postwar exceptionalism—left black Missourians vulnerable at the local level and spurred rather than retarded black activism. The nature of state politics in Missouri indeed produced a period of unprecedented political influence for black Missourians, but it lasted months not years. Although the state's first generation of postwar black political leaders were certainly among the black elite, they were also a diverse group distinguished more by wartime service than membership in the antebellum "colored aristocracy." They remained largely united in their goal of achieving black men's suffrage rights through 1868, but they were increasingly pulled apart by ratification of the Fifteenth Amendment and the Liberal bolt—developments that themselves accentuated preexisting cleavages among black Missourians. Although divisions among black people cannot be said to have *caused* Republican factionalism in Missouri, black efforts to define freedom and seize political influence certainly heightened tensions within the Republican Party during the crucial period following the amendment's ratification.[78] These tensions were particularly intense in St. Louis, where class divisions were pronounced and where Liberalism seemed most advantageous. Far from simply following Turner or any other black politician, black Missourians staked out a number of positions reflecting the dynamics of local political alignments. Although support for disfranchisement waned in the wake of the Liberal bolt, the state's recently freed black majority held on to the promise of a biracial loyalist alliance longer than most of their more privileged leaders. Indeed, in a sense, it was Turner who followed them, at least until McClurg's reversal on disfranchisement and ultimate defeat forced him to scramble to find a place in the quickly shifting sands of Missouri and national politics. But with Republicans—black and white—divided, Democrats returned to power in the state—a position they would hold for the rest of the nineteenth century—leaving black men and women to continue their struggle to find a measure of power and protection in a new white supremacist order.

Chapter 13

"A Little Different than in Alabama": Sectional Narratives and the Rhetoric of Racist Violence*

Brent M. S. Campney

"[The South] is as much a fiction, a story we tell and are told, as it is a fixed geographic space," asserts scholar Tara McPherson. "If one is to understand the many versions of the South that circulate throughout U.S. history and culture, one has always to see them as fundamentally connected to, and defined in relation to, the non-South." Eschewing the possibility of elucidating any "real" South, she explores what she calls the "imagined South." In urging this examination, she echoes geographer Doreen Massey, who argues that places are products of human thought and action rather than products of nature, and reproves "all attempts to institute horizons, to establish boundaries, to secure the identity of places." In fact, scholars across a range of disciplines agree that places are "open and porous," "mental territories" constructed through a multiplicity of relations with "other" places.[1]

The rapidly expanding academic literature on white-on-black racist violence has demonstrated an impressive sensitivity to spatial and temporal variation in the intensity of violence within and among the various states and regions of the South. Despite this sensitivity, it has until very recently focused almost exclusively on this one section of the country. Although whites brutalized blacks throughout the United States, the prevailing impression remains that this was, in the words of historian Paul A. Gilje, "largely a southern phenomenon and needs to be understood within the southern context."[2]

White Southerners certainly earned their association with racist vio-

*The editors would like to thank the online journal *Southern Spaces* for the permission to publish a revised version of the essay "'This is Not Dixie': The Imagined South, the Kansas Free State Narrative, and the Rhetoric of Racist Violence." Published Sept. 6, 2007 at http://www.southernspaces.org.

lence, employing relentless terror to enforce white supremacy. However, those who foster the idea that racist violence was overwhelmingly Southern hinder a comprehensive appraisal of it in other sections of the country. In his study, sociologist James W. Loewen marvels at the intractability of this mindset. "Over and over I tell historians and social scientists about my research, and they assume I'm studying the Deep South," he reports. "I tell a sociologist friend that I've just spent months researching sundown towns in the Midwest. Ten minutes later he has forgotten and again assumes I have been traveling through the South."[3]

If the imagined South has acquired this unenviable position in the popular and scholarly mind, the imagined Midwest has developed a very different position. In the late nineteenth century, according to geographer James R. Shortridge, "two concepts—pastoralism and the Middle West—which initially were similar in several respects, rapidly intertwined and soon became virtually synonymous," creating thereby an image of the Midwest as a land of "bucolic virtue, of sturdy, thriving agrarians inhabiting a blissful Middle Landscape." In addition, "two pairs of bonded concepts: slavery and labor, equality and race," forged during the Civil War and nurtured thereafter, evolved into a second image, which historians Andrew R. L. Cayton and Susan E. Gray have called the image "of the Midwest as a land of freedom." Both images bolstered the Turner thesis that characterized the Midwest as a place where social status was fluid, individuals achieved through hard work and innate ability, and the challenges of the frontier left little space for bigotry.[4]

In the 1880s and 1890s, Kansas and Nebraska were first designated the Middle West, "not in relationship to the 'Far' West, as is commonly believed, but as part of a north-south ordering of space on the plains frontier," a moniker used to distinguish "the comparatively settled and stable 'middle' states both from the frontier 'North West' in the Dakotas and from the culturally different 'South West' in Texas and Indian Territory." Although popular conceptions of the Midwest shifted, Kansas remained at its "core" historically and geographically.[5]

Like the Midwest generally, Kansas has been identified with pastoralism and racial harmony. Unlike its sister states, it was literally defined by race at its inception. Beginning with the Kansas-Nebraska Act of 1854, Kansas became the site of a struggle between white Northern and Southern settlers over the extension of slavery. Some Northerners opposed slavery on moral grounds, but most opposed it on economic grounds, arguing that it choked out opportunity for white men. As historian Eugene H. Berwanger notes, "a large group of settlers was more anti-Negro than anti-slavery." Northerners were divided over many issues but were pushed into a free state alliance by the heavy-handed effort of proslavery advocates—primarily Missourians—to impose their peculiar institution. "Slavery's establishment was to be accomplished by disregarding the 'wishes' of the majority of white settlers, thereby enslaving voters to the proslavery agenda," writes historian Nicole Etcheson. "These events united free-state settlers in the conviction that their political rights and liberties were being trampled by a government determined to impose slavery upon them."[6]

Amidst the sectional conflicts during the Civil War and Reconstruction, white Kansans reshaped the memory of the free-state struggle, framing it as a fight not only for white political and economic freedom but for the liberation of slaves as well. In discussing the possibility of a university in Lawrence, one booster declared in 1856 that such an institution would be a "monument to perpetuate the memory of those martyrs of Liberty who fell during the recent struggles," and prophesized that the university "shall burn the light of Liberty which shall never be extinguished until it illumines the whole continent. It shall be called the 'Free State College' & all the friends of Freedom shall be invited to lend it a helping hand."[7] As Berwanger observes, contemporaries, "recalling events in the territory from 1854 to 1860," later chose to ignore "other issues, stressing the struggle over slavery and describing their efforts as a valiant attempt to prevent the fastening of Negro servitude on the territory."[8]

Throughout the remainder of the century, white Kansans consolidated the free-state narrative. During the Kansas Exodus of 1879–1881, when thousands of blacks from the Deep South migrated to the state, some whites—often state politicians and newspaper editors—recognized that this influx would affirm their superiority to the South, place greater responsibility upon themselves to honor their ideals, and increase national scrutiny of their actions—expectations borne out by increased white middle-class opposition to lynching at the time and thereafter. The *Junction City Tribune* pondered this at the height of the migration. "For years the north has complained that the south has been cruel to the negroes," it reflected. "The south now sends us a few boat loads of darkies, merely to give us a taste. In some places they are met with a flourish of patriotism and charity, in others with shot-guns and pitch-forks." White Kansans could either stifle violence or admit hypocrisy: "Denial or explanation does no good."[9]

With the escalation of violence around the turn of the century, middle-class whites grew increasingly anxious about the impact of lynching on the reputation of the state, about the implications of racist violence for its economic development, and about the necessity of shoring up the distinctions between Kansas and the South. The *Topeka Daily Capital* typified this view in the aftermath of an incident that garnered national headlines in 1901. Responding to the immolation of Fred Alexander by a mob of 5,000 in Leavenworth, it pleaded its case with language melodramatic even by contemporary standards. "Kansas has no extenuation to plead," it cried. "Our people are profoundly shocked at the humiliating stain that has fallen upon our escutcheon. We cover ourselves in sackcloth and ashes. A rose has fallen from our chaplet but it is not lost!"[10]

With John Brown as their symbol, free staters had successfully spun a romantic narrative, rehabilitating white supremacists as righteous soldiers in a struggle for human dignity. As historian Michael Lewis Goldberg argues:

Yankee Kansans believed their state's founding was a profoundly moral act, the triumph of freedom and progress over the barbarity of slavery. Northerners who had rushed to settle Kansas in the years before the Civil War had done so to halt the expansion of slavery. . . Free State settlers had suffered like martyrs at the hands of Southern proslavers, whose marauding ways had inspired the national epithet *Bleeding Kansas*. But in the end, through the perseverance of the Free Staters and the will of God, the righteous triumphed and were rewarded. The lesson of this story, oft repeated, was that Kansans, compared with their relatively benighted counterparts in other states, now possessed a certain moral superiority.[11]

White Kansans generally embraced the free-state narrative. Scholars might underscore "the bald fact that local and personal economic objectives had commonly overshadowed the national and moralistic antislavery crusade in governing the behavior of individual colonists," notes historian Robert Smith Bader, but "the general populace did not overly concern itself with such refinements. It loved to tell and retell the heroics of the Free State champions."[12]

In reality, however, many white Kansans utilized violence systematically and continuously in the state after the Civil War. Between 1864 and 1874 alone, white mobs lynched at least thirty-three black men; throughout the remainder of the century white mobs and individuals murdered or grievously injured innumerable black victims. Assessing the nature of race relations in the state in 1903, a black civil rights activist was blunt. "In Kansas," he declared, whites "burn Negroes alive, and when they are not burning them, they are . . . [denying them] their rights."[13]

This essay explores the ways in which white Kansans employed images of the "South" and its association with racist violence to constitute the free-state identity since the end of the Civil War. It argues that prevailing assumptions about "Dixie" functioned as a durable framework through which white Kansans understood the racist violence in their own midst. On the one hand, the "South" and the bloodshed that took place there provided a means to obscure, dismiss, and justify incidents in Kansas, enabling commentators to cultivate a sort of historical amnesia, to deem each successive episode an anomaly, the exception that proved the rule of Midwestern virtue. On the other hand, the idea of the "South" constituted a powerful incentive for opposing racist violence among white Kansans fearful of becoming associated with it. The conclusion assesses the impact of the narrative on both the history of the state and its historiography, suggesting the possibility of an equally powerful "Southern" narrative that seems to have seduced contemporaries and scholars into the belief that white Southerners had no alternative but the use of violence to control black populations in "Dixie."

The white Kansans who crafted the free-state narrative—principally newspaper editors and Republican politicians, as previously noted—presented Kansas as a foil to the "Negro-Hating South" where "black men have no rights which white men are bound to respect." While theirs was a truthful, if hyperbolic, assessment of racism and violence in the South, they often linked it to the more dubious claim that racist violence was primarily confined to that section of the nation. The *Topeka Daily Capital* articulated this view clearly when it condemned the mob in Georgia that burned Sam Hose in a well-known 1899 lynching. "The sickening story of recent lynching bees in Georgia has no parallels in the history of civilization, outside of the southern states," it concluded. "The vengeance of the southern whites on negro ravishers shows that the elemental man, or the elemental savage, is still there."[14]

Free-state proponents envisioned their state as the anti-South, standing in stark contrast to Southern traditions and "occupying a position in the foreground of enlightened progress." Kansas had been born of the struggle for freedom for all people and baptized with the blood of abolitionists, they insisted. Forged of this purpose and "leading the van in all that goes to make an enlightened and Christian civilization," the state would remain a place where people of all races could achieve success through hard work and where racism was anathema. "There is no State in the Union where a colored man has a better [chance] to ask for a solid Republican support than in the State of Kansas," declared the *Leavenworth Times*. "Blood was shed on Kansas soil for the negro." Ignoring the fact that free-soil ideology had proven quite compatible with racism, whites routinely invoked their origin story as prima facie evidence of their subsequent commitment to racial equality.[15]

Whites could acknowledge acts of racist violence in Kansas but minimize their significance by declaring each an aberration—infrequent, uncharacteristic, and even unprecedented—rather than evidence of a pattern. In the aftermath of the Alexander burning, white Kansans debated extensively over its implications for the state's legacy. The *Topeka Daily Capital* ignored dozens of lynchings stretching back to the Civil War—including another burning—when it insisted that "this sad, solitary misstep is not excused or palliated by the people of the Sunflower state."[16] Governor William E. Stanley pondered the anomaly. "'Thing[s] like this have happened in the south many times but [do] not seem so horrible there as they do here.'"[17]

When a white man attacked a laborer at the Bourbon County Fair in 1883, the *Fort Scott Daily Monitor* depicted the incident as atypical in a land defined by pastoral virtue, prefacing its report with a paean to the fair itself, which, it insisted, epitomized the state's bucolic egalitarianism. "The products of the field were there arrayed . . . giving evidence of the virgin excellence of our soil" and of the "industry and intelligence of a people who have combined to a greater degree than any other people on earth the true dignity of manhood with the necessity that all men earn their bread by the sweat of the brow." Transitioning to the violence, the *Monitor* fused this bounty with biblical transgression, depicting the attack as a betrayal of the state's nonracist essence by an unrepresentative son. "This collection might well be compared to the Garden of Eden in its combination of excellences and like the Garden of Eden, it had just one serpent to mar its harmony and beauty."[18]

More commonly, white Kansans cloaked indigenous incidents of racist violence in narratives about the "South" and the "Free State," characterizing them as contaminants, misplaced and inherently "Southern" phenomena not indigenous to their state. The *Wichita Daily Eagle* blamed the Leavenworth incident on the cultivation of a southern crop in the inhospitable soil of the Midwest. "A negro rapist has been . . . burned at the stake, chained, kerosened and burned alive, in strict accordance with the method employed by the prejudiced south. . . . Such tragedies are unlooked for and unexpected at the hands of western people where the hanging of horse thieves has proved about the only exception to the regular rule of trial by jury."[19]

Despite the varied sectional origins of most settlers in Kansas, commentators seldom remarked upon those of the perpetrators of racist violence, suggesting that they regarded most assailants as fully assimilated "Kansans" motivated by other concerns. However, when individuals identified as *Southerners* perpetrated this violence, whites ascribed great explanatory power to their origins. Reporting the attempted hanging of John E. Lewis near Topeka, the *Topeka Daily Capital* emphasized a Texas connection. Lewis, it reported, "is grand chancellor of the colored Knights of Pythias of the state, and it was his Pythias badge that aroused the southern hostility of the Texans. They didn't like to see a 'nigger' putting on such airs, and proceeded to adopt the regulation Dixie method for teaching the negro his place." Similarly, when newcomers of unknown origins committed racist acts of violence, whites interpreted those as de facto evidence of the perpetrators' origins. The *Hutchinson Semi-Weekly Gazette* typified this inclination, concluding that the murderer of a black resident "was almost a stranger in town, and probably a southerner."[20]

At times, Kansans flouted the superiority of the free state on the basis of the rather modest distinctions in the responses of Kansans and Southerners to local racist violence. In the wake of the Alexander incident, the *Topeka Daily Capital* speculated on the likely public responses of the state's senators and contrasted them with those characteristic of Southern politicians, as typified by the one-eyed South Carolina senator, Ben "Pitchfork" Tillman. Should the former be asked about the incident, "judge, all the earth, of the difference of their utterances [t]o the brazen exultation of the Carolinian Cyclops discoursing on similar tragedies within his state." Although the actions of the mob and the support for those actions among white residents revealed more similarities than differences between Kansas and the South, the *Capital* put considerable stock in oratory: "the ringing resolutions of the Kansas legislature, the utterances of her public men and her public press are proof to all the world that the melancholy affair is not excused or condoned in Kansas."[21]

The *Belle Plaine News* epitomized the way that the free-state narrative could be used to establish the virtue of Kansas and the depravity of the South, no matter how fine the distinctions. When Frank Abbott, a Southerner, killed a black laborer, the *News* freely (and correctly) intimated that the perpetrator would face no penalty—the same result that would undoubtedly have awaited him in the "prejudiced south." Nevertheless, it insisted that the inconvenience of Abbott's arrest and trial before his inevitable acquittal proved the moral superiority of Kansas. "Being arrested for killing a 'nigger' was no doubt a surprise to Mr. Abbott, who, reports have it, has killed other negros [sic]," it reported. "The man may come clear but he will find it a little different than in Alabama and may wait till he gets out of Kansas before being to [sic] hasty again."[22]

Few incidents could underscore the degree to which the free-state narrative could mold perceptions than a custody dispute between officials in Leavenworth and in neighboring Platte County, Missouri—the state that, for reasons of history and proximity, constituted a surrogate for the "South." Officials in both municipalities claimed jurisdiction when Frank Garrison killed a white man on an island in the Missouri River. Having custody of the prisoner and intent upon asserting their boundary claims, those in Leavenworth refused to relinquish control, insisting with haughty superiority that "if Garrison was taken to Missouri he would be lynched." The *Leavenworth Times* seemed oblivious to the irony when it reported that the sheriff had spirited the prisoner to the Leavenworth Federal Penitentiary to protect him from lynch-minded Kansans. "County officials were advised yesterday that an attempt was being made to form a mob to hang Garrison. It was said that some of the men who were in the mob that dragged a colored man to death [in Leavenworth] ten years ago were back of the movement."[23]

Similarly, free-state enthusiasts characteristically blamed racist violence on or near the Kansas-Missouri border on Missourians bent on instigating trouble or on settlers from Missouri with unrepresentative "southern" attitudes. The *Lawrence Journal* took this position when a mob lynched two blacks in Wyandotte, suggesting that only Northerners could be trusted to deal fairly with blacks: "When lynching *does* become necessary in Kansas, we should prefer some other class than the conservatives of Kansas City, and the border to take it in hand." The *Leavenworth Conservative* agreed.

"We are not quite ready to charge upon Kansas, as a State, the perpetration of [the] deed." It proposed a legislative remedy to punish the offending county and its border ruffian residents: "We call upon the Legislature . . . to annex Wyandotte county to some other for judicial purposes, until her citizens shall have virtue."[24]

While white Kansans employed the free-state narrative to obscure, dismiss, and justify racist violence, they also refashioned it as a tool of resistance, seeking to protect the state's self-created image and, consequently, its economic fortunes through an appeal to this same mythology. Accordingly, they expressed concern that racist violence would make Kansas indistinguishable from the "South." "We are told that we have violated all our noble traditions," worried the *Topeka Daily Capital* after the Alexander affair, "that the stain can never be washed away, that the citadel of equal rights established by John Brown has been crushed to earth, that the land consecrated by freedom's blood to law, and order and race equality has degenerated to the level of South Carolina." Free-state boosters celebrated the prevention of mob violence as the inoculation of Kansas from the infection of "Southern" tendencies. The *Leavenworth Times* applauded whites in Eskridge when they condemned a mob. "A poor negro was treated to the methods employed by the old ku-klux gangs of Georgia," it reported. "As soon as the facts came out a large indignation meeting was held by the farmers, and the outrageous action was denounced as it should be in free Kansas."[25]

Rhetoric notwithstanding, prominent whites were often more concerned about upholding their state's reputation than about serving justice. One opposed legal segregation on trains in Kansas not because it was morally wrong but because "it does not look right to outsiders." After the killing of Alexander, the *Atchison Daily Globe* frankly acknowledged that the hand-wringing among state officials was primarily about preserving the name of Kansas for the national audience. "'We will keep ourselves right with the record,' as the politicians say, and there the matter will end for all time," it conceded. "'It will not look right to eastern people if we do not condemn the lynching,' said one legislator yesterday, 'but personally I approve of it.'"[26]

As they deployed the free-state narrative, some white Kansans internalized it, absorbing it into their geographical imaginations where it could constrain behavior. The *Olathe Mirror* typified this view when whites threatened to lynch Alfred Brown. "There are too many such fellows as

Brown in this county, and they should thank their stars they do not live south of the Mason and Dixon line." In 1905, the *Emporia Times and Emporia Republican* expressed its desire for a lynching with headlines shrieking "Nigger Assaults White Woman" and "Many People in for Hanging." Then, revealing the power of the free-state narrative, it concluded that the essence of Kansas made a "Southern" lynching untenable. "This is Not Dixie," it lamented. "He Will Probably Be Left for the Law to Handle."[27] In such instances, they obviously yearned to be in the "Negro-Hating South" where, they believed, the essence of place sustained murderous impulses; grudgingly accepting what they saw as the essence of Kansas, however, they foreswore their yearnings.

Some whites were so intent on preventing the "South" from infiltrating the free state that they proposed extraordinary measures to insulate themselves against it. After the torrent of national condemnation following the Leavenworth burning, state legislators devised a novel method for suppressing racist violence within state boundaries—they would simply redraw them. The *Atchison Daily Globe* noted that "the 'joke' on Leavenworth has been carried to that point where it is proposed to put Leavenworth county into Missouri." If burning was inherently "southern" and antithetical to the "Free State," proponents would simply amputate the offending county and confer it upon their neighbor, a "southern" state where such atrocities were expected and, perhaps, inevitable.[28] Although the proposal was essentially symbolic, legislators had demonstrated that, if racist violence was incompatible with state lore and if Leavenworth was synonymous with racist violence, they would simply excise the county and preserve the imagined.

Whether they employed the free-state narrative to obscure, dismiss, and justify racist violence or to oppose it, white Kansans rarely challenged its underlying assumption that blacks had little cause for complaint. On occasion, however, whites did challenge their own mythology overtly, suggesting that Kansas was not really a racial utopia and, perhaps, that it was not much different from the "South." When students at the University of Kansas raided the dissection laboratory, seized the cadaver of an unknown black man, and hanged it on campus in a "sham lynching," the *Horton Commercial* complained that many Kansas papers had suppressed an incident that undermined state lore. "Had this lynching of a dead Negro occurred in Louisiana or Texas, it would be termed 'another Democratic outrage in the South' by Republican papers of Kansas. But as it occurred in

Kansas they deem it wise to keep mum." Others cautioned Kansans to practice humility in denouncing the South given their own propensity for
inflicting similar violence against blacks. "Let us not howl at the south for
murdering 'niggers,'" noted an editor. "Up at Salina a mob hung a darkey
for slashing but not killing a man."[29]

Less frequently, commentators not only admitted that the reality in
Kansas bore little relationship to the mythology; they openly refused to
apologize for racist violence, even if that refusal wounded the state's image
and prospects. The *Fort Scott Herald* accepted responsibility on behalf of
Kansas when a mob lynched a prisoner there in 1879: "Neither do we pre-
tend to get out of it by claiming that a large proportion of the men engaged
in it were from Missouri." Exasperated by homilies from elsewhere after the
1901 burning, the *Lawrence Daily Journal* revealed that the free state was
better at doling out condemnation than at accepting it, warning that "other
states should understand that this is a family affair, and if they don't keep
their hands out of it, Kansas is likely to back Leavenworth up to sail in and
do it again. Kansas demands for herself the privilege of doing the criticiz-
ing."[30]

After the Civil War, the free-state narrative was deployed by white
Kansans to lavish praise upon themselves for their devotion to black
rights—even as they were working furiously to negate them. In the same
period, as John W. McKerley and Jeremy Neely illustrate in their contributions to this volume, "a tenuous reconciliation," predicated upon a
mutual commitment to white supremacy, was being pursued by former
white antagonists in the North and South. It was a "slow and uneven
process of national reunion," based upon what Neely called "a selective
remembering of the war and its meanings." Nonetheless, the selective
strains of memory that enabled both the free-state narrative and white
national reunion were endlessly tangled, facilitating reconciliation between
white Northerners and Southerners generally while simultaneously pitting
white Kansans against their Southern counterparts in a hypocritical effort
to justify their own betrayal of the promise of racial justice.

The free-state narrative cast a long shadow. For white Kansans from the
Civil War to the Jim Crow era, an imagined South served as an absent con-
stituent of free-state identity. This durable foil provided a means for obscuring, dismissing, and justifying homegrown racist violence, and for
promoting opposition to it. A "Dixie" largely defined by racism and violence created an imaginary and repulsive Other used simultaneously to dis-

tinguish Kansas and to express fears about its future course. The free-state narrative maintained its potency after World War I, as socialist and feminist writer Marcet Haldeman-Julius illustrated repeatedly in a 1927 article on "Negroes in Kansas Colleges." Documenting a darkening atmosphere for blacks on college campuses, she attributed the expanding Jim Crow system to the contaminating influence of white Southerners, not to "the real temper of Kansas."

> Kansas, you must realize, has always been a borderline state. We stand here cheek by jowl with Missouri and, looking over her shoulder and Oklahoma's, nod to Arkansas. People from these three states steadily pour into our midst. And the fact that Lawrence, where our University is located, is so near Kansas City, Missouri, induces to that school a large influx of Missouri students. The result is that never, not even in those days when we were "Bleeding Kansas," has this state passed through a more delicate, critical period so far as the health of her coming generations is concerned than that in which she now finds herself.[31]

Following World War II, a new generation of activists undertook to dismantle Jim Crow. They clashed repeatedly with white conservatives who, though compelled to retreat on some issues, fought aggressively to maintain the status quo. From across the political spectrum, whites responded to the movement by resurrecting the free-state narrative and by marrying fanciful claims about Kansas to assertions about the essentially Southern nature of racism and racist violence. Subscribing to this narrative, many believed that blacks had little to gripe about. In response to civil rights protests in 1947, they stubbornly maintained that "there isn't any racial discrimination at all." At the University of Kansas in 1956, a student watched unrest at the University of Alabama with smug pride. "We should be thankful that the people in this area are well ahead of the narrow thinking of a few in the South."[32]

More liberal whites employed the free-state narrative to different ends, fashioning it as a tool of resistance to Jim Crow. In 1970, an integrationist used it to persuade whites to deal fairly with blacks. "Evoking the spirit of John Brown and Bleeding Kansas," he "lamented that 'too many people' ignore racial exclusion. 'Kansas history is based on freedom, tolerance, the Christian way and fair play; we must not lose this foundation.'"[33] By comparing race relations in Kansas unfavorably to those in Arkansas, a student resorted to the sheer humiliation of his fellow Kansans to change minds. "In Arkansas, at least, they can claim a southern tradition of intolerance and tyranny," he wrote. "In Lawrence we have our own version, home-grown and free-lance, just as vicious, and just as stupid."[34]

Steeped in the free-state mythology, white residents and newcomers alike absorbed the narrative into their geographical imaginations and often acted within the constraints imposed by it. A University of Kansas football player restrained himself from beating the activists who led a sit-in at an eatery in 1947. He, along with several of his teammates, had been summoned by the owner to eject the protesters. Although he yearned for violence, he doubted that his current state of residence would tolerate the murderous impulses that would find favor in his more "Southern" home state. "It is a good thing I'm not running this place," he growled at the protesters. "And it is a good thing you are not down in Oklahoma." Another declared: "You know how we treat them [blacks] down in Texas." A third agreed. "If I had my way," he declared, pointing at a black youth, "I'd shoot him."[35]

At the same time white Kansans also exercised the "Midwestern narrative," depicting "the rural heartland as a place of pastoral virtue, inherently antithetical to the kind of racist violence associated with the American South." A prominent writer happened to be in Lawrence on the night when a police officer killed a black youth in 1970, precipitating racial unrest. Later Bill Moyers had considerable difficulty

> reconciling the event with what he perceived as the bucolic essence of the town. "The man who invited me . . . said that Lawrence is a pleasant place to live and to visit—'A university town in the heart of Middle America should give you a chance to catch your breath,' he had suggested—and I half expected to enjoy a brief respite from my work before heading west. . . . With the early sun behind my back and the twin prairies of sky and grassland racing westward ahead of me, there was no warning of what was to come."[36]

Even more recently, a well-known political commentator breezily reflected these same views in examining the triumph of conservatism in the so-called Heart of America at the turn of the twenty-first century. Kansans today are conservative in many respects, wrote Thomas Frank, but not susceptible to the racism that for him defines the South.

There are undeniably a great number of places where this analysis holds true, but today's Kansas is not one of them. The state may be 88 percent white, but it cannot be easily dismissed as a nest of bigots. Kansas does not have Trent Lott's disease. It is not Alabama in the sixties. It was not tempted to go for George Wallace in 1968. Few here get sentimental about the Confederate flag. Kansas may burn to restore the gold standard; it may shriek for concealed carry and gasp at imagined liberal conspiracies; but one thing it doesn't do is racism.[37]

Many historians have been similarly influenced by the free-state narrative, basing assessments of Kansas not on its record but on that of its Southern foil. Examining the horrific lynching of three blacks in Lawrence in 1882, historian Katie H. Armitage hastens to add that "assaults on blacks and incidents of racial hostility in Kansas . . . were not as horrific as in the South." In making her assertion, she relies on the acceptance of the free-state assumption. Without it she could not explain why identical behavior—the murder of black people by racist mobs—was "not as horrific" when it happened in Kansas as it was when it happened in the South.[38] Other scholars lend credence to the free-state narrative by their acceptance of the view that most white Kansans—of Northern origins—were largely committed to racial equality and justice. "The women of Kansas had become inured to hardship and danger," noted historian Kenneth S. Davis in a discussion of the free-state coalition of the 1850s, "and used to thinking of themselves as the companions of warriors for freedom."[39]

Like white Kansans after the Civil War, scholars have frequently accepted the depiction of the Midwest as a land of pastoral virtue—a "Garden of Eden"—where racist violence was anomalous. In his study of an Indiana lynching, James H. Madison inadvertently presented a Midwest fundamentally incompatible with racist violence even as he documented evidence to the contrary. He seemed to suggest that if white supremacy could exist in the "Heartland," a place he viewed as profoundly antithetical to such things, then it could exist anywhere. "Grant County was an ordinary place," he argued, "a place that celebrated as its heroes its ordinary people, the pioneers who built farms and homes on the flatlands of the Midwest." Nevertheless, he added, there remained whites even "in this ordinary place in America's heartland who continued to believe in 'us' and 'them.'" Historian Leslie A. Schwalm relied on a similar sense of incongruity, concluding her study of Reconstruction in Iowa, Minnesota, and

Wisconsin with a discussion of the "social dislocation that emancipation induced—even in the midwest."[40]

Mimicking the penchant of contemporary white Kansans in the decades after the Civil War to ascribe great explanatory power to origins when a perpetrator of racist violence hailed from the South, contemporary scholars often fault those same origins in their own investigations of racist violence outside the South. Stephen J. Leonard put great stock in Southern heritage in his study of Colorado. Examining the burning of a youth in 1900, Leonard noted that blacks across the state protested this atrocity. "These . . . protests," he observed, "did not move Colorado's Georgia-born governor Charles S. Thomas, whose southern roots and grasp of practical politics apparently overrode his commitment to the law." In her study of racist violence in southwest Missouri, Kimberly Harper noted that the region claimed a heterogeneous population composed of settlers from both the North and South but left little doubt about which settlers she viewed as responsible for the bloodshed. "Southwest Missouri . . . was entrenched in a southern mindset," she wrote, a result of "the region's southern heritage of violence." Southwest Missouri "was a land and people not quite southern, but definitely children of the Confederacy, still locked in the traditions and customs of their rebellious forefathers."[41]

This study illustrates that sectional and regional differences are attributable not only to commonly understood variables, such as history, economics, and demography, but also to the power of stories told about places. When applied to the South, this finding may suggest that white Southerners adhered to an equally powerful Southern narrative that persuaded them, and many of their Northern contemporaries, that they had no alternative other than the use of violence to subjugate the black populations in that section.

The *Kansas Daily Tribune* certainly promulgated a Southern narrative along those lines. It voiced this view shortly after the Civil War, conceding that there was a high crime rate in the North but insisting that criminality *defined* the South. "In the South it is a deep, settled, murderous principle—a premeditated determination to kill when the opportunity offers," it declared. "[The Northern murderer] is a murderer by chance," while the Southern one "acts by rule," killing as "a deliberate thing." Just as the South was unalterably criminal, it was also unalterably racist. "The reconstructed rebels have added another most atrocious and wholesale massacre to their appalling list of crimes," observed the *Tribune* after the 1866

New Orleans race riot. "Its horrible details put into the shade the Memphis slaughter, the Norfolk outbreak, and all the other evidences of 'repentant' and 'reconstructed' hearts with which the demons of the South have heretofore shocked the world."[42]

Although white Southerners resented Northern hypocrisy, they shared Northern assumptions that racism and violence were inevitable in the South. Sharing these assumptions, they reinforced them in word and deed. Following an early-twentieth-century lynching, a white Floridian touted the Southern narrative, telling a Northern critic that the "people of the South dont [sic] think any more of killing the black fellows than you would think of killing a flea." Reflecting his belief in a static South, he asserted confidently that "if I was to live 1,000 years that would be my opinion and [that of] every other Southern man." "Down here," a young white Southerner told a Northerner on another occasion, "we feel like killing a nigger whether he has done anything or not."[43]

Just as scholars reinforce the free-state and Midwestern narratives, so too do they seem to reinforce a Southern one, depicting a "South" somehow *inherently* racist and *inherently* violent—racist and violent in a way impossible elsewhere. In the 1940s, Wilbur Cash reiterated the views of the *Kansas Daily Tribune* that the violent Southerner "acts by rule" and does so as "a deliberate thing." In the 1980s, Stephen J. Whitfield seconded him. Writing of the Emmett Till case in Mississippi, Whitfield wrote that his lynchers "could have stepped from the pages of *The Mind of the South.* 'When confronted with a crime that aroused his anger,' W. J. Cash had written over a decade earlier with an insider's perspicacity, the Southerner demanded 'immediate satisfaction for itself—catharsis for personal passion . . . now, within the hour—and not some ponderous abstract justice in a problematic tomorrow.'"[44]

Indeed scholars seem especially habituated with the application of the Southern narrative in their research on Mississippi. Anthony Walton conveyed this starkly in his meditation on the state. "I have gone over a river from familiar places and into the state of Mississippi," he observed. "Mississippi can be considered one of the most prominent scars on the map of this country." Relying on popular perception more than tangible evidence, he added that there "is something different about Mississippi, something almost unspeakably primal and vicious; something savage unleashed there that has yet to come to rest." James C. Cobb betrayed this tendency in the title of his history of the Mississippi Delta, calling it "The Most Southern

Place on Earth." With this phrase, he made "Southern Place" synonymous with racism and violence, identifying the region as "A World Apart." Historian Joseph Crespino recognized the degree to which historians reinforce overlapping Southern narratives in his discussion of "Mississippi as Metaphor." Historians, Crespino wrote, have often "viewed Mississippi as the South on steroids, the South in all of its gothic racist horror."[45] In recognition of the significance of stories to the history and historiography of places, those investigating racist violence should certainly heed the cautionary advice of historian Christopher Waldrep, who warned that "our history never 'caused' us to be violent" even if "scholars have often argued that Americans cannot help themselves."[46]

Chapter 14

The Quantrill Men Reunions: The Missouri-Kansas Border War, Fifty Years On

Jeremy Neely

Looking upon the sprawling picnic he had organized, the retired outlaw spied in attendance some three dozen former comrades and at least five hundred friends, well-wishers, and other curious folk. Virtually everyone in attendance knew, or knew of, the old man, who could reasonably claim to be among the most famous people in Missouri. That fame had blossomed from 1868 to 1876, when he had been a criminal of extraordinary skill and daring. Once a robber of banks and trains, he had been accused of murder and had a $10,000 government bounty put upon his head. He was also, of course, older brother to Jesse James, the most celebrated bandit in American history. Yet as Frank James leaned against the worm rail fence that cool afternoon in September 1898, he was the center of attention less for that legendary reputation than for his part in the Missouri-Kansas border war some three decades earlier.[1]

Days after the Confederate attack on Fort Sumter, eighteen-year-old Frank had enlisted as a private in a local company of Southern sympathizers. He had fought at the Battle of Wilson's Creek as a member of Sterling Price's Missouri State Guard, but soon thereafter contracted measles and was captured by advancing Union soldiers. In exchange for a promise not to take up arms against the Union once more, federal troops had paroled Frank, and he had returned to Clay County and signed an oath of loyalty to the United States. Yet barely one year later, the elder James brother had taken to the brush as a pro-Confederate guerrilla; by the summer of 1863, he had joined the band of partisans captained by William Clarke Quantrill. It was this final association, more than Frank James's famed criminal exploits, that drew an admiring throng to the shady grove near Blue Springs, site of the first reunion of men who had fought under the most notorious guerrilla of the entire Civil War.[2]

Quantrill's raiders were not the only irregular fighters to have stalked the Missouri-Kansas line, an area roiled by a near-decade of partisan bloodshed, but their unmatched boldness and ferocity made them its most polarizing figures. The guerrillas, as they later explained, fought for a variety of reasons: to resist the Union army and its occupation of Missouri; to defend their families and property, including slaves, against the depredations of federals and abolitionists; and to avenge the grievances wrought by such foes.[3] Critics, meanwhile, charged that such Bushwhackers unleashed terror upon enemies and innocents alike, and that wanton bloodlust, rather than principle, fueled their campaign of plunder and terror. The worst atrocity committed by Quantrill's men came on the morning of August 21, 1863, when the guerrillas descended upon the sleeping town of Lawrence, Kansas, and killed more than 150 men and boys.[4]

Thirty-five years later these self-described "terrors of the border" hardly looked the part. With his stylish clothes and patent leather shoes, Frank James, now fifty-five, looked like an operator at the local board of trade, according to one eyewitness. James had surrendered himself to Missouri governor Thomas Crittenden on October 5, 1882, but ultimately avoided conviction for any of the crimes committed by the James gang during its outlaw heyday. Crittenden's successor, John Sappington Marmaduke—himself a former Confederate general—had reportedly urged Frank to "keep out of the newspapers. Keep away from the fairs and fast horses, and to keep strictly out of sight for a year." Heeding Marmaduke's advice, the retired bandit maintained a relatively low profile, drifting between a series of jobs: shoe salesman, telegraph operator, livestock trader, horse-race starter, and doorman for a St. Louis burlesque house. In the early twentieth century, he and fellow guerrilla-cum-bandit Coleman Younger attempted to parlay their colorful past into greater fame and fortune with the staging of a short-lived traveling pageant dubbed, "The Great Cole Younger and Frank James Historical Wild West."[5] Other former members of Quantrill's band seemed every bit the prosperous, grandfatherly farmers and merchants that they had become. In the view of one observer, the old guerrillas "have buried the hatchet and are as patriotic, home-loving and peaceable a set of men as could be found anywhere." Some guerrillas, however, never made the transition to a peaceful civilian life. "Quantrell," as many contemporaries spelled it, was long dead, having been shot in Kentucky during the spring of 1865; Archie Clement and "Bloody" Bill Anderson, each renowned for his exceptional brutality, had likewise been gunned down. For those men who did attend that first reunion, the plainness of their appearance, like the banality of their postwar lives, masked a vicious history that bound them in memory.[6]

Frank James and the other Quantrill men organized the 1898 reunion as a strictly social gathering. Conceived in a spirit of nostalgic fellowship, the dinner provided an opportunity to share jokes and war stories, but its tone was to remain decidedly nonpartisan. Falling in an election year, the gathering also gave Democratic and Republican office seekers a chance to deliver stump speeches about the proper coinage of gold and silver, and the peace terms of the recently ended Spanish-American War. "The Blue Springs picnic," explained the *Kansas City Star*, "differed in nothing from the dozen other country picnics which have been held this year." It was no small coincidence, though, that the first and featured speaker was Francis M. Cockrell, a United States senator, former Confederate general, and namesake of the Warrensburg chapter of the United Daughters of the Confederacy (UDC).[7] Despite the professed intentions of that first picnic's organizers, the very gathering of those men together, assembling proudly and in public, was an inescapably political act.

The Quantrill men reunions were no ordinary country picnics, for they illuminated the complex ways that memories of the border war served at once to unify and to divide people along the Missouri-Kansas line well into the twentieth century. The quarter-century after the Civil War witnessed a tenuous reconciliation between many former antagonists in the North and the South. Union and Confederate veterans played a central role within this slow and uneven process of national reunion, which emerged from both a softening of bitter feelings and a selective remembering of the war and its meanings. For many whites, the Civil War came to represent the crucible of American Union, a triumph forged through the mutual valor and sacrifice of soldiers on both sides. Often forgotten within this celebration of American devotion was the war's other central accomplishment, the emancipation of four million African American slaves. The unfortunate eclipse of this "emancipationist" memory of the Civil War carried sweeping consequences for freed people, including the negation of civil rights won during Reconstruction and the racialized violence and segregation that came to mark the Jim Crow era.[8]

This chorus of reconciliation echoed across much of Kansas and Missouri, where white veterans exhibited both a growing willingness to forgive old foes and a general indifference toward the advancement of former slaves.⁹ Yet discordant notes also continued to ring along the long-enflamed state line. The Quantrill men reunions were at once part of and outside of this narrative of national reunion. On one hand, former guerrillas voiced patriotic sentiments like those heard at cemetery observances across America; on the other hand, they revealed that loyalties, identities, and animosities formed during the war continued to persist a half-century after its conclusion. Divisive feelings no doubt still lingered in other parts of America, but the controversy surrounding the Quantrill men reunions shows that nowhere were they as bitterly and acutely evident for such a long period of time. The animated public outcry sparked by these gatherings revealed sharp limits to the reconciliation of people once engaged in a border struggle that was so protracted, brutal, and personal.

Decades before the first Quantrill men reunion in 1898, Decoration Day had become the most well established ritual in Americans' efforts to memorialize the Civil War. Former soldiers, mobilized within fraternal associations such as the Grand Army of the Republic (GAR) and the United Confederate Veterans, gathered each spring in local cemeteries to honor the memories and decorate the graves of fallen comrades. The observance of Decoration Day, which was first organized by the GAR on May 30, 1868, spread quickly across the North. Southern men and women also marked Decoration Day, some as early as 1866, and used the occasion not only to honor those who had died but also to affirm the Confederate loyalties of those still living. The actual date of Southern observances varied by state; North and South Carolina, for example, adopted May 10 to commemorate the death of Stonewall Jackson, and several Deep South states chose April 26, the day of Johnston's surrender to Sherman.¹⁰

Decoration Day evolved by the late nineteenth century into a unifying spectacle, drawing together citizens from opposite sides of the wartime divide. Each year, innumerable Americans gathered in cemeteries to witness the poignant ritual of Union and Confederate veterans laying flowers at the graves of the war dead. These scenes played out in much of the country but were perhaps more common in border states, where the propinquity of former combatants was greatest. The powerful symbolism of such displays was impossible to miss, especially in a state as deeply divided as Missouri. "The sight of Federal soldiers decorating with flowers the graves of Confederate dead, and vice versa, against whom they had fought so hard, was often witnessed, and so great and sublime a thought was such forgiveness that it made our own petty trials sink into insignificance by comparison," wrote one Missouri editor.[11] Columbus C. Blankenbecker, a former Confederate from Bates County, Missouri, likewise stressed the value of leaving behind the violent past and instead looking forward toward a more peaceful coexistence. "When I laid down my musket I considered the war at an end," said Blankenbecker. "The past is behind us, our duty is to the future and as patriotic Americans we should turn our eyes in that direction."[12]

The expressions of friendship and forgiveness that prevailed at these inclusive reunions often depended on a carefully circumscribed memory of the war. Foremost among the potentially explosive subjects that attendees ignored were the sources of sectional tension. With slavery, secession, and the Kansas troubles taken off the table, people acknowledged the conflict in the most general terms, avoiding criticisms and sparing unseemly details of wartime hardships. Speakers typically withheld any kind of moral judgment on the righteousness of the Union or Confederate causes, except perhaps to herald the preservation of the United States of America as the war's central accomplishment. "The bitter sectional hate of a few years ago is gone," observed Reverend O. P. Shrout of Belton, Missouri. "As we thus look upon the remnant of reunited heroes of other days, we feel in our hearts that they are indeed brethren and all loyal sons of a common country."[13] From this vantage, the question of whether the North or the South had been right or wrong hardly mattered, for both sections had, in memory, been redeemed by their soldiers' mutual valor and patriotism.

Most Decoration Day addresses were largely silent about the war's other major accomplishment, the emancipation of several million slaves. To the extent that African Americans had a part in the ritual gatherings of veterans and mourners, they were usually quiet, peripheral witnesses. Such exclusion was not limited to cemeteries in Missouri and the South. Local GAR posts were racially segregated, and the city fathers of Lawrence, Kansas, typically did not invite African Americans, including the men of the all-black Sam Walker Post No. 365, to participate in Decoration Day services there. African American veterans and observers were likewise marginalized years later at the semicentennial of the Battle of Gettysburg, arguably the most publicized commemoration of the postwar period.[14]

White women, meanwhile, occupied a position of relative privilege and authority within the culture of postwar memorialization, particularly in the South. The cultivation and preservation of Civil War memory offered to women an opportunity for self-definition and empowerment not otherwise available to them in late nineteenth-century public life. In addition to decorating soldiers' graves and erecting historical monuments, Southern women, especially within the United Daughters of the Confederacy, wielded considerable cultural influence in shaping and advancing what they believed to be the "true history" of the South. In stretching the gendered spheres of postbellum society, these women assumed public roles that were deemed uncontroversial and instead heralded as expressions of uniquely feminine devotion. Many commemorations also celebrated the sacrifices and vital contributions of women during the war.[15] Quantrill's men, for example, often paused to recognize the critical support of female kinfolk, who provided the raiders with food and shelter, and helped to sustain the guerrillas in wartime. "We must not forget the good women who with their heroism, made it possible for us to live in the midst of so brutal an enemy as that with which we had to contend," said former raider Bill Gregg.[16]

Conspicuously absent from newspaper accounts of Decoration Day pageantry were the Quantrill men and other erstwhile guerrillas. Raiders who had also fought in pro-Confederate militias, such as Frank James, may have attended military reunions or paid their respects at cemeteries, but guerrilla bands were not formally recognized at Civil War observances on the Missouri side of the border. Such exclusion in part reflected regular soldiers' enduring misgivings about guerrillas. The leaders of the Confederacy had once looked upon irregular partisans with wary ambivalence, conceding those fighters' military value but scorning their undisciplined, often vicious tactics.[17] Some guerrillas noted that Quantrill had sought and obtained a military commission as a partisan ranger and that his raiders functioned as regular Confederate soldiers. Their apparent exclusion from Decoration Day observances can be explained less by doubts about those claims than by outrage among many citizens over their notorious part in the border war. For a great many Unionists and other civic leaders, no measure of postwar rehabilitation could restore the old guerrillas to equal footing with surviving veterans.[18]

Confederate veterans in Missouri, so often flanked by Union men, rarely used Decoration Day as a platform to assert their Southern loyalties in an outspoken fashion. That is not to say, however, that former rebels relinquished their pride and affinity for the defeated Confederacy, for the reunion of Quantrill's men demonstrated the durability of Lost Cause mythology. By the turn of the twentieth century, the Lost Cause had emerged as both an attitude toward the past and a conscious effort to shape the way that recent history was explained to current and future generations.

Adherents, including Quantrill's raiders, invoked a familiar Southern refrain: the supremacy of the white race; the honor of noble men who fought valiantly to defend both their homes and their people's cause; the exalted sacrifices of women who supported them; and the faithfulness of contented African American slaves.[19]

The Quantrill men reunions demonstrated that the narrative of postwar reconciliation, however popular at Decoration Day, did not win universal acceptance among old-stock Southern sympathizers. Unlike the boosters who tried to obscure painful tales of Civil War discord, many ex-Confederates worked to keep such memories alive. Mrs. N. M. Harris, a UDC member from Rich Hill, challenged the suggestion that wartime depredations ought be forgotten or at least left unsaid, and her postwar recollections instead took direct aim at the jayhawking raids of Charles Jennison, one of the most controversial Kansans of the border war. "Some contend that it serves no good purpose to chronicle such deeds of outlawry and cruelty as marked Jennison's forays," she wrote. "Why? Isn't this a part of the history of the Civil War? Does any historian spare Quantrill?"[20]

Harris's pointed question reflected a deepening frustration with what many former Confederates saw as an unfair double standard in the emerging history of the border war. Despite its tributes to the worthiness of regular soldiers, the narrative of reconciliation did not often celebrate the honor and courage of former Bushwhackers, who were instead ignored or dismissed with contempt. Some former raiders blamed Kansans and Unionists for spreading a prejudiced view of Civil War history. "Those Kansans have written all the history of Quantrell," said one retired guerrilla. "They don't know half of the facts about the man. We knew his thoughts, his intents, his cause of action. They know only his results."[21] An alternative memory of the border war thus took root among disenchanted Southern sympathizers, eager to rescue pro-Confederate partisans from the undeserved fates of historical obscurity and villainy.

The Quantrill men reunions thus became a public expression of one distinctly local flavor of Lost Cause history. The former guerrillas were living complements to the memory of the border war that had been crafted and advanced by the Missouri UDC. This "true and unbiased history," wrote one UDC member, strenuously defended Quantrill and his men by emphasizing their courage and honor—these were men who never harmed women, it was often said—and by explaining their actions as justifiable responses to plundering Kansans and Unionists.[22] This narrative of the border war was not only a self-conscious reflection of its creators' values and aspirations, but it also reflected their shifting position within Missouri society. After suffering through defeat and the indignities of the Reconstruction era, Missouri Confederates had witnessed a remarkable political comeback by the 1880s, culminating in the election of Senator Cockrell and other prominent former rebels, including Marmaduke, elected governor in 1884, and George Vest, who served in the United States Senate for twenty-four years.[23]

Amid this revival of Confederate influence, the Quantrill men and their supporters made no apology for the guerrillas' part in the border struggle. Missourians, they explained, took up arms against marauding Kansans only as a matter of self-defense. As one sympathetic editor explained it, the Bushwhackers had been mere "farmer boys" who were spurred to fight in order to avenge the cruelties perpetrated against their fathers, mothers, and sisters. Waging such a defensive war was both honorable and morally justified, according to Missouri guerrillas and other Southerners.[24] Many partisans cited the outrageous excesses of federal troops as the catalyst for their own violent actions. David George, for example, joined Quantrill's band after federal soldiers burned down his family's home; Cole Younger came aboard following his father's murder by Union troops. Blame lay not with themselves, but with menacing outsiders, whether Union soldiers or Kansas partisans, who had forced the war upon them. For the Quantrill men, the Civil War was less an abstract conflict over popular sovereignty and states' rights than it was a vengeful and deeply personalized struggle.[25]

Surviving guerrillas even framed the Lawrence massacre, one of the worst atrocities of the entire Civil War, as a defensible reaction to the prior abuses wrought by Kansans. William Gregg maintained that Quantrill's men had attacked Lawrence in 1863 to gain revenge for the litany of outrages that James Lane, Charles Jennison, and Kansas Jayhawkers had inflicted upon the state of Missouri, most notably their destruction of Osceola and other western towns in the fall of 1861. Lawrence became Quantrill's principal target because it was a "hotbed of abolitionism" and the suspected location of goods that had been plundered from Missouri homes during the sack of border communities. For Bill Gregg, justifying the murder of unarmed men and boys was an exercise of some moral and logical dexterity. The raid on Lawrence was a defensible act of war, he maintained, because "Quantrell and his men only killed soldiers in Kansas." In Gregg's estimation, "The entire male populace of Kansas were soldiers, minute men organized and equipped by the government."[26] Quantrill's men

claimed that they had descended upon the town expecting to meet a cred-
ible defense from Union soldiers or Kansas militias. Surprised that they met
so little resistance from unarmed men, just roused from bed, the guerrillas
proceeded with the attack. Decades later, they expressed little contrition
for the gruesomely one-sided slaughter of civilians. Kit Dalton described
that morning as a "terrible slaughter" and "butchery of the bloodiest sort,"
but he concluded that in light of previous provocations, the assault had
been a "just punishment." Gregg echoed such unrepentant anger, saying,
"None of us has ever regretted it." Observers could not help but note that
several of the late-summer Quantrill reunions fell on or near the anniversary of the Lawrence massacre.[27]

In addition to such sharp denials of their own culpability, ex-guerrillas
found their assumptions about the faithfulness of former slaves validated
by the attendance of three elderly African American men at several early
reunions. One account of the first reunion hailed Sam Jackson as the model
of loyal servitude. During the war, Jackson had helped his masters, the Hudspeth family, conceal and provision guerrillas in the nearby woods; when
Union soldiers destroyed the Hudspeth home under General Order No. 11,
he recovered the family Bible from the still-smoldering ruins. Another former slave, John Noland, had accompanied Quantrill as a servant and spy,
and spent several days in Lawrence to gather intelligence about the town's
defenses. Henry Wilson, the third former slave to attend the reunions,
claimed that rather than flee to freedom, he had run nonstop for several
miles to escape from federal troops and instead enlist with the Quantrill
gang, which he served as a cook and bodyguard.[28]

The Confederate army struggled with the issue of slave impressment
throughout the war. Hampered by chronic shortages of manpower, officers
called upon masters to allow their slaves to be used for military labor. Such
demands, however, often alienated masters who were unwilling to relinquish their property to a state that had been conceived for the very purpose
of upholding slaveholders' rights. The actual number of slaves who were
impressed into military service typically fell far below the number requested
by the military, a shortfall explained not only by the opposition of disaffected masters but also by the mass resistance of slaves themselves. In the
case of Quantrill's band, the masters were the very men pressing their slaves
into paramilitary service. The experiences of Noland and Smith, the former raiders maintained, were evidence that such service at times required
little coercion and was instead born of loyalty and even affection.[29]

The apparent fidelity of former slaves strengthened the aging raiders' conviction that slavery had indeed been a benign institution and a minor factor in the border struggle. Missouri slaveholders had long assured themselves that a milder, even familial form of bondage prevailed in the smaller slaveholdings of their state, in contrast to the more brutal forms of slavery that were common to the plantations of the Deep South. Retired guerrillas may have looked upon their relationships with freed slaves and believed that an antebellum social order had somehow survived both emancipation and war. Lost Cause writers often invoked the image of happy and faithful slaves in their idealized portrayals of master-slave relations. Mary Harrison Clagett captured the supposed antebellum idyll of her slaveowning family's Boone County farm, writing, "Life flowed along easily, happily and care free alike for master and slave." Mrs. J. A. B. Adcock, a fellow member of the UDC, charged that marauding outsiders upset this otherwise peaceful order. "The Kansas people and the Federal soldiers were driving the slaves to Kansas," she concluded. "The slaves, as a rule, did not want to go." The experiences of Jackson, Noland, and Wilson were an unusual counterpoint to the thousands of Missouri slaves who had seized the opportunity to gain their freedom during the Civil War, whether of their own accord or with the assistance of others. The Quantrill men's silence about the exodus of so many former slaves, along with the tensions and conflicts endemic to slaveowning households, suggested that the racial dynamics of master-slave relationships were undoubtedly more complicated than white Southerners would readily admit.[30]

For many old-stock Missourians, the retired guerrillas were also a living connection to a rural world that was steadily disappearing from parts of Jackson County. Explosive postwar growth had transformed Kansas City into the bustling fulfillment of booster dreams, a major railroad hub and a teeming cosmopolitan center of some 160,000 residents. Independence, the original county seat, was the largest neighboring town but counted fewer than 7,000 residents in 1900. The outlying towns of eastern Jackson County that hosted most of the Quantrill men reunions had witnessed remarkable growth but were mere hamlets in comparison. Blue Springs, site of the first guerrilla picnic, had but 468 inhabitants at the turn of the century. Most of the former raiders remained fixtures of these rural communities; only three men of the thirty-plus men at the first reunion were identified as residents of Kansas City.[31]

In time, the Quantrill men picnics came to exhibit the kind of effusive

Quantrill's Raiders Reunion, Independence, Missouri, 1906. *In 1906, many of the men who rode with guerrilla William Clarke Quantrill gathered for their annual reunion in Independence, Missouri. Former slave John Noland is pictured in the third row, on the right. Courtesy of the State Historical Society of Missouri*

patriotism that had drawn together Confederate and Union veterans else-where on the border. Political identity was not a strictly either-or proposi-tion, and by the early twentieth century many ex-Confederates could proudly assert their devotion as American patriots without abandoning their affinity as proud Southerners.[32] The guerrillas' inaugural reunion came just weeks after the Spanish-American War, and aging partisans were scarcely immune to the full-throated nationalism that suffused that conflict. Writ-ing at the age of seventy-one, Kit Dalton proudly explained that former ene-mies could now lay common claim to the Stars and Stripes, which he called "the most glorious flag that ever fluttered over a free and courageous peo-ple."[33] At the same time, other Quantrill men claimed that their reunion was perhaps the only place west of the Mississippi River where the Confed-erate flag still flew. The commencement of World War I brought striking changes to the annual picnic. "A Confederate flag swayed here and there," reported one Missouri paper, "while American flags were everywhere." Fol-lowing the arrival of American doughboys in Europe, some ex-raiders re-imagined a Civil War past that better conformed to America's enemy of the moment. "Of all the troops that did things to cause bitter memories in western Missouri during the Civil War, none left so many monuments of hate as the Germans," said one guerrilla. "We'd like to take a crack at the Germans for that reason."[34] For a moment at least, another foe had supplanted jayhawking Kansans as the Missourians' foremost enemy of old.

The unmistakable dissonance of the guerrilla reunions, mingling defiant anger with a yearning for conciliation, reflected the tenuous place that Quantrill's men continued to occupy along the postwar border. One Missouri newspaper found that the former guerrillas exhibited "no evidence of the old spirit" and had "successfully lived down the bad repute of years ago."[35] Observers in Lawrence, Kansas, meanwhile, regarded the old Bushwhackers in a starkly different light and received news of the guerrilla picnics with outrage and disgust. Kansans had been seeking justice against the Quantrill men, without success, ever since that fateful morning in August 1863. The *Lawrence Daily Tribune* suggested in 1869 that survivors present claims from the Quantrill raid to the United States government. After that effort came to nothing, the state of Kansas established a raid commission in 1875 that issued certificates to individuals who presented claims for damages caused by the raid. Legislators failed to appropriate state funds for such a purpose, and it wasn't until 1887, when the Kansas legislature finally approved a compensation bill, that victims were compensated, albeit at a small percentage of their claims. In 1905, former Douglas County prosecutor and raid survivor Sam Riggs suggested that the former guerrillas be returned to Kansas to face trial under indictments that had been issued in November 1863. One Lawrence editorial, though sympathetic with Riggs's idea, doubted its timing, and wrote, "Even though it would be proper, there is no chance of hanging those men who were here from Missouri for the murderous Quantrill raid. It is too late to prosecute them now."[36]

Survivors of the Lawrence Massacre came together for their first formal reunion in 1891, seven years before the inaugural Quantrill men picnic. In the years that followed, a small number of Kansans gathered to memorialize the raid's victims on each August 21. Some Lawrence residents were reluctant to organize a large formal observance, worried that the occasion might devolve into open feuding between residents who favored reconciliation and those who harbored lingering grievances against the Missourians. In 1895, the people of Lawrence erected a Citizens Monument in Oak Hill Cemetery, which they located near the mass grave of raid victims. Its inscription said it had been dedicated to the memory of "the one hundred and fifty citizens who fell defenceless victims to the inhuman ferocity of border guerrillas led by the infamous Quantrell."[37] Over the years that followed, news of the Quantrill men reunions only deepened the anger of the massacre's survivors. "The blood of the old settlers," the *Lawrence Daily Journal-World* found, "still boils when they read each year of the celebrations at Independence of the very men who shot down their friends and neighbors and relatives and burned their homes and stores."[38]

Lawrence hosted a large reunion of raid survivors in 1913 on the fiftieth anniversary of Quantrill's attack. Reunion organizers were concerned with striking the appropriate tone for the semicentennial memorial. Virtually everyone recognized the need to mark such a solemn date with proper reverence, yet some boosters also saw the occasion as a chance to celebrate the city's remarkable progress since its near-destruction a half-century earlier. More than 200 survivors participated in the reunion, with some traveling several hundred miles to return to Lawrence. Speaking at the Bowersock Opera House before an audience of several hundred people, Charles Sumner Gleed delivered memorial remarks in which he eulogized the attack's victims as "martyrs to the cause of freedom and equality." Gleed, a Lawrence businessmen whose family had settled in Lawrence after the Civil War, devoted much of his address to considering what kind of men Quantrill and his raiders had been. The guerrilla captain, he maintained, was a cruel and vile "dry-land pirate with plunder his object and murder his pastime." The raiders, meanwhile, represented "many grades of criminality." Most of the men, Gleed argued, were "thoroughly bad men, criminals by instinct, by training." Others were slightly more reputable, having thwarted the killing of innocents or refusing to commit such murders themselves. A final category included raiders who were merely innocent followers and who later became solid citizens regretful for their part in the Lawrence raid.[39]

William Elsey Connelley, secretary of the Kansas Historical Society and a Quantrill biographer, searched for traces of mercy among the guerrillas in his 1909 recounting of the attack. "Even the worst were touched with pity sometimes and showed kindness," he wrote. Connelley suggested that some raiders offered to remove furniture from the buildings that they set ablaze; others yielded to frantic pleas and spared the homes of Lawrence women. He concludes that such reports of occasional leniency were thoroughly overshadowed by the fiendish and diabolical savagery of Quantrill's men. "Frank James," he pointed out, "was as ferocious and merciless as a hyena."[40]

The *Lawrence Daily Journal-World* suggested that the semicentennial observance served to assuage some of the raw emotions that it had described just four years earlier. "The sorrows of those days live with us, and the memory of heroism cannot be allowed to perish. But the bitterness is gone," the *Journal-World* concluded. For decades, citizens in each state had called upon their neighbors to bury the hatchet, arguing that ancient partisan feuds had no place in a modern, forward-looking America. A spirit of grace and forgiveness even touched a number of Quantrill's former raiders. Tom Nolan announced at the inaugural picnic of 1898 that he would gladly take the hand of Jayhawker Charles Jennison and "shake it with cordiality," if only that notorious Kansan was still alive. Frank James reportedly said, "I believe that if we expect to be forgiven, we must forgive. They did some very bad things on the other side, but we did, too."[41] The surviving Quantrill men gave notice before the 1908 reunion that all Union veterans were welcome at the annual picnic, in order "to let the animosities engendered during the war be forgiven." Subsequent reports gave no evidence that any Union veterans were in attendance that year or in any year thereafter.[42]

The impulse toward reconciliation had its limits. The *Topeka Daily Capitol* sharply disagreed with the *Journal-World*'s assessment and found that raw grievances, now inflamed by the Quantrill men reunions, still gripped the raid's survivors in 1913. According to the Topeka paper, a number of Kansans "still would listen to a proposal to swoop down upon the reunion of the survivors of Quantrell's band, now in progress in Missouri, and wreak a belated vengeance for the blood which was shed in Lawrence fifty years ago."[43] Like the controversial reunion of aging guerrillas, the semicentennial memorial of the attack on Lawrence revealed that hard feelings endured along the Missouri-Kansas border well into the twentieth century. The moral impasse between the perpetrators and survivors of the Lawrence massacre had scarcely budged after fifty years. One Missourian marked the attack's anniversary by reportedly saying that Quantrill should have "wiped out the whole damn town." George Martin, meanwhile, voiced the sharp anger of Kansans who found the romanticized legend of noble guerrillas to be an utter lie. "The Quantrill reunions are the last wrigglings of the dying snake's tail," said Martin. "When the last Quantrill reunion is held the obliteration will be complete—there will be no more reminders of the barbarism of slavery, and Missouri and Kansas, united, will be the choicest piece of God's green earth in sentiment and right living."[44] Some of the border war's survivors, it was clear, would remain divided for as long as they were able to draw breath.

On February 18, 1915, Frank James, the celebrated outlaw and reunion organizer, died at his farm in Clay County; guerrilla captains Bill Gregg and Cole Younger passed away the following year.[45] Yet by simply surviving and assembling for so long, their white-haired, stoop-shouldered peers continued to provoke detractors. One Kansas City writer noted in 1918, "It has been so long since this band committed its outrages that the survivors could have lived down the dishonor by this time if they had gone quietly about their business and given the public a chance to forget it."[46] Despite such criticisms—or perhaps because of it—the dwindling reunions continued, even during a three-year span when just one man, George Noland, showed up. The final get-together came in August 1929, when four men, including former slave Henry Wilson, made the trip to Independence.[47]

The Quantrill men reunions had often been daylong affairs, sometimes filling an entire weekend, and that tradition continued to the end, with picnic lunches extending into long hours of visiting and then finally an evening of dancing and entertainment. The final gatherings centered as much around the guerrillas' admiring descendants as they did the few aged partisans still in attendance. For the daughters and sons of Quantrill's men, the reunions were part of the Lost Cause cultural inheritance that had been passed among Southern families since the end of the Civil War. Fifty years on, that inheritance—a determination to keep alive old stories, feelings, and loyalties, and to nurture the legend of Quantrill and his riders—had itself become a relic, as the refrain of reconciliation swept up many of the guerrillas themselves.

Yet vastly different memories of Quantrill's men persisted across the Missouri-Kansas line, tokens of an insoluble bitterness that made reconciliation ever elusive. That such reunion came more slowly and unevenly there than elsewhere in America affirms the terrible sweep of a guerrilla conflict that quite literally pitted neighbor against neighbor. The border war blurred, and sometimes destroyed, the distinctions between the battlefield and home front, as well as those between combatants and civilians. From such ambiguity came not only the extraordinary devastation wrought by war but also the fierce contest for the social memory of the border war that was waged by its survivors over the ensuing decades. A half century later, that contest was yet unresolved, a sign that the dying embers of the border war were not yet fully extinguished.[48]

Chapter 15

"William Quantrill Is My Homeboy": Or, The Border War Goes to College

Jennifer L. Weber

In a nation besotted with college athletics, the University of Missouri and the University of Kansas share a mythology unique in sports. Their rivalry goes beyond the bounds of traditional college contests, according to modern-day sports journalists, university publicity departments, and fans. Whether on the football field or basketball court, their competitions actually are the sublimation of historical antagonisms, a peaceful way to act out hostilities that began in the violence of Bleeding Kansas in the 1850s—or so today's followers would have us think. Modern-day observers have come to believe that the encounters between the two schools are so intense, so historically predetermined, that the rivalry bears a name that is itself drawn from the Civil War era: the Border War.

It's a marvelous, meaty, historically appealing story. There's just one problem. It is not true. To the contrary, "The Border War," with a capital "T," is a relatively recent moniker that emerged in the 1990s and was adopted officially by the two schools as a marketing gimmick in 2002 and gained broad acceptance in the mid-2000s, when both schools fielded nationally ranked football teams. The story of The Border War as a sports phenomenon is a lesson in historical memory, how quickly it can be shaped and transformed, and how eagerly the public will grab onto a good history story, regardless of its accuracy.

Kansas and Missouri first met on the gridiron in 1891, making theirs the oldest Division I college rivalry west of the Mississippi River. The names of both teams had historical roots. Kansas had taken the name of the Jayhawkers in honor of the antislavery forces, a.k.a. guerrillas, during the Bleeding Kansas period and the Civil War. The name was later shortened to the Jayhawks, which combined the names of two birds: the blue jay, "a noisy, quarrelsome thing known to rob other nests," and the sparrow

259

hawk, "a stealthy hunter," according to KU's web site. "The message here: Don't turn your back on this bird." The school's hometown, Lawrence, had been at the center of Kansas' free-state movement in the 1850s, which had brought all kinds of heartbreak on the community during the Bleeding Kansas and Civil War periods. Founded in 1854 by the abolitionist New England Emigrant Aid Company, the city was such a potent symbol of the antislavery movement that it was sacked twice. In May 1856, Douglas County proslavery sheriff Samuel J. Jones led a posse into Lawrence—the county seat—that burned the Free-State Hotel (one man died there from a stone falling from the building), ruined the equipment of two antislavery newspapers, and looted several other businesses. Seven years later, in August 1863, William Quantrill's Confederate guerrillas burned most of the businesses in Lawrence and about 185 homes in four hours, and killed an estimated 150 to 200 men and boys in an event that came to be known as the Lawrence Massacre. These events so scarred the town that it still observes the anniversary of Quantrill's raid each year, uses an image of flames rising like a phoenix from a building as its crest, and has adopted "from ashes to immortality" as the city motto. The university itself, however, had no direct Civil War connection, having opened in 1866, a year after the war ended.[1]

The University of Missouri has a more obvious tie to the Border War era. It was founded in 1839, and its second president, James Shannon, spent the summer of 1855—the year after the Kansas-Nebraska Act—touring Missouri and making speeches that justified slavery by citing the Bible and natural law. The federal government, he argued, did not have the authority to ban slavery from the territories, and he went so far as to encourage Missourians to invade Kansas to guarantee that the peculiar institution would extend to the new territory. Eight months after the Civil War broke out, federal forces occupied the University Building, the main academic structure on campus, and turned part of it into a prison for people who would not or could not prove their fealty to the United States. After Major General Henry Halleck announced that the university's board and faculty members had to take a loyalty oath, two professors resigned and joined the Confederate army. The military takeover of the campus, meanwhile, was nearly total. Officers used President Benjamin B. Minor's official residence as their headquarters after the Board of Curators ordered him to evacuate the home, the grammar school was converted into a hospital, and the grounds were turned into a giant corral for military horses. During the occupation, the fence around the campus was torn down, the landscaping destroyed, and building fixtures broken. Soldiers were blamed for stealing 467 library books and destroying scientific apparatus. In all, a curators' committee determined that before leaving in mid-August 1863, the military had inflicted more than $3,000 damage to the university, a figure that university historian Frank F. Stephens says was "probably a gross understatement."[2]

Columbia was a town with divided loyalties during the war, but it was the militia unit that held off Confederate General Sterling Price's forces that inspired the school to adopt the tiger as its mascot. In early 1864, many of the Union troops in Missouri were ordered east or south to reinforce the federal war effort outside of Missouri. Seeing an opportunity, Price responded by moving from Arkansas into Missouri in the late summer and fall of 1864. After abandoning his original plan to attack St. Louis, Price targeted Jefferson City in central Missouri, but veered toward Boone County instead after learning of how heavily fortified the capital city was. In Columbia, every man who was physically able had been drafted into the local militia, the Columbia Tigers. Heavily armed and supported by cavalry troops out of Iowa, the city deterred an attack. Price headed west, which ultimately led him to the battle at Westport, Missouri, and the doom of his army.[3]

A generation passed before the two universities met in Kansas City, Missouri, for their inaugural football game. College football was beginning to broaden its appeal in the 1890s. The first college game had been in 1869, between Princeton and Rutgers, and football had remained largely an East Coast game dominated by the elite colleges and universities that now populate the Ivy League. Football grew increasingly attractive to Americans as worries increased about the state of masculinity. The growth of white-collar jobs, work done by machines, and the closing of the frontier caused many to fret that Americans' interest in violent sports rose as an antidote for their anxieties. Athletics also came to be seen as a peacetime alternative for war and a way to imbue men with qualities—competitiveness, teamwork—they would use throughout their lives, historian Anthony Rotundo points out. Boxing, which became a vehicle out of poverty for immigrants, poor whites, and African Americans, enjoyed wide popularity. So did football, although its participants tended to be from the more elite classes of society, higher education still being out of reach of most Americans. Woodrow Wilson and Theodore Roosevelt advocated the sport. From its earliest days, football was brutal and bloody. Eighteen players died of injuries suffered on the field in 1905, thirteen in 1908, and twenty-six in 1909, including ten at the college level. This prompted some college administrators to ban the game on campus (TR summoned the presidents of Harvard, Princeton, and Yale to the White House and told them to modify the game before Harvard did away with its team) and others to try to protect players with pads, helmets, and stricter rules. The ideal balance between onlookers' bloodlust and the well-being of the players is one that still eludes those who make the rules on both the professional and college levels.[4]

Each school had fielded a football team for only about a year when the first Kansas-Missouri game was held in Kansas City over Thanksgiving weekend in 1891. Both the timing and the location were meant for more than the convenience of the fans, historian John Sayle Watterson says. Having the game over a holiday weekend in the biggest city between the two schools was a choice designed to bring the largest turnout and generate maximum revenue.[5] (As with safety, money has long been a point of controversy in college football.) The inaugural meeting, which Kansas won, 22–8, drew a crowd of 3,000, but outside of the Kansas City area the game attracted little attention. The *Abilene Weekly Reflector*, for instance, covered the contest in a single sentence—not even a headline—in the bottom right corner of the newspaper's last page: "The Kansas university beat the Missouri team at football at Kansas City, Mo." What are now the Ivy League schools, and particularly the programs at Harvard, Princeton, and Yale, dominated college football, and their games drew considerably more coverage than Missouri and Kansas in papers in both states. The disproportional coverage of Ivy League teams over local "elevens," as they were called, remained true the next year, when *The Iola Register* reported that 6,000 people turned out to see Kansas beat Missouri, 12–4, in the "grandest struggle for football honors that was ever seen in the west." Along with a very brief account of the game, which also featured overzealous fans crowding onto the field, the story devoted a significant amount of space to the fact that the referee, a man named Cornell, was a Harvard graduate, and the umpire was "a Williams man." By the third meeting, where Missouri "finally down[ed] the haughty Kansans," 12–4, the competition was clearly established. Unlike football games elsewhere, this particular one was "reasonably free from slugging," the *Kansas City Times* reported, while Kansas City police and a squad of Pinkerton agents kept the crowd under control. Even so, one has to wonder whether Kansas and Missouri were the main attractions. The stands for this game featured special sections for alumni of Harvard, Princeton, and Yale, each area bedecked in the colors for those schools, while "what space that was left . . . was occupied by friends and followers of the contesting teams," according to the *Times*.[6]

Although the MU-KU meetings did not attract nearly the press that they would a century later, these early clashes on the football field have sparked tremendous historical imagination among some in the modern-day press booth. Blair Kerkhoff of the *Kansas City Star* has covered the rivalry extensively in his years with the paper and by his own account is "fascinated by the subject." More than any other single journalist, he seems to have done most to advance the story line in the 1990s and early 2000s that The Border War matchup was an extension of nineteenth-century animosity. In a lengthy article in 2007 about the history of The Border War, for instance, he explained that the hostilities between the two states "date to pre–Civil War days and involve the issues that tore apart a nation," and he speculated that "there had to have been direct descendents of the chaos sitting among the 3,000 at Kansas City's Exposition Park in 1891," at that first game. Bad feelings may have existed between the two states, but they seem not to have made their way onto the playing fields, at least not according to contemporary accounts.[7]

The lack of early references to the actual border war is not to suggest that the two schools were not highly competitive, even at the beginning of the rivalry. The schools' meetings were so intense by 1895 that Missouri's yearbook said that "Missouri and Kansas are rivals in so many things that each would rather defeat the other than gain victories over all the rest of the world." The rivalry was so established by 1900 that the alternative student newspaper at MU called the football matchup with KU "The Great Game." The significance of the matchup was evident six years later when the same student previewed that year's contest: "Missouri and Kansas are putting on the gloves, figuratively speaking, for their great annual battle in Kansas City," the *Independent* said, and it suggested a special ferocity to this game when it reported that every Missouri player was "ready to put up the fight of his life." After that particular encounter, in which neither team scored, the *Kansas City Journal* splashed this headline across its front page: "Missouri-Kansas Record: No Dead, No Score; No Injured, No Red Cross; Simply Mud."[8]

Context here is important, though. While the Kansas-Missouri matchups may have been intense, each school had other rivals that for many years were equally important: Kansas with Kansas State University, the first university in the state, though not the flagship; and Missouri with Washington University until the St. Louis school refused to play any more and then with the universities of Iowa, Nebraska, and Oklahoma. These other rivalries are important to note not just for their own sakes but also to underscore the fact that neither KU nor Mizzou regarded their competition as having any historical roots outside of athletics. Indeed, the first time that Missouri's yearbook, the *Savitar*, referred to a "border war" was in 1995, and the opponent was Illinois.[9]

For decades, the Missouri-Kansas rivalry seemed to play out along the lines of any other memorable college matchup (think Army-Navy, Harvard-Yale, Stanford-Cal, Ohio State–Michigan). The opponents had a special traveling trophy that went to the winner of the football game each year. For MU and KU, this tradition began in the mid-1930s (dates vary from 1935 to 1937). Interest in the annual faceoff had been declining for some time because of the Depression and the Tigers' lack of success on the field. The trophy was a war drum that supposedly had been crafted by the Osage Indians, who had long roamed the area that became Kansas and Missouri. It was a romantic story, but untrue. The drum was from a pawnshop in Kansas City, Missouri. When it was lost in the 1980s, Taos Indians from New Mexico replaced it. (The original was discovered in the basement of Read Hall at MU and is now in the College Football Hall of Fame.) The Taos drum has since been replaced with a standard-issue snare drum.[10]

Football may have been where the rivalry began and where it remained most intense, but the competition between Kansas and Missouri spilled into other endeavors, including debate, women's sports, and athletic competitions that attracted smaller audiences and less money. Even charity got involved, as the two schools engaged in the early 2000s in a "Border Hunger Showdown" to see which university could collect more food for the needy. After football, though, the KU-MU fight played out most prominently over the years on the basketball court. The first men's hoops matchup between the two schools was in 1907, sixteen years after Kansas coach James Naismith had invented the game in Springfield, Massachusetts, and nine years after KU fielded its first men's team. And it was a basketball coach, KU's legendary Forrest "Phog" Allen, who is the first coach on record who was willing to twist history to inspire a player. Allen took aside one of his key players, Tusten Ackerman, during a game in 1923. He knew that as a boy Ackerman had idolized KU's first great football player,

Tommy Johnson, who had died in 1912. Two years before Johnson's death, a pair of Missouri players had delivered a "vicious hit" on him during a game. There was never any evidence that any connection existed between that hit and Johnson's death, but Allen told Ackerman: "I thought they had done Tommy Johnson wrong. Tonight, you're Tommy Johnson." Ackerman bit on Allen's fable and scored a game-high 11 points.[11]

Partly because of the crowd's proximity to the court, basketball games seemed to be where the most frightening clashes between the two schools took place. In 1951, Missouri's basketball coach, Sparky Stalcup, prevented angry partisans from starting a large fight after a Jayhawk player stepped on the stomach of a Missouri guard. The referee ejected the Kansan, but the Tigers in the crowd would not be placated. Finally Stalcup stepped up to a microphone, commended KU's Phog Allen on his coaching, and inspired his own players to make peace spontaneously with the Jayhawk team. Norm Stewart, who would later coach Missouri's basketball team, recalled that in his own days on the team in the mid-1950s, Tigers would run through the Allen Fieldhouse before games with Kansas to practice ducking cans and other objects that Jayhawk fans would throw at them. In the fall of 1960, the KU football team had beaten Mizzou, which to that point had been ranked No. 1 in the country. The loss ended MU's chance at a national title. Then officials discovered that the Jayhawks' running back had violated NCAA rules by accepting a plane ticket. Kansas fans suspected that someone at Missouri had discovered this and reported it as a way of getting back at KU. At the basketball game the following March, the benches of both teams cleared in a wild fight that featured punching, kicking, and wrestling and drew hundreds of fans onto the floor of Missouri's field house. By beating the Jayhawks, 79–76, the Tigers robbed KU of its shot at a conference title and ended a ten-game winning streak that KU hoopsters had begun in 1959.[12]

Judging the historical importance of that game is difficult. Did it mark the end of a gentler era, or was it an anomaly more in line with the 1951 episode? Were the objects flying at the Mizzou players in mid-decade something new, a harbinger of what was to come? That is murky from this distance, but the 1960s certainly marked the time when what had been mostly a civil rivalry began to degenerate into pure animosity. The coaches bear much of the blame for this trend. Consider, for instance, that in 1952, Mizzou's football coach, Don Faurot, whose team had just edged out Kansas, 20–19, adopted a humble tone when he told reporters: "We are happy to win, but it's no discredit to Kansas. The Jayhawks lost [two players], and that hurt. If we lost [two] from our backfield, picture our position." This sportsmanlike statement was typical for coaches for most of the twentieth century. Compare that, then, with the 1969 gridiron matchup of the two teams. Before the game, Jayhawk coach Pepper Rodgers had bad-mouthed Mizzou's Dan Devine in an interview with *Sports Illustrated*. After MU won that game 69–21, "I gave Dan the peace sign and got half of it back," Rodgers said. Devine denied that he had flipped off Rodgers and added that his own fans were upset that he hadn't rolled up the score to an even 70. In 1995, Kansas threw a touchdown pass with 88 seconds left in the game, despite its already dominating, 42–23. Furious, Missouri coach Larry Smith "offered a one-armed salute" to KU's Glen Mason. "Good," Mason told reporters. "Maybe this is getting to be a heated rivalry again." Note, however, that nothing the coaches said had any sort of historical reference, and certainly not to the 1850s or 1860s. In basketball, meanwhile, Norm Stewart, who had become a coaching legend, famously hated Kansas to the point that he would not spend a penny in the state. Whenever his team faced the Jayhawks they spent the night before in Kansas City, Missouri, and gassed up the bus before crossing the state line.[13]

Don Fambrough, who coached Kansas football from 1971 to 1974 and 1979 to 1982, appears to have been the first person to introduce historical memory into the rivalry. For him, there was never a moment when the rivalry was anything but white-hot. "I dislike 'em," he told a reporter, "and I don't give a damn who knows it." Like Stewart, he did not like to cross the state line, even refusing to see a recommended surgeon in Missouri. "I wouldn't go," he said. "I'd rather die. I'd rather die than have some Missouri bastard cut on me." He was well known for his annual pep talk to the football team before games. By the early twenty-first century, his message went about like this: "It's (expletive) war! They started the war! They sent that (expletive) (William) Quantrill over here! That (expletive) killed all the men, raped all the women, burned the town down!" He once told the team that Quantrill was a Missouri graduate, although that was not true. He was amused when the history department objected to his interpretation and promised to leave history to the historians. But he did not.[14]

Despite Fambrough's analysis, the historical angle to the rivalry did not seep into the popular imagination until the 1990s. The earliest mention of a "border war" between the two schools appeared in 1990, and it showed up in two venues. One was *Sports Illustrated*, which mentioned the Civil

War experience as a backdrop for the modern rivalry. But the reference was brief and oddly light-hearted as the reporter described the 1863 attack on KU's home town this way: "Quantrill's Raiders—now we're talkin' serious woofing—slam-dunked across the border from Missouri and burned Lawrence to the ground." The other reference, in the *Kansas City Star*, was even more brief, as Kerkhoff wrote that the hoops "battle for the nation's No. 1 ranking boils down to a border war" between the two schools. But the notion of this being a rivalry that always had historical roots did not take hold until the middle of that decade. It is hard to know quite why that is, but it may be the interest that Kerkhoff has in history. In his years with the *Kansas City Star*, he has written repeatedly about both the historical and the more sports-oriented Border Wars and claimed that history has infected the rivalry. For the 1995 meeting, for instance, his lead referred to the matchup as the "104th Border War." By about 1997, there is considerable evidence that both sides began to regard the animosity as being historically predetermined. The periodization squares with the memories of Erik Ashel, who would later produce a documentary about the football game:

> I grew up loving Kansas and hating Missouri, but until I got to KU in the fall of 1996, I never really knew why. I figured proximity was probably the best explanation for the animosity. I was only half right. When you get to Lawrence, just as I assume is the case when you arrive in Columbia, it doesn't take long to be indoctrinated into the bitter feud that existed prior to either university.[15]

The open animus of the coaches and the appeal of this being a rivalry with deep historical roots infected the fans. For many, what had been a standard athletic rivalry with great sportsmanship was replaced by a historically determined hatred of the opposition. The 1996 Missouri yearbook, for instance, wrote about the Jayhawks as the Tigers' "hated rival," even as it described the annual gridiron meeting as "a classic." The new, hardened attitude left older observers puzzled. Van Robinson played football for the Tigers in 1944. He was shocked when he attended a Missouri-Kansas game in the early 2000s and encountered considerable hostility on the part of KU fans toward Missouri. "This was stuff I never heard when I was playing," he said. He was especially offended by Jayhawks wearing T-shirts that said, "Muck Fizzou." Bewildered, someone in his group finally asked a

Kansas fan why they were so angry. "Because you had slaves," the man said. Robinson said he thought, "My god, they're living in the 19th century. What's going on?"[16]

In 2002 the two schools decided to declare war officially. They adopted "The Border War" as the formal title of almost every athletic meeting and established a Border War Series. This awarded points to each school for winning head-to-head contests in baseball, basketball, football, soccer, softball, women's swimming, women's tennis, and volleyball. More points would accrue to whichever school's cross-country, golf, or track team finished higher at Big 12 championship events. Bonus points were given for postseason competitions that involved the two universities.

This was about more than sports, however. The institutions had figured out a way to exploit the competition financially. The Midwest Ford Dealers paid to underwrite the new program, in which a traveling trophy was awarded, and the schools could collect royalties on "The Border War" for every T-shirt or other item with the term. As has been the case since the early days of college sports, the universities found a new way to generate revenue from their teams. This was not even the first time one of these two schools in particular had capitalized on their rivalry to boost income. Missouri had used the opportunity of the 1911 meeting of the teams to invite its alumni to come back and attend the game. One of the great benefits of homecomings, of course, is that they tend to prompt nostalgic alumni to give money to the institution.[17]

Two years later, however, the schools backed off the phrase in favor of "The Border Showdown." In a perplexing statement, given that "The Border War" had been adopted after the September 11 terrorist attacks, KU athletic director Lew Perkins said, "We feel that in the aftermath of September 11, 2001, and the ensuing events around the world, it is inappropriate to use the term 'war' to describe intercollegiate athletics events." Ashel, the television producer and KU alumnus, decried the "political correctness" that led the schools to rename the rivalry, writing: "If any series deserves to be called a 'war,' it's this one. A rivalry with so much meaning to so many people needs a name that represents its level of historical importance." And then Ashel quoted former Kansas coach "and legendary Missouri hater" Fambrough in saying, "Border Showdown sounds like we're going to a tea party . . . not a football game."[18]

"The Border Showdown" has never taken hold in the public imagination, though. In 2007, the Jayhawks were ranked No. 2 nationally and the

Tigers No. 3 by the time the teams faced off in late November. For the first time, the rivalry gained national attention, and "The Border War" was a great hook for the sports media. Bewildered by an antagonism that was just coming to his notice, a *Sports Illustrated* writer interviewed two of his colleagues—one a Jayhawk, the other a Tiger—about the contest. Once again, history appeared to be at the bottom of the hostility. "It's more than the schools," supervising producer and KU grad Dan George said, "it's a state thing going back to the Civil War, when William Quantrill's Confederate guerrillas burned Lawrence and murdered nearly 200 people. Neither Missouri nor Kansas folks have forgotten it. As the saying goes, the only good thing to come out of Missouri is I-70." When asked what he would do if the hated Jayhawks won the national title, Adam Levine, SI.com's executive editor, also hearkened back to the mid-nineteenth century. He said he would "lead a war party down to Lawrence and burn that mother down."[19]

With the two football teams performing so well and with such an appealing peg, the media could not stop themselves from drawing dramatic connections between the athletic Border War and the historical one. "Digital bushwhackers and jayhawkers" still fought, the *Kansas City Star* wrote, just without bullets. Now they were using "today's fan weapon of choice—keyboard strokes and the 'send' button." Metro Sports, Kansas City's local sports station, was graver in its approach. "Kansas is no longer a matter of life and death, although to the fans of these two schools, it definitely feels like it," intoned the promotional material for a documentary about the rivalry. This competition is "one of the most heated and historically significant rivalries in all of sports," according to Metro Sports, which produced the film. The hyperbolic tone continued as the anonymous writer claimed that the KU-MU game was "the only American college rivalry derived from actual warfare."[20]

T-shirt vendors helped bring considerable attention to the game through their questionable taste. Now Missouri fans could wear a top that featured a photo of William Quantrill and said "Quantrill Is My Homeboy." Another unlicensed tee showed Lawrence in flames with the word "Scoreboard" and the Tigers' logo underneath. On the back was Quantrill's slogan: "Raise the black flag and ride hard, boys. Our cause is just and our enemies many." The shirt drew attention from across the country, most of it negative. "Talk about going straight past normal levels of fan behavior and making a hard right turn into loony land, that might be the single most offensive game day t-shirt I've ever seen," AOL News blogger Nathan

Fowler wrote in a piece called "We Burned Your Town to the Ground!" Kansas supporters struck back with their own unlicensed shirts featuring John Steuart Curry's depiction of John Brown that said "Kansas: Keeping America Safe from Missouri since 1854." The sartorial imbroglio made Fowler worry what might happen on game day.

> This game is going to be played on a neutral site at Arrowhead Stadium in Kansas City—home to huge parking lots for tailgating and beer sales in the stadium during the game. It's going to be for a berth in the Big XII Championship Game at the very least, and a shot at the National Championship at the most. Liquored up fans sharing the same parking lots and stadium, some who are celebrating their history of brutal violence against each other? Two fan bases who hate each other, with the chance to not only continue their own dream season but also to end the chance of glory for their rivals? Yeah, no way that doesn't end up without at least a few folks in the slammer. It's going to be a fun Saturday for the KCPD and Jackson County Sheriffs.[21]

Happily, his fears of serious trouble did not bear out, but his concern underscored how the rivalry had transformed into something nearly out of control.

Three years and three more hard games on the gridiron did nothing to ease tensions, at least among the players. As the football teams geared up for their annual meeting, the *Kansas City Star* quoted Missouri's safety Jarrell Harrison as saying, "There's hate within that rivalry. They don't want to see us succeed. We don't want to see them succeed. They want to spoil our season. They don't want us to go to any big bowl game." MU coach Gary Pinkel tried to turn down the rhetoric, saying, "Certainly, we don't teach hate."[22]

By 2011, the historical demonization of each side by the other was complete. Convinced that the athletic "Border War" indeed represented the modern extension of the hostilities of the 1850s, the aldermen of Osceola, Missouri, adopted a resolution in September demanding that the University of Kansas drop "Jayhawk" as its name and mascot. Commemorating the 150th anniversary of a raid by Kansans that left the town in ruins, the board of aldermen condemned "the celebration of this murderous gang of terrorists by an institution of 'higher education' in such a brazen and malicious manner." The resolution called on Missouri residents to stop capitalizing

University of Kansas Students, Allen Field House, 2009. *University of Kansas students displayed an enlarged (and modified) version of John Steuart Curry's "Tragic Prelude" mural, featuring abolitionist John Brown holding the 2008 National Championship trophy instead of a rifle, during a 90–65 basketball victory over the University of Missouri at Allen Fieldhouse in 2009. Photo Nick Krug. Courtesy of the* Lawrence Journal-World

Kansas or KU, as "neither is a proper name or a proper place." And it asked the University of Missouri to make the public more aware of the broader history of the border war beyond Quantrill's raid. The aldermen noted that during the attack on Lawrence, many guerrillas shouted "Remember Osceola!" "I don't expect [KU] to do anything," said Rick Reed, who introduced the resolution. "They are so arrogant and uppity."[23]

Though both schools reveled in the rivalry for decades, the contest is now dormant and perhaps dead. When Missouri left the conference it had shared with Kansas since 1907 and joined the Southeastern Conference in 2012, the Jayhawks announced they would no longer compete with the Tigers, even in nonconference games. Kansas was not particularly gracious in sending off its old adversary. The school's public relations office posted this online through @KUNews: "Missouri forfeits a century old rivalry. We win."[24]

Kansas vs. Missouri Football

Date	Location	Winner	Score
1891—October 31	(at KC)	KU	22–8
1892—November 26	(at KC)	KU	12–4
1893—November 30	(at KC)	MU	4–12
1894—November 31	(at KC)	KU	18–12
1895—November 28	(at KC)	MU	6–10
1896—November 26	(at KC)	KU	30–0
1897—November 25	(at KC)	KU	16–0
1898—November 24	(at KC)	KU	12–0
1899—November 30	(at KC)	KU	24–6
1900—November 29	(at KC)	Tie	6–6
1901—November 28	(at KC)	MU	12–18
1902—November 27	(at KC)	KU	17–5
1903—November 26	(at KC)	KU	5–0
1904—November 24	(at KC)	KU	29–0
1905—November 30	(at KC)	KU	24–0
1906—November 29	(at KC)	Tie	0–0
1907—November 28	(at St. Joseph)	KU	4–0
1908—November 26	(at KC)	KU	10–4
1909—November 26	(at KC)	MU	6–12
1910—November 24	(at KC)	Tie	5–5
1911—November 23	at Kansas	Tie	3–3
1912—November 23	at Kansas	KU	12–3
1913—November 22	at Missouri	MU	0–3
1914—November 21	at Kansas	MU	7–10
1915—November 27	at Missouri	KU	8–6
1916—November 30	at Kansas	MU	0–13
1917—November 29	at Kansas	KU	27–3
1918*			
1919—November 29	at Kansas	MU	6–3
1920—November 27	at Missouri	MU	7–16
1921—November 24	at Kansas	KU	15–9
1922—November 30	at Missouri	MU	7–9
1923—November 29	at Kansas	Tie	3–3
1924—November 27	at Missouri	MU	0–14
1925—November 21	at Kansas	KU	10–7
1926—November 20	at Missouri	MU	0–15
1927—November 19	at Kansas	KU	14–7
1928—November 24	at Missouri	MU	6–25

1929—November 23	at Kansas	MU	0–7
1930—November 22	at Missouri	KU	22–0
1931—November 21	at Kansas	KU	14–0
1932—November 12	at Missouri	KU	7–0
1933—November 30	at Kansas	KU	27–0
1934—November 29	at Missouri	KU	20–0
1935—November 28	at Kansas	Tie	0–0
1936—November 26	at Missouri	MU	3–19
1937—November 25	at Kansas	Tie	0–0
1938—November 25	at Missouri	MU	7–13
1939—November 25	at Kansas	MU	0–20
1940—November 21	at Missouri	MU	20–45
1941—November 22	at Kansas	MU	6–45
1942—November 26	at Missouri	MU	13–42
1943—November 20	at Kansas	KU	7–6
1944—November 23	at Kansas	MU	0–28
1945—November 24	at Kansas	MU	12–33
1946—November 28	at Missouri	KU	20–19
1947—November 22	at Kansas	KU	20–14
1948—November 25	at Missouri	MU	7–21
1949—November 19	at Kansas	MU	28–34
1950—November 23	at Missouri	MU	6–20
1951—December 1	at Kansas	KU	41–28
1952—November 22	at Missouri	MU	19–20
1953—November 21	at Kansas	MU	6–10
1954—November 20	at Kansas	MU	18–41
1955—November 19	at Kansas	KU	13–7
1956—December 1	at Missouri	MU	13–15
1957—November 23	at Kansas	KU	9–7
1958—November 22	at Missouri	Tie	13–13
1959—November 21	at Kansas	MU	9–13
1960**—November 19	at Missouri	KU	23–3
1961—November 25	at Kansas	MU	7–10
1962—November 24	at Missouri	Tie	3–3
1963—November 30	at Kansas	MU	7–9
1964—November 21	at Missouri	MU	14–34
1965—November 20	at Kansas	MU	20–44
1966—November 19	at Missouri	MU	0–7
1967—November 25	at Kansas	KU	17–6
1968—November 23	at Kansas	KU	21–19

(continued)

Kansas vs. Missouri Football (continued)

Date	Location	Winner	Score
1969—November 22	at Kansas	MU	21–69
1970—November 21	at Missouri	MU	17–28
1971—November 20	at Kansas	KU	7–2
1972—November 25	at Missouri	KU	28–17
1973—November 24	at Kansas	KU	14–13
1974—November 23	at Missouri	MU	3–27
1975—November 22	at Kansas	KU	42–24
1976—November 20	at Missouri	KU	41–14
1977—November 19	at Kansas	KU	24–22
1978—November 11	at Missouri	MU	0–48
1979—November 22	at Kansas	MU	7–55
1980—November 22	at Missouri	MU	6–31
1981—November 21	at Kansas	KU	19–11
1982—November 20	at Missouri	MU	10–16
1983—November 19	at Kansas	KU	37–27
1984—November 17	at Missouri	KU	35–21
1985—November 23	at Kansas	KU	34–20
1986—November 22	at Missouri	MU	0–48
1987—November 21	at Missouri	MU	7–19
1988—November 19	at Kansas	MU	17–55
1989—November 18	at Missouri	KU	46–44
1990—November 17	at Kansas	MU	21–41
1991—November 23	at Kansas	KU	53–29
1992—November 21	at Missouri	MU	17–22
1993—November 20	at Kansas	KU	28–10
1994—November 19	at Missouri	KU	41–31
1995—November 4	at Kansas	KU	42–23
1996—November 23	at Missouri	MU	25–42
1997—September 13	at Kansas	KU	15–7
1998—September 12	at Missouri	MU	23–41
1999—October 23	at Kansas	KU	21–0
2000—October 14	at Missouri	KU	38–17
2001—October 20	at Kansas	MU	34–38
2002—October 26	at Missouri	MU	12–36
2003—September 27	at Kansas	KU	35–14
2004—November 20	at Missouri	KU	31–14
2005—October 29	at Kansas	KU	13–3
2006—November 25	at Missouri	MU	14–42

2007—November 24	(at KC)	MU	28–36
2008—November 28	(at KC)	KU	40–37
2009—November 28	(at KC)	MU	39–41

*Season shortened because of influenza outbreak
**KU later had to forfeit because of an ineligible player

NOTES

Introduction

1. William Elsey Connelley, *Quantrill and the Border Wars: The Story of the Border* (Cedar Rapids, Iowa: Torch Press, 1910), 288.

2. John Edwards, *Noted Guerrillas, or The Warfare on the Border* (St. Louis: Bryan, Brand, 1877); T. Coleman Younger, *The Story of Cole Younger, by Himself* (1903); Wiley Britton, *The Civil War on the Border: A Narrative of Operations in Missouri, Kansas, Arkansas, and Indian Territory during the Years, 1861–62* (New York: J. P. Putnam's Sons, 1891); Connelley, *Quantrill and the Border Wars*; Charles Robinson, *The Kansas Conflict, 1892* (Lawrence: Journal Publishing, 1898).

3. Richard Brownlee, *Gray Ghosts of the Confederacy: Guerrilla Warfare in the West, 1861–1865* (Baton Rouge: Louisiana State University Press, 1958); Albert Castel, *William Clarke Quantrill: His Life and Times* (New York: Frederick Fell, Inc., 1962); Albert Castel, *A Frontier State at War: Kansas, 1861–1865* (Ithaca: Cornell University Press, 1958); Albert Castel, "Order No. 11 and the Civil War on the Border," *Missouri Historical Review* 54, no. 4 (1963); Albert Castel, *General Sterling Price and the Civil War in the West* (Baton Rouge: Louisiana State University Press, 1968); Jay Monaghan, *Civil War on the Western Border, 1854–1865* (Boston: Little, Brown, and Co., 1955); Allen Crafton, *Free State Fortress: The First Ten Years of the History of Lawrence, Kansas* (Lawrence: World Co., 1954); Alice Nichols, *Bleeding Kansas* (New York: Oxford University Press, 1954); William Parrish, *Turbulent Partnership: Missouri and the Union, 1861–1865* (Columbia: University of Missouri Press, 1963); Thomas Goodrich, *Bloody Dawn: The Story of the Lawrence Massacre* (Kent, Ohio: Kent State University Press, 1991); Donald Gilmore, *Civil War on the Missouri/Kansas Border* (Gretna, La.: Pelican Press, 2006); Thomas Goodrich, *Black Flag: Guerrilla Warfare on the Western Border, 1861–1865* (Bloomington: Indiana University Press, 1995); Edward Leslie, *The Devil Knows How to Ride: The True Story of William Clarke Quantrill and His Confederate Raiders* (New York: Random House, 1996); Albert Castel and Thomas Goodrich, *Bloody Bill Anderson: The Short, Savage Life of a Civil War Guerrilla* (Mechanicsburg, Pa.: Stackpole Books, 1998); O. S. Barton, *Three Years with Quantrill: A True Story Told by His Scout, John McCorkle*

277

278 Notes to Pages 6–12

(Norman: University of Oklahoma Press, 1992); Thomas Goodrich, *War to the Knife: Bleeding Kansas, 1854–1861* (Lincoln: University of Nebraska Press, 2006).

4. Michael Fellman, *Inside War: The Guerrilla Conflict in Missouri during the Civil War* (New York: Oxford University Press, 1990).

5. Nicole Etcheson, *Bleeding Kansas: Contested Liberty in the Civil War Era* (Lawrence: University Press of Kansas, 2006); Jonathan Earle, *Jacksonian Antislavery and the Politics of Free Soil* (Chapel Hill: University of North Carolina Press, 2004); Jonathan Earle, *John Brown's Raid: A Brief History with Documents* (New York: Bedford St. Martins, 2008); Tony R. Mullis, *Peacekeeping on the Plains: Army Operations in Bleeding Kansas* (Columbia: University of Missouri Press, 2004).

6. Daniel Sutherland, *A Savage Conflict: The Decisive Role of Guerrillas in the American Civil War* (Chapel Hill: University of North Carolina Press, 2009); Stanley Harrold, *Border War: Fighting over Slavery before the Civil War* (Chapel Hill: University of North Carolina Press, 2010); Diane Mutti Burke, *On Slavery's Border: Missouri's Small-Slaveholding Households, 1815–1865* (Athens: University of Georgia Press, 2010); Kristen Tegtmeier Oertel, *Bleeding Borders: Race, Gender, and Violence in Pre–Civil War Kansas* (Baton Rouge: Louisiana State University Press, 2009); Marilyn S. Blackwell and Kristen Tegtmeier Oertel, *Frontier Feminist: Clarina Howard Nichols and the Politics of Motherhood* (Lawrence: University Press of Kansas, 2010); LeeAnn Whites, "Forty Shirts and a Wagon Load of Wheat," *Journal of the Civil War Era* 1, no. 1 (March 2011): 56–78. Christopher Phillips, *Missouri's Confederate: Claiborne Fox Jackson and the Creation of Southern Identity in the Border West* (Columbia: University of Missouri Press, 2000); Aaron Astor, *Rebels on the Border: Civil War, Emancipation, and the Reconstruction of Kentucky and Missouri* (Baton Rouge: Louisiana State University Press, 2012); T. J. Stiles, *Jesse James: Last Rebel of the Civil War* (New York: Alfred A. Knopf, 2002); Mark Geiger, *Financial Fraud and Guerrilla Violence in Missouri's Civil War, 1861–1865* (New Haven, Conn.: Yale University Press, 2010); Louis Gerteis, *The Civil War in Missouri: A Military History* (Columbia: University of Missouri Press, 2012); Louis Gerteis, *Civil War St. Louis* (Lawrence: University Press of Kansas, 2001); William G. Piston, *Wilson's Creek: The Second Battle of the Civil War and the Men Who Fought It* (Chapel Hill: University of North Carolina Press, 2000); Jeremy Neely, *The Border between Them: Violence and Reconciliation on the Kansas-Missouri Line* (Columbia: University of Missouri Press, 2007).

Chapter 1. "I Came Not to Bring Peace, but a Sword"

1. This discussion of the Crusades is grounded in Jonathan Riley Smith, *The Crusades: A History*, 2nd ed. (New Haven, Conn.: Yale University Press, 2005), quotations, 302.

2. Charles Firth, *Oliver Cromwell and the Rule of the Puritans in England* (London: G. P. Putnam's Sons, 1900; reprinted: Amazon/Nabu Press, 2010), 260.

3. Nicholas P. Canny, "The Ideology of English Colonization: From Ireland to America," *William and Mary Quarterly*, 3rd. ser., 30 (Oct. 1973): 575–598. For a fuller discussion of the historically grounded cultural anthropology of Christian warrior rationalizations for slaughter of the Other, see my essay, "At the Nihilist Edge: Reflections on Guerrilla Warfare during the American Civil War," in *On the Road to Total War: The American Civil War and the German Wars of Unification, 1861–1871*, ed. Stig Forster and Jorg Nagler (Cambridge: Cambridge University Press, 1997), 519–540.

4. Entry for Feb. 2, 1863, Fordyce, Diary of Timothy Phillips, Wisconsin State Historical Society, quoted in Michael Fellman, *Inside War: The Guerrilla Conflict in Missouri during the American Civil War* (New York: Oxford University Press, 1989), 186.

5. Colonel W. R. Pennick to Brigadier General Benjamin Loan, Independence, Jan. 11, 1863, Letters Received File 2593, Record Group 393, National Archives, Washington D.C., quoted in *Inside War*, 188.

6. Brigadier General Clinton B. Fisk to Lieutenant Colonel Daniel M. Draper, Macon, Apr. 18,1864, in *The War of the Rebellion: A Compilation of the Official Records of the Union and Confederate Army*, 130 vols. (Washington, D.C., 1880–1902), Series 1, XXXIV (3), 216. Entry for Oct. 20, 1864, Diary of Webster Moses, Kansas Historical Society, quoted in *Inside War*, 185–186.

7. John J. Ingalls to his Brother, Atchison, Kansas, Jan. 2, 1862, John J. Ingalls Collection, Kansas Historical Society, quoted in *Inside War*, 151. Emphasis in the original.

8. Entries for July 4, 5, 10, 1862; Aug. 4, 21, 24, Sept. 26, Oct. 1, 4, 1863; Sept. 20, 1865, Diary of Sherman Bodwell, Kansas Historical Society, quoted in *Inside War*, 189–192.

9. King James Version of the Bible, Matthew 5:9, 38.

10. Matthew 10:34, 38

11. Matthew 11:12.

12. Williams is quoted in Jill Lepore, *The Name of War: King Phillip's War and the Origins of American Identity* (New York: Random House, 1999), 120. Emphasis in the original.

13. On the White Line Movement in 1875 in Mississippi, from which these generalizations are taken, see my chapter, "Blood Redemption: The Counterrevolutionary White-Terrorist Destruction of Reconstruction," in *In the Name of God and Country: Reconsidering Terrorism in American History* (New Haven, Conn.: Yale University Press, 2010), 97–142.

14. This discussion of the Haymarket is drawn from my chapter, "The Haymarket: Terrorism and Class Conflict," in *In The Name of God and Country*, 143–185.

15. Parsons, speech at the Haymarket, Nov. 29, 1884, in *In the Name of God and Country*, 153. Parsons quoted from James 10:1–4.

16. The quotations in this paragraph come from *In the Name of God and Country*, 144–145.

17. David A. Noble, "Christianity and the Red Flag: A Sermon Preached at the Union Park Congregational Church, May 9, 1886," Haymarket Affair Digital Collection, Chicago Historical Society, quoted in *In the Name of God and Country*, 168–169. Noble quoted Isaiah 59:7–8.

18. David Blight, *Race and Reunion: The Civil War in American Memory* (Cambridge, Mass.: Harvard University Press, 2001).

19. The clearest and most recent elucidation of this effort to marginalize guerrilla warfare, and to deny extreme practices by Civil War warriors more generally, is Mark Neely, *The Civil War and the Limits of Destruction* (Cambridge, Mass.: Harvard University Press, 2007). I take issue with this book and others of its persuasion in "Reflections on *Inside War*," in *Views from the Dark Side of American History* (Baton Rouge: Louisiana State University Press, 2011), 136–151.

20. Sanborn is discussed in *Inside War*, 127, 265–266. Sanborn quoted 2 Samuel 23:3.

Chapter 2. Before the Border War

1. W. Darrell Overdyke, "A Southern Family on the Missouri Frontier: Letters from Independence, 1843–1855," *Journal of Southern History* 17, no. 2 (May 1951): 218.

2. Ibid.

3. Ibid., 219, 223.

4. I use the term "household" to reference both the free and the enslaved individuals who lived on the farm or plantation. This aligns with Elizabeth Fox-Genovese's description of the household as "a basic social unit in which people, whether voluntarily or under compulsion, pool their income and resources" (Elizabeth Fox-Genovese, *Within the Plantation Household* [Chapel Hill: University of North Carolina Press, 1988], 31).

5. My definition of "frontier" is based on Stephen Aron and Jeremy Adelman's determination that a frontier is "a meeting place of peoples in which geographic and cultural borders were not clearly defined" (815). See Jeremy Adelman and Stephen Aron, "From Borderlands to Borders," *American Historical Review* 104, no. 3 (June 1999): 814–841. Also, I adopt Christopher Phillips's definition of "Southernness"; namely, that the South was defined by its strong religious and conservative roots, white cultural homogeneity, humid climate, reliance on cash crops cultivated with slave labor, a predominantly agrarian population, and the presence of large African American communities (Christopher Phillips, "'The Crime Against Missouri': Slavery, Kansas, and the Cant of Southernness in the Border West," *Civil War History* 48, no. 1 [Mar. 2002]: 61). Although, as Phillips correctly points out, Missouri cannot be neatly categorized as Southern since it was also a Western state.

6. Arvarh E. Strickland, "Aspects of Slavery in Missouri, 1821," *Missouri Historical Review* 65, no. 4 (July 1971): 513.

7. This chapter focuses on seven counties in western Missouri—the modern-day counties of Buchanan, Platte, Clay, Jackson, Cass, Bates, and Vernon—and the modern-day Kansas counties of Leavenworth, Wyandotte, Shawnee, Douglas, Bourbon, Miami, and Linn.

8. In an abroad marriage, the man and woman lived in separate households.

9. Diane Mutti Burke, *On Slavery's Border* (Athens: University of Georgia Press, 2010), 32.

10. Ibid., 50.

11. By one estimate, there were approximately 1,400 white inhabitants in northern Indian Territory. See William G. Cutler, *History of the State of Kansas*, vol. 1 (Chicago: A. T. Andreas, 1883), 82.

12. Mutti Burke, *On Slavery's Border*, 19.

13. For instance, according to the population schedules for the 1850 census, residents from the states of Kentucky, Tennessee, Virginia, and North Carolina composed 88.5 percent of the population in Washington Township, Clay County. This was the first census to record the birthplace of each white individual. See U.S. Bureau of the Census, *Seventh Census of the United States*, 1850, Population Schedules (Washington, D.C.: Government Printing Office, 1853).

14. William E. Foley, *The Genesis of Missouri* (Columbia: University of Missouri Press, 1989), 241.

15. Lorenzo J. Greene, Gary R. Kremer, and Antonio F. Holland, *Missouri's Black Heritage*, rev. ed. (Columbia: University of Missouri Press, 1993), 8–9.

16. Ibid., 10–12.

17. Greene et al., *Missouri's Black Heritage*, 17–20.

18. Foley, *The Genesis of Missouri*, 143–144, 151. The territory was divided along the thirty-third parallel. The northern portion was called Upper Louisiana (officially the "District of Louisiana") and the southern portion designated the Territory of Orleans. See ibid., 134–135, 149.

19. Ibid., 114.

20. Mutti Burke, *On Slavery's Border*, 23.

21. Michael Holt, *The Political Crisis of the 1850s* (New York: W. W. Norton, 1978), 19–20.

22. U.S. Bureau of the Census, *Fourth Census of the United States*, 1820, Population Schedules (Washington, D.C: Government Printing Office, 1821); U.S. Bureau of the Census, *Fifth Census of the United States*, 1830, Population Schedules (Washington, D.C.: Government Printing Office, 1831).

23. Pearl Wilcox, *Jackson County Pioneers* (Independence, Mo.: Jackson County Historical Society, 1990), 22–23, 27.

24. Dorothy Brandt Marra, *Cher Oncle, Cher Papa: The Letters of Francois and*

Berenice Chouteau, ed. David Boutros, trans. Marie-Laure Dionne Pal (Kansas City, Mo.: Western Historical Manuscript Collection–Kansas City, 2001), 161–162.

25. Ibid., 24.

26. Ibid., 19.

27. Phyllis Edwards Kite, "History of Westport Methodist Church," 1964, in Monograph Collection, Jackson County (Mo.) Historical Society and Archives, Independence, Missouri.

28. Perry McCandless, *A History of Missouri*, vol. 2, 1820–1860 (Columbia: University of Missouri Press, 1971), 133.

29. Wilcox, *Jackson County Pioneers*, 120–121.

30. Ibid., 122–123, 137.

31. Ibid., 171, 179.

32. McCandless, *A History of Missouri*, 132.

33. Wilcox, *Jackson County Pioneers*, 142–144.

34. William H. Harris, "A Brief History of Old Westport," *Kansas City Genealogist* 44, no. 3 (Spring 2004): 115.

35. Ibid., 115.

36. Martha J. Lamb, ed., *Magazine of American History with Notes and Queries*, vol. 26, July–December 1891 (New York: Historical Publication Company, 1891), 111–112.

37. Rudolph Friederich Kurz, *Journal of Rudolph Friederich Kurz: An Account of His Experiences among Fur Traders and American Indians on the Mississippi and the Upper Missouri Rivers during the Years 1846 to 1852*, ed. J. N. B. Hewitt, and trans. Myrtis Jarrell (Washington, D.C.: Government Printing Office, 1937), 29.

38. *The History of Buchanan County, Missouri* (St. Joseph, Mo.: Union Historical Company, 1881), 286.

39. Ibid., 430.

40. George Remsburg, "Old Weston," *Globe*, Apr. 18, 1908.

41. W. H. Woodson, *History of Clay County, Missouri* (Topeka, Kans.: Historical Publishing Company, 1920), 74.

42. Ibid., 149.

43. Wilcox, *Jackson County Pioneers*, 171; Woodson, *History of Clay County*, 153. The Estes family emigrated from either Kentucky or Tennessee. In the 1850 census there are a number of Searcys listed in Platte and Clay Counties; all were from Kentucky. See U.S. Bureau of the Census, *Seventh Census of the United States*, 1850, Population Schedules (Washington, D.C.: Government Printing Office, 1853).

44. R. Douglas Hurt, *Agriculture and Slavery in Missouri's Little Dixie* (Columbia: University of Missouri Press, 1992), 105, 121.

45. Ibid., 109–111; Anne Chiarelli, "A Look at Slavery in Missouri," *Jackson County Historical Society Journal* 28 (Winter 1986): 13–14.

46. For more on hemp growing, see Jeffrey C. Stone, *Slavery, Southern Culture, and Education in Little Dixie, Missouri, 1820–1860* (New York: Routledge, 2006), 26.

47. "Hemp and Produce Commission House," *Liberty Tribune*, Mar. 20, 1847.

48. Hurt, *Agriculture and Slavery in Missouri's Little Dixie*, 80, 86, 101.

49. "The Great Depression," *Liberty Tribune*, Sept. 19, 1846. Chariton County is in central Missouri, while Camden is in Ray County, which shares a border with Clay County.

50. "United States Congress, Indian Removal Act, May 28, 1830," in Theda Purdue and Michael Green, eds., *The Cherokee Removal*, 123–125 (Boston: Bedford St. Martins, 2005), 123.

51. Isaac McCoy, "Names and Numbers of Indian Tribes Which Must Have Possessions in the Indian Territory," Nov. 1, 1832, in Isaac McCoy Papers, Library and Archives Division, Kansas Historical Society, Topeka, Kansas (hereafter KHS).

52. William E. Unrau, *Indians of Kansas* (Topeka: Kansas Historical Society, 1991), 56–59.

53. Ibid., 42–49.

54. Annie Heloise Abel, *The American Indian as Slaveholder and Secessionist* (Lincoln: University of Nebraska Press, 1992), 2.

55. Adrienne Christopher, "Captain Joseph Parks: Chief of the Shawnee Indians," *Westport Historical Quarterly* 5, no. 1 (June 1969): 13.

56. Martha B. Caldwell, comp., *Annals of Shawnee Methodist Mission and Indian Manual Labor School*, 2nd ed. (Topeka: Kansas Historical Society, 1977), 17.

57. Ibid., 58.

58. Kevin Abing, "Before Bleeding Kansas: Christian Missionaries, Slavery, and the Shawnee Indians in Pre-Territorial Kansas, 1844–1854," *Kansas History* 24, no. 1 (Spring 2001): 58.

59. Christopher, "Captain Joseph Parks,"14.

60. "Wyandott County, Our Recollection of By-Gone Days," *Wyandott Herald*, July 6, 1876, in Wyandotte County Clippings, vol. 3, KHS.

61. William E. Connelley, *The Emigrant Indian Tribes of Wyandotte County* (Topeka, Kans.: Crane and Company, 1901), 18–19.

62. Ibid., 14.

63. See J. Patrick Hughes, *Fort Leavenworth* (Topeka: Kansas Historical Society, 2000), 10.

64. Ibid., 1, 3–4.

65. Ibid., 7.

66. The town of Leavenworth was not officially founded until 1854, and thus falls outside this article's temporal scope.

67. Lewis B. Dougherty, "Biographical Sketch of John Dougherty," in John Dougherty Papers, KHS.

68. His house still stands at 611 Scott Street. See "Occupants of 611 Scott,"

memorandum, in "Fort Leavenworth—Topical—Buildings—Sutler's House" Vertical File, Combined Arms Research Library, Fort Leavenworth, Kansas.

69. Henry Schindler, "A Post Trader, a King Here in the Early Days," *Leavenworth Times*, Nov. 19, 1911, in History of Fort Leavenworth Clippings, KHS.

70. L. Candy Ruff, "Musettes Homes Tour Has Stories to Tell, Sutler Is Rich to Remember," *Leavenworth Times*, Apr. 9, 1989.

71. Henry Schindler, "When Slaves Were Owned in Kansas by Army Officers," *Leavenworth Times*, Oct. 13, 1912, in History of Fort Leavenworth Clippings, KHS. The term "sound on the goose" was code for identifying oneself as a proslavery partisan.

72. Henry Schindler, "A Post Trader, a King Here in the Early Days," *Leavenworth Times*, Nov. 19, 1911, in History of Fort Leavenworth Clippings, KHS.

73. Kristen Tegtmeier Oertel, *Bleeding Borders* (Baton Rouge: Louisiana State University Press, 2009), 39.

74. See Jonathan D. Martin, *Divided Mastery* (Cambridge, Mass.: Harvard University Press, 2004).

75. Sarah S. Hughes, "Slaves for Hire," *William and Mary Quarterly*, 3rd ser., 35, no. 2 (Apr. 1978): 260–286; Clement Eaton, "Slave-Hiring in the Upper South," *Mississippi Valley Historical Review* 46, no. 4 (Mar. 1960): 663–678.

76. Martin, *Divided Mastery*, 2. It is difficult to establish concrete percentages of how many slaves were hired out, since census records do not distinguish between hired slaves and those owned by the slaveholder.

77. Leo E. Oliva, *Fort Scott*, rev. ed. (Topeka: Kansas Historical Society, 1996), 1–4, 15.

78. Hiero T. Wilson Daybook, vol. 1, 1844–1845, KHS.

79. T. F. Robley, *History of Bourbon County, Kansas, to the Close of 1865* (Fort Scott, Kans.: [Press of Monitor Book & Printing], 1894), 12.

80. Clifford H. Lyman, *Aaahh Bourbon, 1842–1865* (Self-published, 1984), 23–25.

81. William E. Connelley, "Hiero T. Wilson," *A Standard History of Kansas and Kansans* (Chicago: Lewis Publishing, 1918), http://skyways.lib.ks.us/genweb/archives/1918ks/biow/wilsonht.html.

82. Robley, *History of Bourbon County*, 44–48.

83. "Aunt Ann's Story, More than Thirty Years in Kansas," May 12, 1875, in George Allen Root Papers, KHS.

84. Ann Archbold to Julia Anne McBride, May 6, 1848, in Indians History Collection, KHS.

85. U.S. Bureau of the Census, *1855 Territorial Kansas Census* (Washington, D.C.: Government Printing Office, 1855).

86. Alexander S. Johnson, "Slaves in Kansas Territory," Apr. 20, 1895, in Alexander Johnson Miscellaneous Collection, KHS; and Oertel, *Bleeding Borders*, 39.

87. W. R. Bernard to George W. Martin, July 24, 1905, in W. R. Bernard Miscellaneous Collection, KHS.

88. Caldwell, *Annals of Shawnee Methodist Mission*, 12, 25–26.

Chapter 3. The Goose Question

1. Abraham Lincoln, "First Inaugural Address," Mar. 6, 1861, in *Collected Works of Abraham Lincoln*, ed. Roy P. Basler, 9 vols. (New Brunswick: Rutgers University Press, 1953), 4:263–271.

2. "Declaration of the Immediate Causes Which Induce and Justify the Secession of South Carolina from the Federal Union," Avalon Project (http://avalon .law.yale.edu); "Georgia Secession," ibid.; "A Declaration of the Immediate Causes Which Induce and Justify the Secession of the State of Mississippi from the Federal Union," ibid.; "A Declaration of the Causes Which Impel the State of Texas to Secede from the Federal Union," ibid. For a discussion of why lower South states, which had few runaway slaves, so emphasized violations of the Fugitive Slave Law, see John Ashworth, *Slavery, Capitalism, and Politics in the Antebellum Republic*, vol. 2: *The Coming of the Civil War, 1850–1861* (Cambridge: Cambridge University Press, 2007), 131–133.

3. Michael W. Flamm, *Law and Order* (New York: Columbia University Press, 2005).

4. Phillip S. Paludan, "The American Civil War Considered as a Crisis in Law and Order," *American Historical Review* 77 (Oct. 1972): 1013–1034; Russell McClintock, *Lincoln and the Decision for War* (Chapel Hill: University of North Carolina Press, 2008), 276–277.

5. Gerald W. Wolff, *The Kansas-Nebraska Bill* (New York, N.Y.: Revisionist Press, 1977), 37–46; Don E. Fehrenbacher, *The South and Three Sectional Crises* (Baton Rouge: Louisiana State University Press, 1980), 43; Michael A. Morrison, *Slavery and the American West* (Chapel Hill: University of North Carolina Press, 1997), 142–156; William E. Parrish, *David Rice Atchison of Missouri: Border Politician* (Columbia: University of Missouri Press, 1961), 142–151; Roy F. Nichols, "The Kansas-Nebraska Act: A Century of Historiography," *Mississippi Valley Historical Review* 43 (Sept. 1956): 201–204; Robert W. Johannsen, *Stephen A. Douglas* (New York: Oxford University Press, 1973), 390–400, 405–418.

6. C. F. Jackson to [D. R. Atchison], Jan. 18, 1854, folder 4, David Rice Atchison Papers, State Historical Society of Missouri, Manuscript Collection, Columbia, Mo.

7. Robert Toombs to W. W. Burwell, Feb. 3, 1854, in *The Correspondence of Robert Toombs, Alexander H. Stephens, and Howell Cobb*, ed. Ulrich Bonnell Phillips (New York: Da Capo, 1970), 342–343; *New York Times*, Feb. 24, 1854.

8. *New York Times*, Apr. 26, 1854.

9. Robert R. Russel, "The Issues in the Congressional Struggle over the Kansas-Nebraska Bill, 1854," *Journal of Southern History* 29 (May 1963): 208–209.

10. Ibid., 205; William J. Cooper Jr., *The South and the Politics of Slavery, 1828–1856* (Baton Rouge: Louisiana State University Press, 1978), 358.

11. Alice Nichols, *Bleeding Kansas* (New York: Oxford University Press, 1954), 24; Emmett Redd and Nicole Etcheson, "'Sound on the Goose': A Search for the Answer to an Age Old Question," *Kansas History* 32 (Autumn 2009): 205–217.

12. *New York Times*, Oct. 25, 1854.

13. Eli Thayer, *A History of the Kansas Crusade, Its Friends and Its Foes* (New York: Harper, 1889), 187.

14. Territory of Kansas Census of 1855, Kansas Historical Society, Topeka, Kans., microfilm, 1951.

15. Russell K. Hickman, "The Reeder Administration Inaugurated: Part I—The Delegate Election of November, 1854," *Kansas Historical Quarterly* 36 (Autumn 1970): 305–340, esp. 322–323, 334–335; *New York Times*, Apr. 18, 1855; James A. Rawley, *Race and Politics* (Philadelphia: Lippincott, 1969), 87–89; Nichols, *Bleeding Kansas*, 28.

16. Russell K. Hickman, "The Reeder Administration Inaugurated: Part II—The Census of Early 1855," *Kansas Historical Quarterly* 36 (Winter 1970): 402–455, esp. 430; Edward Everett Hale, *Kanzas and Nebraska . . .* (Boston: Phillips, Sampson, 1854), 234. For descriptions of Missouri voting, see House of Representatives, Report No. 200, 34 Cong., 1 sess., serial 869, vol. 2 (Washington, D.C., 1856).

17. *New York Times*, May 9, 1857.

18. Kenneth J. Winkle, *The Politics of Community: Migration and Politics in Antebellum Ohio* (Cambridge, Eng.: Cambridge University Press, 1988), 63; Nicole Etcheson, *Bleeding Kansas: Contested Liberty in the Civil War Era* (Lawrence: University Press of Kansas, 2004), 58.

19. David Grimsted, *American Mobbing, 1828–1861: Toward Civil War* (New York: Oxford University Press, 1998), 181–185; Francis A. Hart, House of Representatives, Report No. 200, 389–392; E. R. Zimmerman, ibid., 363–365; Benjamin Harding, ibid., 308–311; Dana Fizer, ibid., 351–353.

20. George H. Keller, House of Representatives, Report No. 200, 27–30.

21. John A. Wakefield, ibid., 187–190.

22. *New York Times*, Dec. 1, 1854.

23. House of Representatives, Report No. 200, 927–930.

24. *New York Times*, May 11, 1855.

25. John H. Stringfellow, House of Representatives, Report No. 200, 925–927.

26. Locke Hardeman to Gen. G. R. Smith, June 10, 1855, General George R. Smith Collection, Missouri Historical Society, St. Louis, Mo.

27. "Kansas Election!" n.d., 1855, folder 6, Frederick Starr Jr. Papers, State Historical Society of Missouri Manuscript Collection.

28. Richard Tuck, House of Representatives, Report No. 200, 343–346; Andrew Johnson, ibid., 259–261; Dr. B. C. Westfall, ibid., 225–227.

29. J. N. Mace, ibid., 174–176.

30. Rev. Henry B. Burgess, ibid., 192–199; Harrison Burson, ibid., 168–170; James B. Abbott, ibid., 154–155; C. S. Pratt, ibid., 149–150.

31. N. B. Blanton, ibid., 148–149.

32. Election of Mar. 30, 1855, "Executive Minutes," *Transactions of the Kansas State Historical Society* (Topeka: Kansas Publishing House, 1886), 3:271–273; Etcheson, *Bleeding Kansas*, 66–68; S. D. Lecompte and Rush Elmore with A. J. Isaacks concurring, July 30, 1855, "Governor Reeder's Administration," *Transactions of the Kansas State Historical Society* (Topeka: Kansas State Printing Co., 1896), 5:213–222.

33. B. F. Stringfellow to ——, Oct. 6, 1855, in *Atchison Squatter Sovereign*, Dec. 4, 1855.

34. Daniel W. Wilder, *The Annals of Kansas* (Topeka: Kansas State Historical Society, 1875), 56–58; *The Border Ruffian Code in Kansas* [1856], 1–4.

35. For the Topeka Constitution, see *Lawrence Herald of Freedom*, Nov. 24, 1855.

36. *Atchison Squatter Sovereign*, Oct. 23, 1855; *St. Louis Missouri Democrat*, Nov. 21, 26, 1855.

37. *St. Louis Missouri Democrat*, Nov. 26, 1855.

38. Wilson Shannon to Col. Sumner, May 21, 1856, House of Representatives, Executive Documents, No. 1, 34 Cong., 3 sess., serial 894, vol. 2 (Washington, D.C., 1856), 38–39.

39. *St. Louis Missouri Democrat*, Nov. 28, Dec. 8, 1855; Kenneth M. Stampp, *America in 1857: A Nation on the Brink* (New York: Oxford University Press, 1990), 153; *Lawrence Herald of Freedom*, Jan. 24, July 25, 1857.

40. *New York Times*, Jan. 26, 1856.

41. Wm. O Yager to Danl. Woodson, Aug. 31, 1856, Daniel Woodson Papers, Kansas Historical Society; H. J. Strickler to Danl. Woodson, Aug. 30, 1856, ibid.

42. S. Cooper to Maj. Gen. P. F. Smith, Sept. 24, 1856, House of Representatives, Executive Documents, No. 1, 33–34.

43. Jno. W. Geary to James Buchanan, Jan. 16, 1857, roll 31, James Buchanan Papers, Historical Society of Pennsylvania, Philadelphia, Pa.; *Lecompton Union*, Jan. 7, Feb. 7, 1857; *Atchison Squatter Sovereign*, Dec. 16, 1856; R. J. Walker to Lewis Cass, Sept. 26, 1857, "Governor Walker's Administration," *Transactions of the Kansas State Historical Society* (Topeka: Kansas State Printing Co., 1896), 5:384–387.

44. *Kansas City* (Mo.) *Enterprise*, Mar. 22, 1856.

45. A. P. Butler to D. R. Atchison, Feb. 28, 1856, folder 5, Atchison Papers.

46. Wm. Brindle to Col. Geary, Aug. 5, 1856, reel 2, John White Geary Papers, Yale University Library, New Haven, Conn.

47. Special Message of Jan. 24, 1856, in *A Compilation of the Messages and Papers*

of the Presidents, 1787–1897, ed. James D. Richardson (Washington, D.C.: Congress, 1900), 5:359; First Annual Message, Dec. 8, 1857, ibid., 455; Roy Franklin Nichols, *Franklin Pierce* (Philadelphia: University of Pennsylvania Press, 1958), 361, 400–406; Allan Nevins, *The Emergence of Lincoln*, vol. 1: *Douglas, Buchanan, and Party Chaos, 1857–1859* (New York: Scribner, 1950), 314–315; Grimsted, *American Mobbing*, 254–255.

48. For details of the murder and ensuing events, see Etcheson, *Bleeding Kansas*, 79–88.

49. Wilson Shannon to Franklin Pierce, Nov. 28, 1855, "Executive Minutes," *Transactions of the Kansas StaHistorical Society* (Topeka: Kansas Publishing House, 1886), 3:292–294; Proclamation of Governor Shannon, Nov. 29, 1855, ibid., 294–295; Wilson Shannon to Major General Richardson, Dec. 2, 1855, ibid., 295–296; Wilson Shannon to Col. Sumner, Dec. 1, 1855, Woodson Papers; Wilson Shannon to Sheriff Jones, Dec. 2, 1855, "Executive Minutes," *Transactions*, 3:295.

50. George W. Clarke to Wilson Shannon, Dec. 3, 1855, "Executive Minutes," *Transactions*, 3:297–298.

51. Christopher Phillips and Jason L. Pendleton, eds., *The Union on Trial* (Columbia: University of Missouri Press, 2005), 149.

52. Wm. T. Davis to Catharine, Dec. 5, 1855, folder 1, Davis-Hughes Correspondence, State Historical Society of Missouri Manuscript Collection.

53. Wilson Shannon to General Strickler, Dec. 8, 1855, "Executive Minutes," *Transactions*, 3:298; Wilson Shannon to General Richardson, Dec. 8, 1855, ibid., 298; Wilson Shannon to S. J. Jones, Dec. 8, 1855, ibid.

54. Wm. J. Preston, J. C. Anderson, W. F. Donaldson, Apr. 28, 1856, Senate, Executive Documents, No. 17, 35 Cong., 1 sess., serial 923, vol. 6 (Washington, D.C., 1858), 7–8; Wilson Shannon to Sec. of State Marcy, Apr. 27, 1856, ibid., 2–5; Axalla to Brother, Apr. 27, 1856; William Stanley Hoole, "A Southerner's Viewpoint of the Kansas Situation, 1856–1857: The Letters of Lieut. Col. A. J. Hoole, C.S.A.," *Kansas Historical Quarterly* 3 (Feb. 1934): 47–48; *Atchison Squatter Sovereign*, Apr. 29, 1856.

55. *Lecompton Union*, n.d., 1856.

56. Wilson Shannon to Franklin Pierce, May 31, 1856, Senate, Executive Documents, No. 17, 16–19.

57. *New York Times*, May 13, 1856; Wilson Shannon to Col. Sumner, May 21, 1856, "Executive Minutes," *Transactions*, 3:310; Charles Robinson, *The Kansas Conflict* (Lawrence: Journal Publishing, 1898), 234–238; [Andrew H. Reeder], "Governor Reeder's Escape from Kansas," *Transactions*, 3:205–223; Nichols, *Franklin Pierce*, 473–480; Albert D. Richardson, *Beyond the Mississippi* (Hartford: American Publishing Co., 1867), 82; Stampp, *America in 1857*, 181.

58. Major L. Wilson, *Space, Time, and Freedom: The Quest for Nationality and the Irrepressible Conflict, 1815–1861* (Westport: Greenwood Press, 1974), 183–184.

59. *Richmond Enquirer*, Mar. 21, 1857.

60. *Lecompton Kansas National Democrat*, June 17, 1858.

61. James Buchanan to Robert J. Walker, July 12, 1857, House of Representatives, Report No. 548, 36 Cong., 1 Sess., serial 1071, vol. 5 (Washington, D.C., 1860), 112–113; M. J. Crawford to [Alexander Stephens], June 19, 1857, Alexander H. Stephens Papers, Library of Congress, Washington, D.C.; Stampp, *America in 1857*, 266–268, 272–275; Roy Franklin Nichols, *The Disruption of American Democracy* (New York: Collier, 1948), 117–131; Wilder, *Annals of Kansas*, 134–147.

62. *New York Times*, Jan. 26, 1858; Stampp, *America in 1857*, 32.

63. Richardson, *Compilation of the Messages and Papers of the Presidents*, 5:471–481; Stampp, *America in 1857*, 282–285; Rawley, *Race and Politics*, 225–226; Annual Message, Dec. 3, 1860, Richardson, *Compilation of the Messages and Papers of the Presidents*, 646–647. In contrast, Buchanan called the free-state movement a "revolutionary organization." Annual Message, Dec. 8, 1857, ibid., 449–454.

64. J. S. Black, Sept. 25, 1857, roll 6, Jeremiah S. Black Papers, Library of Congress, Washington, D.C.

65. *Congressional Globe*, 35 Cong., 1 sess., 1087–1101 [Speech by Senator Charles E. Stuart]; Stampp, *America in 1857*, 266–268; R. M. T. Hunter to Shelton F. Leake, Oct. 16, 1857, Charles Henry Ambler, ed., *Correspondence of Robert M. T. Hunter, 1826–1876* (New York: Da Capo Press, 1971), 2372–2341; *Congressional Globe*, 35 Cong., 1 sess. (Washington, D.C., 1858), 521–527, 1025–1035; *Congressional Globe Appendix*, 35 Cong., 1 sess. (Washington, D.C., 1858), 289–298, 277–289.

66. Senate Report No. 34, 34 Cong., 1 sess., serial 836, vol. 1 (Washington, 1856), 38.

67. *Congressional Globe Appendix*, 34 Cong., 1 sess. (Washington, D.C., 1856), 545.

68. S. A. Douglas to J. A. McClernand, Nov. 23, 1857, box 1, John A. McClernand Papers, Illinois State Historical Library, Springfield, Ill.; *Congressional Globe Appendix*, 35 Cong., 1 sess. (Washington, D.C., 1858), 174–204; *New York Times*, Dec. 1, 10, 1857; Don E. Fehrenbacher, *The Dred Scott Case* (New York: Oxford University Press, 1978), 465–466.

69. Johannsen, *Stephen A. Douglas*, 590.

70. *Lawrence Herald of Freedom*, Jan. 9, 1858.

71. Rawley, *Race and Politics*, 246–250; Frank Haywood Hodder, "Some Aspects of the English Bill for the Admission of Kansas," *Annual Report of the American Historical Association for the Year 1906*, 2 vols. (Washington, D.C., 1908), 1:199–220; William J. Cooper Jr., *Liberty and Slavery: Southern Politics to 1860* (New York, 1983), 259–262; Stampp, *America in 1857*, 327–328; Nichols, *Disruption of American Democracy*, 170–175.

72. Nichols, *Disruption of American Democracy*, 170–175; *Congressional Globe*, 35 Cong., 1 sess. (Washington, D.C., 1858), 1900–1906, 1868–1880.

73. Joseph E. Brown to Alexander H. Stephens, May 7, 1858, *Correspondence of Toombs, Stephens, and Cobb*, 434.

74. *New York Times*, May 3, 1858.

75. Fehrenbacher, *The South and Three Sectional Crises*, 54–55; Etcheson, *Bleeding Kansas*, 184; *Lecompton Kansas National Democrat*, Jan. 27, 1859; *Lawrence Herald of Freedom*, May 14, 1859.

76. Geret Findley Patterson to James Buchanan, May 17, 1859, roll 37, Buchanan Papers.

77. John H. Stringfellow to James Buchanan, Jan. 5, 1858, roll 34, ibid.

78. *St. Louis Missouri Republican*, Aug. 27, 1859.

79. William H. Seward, "Freedom in the Territories," http://www.senate.gov/artandhistory/history/resources/pdf/SewardNewTerritories.pdf; David M. Potter, *The Impending Crisis, 1848–1861* (New York: Harper & Row, 1976), 102; R. M. T. Hunter speech, Oct. 1, 1856, roll 1, R. M. T. Hunter Papers, University of Virginia, Charlottesville, Va.

80. Wendell Phillips, "A Discourse Delivered before the Twenty-Eighth Congregational Society," in James Redpath, *Echoes of Harper's Ferry* (1860; reprint: New York: Arno Press, 1969), 109.

81. Wm. Bigler to James Buchanan, Oct. 22, 1859, roll 38, Buchanan Papers, Historical Society of Pennsylvania, Philadelphia, Pa.

82. U.S. Senate, Report No. 278, 36 Cong., 1 sess. (Washington, D.C., 1860), 2.

83. James Oakes, *The Ruling Race* (New York: Norton, 1982), 233–234; Stephen B. Oates, *To Purge This Land with Blood* (New York: Harper & Row, 1970), 320–324.

84. *New York Times*, Feb. 16, 1860; Johannsen, *Stephen A. Douglas*, 829–830; Nichols, *Disruption of American Democracy*, 475.

85. William W. Freehling, *The Road to Disunion*, vol. 2 (New York: Oxford University Press, 2007), xii, xiv, 59.

Chapter 4. *"Nigger-Worshipping Fanatics" and "Villain[s] of the Blackest Dye"*

1. Senator Charles Sumner, "The Crime against Kansas" (Boston: John P. Jewett, 1856), 5–6, reprint at http://books.google.com/books?dq=crime+against+Kansas+Sumner. See David Herbert Donald, *Charles Sumner and the Coming of the Civil War* (New York: Ballantine Books, 1989), 278–311, for an analysis of the speech and the caning. The ideas for this chapter were first presented at the 2009 meeting of the Organization of American Historians, and I thank the session chair, Amy Greenberg, for her helpful comments. I also acknowledge the insightful critiques provided by my fellow colleagues at the Border Wars conference in 2011.

2. *Boston Courier*, May 23, 1856, Secession Era Editorials Project, http://history

.furman.edu/benson/docs/mabcsu560523a.htm. For a discussion of the political fall-out of the caning see William Gienapp, "The Crime against Sumner," *Civil War History* 25 (Sept. 1979): 218–245.

3. Kristen Tegtmeier Oertel, *Bleeding Borders* (Baton Rouge: Louisiana State University Press, 2009); Amy Greenberg, *Manifest Manhood and the Antebellum American Empire* (New York: Cambridge University Press, 2005); and Michael Kimmel, *Manhood in America* (New York: Free Press, 1996). All three authors identify the mid-nineteenth century as an especially salient time in which men struggled over competing definitions of manhood.

4. Anthony Rotundo, *American Manhood* (New York: Basic Books, 1993), 2–7, 281–283; and Gail Bederman, *Manliness and Civilization* (Chicago: University of Chicago Press, 1995), 170–216.

5. I began to answer these questions in *Bleeding Borders*, but I hope to explore more fully the racial and racist foundations of white manhood in this article.

6. "Possuming," *Richmond* (Virginia) *Whig*, May 31, 1856, Secession Era Editorials Project, http://history.furman.edu/benson/docs/varwsu56531a.htm.

7. *Charleston Mercury*, May 28, 1856, Secession Era Editorials Project, http://history.furman.edu/benson/docs/sccmsu56528a.htm.

8. "The Progress of the Revolution," *Richmond* (Virginia) *Whig*, June 4, 1856, Secession Era Editorials Project, http://history.furman.edu/benson/docs/varwsu56604a.htm.

9. Darlene Clark Hine and Earnestine Jenkins, eds., *A Question of Manhood*, vol.1 (Bloomington: Indiana University Press, 1999), 1, 45.

10. *Lawrence Republican*, June 14, 1860, cited in Richard Sheridan, *Freedom's Crucible* (Lawrence: University Press of Kansas, 1998), 63–64.

11. Dr. John Rock, *Liberator*, Mar. 12, 1858, cited in Mia Bay, *The White Image in the Black Mind* (New York: Oxford University Press, 2000), 58.

12. David Walker, cited in Merton Lynn Dillon, *Slavery Attacked* (Baton Rouge: Louisiana State University Press, 1990), 146.

13. Lorri Glover, *Southern Sons* (Baltimore: Johns Hopkins University Press, 2007), 2, 34.

14. *Southern Literary Messenger*, Mar. 11, 1861, 164, cited in Linda Frost, *Never One Nation* (Minneapolis: University of Minnesota Press, 2005), 98.

15. "Black Republican Balderdash," *Charleston Mercury*, May 12, 1856, 19th-Century U.S. Newspapers database, University of Tulsa. In a recent search of this database, the phrase "Black Republican" resulted in 2,910 hits in newspapers across the country between 1856 and 1858.

16. "The Black Republican Notion of Negro Equality," *Jackson Mississippian*, Nov. 5, 1858, 19th-Century U.S. Newspapers database, University of Tulsa.

17. "Senator Seward," *Weekly Raleigh* (N.C.) *Register*, 1 Dec. 1858, 19th-Century U.S. Newspapers database, University of Tulsa.

18. Christopher Phillips, *The Making of a Southerner* (Columbia: University of Missouri Press, 2008), 71, 70.

19. Doyle testimony quoted in Oertel, *Bleeding Borders*, 128.

20. "John Brown a Ferocious and Bloody Savage!" *New York Journal of Commerce*, cited in *Liberator*, Dec. 2, 1859, 19th-Century U.S. Newspapers database, University of Tulsa.

21. "Slavery Extension Beneficial to the North," *Richmond* (Virginia) *Enquirer*, cited in the *New York Herald*, July 19, 1856, 19th-Century U.S. Newspapers database, University of Tulsa.

22. These examples support the argument that Linda Frost makes about the contradictory but integral place of slaves within the Confederate nation: "Slaves are ideologically and practically included within the boundaries of the Confederacy, and the morally and racially problematic Yankee is cast out." See Frost, *Never One Nation*, 105.

23. "Slavery Extension Beneficial to the North," *Richmond* (Virginia) *Enquirer*, cited in the *New York Herald*, July 19, 1856, 19th-Century U.S. Newspapers database, University of Tulsa.

24. "Attack on Mr. Sumner," *Boston* (Mass.) *Bee*, May 23, 1856, Secession Era Editorials Project, http://history.furman.edu/benson/docs/mabbsu56523a.htm.

25. *Pittsburgh* (Pa.) *Gazette*, May 24, 1856, Secession Era Editorials Project, http://history.furman.edu/benson/docs/papgsu56524a.htm.

26. *New York Tribune*, May 23, 1856, Secession Era Editorials Project, http://history.furman.edu/benson/docs/nytrsu56523a.htm.

27. William Lloyd Garrison, cited in the *Liberator*, reprinted in the *New York Herald*, July 19, 1856, 19th-Century U.S. Newspapers database, University of Tulsa.

28. Quoted from diary of H. Miles Moore, *Early History of Leavenworth* (Leavenworth, Kans.: Samuel Dodsworth Book Co., 1906), Kansas Historical Society, Topeka, Kans. (KHS).

29. *Boston Daily Atlas*, May 23, 1856, 19th-Century U.S. Newspapers database, University of Tulsa.

30. Julia Louisa Lovejoy Diary, July 8, 1856, and Aug. 20, 1856, cited in Oertel, *Bleeding Borders*, 99.

31. James Manning Winchell Papers, undated, Library and Archives Division, KHS.

32. James Leiby to Samuel Leiby, with addendum by Mrs. Leiby, Sept. 8, 1856, James Leiby Papers, Library and Archives Division, KHS.

33. "Meeting of Ministers," *Liberator*, June 27, 1856, 19th-Century U.S. Newspapers database, University of Tulsa (emphasis added).

34. "The Voice of Bunker Hill," *Boston Daily Atlas*, May 29, 1856, 19th-Century U.S. Newspapers database, University of Tulsa.

35. *Frank Leslie's Illustrated Newspaper*, May 17, 1862, and *Harper's Weekly*, June 7, 1862, both cited in Frost, *Never One Nation*, 20–21.

36. William Henry Seward, "On the Irrepressible Conflict," Oct. 25, 1858, reprinted at New York History Net, http://www.nyhistory.com/central/conflict.htm.

37. William Lloyd Garrison found in the *Liberator*, reprinted in the *New York Herald*, July 19, 1856. 19th-Century U.S. Newspapers database, University of Tulsa (emphasis added).

38. *New York Tribune*, May 23, 1856, Secession Era Editorials Project, http://history.furman.edu/benson/docs/nytrsu56523a.htm.

Chapter 5. "The Noise of Democracy"

1. James Buchanan, "First Annual Message," Dec. 8, 1857, in *The Works of James Buchanan*, ed John Bassett Moore (Philadelphia: J. B. Lippincott, 1910), 10:151.

2. John Speer, *Life of Gen. James H. Lane* micropublished in "Western Americana: Frontier History of the Trans-Mississippi West, 1550–1900" (New Haven, Conn.: Research Publications, 1975), no. 5084 (reel 507), 175. His tally includes acting governors.

3. "Documentary History: Kansas Governor Biographies," in *Transactions of the Kansas State Historical Society* (Topeka: Kansas Publishing House, 1886–1896), 5:160; James W. Denver, "Address of Ex-Governor James W. Denver, September 3, 1884," in *Publications of the Kansas State Historical Society* (Topeka: T. D. Thacher, State Printer, 1886), 167–168.

4. Denver, "Address to the People of Kansas," *Transactions*, 5:465, 467–468.

5. "Proclamation by Governor James W. Denver," Dec. 26, 1857, ibid., 468–469.

6. Denver to Mrs. Denver, Jan. 4, James William Denver Papers, Kansas Historical Society, Topeka, Kans. (KHS).

7. George C. Barns, *Denver, the Man: The Life, Letters, and Public Papers of the Lawyer, Soldier and Statesman* (Wilmington, Ohio: Shenandoah Publishing House, 1949), 155–156; and E. Duane Elbert, "The English Bill: An Attempt to Compromise the Lecompton Dilemma," *Kansas History* 1, no. 4 (Winter 1978): 221n13.

8. Barns, *Denver, the Man*, 159–161.

9. Denver, "Address of Ex-Governor James W. Denver," 170–171; Jeremiah Black, "Opinion of Attorney General J. S. Black to Secretary Cass," Mar. 10, Records of the Territorial Executive Department: Kansas Territory (RTED), KHS; Alice Nichols, *Bleeding Kansas* (New York: Oxford University Press, 1954), 216–218; and Charles Robinson, *The Kansas Conflict* (Lawrence, Kans.: Journal Publishing, 1898; reprint, Freeport, N.Y.: Books for Libraries Press, 1972), 381–382.

10. Buchanan to Joseph Baker, Jan. 11, 1858, *Works of James Buchanan*, 10:177.

11. James W. Davidson, June 14, 1860, House of Representatives, 36th Cong., 1st Sess., *House Report 648: Select Committee on Alleged Corruptions in Government: The Covode Investigation* (Washington, D.C.: n.p. 1860), 323.

12. *National Intelligencer*, Feb. 15, 1858.

13. James Buchanan, *Mr. Buchanan's Administration on the Eve of the Rebellion* (New York: D. Appleton, 1866), 40.

14. Ibid., 42.

15. Buchanan, "Message on the Constitution of Kansas," in *Works of James Buchanan*, 10:180, 186.

16. Ibid., 186–188, 189–192.

17. Thomas C. Wells to Mrs. Thomas P. Wells, Feb. 27, Thomas C. Wells, "Letters of a Kansas Pioneer," *Kansas Historical Quarterly (KHQ)* 5, no. 4 (Nov. 1936): 384.

18. *Charleston Mercury*, Mar. 9.

19. Reprinted in *Charleston Mercury*, Apr. 17. Also see the *Mobile Register* reprinted in the same issue.

20. Douglas to Forney, et al., Feb. 6, in *The Letters of Stephen A. Douglas*, ed. Robert W. Johannsen (Urbana: University of Illinois Press, 1961), 409.

21. Stanton, "Address of Ex-Governor Frederick P. Stanton, September 2, 1884," in *Publications of the KSHS*, 159.

22. Stanton, "Address of Hon. F. P. Stanton, of Tennessee, January 29, 1858," in *Democratic Protests against the Lecompton Fraud* (n.p., 1858), 2.

23. Walker to the Indiana Anti-Lecompton Democratic Convention, Feb. 20, reprinted in *National Intelligencer*, Mar. 1.

24. Buchanan, "Message on the Constitution of Kansas," in *Works of James Buchanan*, 10:180–183.

25. Buchanan, *Mr. Buchanan's Administration*, 43.

26. See Maclay to John C. Mather et al., Dec. 16, 1857, 2; Maclay to the Chairman of Committee of Arrangements, Dec. 22, 1857, 3–4; and Maclay to William Wilson et al., 6–10, William B. Maclay, *Letters from the Hon. William B. Maclay, Member of Congress from Fifth District of New York, on the Admission of Kansas under the Lecompton Constitution* (n.p., 1858).

27. Douglas to Samuel Treat, Feb. 28, in *Letters of Stephen A. Douglas*, 418.

28. J. Collamer and B. Wade, Feb. 18, in *Views of the Minority on the Constitution of Kansas* (Washington, D.C.: n.p., 1858?), 7, and Douglas, *Report of Senator Douglas, of Illinois, on the Kansas-Lecompton Constitution, February 18, 1858* (Washington, D.C.: Lemuel Towers, 1858), 1, 16.

29. James H. Hammond, *Kansas-Lecompton Constitution: Speech of Hon. James H. Hammond, of South Carolina, on the Admission of Kansas, Delivered in the Senate of the United States, March 4, 1858* (Washington, D.C.: n.p., 1858?), 4, 7, 9.

30. Lafayette Sabine Foster, *Speech of Hon. L. F. S. Foster, of Connecticut, on the Lecompton Constitution; Delivered in the Senate of the United States, March 8 and 19, 1858* (Washington, D.C.: Congressional Globe, 1858), 14–15.

31. Philip G. Auchampaugh, "The Buchanan-Douglas Feud," *Journal of the Illinois State Historical Society* 25 (Apr. 1932–Jan. 1933), 17.

32. *New York Times*'s Washington correspondent, Jan. 14, 1858, *Freedom's Champion*, Feb. 20, 1858.

33. Conrad Swackhamer, "Kansas Congressional Record," *United States Democratic Review* 41, no. 6 (June 1858): 446; and Philip Shriver Klein, *President James Buchanan: A Biography* (University Park: Pennsylvania State University Press, 1962), 310.

34. Swackhamer, "Kansas Congressional Record," 447–448; Klein, *President James Buchanan*, 310; Daniel Webster Wilder, *The Annals of Kansas* (Topeka: T. Dwight Thacher, Kansas Publishing House, 1886; reprint: New York: Arno Press, 1975), 215; and Elbert, "The English Bill," 221.

35. Buchanan to Denver, Mar. 27, 1858 in *Works of James Buchanan*, 10:201–202. For a similar view, see R. S. Stevens to Denver, Apr. 25, 1858, Denver Papers, KHS.

36. Harris to J. Forney et al., "February 5, 1858," in *Democratic Protests*, 5–6.

37. Marcus J. Parrott, *Kansas—the Lecompton Constitution: Speech of Hon. Marcus J. Parrott, Delegate from Kansas, Delivered in the House of Representatives, March 31, 1858* (Washington, D.C.: n.p., 1858), 5, 8.

38. James F. Dowdell, *The Kansas Issue: Remarks of Hon. James F. Dowdell, of Alabama, in the House of Representatives, March 10, 1858, Advocating the Necessity of Additional Guarantees for the Protection of Southern Rights* (Washington, D.C.: Congressional Globe Office, 1858), 1, 6–7.

39. Samuel Cox, *Lecompton Constitution of Kansas: Speech of Hon. Samuel S. Cox, of Ohio, on the President's Message, Delivered in the House of Representatives, December 16, 1857* (Washington: Lemuel Towers, 1857), 9.

40. Elbert, "The English Bill," 222.

41. D. W. Gooch, *The Lecompton Constitution, and the Admission of Kansas into the Union: Speech of Hon. D. W. Gooch, of Mass., delivered in the House of Representatives, March 29, 1858* (n.p., 1858), 7.

42. Wilder, *Annals of Kansas*, 215.

43. *Leavenworth Ledger*, Apr. 19, reprinted in *National Intelligencer*, Apr. 27.

44. Frank Heywood Hodder, "Some Aspects of the English Bill for the Admission of Kansas," in *Annual Report of the American Historical Association for the Year 1906*, vol. 1 (Washington, D.C.: Government Printing Office, 1908), 203–204.

45. Samuel Cox, May 31, 1860, *House Report 648*, 229–230, 290.

46. Wilder, *Annals of Kansas*, 234.

47. Buchanan to William Reed, July 31, in *Works of James Buchanan*, 10:225.

48. *Washington Union*, May 2: Philemon Bliss, *Success of the Absolutists. Their Idealism; What and Whence is it? Speech of Hon. Philemon Bliss, of Ohio, in the House of Representatives, May 24, 1858* (Washington, D.C.: Buell & Blanchard, 1858), 6.

49. Swackhamer, "Kansas Congressional Record," 465.

50. *Freedom's Champion*, May 8.

51. Cass to Denver, May 7, Kansas Territory, Executive Department Correspondence (EDC), KHS.

52. Geary to Pierce, Dec. 15, 1856, "John White Geary: Letters and Papers, 1855–1871, Executive Minutes Diary of Kansas Territory," 290, KHS.

53. Paul Wallace Gates, *Fifty Million Acres: Conflicts over Kansas Land Policy, 1854–1890* (Ithaca, N.Y.: Cornell University Press, 1954), 4. Also see, James C. Malin, *John Brown and the Legend of Fifty-Six* (Philadelphia: American Philosophical Society, 1942), 507–508.

54. Gates, *Fifty Million Acres*, 5.

55. Ibid., 77, 93.

56. John to Everett Family, May 28, John and Sarah Everett, "Letters of John and Sarah Everett," *KHQ* 8, no. 3 (Aug. 1939): 298. Buchanan's decision was widely assailed as motivated by revenge. See *Freedom's Champion*, Apr. 3.

57. See Denver to Buchanan, Aug. 26, in *Transactions*, 5:543.

58. John S. Cummings to Stanton, Dec. 13, 1857, in *Transactions*, 5:318–319.

59. Denver to Cass, June 23, 1858, in ibid., 534, 532.

60. Ibid., 532–533.

61. J. P. Jones and Ben. J. Newsom to Denver, June 3, 1858, in ibid., 526–528.

62. Denver to Cass, June 7, 1858, in ibid., 528–530.

63. Ibid., 530.

64. John Hamilton, T. R. Robert, and J. W. Denver, Resolution at Mass-Meeting of the Citizens of Bourbon County, June 15, 1858, in ibid., 494–495.

65. Sherman to Denver, June 28, 1858, in ibid., 537; Denver to Sherman, June 29, 1858, in ibid., 538.

66. Denver to Cass, Aug. 24, 1858, in ibid., 540–542.

67. R. M. Stewart to Governor Denver, Aug. 7, 1858, EDC.

68. Thompson to Denver, June 21, 1858, quoted in Barns, *Denver, the Man*, 183.

69. Ibid.

70. *Richmond South*, Sept. 27, 1858 quoted in *Freedom's Champion*, Oct. 23.

71. *New Orleans Daily Picayune*, Aug. 20, 1858.

72. Denver to Cass, Sept. 1, 1858, in *Transactions*, 5:544.

73. Thompson to Denver, Oct. 10, 1858, Denver Papers, KHS.

74. Denver, "Proclamation Issued upon His Resignation," Oct. 9.

75. Denver, "Address of Ex-Governor James W. Denver," 168.

76. Homer E. Socolofsky, *Kansas Governors* (Lawrence: University Press of Kansas, 1990), 67.

77. Quoted in J. H. St. Matthew, "Walker's Administration in Kansas," *Overland Monthly* 5, no. 6 (Dec. 1870): 556.

78. Denver to Cass, in *Transactions*, 5:544.

79. See Medary, *House Report 648*, 135–136.

80. Wilder, *Annals of Kansas*, 244.

81. William Frank Zornow, *Kansas: A History of the Jayhawk State* (Norman: University of Oklahoma Press, 1957), 84.

82. Ibid., 86.

83. Lovejoy, Letter to the Editor, *Boston Zion's Herald*, Oct. 6, 1859, "Letters of Julia Louisa Lovejoy," *KHQ* 16, no. 1 (Feb. 1948): 70.

84. Wilder, *Annals of Kansas*, 295.

85. Zornow, *Kansas*, 88.

86. Buchanan, *Mr. Buchanan's Administration*, 46.

87. *Freedom's Champion*, May 15, 1858. Also see *Charleston Mercury*, July 27, 1858.

88. Bruce W. Collins, "The Democrats' Electoral Fortunes during the Lecompton Crisis," *Civil War History* 24, no. 4 (Dec. 1978): 314–331.

89. Buchanan to Harriet Lane, Oct. 15, 1858, in *Works of James Buchanan*, 10:229–230.

90. Buchanan, "Second Annual Message," Dec. 6, 1858, in *Works of James Buchanan*, 10:237–238.

91. Ibid., 241.

92. Buchanan, *Mr. Buchanan's Administration*, 55.

93. Ibid., 50–51.

94. Ibid., 56.

95. R. G. Horton, *The Life and Public Services of James Buchanan* (New York: Derby & Jackson, 1856), 397, 428, 403–404.

Chapter 6. The Illusion of Security

1. "Jayhawker" is an umbrella term that described Kansans such as James Montgomery and Charles R. Jennison and their motivated followers who operated outside the law and employed guerrilla tactics to free slaves and aid fugitives. Many also liberated horses, money, and other items of value, which compromised the Jayhawkers' image as a moral agent to eradicate slavery. Jayhawkers were pro-Unionists once the Civil War began. They continued their guerrilla operations in Missouri under federal authority and ostensibly within the law. The sacking of Osceola in September 1861 was one example of the excessive brutality that characterized the Civil War along the Kansas-Missouri border. The most famous or infamous Missouri guerrilla or Bushwhacker assault was William Quantrill's raid on Lawrence in August 1863. Thanks to Jonathan Earle, Diane Mutti Burke, Michael Fellman, Sam Watson, and all the other contributors for their comments and suggestions for this chapter and for the entire volume.

2. T. F. Robley, *History of Bourbon County, Kansas to the Close of 1865* (Fort Scott, Kans.: n.p., 1894), 150. See also, "Troubles in South-Eastern Kansas," *Kansas National Democrat*, Nov. 23, 1860. See Parsons to Stewart, Dec. 8, 1860, Box 2, Folder 31, Missouri-Kansas Border War Collection, Southwest Expedition Collection (MK/SEC), Missouri State Archives, Jefferson City, Mo., for more information about Scott. See also, "ANOTHER OUTBREAK IN KANSAS.; Capt. Montgomery Again in the Field—Marauding and Murder—Reported Outrages upon Settlers," *New York Times*, Nov. 22, 1860, http://www.nytimes.com/1860/11/22 /news/another-outbreak-kansas-capt-montgomery-again-field-marauding-murder-reported.html?scp=1&sq=another+outbreak+in+kansas &st=p. See Dale E. Watts, "How Bloody Was Bleeding Kansas? Political Killings in Kansas Territory, 1854–1861," *Kansas History* 18, no. 2 (Summer 1995): 129.

3. Charles R. "Doc" Jennison was perhaps the most notorious of all Jayhawkers. His "Red Legs" were the most feared and hated forces in Missouri during the Civil War. The government established Fort Scott as a military installation in 1842. It was deactivated in 1853, and the location became the proslavery community of Fort Scott during the territorial period.

4. For specific guidance, see "Abstract from instructions to Governor Walker, Dated July 25th 1857,"Adjutant General's Office to Department of the West, Fort Leavenworth, Department of the West enclosure from the War Department, Feb. 21, 1859, Box 6, Letters Received, Department of the West (LR DW), RG 393, National Archives and Records Administration, Washington, D.C. (NARA).

5. Cooper to Harney (telegram), Nov. 22, 1860, Box 8, Letters Received, LR DW, RG 393, NARA.

6. Cooper to Harney (telegram), Nov. 28, 1860, Box 9, LR DW, RG 393, NARA.

7. Stewart to Medary, Apr. 8, 1859, Box 1, Folder 38, MK/SEC.

8. Frost to Harney, Headqusrters, Southwest Expedition (HQ SWE), Camp Parsons, Nov. 24, 1860, Box 8, LR DW, RG-393, NARA. See also George Rollie Adams, *General Williams S. Harney* (Lincoln: University of Nebraska Press, 2001), 219.

9. Frost to Harney, HQ SWE, Camp Parsons, Nov. 24, 1860, Box 8, LR DW, RG-393, NARA.

10. Frost to Stewart, HQ SWE, Camp Daniel Boone, Dec. 5, 1860, Box 2, Folder 30, MK/SEC.

11. Augustus Wattles to Thaddeus Hyatt, Dec. 3, 1860, http://www.territorial kansasonline.org/~imlskto/cgi-bin/index.php?SCREEN=show_transcript&docu ment_id=101607SCREEN=keyword&submit=&search=&startsearchat=35&search for=&printerfriendly=&county_id=&topic_id=&document_id=101607&selected_ keyword=Montgomery,%20James,%201814-1871.

12. Augustus Wattles to Thaddeus Hyatt, Dec. 3, 1860, http://www.territorial

kansasonline.org/~imlskto/cgi-bin/index.php?SCREEN=show_transcript&docu ment_id=101607SCREEN=keyword&submit=&search=&startsearchat=35&search for=&printerfriendly=&county_id=&topic_id=&document_id=101607&selected_ keyword=Montgomery,%20James,%201814-1871.

13. Augustus Wattles to Thaddeus Hyatt, Dec. 3, 1860, http://www.territorial kansasonline.org/~imlskto/cgi-bin/index.php?SCREEN=show_transcript&docu ment_id=101607SCREEN=keyword&submit=&search=&startsearchat=35&search for=&printerfriendly=&county_id=&topic_id=&document_id=101607&selected_ keyword=Montgomery,%20James,%201814-1871.

14. Montgomery to Stearns, Mound City, Nov. 27, 1860, http://www.territori alkansasonline.org/~imlskto/cgi-bin/index.php?SCREEN=show_transcript&docu ment_id=100493SCREEN=keyword&submit=&search=&startsearchat=35&search for=&printerfriendly=&county_id=&topic_id=&document_id=100493&selected_ keyword=Montgomery,%20James,%201814-1871.

15. Montgomery to Stearns, Mound City, Nov. 27, 1860, http://www.territori alkansasonline.org/~imlskto/cgi-bin/index.php?SCREEN=show_transcript&docu ment_id=100493SCREEN=keyword&submit=&search=&startsearchat=35&search for=&printerfriendly=&county_id=&topic_id=&document_id=100493&selected_ keyword=Montgomery,%20James,%201814-1871.

16. See Welch, *Border Warfare*, 187–190, and Robley, *History of Bourbon County*, 127–133. Proslavery elements arrested Ben Rice for murder and held him prisoner at the Fort Scott Hotel. James Montgomery deemed his arrest illegal and formed a band to rescue Rice from his incarceration on December 16, 1858. During the raid, Montgomery's men exchanged gunfire with local residents. John Little, former deputy marshal, was mortally wounded in the melee. Judge Williams issued a writ for Montgomery's arrest for Little's death.

17. Montgomery to Stearns, Mound City, Nov. 27, 1860, http://www.territorial kansasonline.org/~imlskto/cgi-bin/index.php?SCREEN=show_transcript&docu ment_id=100493SCREEN=keyword&submit=&search=&startsearchat=35& search for=&printerfriendly=&county_id=&topic_id=&document_id=100493&selected _keyword=Montgomery,%20James,%201814-1871.

18. Montgomery to Stearns, Mound City, Dec. 12, 1860, http://www.territori alkansasonline.org/~imlskto/cgi-bin/index.php?SCREEN=show_transcript&docu ment_id=100495SCREEN=keyword&submit=&search=&startsearchat=40&search for=&printerfriendly=&county_id=&topic_id=&document_id=100495&selected_ keyword=Montgomery,%20James,%201814-1871.

19. Montgomery to Stearns, Mound City, Dec. 14, 1860, http://www.territori alkansasonline.org/~imlskto/cgi-bin/index.php?SCREEN=show_transcript&docu ment_id=100497SCREEN=keyword&submit=&search=&startsearchat=40&search for=&printerfriendly=&county_id=&topic_id=&document_id=100497&selected_ keyword=Montgomery,%20James,%201814-1871.

20. Montgomery to F. B. Sanborn, Mound City, Linn Co, KT, Jan. 14, 1861, Stearns Collection, Kansas Historical Society, Topeka, Kans. (KHS).

21. See Fort Leavenworth Post Return, Nov. 1860, *Returns from US Military Posts*, M617, Reel 611, RG-94, NARA, and Fort Riley Post Return, Nov. 1860, *Returns from US Military Posts*, M617, Reel 1011, RG-94, NARA.

22. Montgomery to Stearns, Mound City, Dec. 14, 1860, http://www.territori alkansasonline.org/~imlskto/cgi-bin/index.php?SCREEN=show_transcript&docu ment_id=100497SCREEN=keyword&submit=&search=&startsearchat=40&search for=&printerfriendly=&county_id=&topic_id=&document_id=100497&selected_ keyword=Montgomery,%20James,%201814-1871.

23. Montgomery to F. B. Sanborn, Mound City, Linn Co, KT, Jan. 14, 1861, SHS.

24. The Wide Awake Organization was one of several known or suspected secret antislavery societies that existed in and around territorial Kansas. According to G. Murlin Welch, the Linn County version emerged from a free-state reaction to a claim dispute in June 1857. The proslavery supporters formed secret societies known as "Dark Lantern Societies" or "Blue Lodges" to force free-state supporters out of their communities. See Welch, *Border Warfare*, 14, 33, 39, 163–164, 178, and 234, for more information on secret societies.

25. Montgomery to Stearns, Mound City, Dec. 12, 1860, http://www.territori alkansasonline.org/~imlskto/cgi-bin/index.php?SCREEN=show_transcript&docu ment_id=100495SCREEN=keyword&submit=&search=&startsearchat=40&search for=&printerfriendly=&county_id=&topic_id=&document_id=100495&selected_ keyword=Montgomery,%20James,%201814-1871; Montgomery to Stearns, Mound City, Dec. 14, 1860, http://www.territorialkansasonline.org/~imlskto/cgi-bin/ index.php?SCREEN=show_transcript&document_id=100497SCREEN=keyword& submit=&search=&startsearchat=40&searchfor=&printerfriendly=&county_id=& topic_id=&document_id=100497&selected_keyword=Montgomery,%20James,%20 1814-1871.

26. Department of the Army, FM 3-24, *Counterinsurgency* (Washington D.C.: Government Printing Office, 2006), 1–2.

27. Montgomery to F. B. Sanborn, Mound City, Jan. 14, 1861, Stearns Collection, KHS.

28. Ibid.

29. Stewart to Snyder, Jefferson City, Nov. 20, 1860, Box 2, Folder 3, MK/SEC.

30. Exec Dept to Parsons, Jefferson City, Mo., Apr. 5, 1859, Box 1, Folder 37, MK/ SEC.

31. Robert W. Coakley, *The Role of Federal Military Forces in Domestic Disorders, 1789–1878* (Washington, D.C.: Center for Military History, 1988), 187.

32. Montgomery to F. B. Sanborn, Mound City, Jan. 14, 1861, Stearns Collection, KHS.

33. "AFFAIRS IN KANSAS.; Advices Direct from Fort Scott—United States Troops in Possession—The Land Sales—The Actual Condition of Matters," *New York Times*, Dec. 4, 1860, http://www.nytimes.com/1860/12/22/news/affairs-kansas-advices-direct-fort-scott-united-states-troops-possession-land.html?scp=2&sq=affairs+in+kansas+dec+22+1860&st=p.

34. Ibid.

35. Ibid.

36. See Mullis, *Peacekeeping on the Plains* (Columbia: University of Missouri Press, 2004), 61–95.

37. Denver to Stewart, Lecompton, Aug. 18, 1858, Box 1, Folder 21, MK/SEC.

38. J. F. Snyder (from Bolivar) to Stewart (HQ 6th Div Mo Militia), Aug. 7, 1858, Box 1, Folder 20, MK/SEC.

39. "To the People of Kansas," Lecompton *Kansas National Democrat*, Dec. 20, 1860.

40. Montgomery to F. B. Sanborn, Mound City, Jan. 14, 1861, Stearns Collection, KHS.

41. For more on General Order No. 11, see Michael Fellman, *Inside War: The Guerrilla Conflict in Missouri during the American Civil War* (New York: Oxford University Press, 1989), 95–96.

42. For an example of a secret code see Brian R. Dirck, "By the Hand of God: James Montgomery and Redemptive Violence," *Kansas History: A Journal of the Central Plains* 27 (Spring–Summer 2004): 109.

43. Hackney to Stewart, June 1 or 6, 1858, Box 1, Folder 5, MK/SEC.

44. Denver to Stewart, Lecompton, Aug. 18, 1858, Box 1, Folder 21, MK/SEC.

45. For other explanations, see Nicole Etcheson, *Bleeding Kansas: Contested Liberty in the Civil War Era* (Lawrence: University Press of Kansas, 2004); Jeremy Neely, *The Border between Them: Violence and Reconciliation on the Kansas-Missouri Line* (Columbia: University of Missouri Press, 2007); Coakley, *The Role of Federal Military Forces in Domestic Disorders*; and Robley, *History of Bourbon County*.

Chapter 7. "If I Went West, I Think I Would Go to Kansas"

1. The flag now resides in the main gallery of the Kansas Museum of History in Topeka.

2. Lincoln was not even renominated for a second term in the House by the Whigs of central Illinois. Kansas was admitted as the thirty-fourth state on January 29, 1861, after South Carolina, Mississippi, Florida, Alabama, Georgia, and Louisiana had left the Union (and three days before Texas seceded).

3. Lincoln has come in first in a large majority of the polls of historians and political scientists since Arthur Schlesinger Sr. first conducted a survey in 1948, as well as most polls conducted by media organizations—despite being one of the most divisive chief executives in American history during his own time. See William A.

Degregorio, *The Complete Book of U.S. Presidents* (New York: Barricade Books, 2013); William J. Ridings Jr. and Stuart B. McIver, *Rating the Presidents: A Ranking of U.S. Leaders, from the Great and Honorable to the Dishonest and Incompetent* (New York: Citadel Press, 1997).

4. Robert A. Taft, "A Century of Kansas History: Abraham Lincoln in Kansas," *Kansas Teacher* 63, no. 6 (Feb. 1955): 40. A talented local historian wrote a book that is full of excellent primary sources for Lincoln's visit to Kansas. See Carol Dark Ayres, *Lincoln and Kansas: Partnership for Freedom* (Manhattan, Kans.: Sunflower University Press, 2001). Fred W. Brinkerhoff's essay is also very informative. See Fred W. Brinkerhoff, "Address of the President: The Kansas Tour of Lincoln the Candidate," *Kansas Historical Quarterly* 12, no. 5 (1945): 294–307.

5. David Donald, *Lincoln* (New York: Simon & Schuster, 1995), 132–133.

6. Ibid., 140–141.

7. Michael Burlingame, *Abraham Lincoln: A Life* (Baltimore: Johns Hopkins University Press, 2008), 1:309–362. As the author notes, Lincoln spent this "midlife crisis" growing as both a politician and a person, instead of running off with a younger woman or buying a particularly fast horse and carriage.

8. Herndon to W. H. Lamon, March 6, 1870, Lamon MSS, Huntington Library, San Marino, Calif.

9. While Douglas said the phrase several times, it was made especially famous in Lincoln's "House Divided" speech. See Roy P. Basler, ed., *Collected Works of Abraham Lincoln* (New Brunswick, N.J.: Rutgers University Press, 1953), 2:461–468.

10. *Congressional Globe*, 33 Cong., 1 Sess., Appendix, 769.

11. "Appeal of the Independent Democrats in Congress to the People of the United States," in *Diary and Correspondence of Salmon P. Chase, Annual Report of AHA*, vol. 2 (Washington, D.C., 1902).

12. Opposition to the Kansas-Nebraska Act led to immense public meetings in Wisconsin, Michigan, Vermont, Maine, Ohio, Indiana, and Iowa. The new movement carried with it different names, but the name "Republican"—first used in Ripon, Wisconsin, in February 1854—was the one that stuck.

13. Lincoln, Speech at Peoria, Ill., Oct. 16, 1854, in Basler, *Collected Works*, 2:275.

14. Ibid.

15. D. W. Bartlett, *Presidential Candidates of 1860* (New York, 1859). Bartlett's guide to the Republican field contained biographical sketches of twenty-one potential candidates, but neglected to provide one on Lincoln.

16. On the Cooper Union address, see Harold Holzer's *Lincoln at Cooper Union: The Speech That Made Abraham Lincoln President* (New York: Simon & Schuster, 2006).

17. "Lincoln in Kansas," *Transactions of the Kansas State Historical Society* 7 (1901–1920): 536–537.

18. Basler, *Collected Works*, 3:496.

19. *New York Tribune*, December 3, 1859.

20. I am grateful to Michael Fellman for this insight. See his excellent chapter on John Brown in *Views from the Dark Side of American History* (Baton Rouge: Louisiana State University Press, 2011).

21. One could say the Cooper Union speech was to Lincoln what the keynote address at the 2004 Democratic National Convention in Boston was to another little-known Illinois lawyer with lofty political aspirations.

22. *Leavenworth Weekly Herald*, Dec. 10, 1859; see also *Kansas Historical Quarterly* 20 (1951–1953): 530–532; Ayres, *Lincoln and Kansas*, 109–110.

23. *Leavenworth Daily Times*, Dec. 5, 1859; Ayres, *Lincoln and Kansas*, 108.

24. Holzer, *Cooper Union*, passim.

25. *New York Times*, Oct. 3, 1860.

Chapter 8. "A Question of Power Not One of Law"

We would like to thank the Kansas City Public Library and the Kentucky Historical Society for permission to the republish portions of this essay that appear on the *Civil War on the Western Border* website, http://www.civilwaronthewesternborder.org, and in the *Register of the Kentucky Historical Society*: Christopher Phillips, "Netherworld of War: The Dominion System and the Contours of Federal Occupation in Kentucky," *Register of the Kentucky Historical Society* 11, nos. 3 and 4 (Summer/Autumn 2012).

1. George Caleb Bingham to Ja[me]s. S. Rollins and W[illia]m. A. Hall, Feb. 12, 1862, in James Rollins, ed., "Letters of Bingham to Rollins—Part V, Letters: Jan. 22, 1862–Nov. 21, 1871," *Missouri Historical Review* (MHR) 33 (Oct. 1938): 53–54.

2. On the debates and decisions on neutrality in the various border slave states, see William C. Harris, *Lincoln and the Border States* (Lawrence: University Press of Kansas, 2011), esp. chaps. 1–4.

3. Stephen V. Ash, *When the Yankees Came* (Chapel Hill: University of North Carolina Press, 1999), 44–45, 84; Abiel Leonard to Jeanette Leonard, Mar. 7, 1862, Abiel Leonard Papers, Mss. 1013, folder 457, State Historical Society of Missouri (SHSM), Manuscript Collection, Columbia, Mo.; Michael Fellman, *Inside War* (New York: Oxford University Press, 1989), 40; H[enry]. W. Halleck to George B. McClellan, Dec. 19, 1861, in *The War of the Rebellion: Official Records of the Union and Confederate Armies* (OR), 4 ser., 128 vols. (Washington, D.C.: Government Printing Office, 1881–1901), ser. 1, 8:448–449. The term "dominion system" is the author's own.

4. On Apr. 28, 1862, Jefferson Davis signed the Confederate War Department's Partisan Ranger Act, and in July, Maj. Gen. Thomas C. Hindman published his "Confederate Partisan Act in Missouri." They authorized the organization of and

military structure for irregular partisan bands. William E. Parrish, *A History of Missouri*, vol. 3: *1860 to 1875* (Columbia: University of Missouri Press, 1973), 51; Fellman, *Inside War*, 98–99.

5. Scout through Saline County, Missouri, Dec. 14, 1861, OR, ser. 1, 8:34–36; *History of Saline County, Missouri* (St. Louis: Missouri Historical Co., 1881), 628–629.

6. Samuel R. Curtis, "Report on Operations of Iowa Troops in Missouri in June, 1861," *Annals of Iowa*, 3ʳᵈ ser., 8 (Apr. 1908): 358–361; Daniel E. Sutherland, *A Savage Conflict* (Chapel Hill: University of North Carolina Press, 2009), 16–17; J. T. K. Hayward to John C. Frémont, Aug. 10, 1861, OR, ser. 1, 3:434; *Clinton* (Missouri) *Advocate*, Aug. 3, 1876; *Carrollton* (Missouri) *Democrat*, Aug. 25, 1876. Curtis's report to Nathaniel Lyon, dated June 27, 1861, was not included in OR.

7. J. T. K. Hayward to John C. Fremont, Aug. 10, 1861, OR, ser. 1, 3:434; David Bailey to Hamilton R. Gamble, Jan. 13, 1862, Record Group 133: Adjutant General Missouri Volunteers, 27th Regiment Infantry, Regimental Correspondence—Miscellaneous, box 1, Missouri State Archives, Jefferson City, Mo.; W[yllis]. C. Ransom to Thomas Ewing Jr., May 30, 1871, Ewing Family Papers, box 212, Manuscripts Division, Library of Congress, Washington, D.C. (LC); 1875 Kansas State Census, microfilm reel K-6, Kansas Historical Society, Topeka, Kansas; Allen, Andrew, File, Aug. 28, 1864, microfilm reel 131, *Union Provost Marshals' File of Papers Relating to Individual Citizens*, Record Group 109: War Department Collection of Confederate Records, 300 microfilm reels [hereafter cited as Provost I], National Archives and Records Administration, Washington, D.C. (NARA); Smith, Seeden, File, Nov. 30, 1864, microfilm reel 251, Provost I; Holmes, James E., File, Aug. 28, 1864, microfilm reel 131, Provost I; Stuck, I. C., File, Mar. 24, 1864, microfilm reel 260, Provost I; General Orders No. 34, Sept. 13, 1863, in U.S. War Department, *Missouri Troops in Service during the Civil War: A Letter from the Secretary of War . . . Showing Various Classes of Missouri Volunteers, Militia, and Home Guards in Service during the Civil War* (Washington, D.C.: Government Printing Office, 1902), 179.

8. Message to Congress in Special Session, July 4, 1861, in *The Collected Works of Abraham Lincoln (CWAL)*, 11 vols., ed. Roy P. Basler (Springfield, Ill.: Abraham Lincoln Association, 1953), 4:426–428.

9. James M. McPherson, *For Cause and Comrades* (New York: Oxford University Press, 1997), 3–13; Proclamation, "To all peaceably-disposed citizens of the State of Missouri, greeting," Nov. 1, 5, 1861, OR, ser. 1, 3:563–564; Ettie Scott to Susan Grigsby, Aug. 3, 1862, Grigsby Family Papers, Mss. A/G857, folder 173, Filson Historical Society, Louisville, Ky. (FHS); Williamson Dixon Ward Civil War Journal, Oct. 12, 1861, entry, Mss. SC627, Kentucky Library and Special Collections, Western Kentucky University, Bowling Green, Ky. (WKU); J[ohn]. M. Schofield to E[dwin]. M. Stanton, May 16, 1862, OR, ser. 1, 13:386; Elvira A. W.

Scott Diary (typescript), Mss. 1053, folder 4, 116–131, SHSM; Samuel S. Hildebrand, *The Autobiography of Sam S. Hildebrand*, comp. James W. Evans and Abraham Wendell Keith (Jefferson City, Mo.: State Times Printing House, 1870), 47; James H. Goodnow to Nancy Goodnow, Aug. 29, 1862, James H. Goodnow Papers, LC.

10. Edward Conrad Smith, *The Borderland in the Civil War* (New York: Macmillan, 1927), 367–368; William Crawford to H[enry]. W. Halleck, Jan. 5, 1862, Record Group 393: Records of the U.S. Army Continental Commands, 1821–1920 (RG 393), pt. 1, ser. 2593: Letters Received, Department of the Missouri, 1862–1867, box 2, NARA; Abraham Lincoln to Samuel R. Curtis, Jan. 5, 1863, *OR*, ser. 1, 22/2:17–18; H[enry]. W. Halleck to George B. McClellan, Dec. 19, 1861, *OR*, ser. 1, 8:448–449.

11. Statement of T[heodore]. M. Ault, Jan. 3, 1862, Francis J. Herron to Benjamin Farrar, Jan. 5, 1862, Affidavit of Samuel Shelton, undated, all in Shelton, Samuel, File, microfilm reel 243, Provost I; Smith, *Borderland in the Civil War*, 373; Ash, *When the Yankees Came*, 84; Dennis K. Boman, *Lincoln's Resolute Unionist* (Baton Rouge: Louisiana State University Press, 2006), 203–205; John M. Schofield to John C. Kelton, June 17, 1862, *OR*, ser. 2, 4:34.

12. General Orders No. 5, Oct. 7, 1861, *OR*, ser. 1, 4:296; J. T. K. Hayward to John C. Frémont, Aug. 10, 1861, *OR*, ser. 1, 3:434; E. Merton Coulter, *The Civil War and Readjustment in Kentucky* (Chapel Hill: University of North Carolina Press, 1926), 148; Smith, *Borderland in the Civil War*, 372; William T. Sherman to W. T. Ward, Nov. 2, 1861, *OR*, ser. 1, 4:327; R. A. Curd to Cal Morgan, June 22, 1862, Hunt-Morgan Family Papers, Mss. 63M202, box 15, folder 9, Special Collections and Archives, University of Kentucky, Lexington, Ky. (UK).

13. Ira Berlin et al., eds., *Freedom: A Documentary History of Emancipation*, ser. 1, vol. 1: *The Destruction of Slavery* (Cambridge: Cambridge University Press, 1986), 398; David Rice Atchison to Col. J[efferson]. Davis, Sept. 24, 1854, David Rice Atchison Papers, Mss. 71, folder 4, SHSM; T. J. Stiles, *Jesse James* (New York: Alfred A. Knopf, 2001), 50, 73–77; James A. Hamilton, "The Enrolled Missouri Militia: Its Creation and Controversial History," *MHR* 69 (July 1975): 416–419; Bruce Nichols, *Guerrilla Warfare in Civil War Missouri, 1862* (Jefferson, N.C.: McFarland, 2004), 103–105. Over 52,000 Missourians were enrolled in seventy EMM regiments, which, unlike the MSM, were confined to service in their home state.

14. Coulter, *Civil War and Readjustment*, 151–153; Lloyd W. Franks, ed., *The Journal of Elder William Conrad: Pioneer Preacher* (Lexington, Ky.: RF Publishing, 1976), 76–77; Ettie Scott to Susan Grigsby, Aug. 3, 1862, Susan Preston Shelby Grigsby Papers, Mss. A/G857, folder 173, FHS; G. Glenn Clift, ed., *The Private War of Lizzie Hardin* (Frankfort: Kentucky Historical Society, 1963), 63; L. C. Turner to J[eremiah]. T. Boyle, Nov. 2, 1862; and Isaac R. Gray to Boyle, Nov. 17,

1862, both in RG 393, pt. 1, ser. 2173: Letters Received, Department of Kentucky, 1862–1869, box 1, NARA; R. A. Curd to Cal Morgan, June 22, 1862, Hunt-Morgan Family Papers, Mss. 63M202, box 15, folder 9, UK.

15. John M. Schofield to John C. Kelton, June 17, 1862, *OR*, ser. 2, 4:34. In Sept. 1862, the federal adjutant general's office issued General Orders No. 140, appointing special provost marshals for each state, with responsibility for investigating charges or acts of treason and arresting deserters, spies, and persons deemed disloyal in order to enforce the militia drafts in the various states. Guards were assigned to the provost marshal to assist in carrying out assigned functions, chief of which was preservation of order. Curtis implemented and expanded the system in Missouri beginning in December 1862, including the disarming of alleged disloyalists. A reorganization of the War Department in 1863 required a provost marshal for each congressional district and a deputy provost marshal for each county. In districts removed from the scene of fighting, provost marshals had expanded powers to administer and enforce the law beyond those in war zones, regulating public places; conducting searches, seizures, and arrests; regulating sermons and printed materials; issuing travel passes to citizens within and beyond federal lines; and recording and investigating citizen complaints. Later in the war, they assumed responsibility for conducting local military drafts, with the assistance of enrollment boards. Smith, *Borderland in the Civil War*, 373; Ash, *When the Yankees Came*, 84; Boman, *Lincoln's Resolute Unionist*, 203–205.

16. F. D. Dickinson to Dear Aunt, May 15, 1863, F. D. Dickinson Letter, Mss. C/D, FHS; Oath of Allegiance, May 19, 1862, William Johnson Stone Papers, Mss. 54M131 [microfilm], UK; J. Howard McHenry to Lt. Col. Chesebrough, Feb. 21, 1863, Hunt-Morgan Family Papers, Mss. 63M202, box 16, folder 9, UK; M. A. Shelby to Susan Grigsby, July 26, [1863], Grigsby Family Papers, Mss. A/G857, folder 179, FHS.

17. William B. Napton Journals (typescript), 318, William B. Napton Papers, box 1, Missouri History Museum, St. Louis, Mo. (MHM); Thomas B. Gordon to Neal M. Gordon, Aug. 12, 1862, Nov. 24, 1863, both in Gordon Family Papers, Mss. 51M40, box 4, UK.

18. Carole Emberton, "Reconstructing Loyalty: Love, Fear, and Power in the Postwar South," in *The Great Task Remaining before Us*, ed. Paul A. Cimbala and Randall M. Miller (New York: Fordham University Press, 2010), 173–174; Printed Oath of Allegiance, Aug. 16, 1864, Thomas S. Crutcher File, Mss. C/C, FHS; Oath of Allegiance of Samuel Jones Denton, Mss. C/D, FHS; Joseph Maple Diary, 7, 12, Cape Girardeau County Archives Center, Jackson, Mo.; Bettie Morton to Pat [Joyes], July 21, 1862, Joyes Family Papers, Mss. A/J89b, folder 18, FHS; Barton Bates to Edward Bates, Sept. 8, 1861, Bates Family Papers, MHM; Coulter, *Civil War and Readjustment*, 151; Mark Grimsley, *The Hard Hand of War* (Cambridge: Cambridge University Press, 1996), 38; Richard S. Brownlee, *Gray Ghosts of the*

Confederacy (1958; reprint: Baton Rouge: Louisiana State University Press, 1984), 164–167; Parrish, *History of Missouri*, 67. On loyalty oaths during the Civil War, see Harold M. Hyman, *Era of the Oath* (New York: Octagon Books, 1954).

19. John S. Morton to Pat [Joyes], July 26, 1862, Joyes Family Papers, Mss. A/J89b, folder 18, FHS; Samuel W. Pruitt to Dear Bettie, Apr. 20, 1863, Samuel W. Pruitt Letters, Mss. C/P, FHS; James Prentiss to John B. Bruner, Sept. 12, 1861, John B. Bruner Papers, Mss. A/B894, folder 17, FHS; C. H. McElroy to Charles Whittlesey, Jan. 2, 1862, Charles Whittlesey Papers, Mss. 3196, Western Reserve Historical Society, Cleveland, Ohio.

20. Fanny Gunn to John and Thomas Gunn, Aug. 16, 1862, Gunn Family Papers, Mss. 73M28, UK; John David Smith and William Cooper Jr., eds., *A Union Woman in Civil War Kentucky* (Lexington: University Press of Kentucky, 2000), 65; Bond of R. B. Steele, Nov. 15, 1862, and W. L. Gibson to S. G. Hicks, Nov. 19, 1863, both in RG 393, pt. 1, ser. 2173: Letters Received, Department of Kentucky, 1862–1869, box 1, NARA; O. D. Williams to Samuel R. Curtis, Dec. 4, 1862, RG 393, pt.1, ser. 2593: Letters Received, Department of the Missouri, 1862–1867, box 7, NARA; Isaac R. Gray to J[eremiah]. T. Boyle, Nov. 17, 1862, RG 393, pt. 1, ser. 2173: Letters Received, Department of Kentucky, 1862–1869, box 1, NARA; Elvira A. W. Scott Diary [transcript], Mss. 1053, 155, SHSM; Abraham Lincoln to Samuel R. Curtis, Jan. 2, 1863, *CWAL*, 6:33–34.

21. Samuel Haycraft Journal, 1849–1873, June 17, 1862, entry, Mss. A/H414, FHS; R. A. Curd to Cal Morgan, June 22, 1862, Hunt-Morgan Family Papers, Mss. 63M202, box 15, folder 9, UK; Thomas B[oston]. Gordon to Neal M. Gordon, Aug. 12, 1862, Gordon Family Papers, Mss. 51M40, box 4, UK; Ettie Scott to Susan Grigsby, Aug. 3, 1862, Grigsby Family Papers, Mss. A/G857, folder 173, FHS; Elvira A. W. Scott Diary [transcript], Mss. 1053, pp. 118–131, SHSM.

22. J[eremiah]. T. Boyle to H[oratio]. G. Wright, Nov. 14, 1862, and Henry Dent to Boyle, Nov. 14, 1862, and responses, Nov. 19–20, 1862, all in *OR*, ser. 1, 30/2:51, 5–6. Boyle to Capt. King, Nov. 14, 1862; Leonidas Metcalfe to Boyle, Dec. 14, 1862; B[enjamin]. H. Bristow to S. D. Bruce, Dec. 21, 1864, all in RG 393, pt. 1, ser. 2173: Letters Received, Department of Kentucky, box 1, NARA. W[illiam]. G. Eliot to H[amilton]. R. Gamble and endorsements [by Gamble and Samuel R. Curtis], Dec. 1, 1862, and John M. Schofield to James S. Thomas, Dec. 5, 1862, all in *OR*, ser. 1, 22/1:801–803, 810–812. On William G. Eliot, see Adam Arenson, *The Great Heart of the Republic: St. Louis and the Cultural Civil War* (Cambridge, Mass.: Harvard University Press, 2011), 140–142.

23. W. F. Evans to J[eremiah]. T. Boyle, Nov. 9, 1862, RG 393, pt. 1, ser. 2173: Letters Received, Department of Kentucky, 1862–1869, box 1, NARA.

24. J. T. K. Hayward to John C. Frémont, Aug. 10, 1861, *OR*, ser. 1, 3:434; "Sermon Delivered in the Lexington Presbyterian Church," June 3, 1862, p. 12, Lyle Family Papers, Mss. 62M49, box 1848–1872, UK; Clift, *Private War*, 51.

25. Frank F. Mathias, ed., *Incidents and Experiences in the Life of Thomas W. Parsons from 1826 to 1900* (Lexington: University Press of Kentucky, 1982), 87–89, 114; Petition of Thomas H. Smith et al., Sept. 1, 1864, and affidavits, RG 393, pt. 1, ser. 2229: Correspondence, Affidavits, Oaths Regarding Civilians Charged with Disloyalty, Department of Kentucky, box 1, NARA.

26. Collins, Perry H., File, Feb. 22, 1862, Provost I, microfilm reel 56, pt. C, NARA.

27. Edwin Smith to Maria Smith, Oct. 14, 1862, Smith Family Papers, CHSL; Clift, *Private War*, 48, 59; Mary A. Crebs to My own dear Husband [Daniel Crebs], Nov. 16, 1863, Mary A. Berry [Crebs] Letters, Misc. vol. 88, Special Collections and Archives, Southern Illinois University, Carbondale, Ill.; T. Harry Williams, "Voters in Blue: The Citizen Soldiers of the Civil War," *Mississippi Valley Historical Review* 31 (Sept. 1944): 199; Martha M. Jones to My dear father, Dec. 21, 1862, Jones Family Papers, Mss. A/J78, folder 1, FHS; Henry Chenoweth to Thomas W. Bullitt, Mar. 1, 1862, Bullitt-Chenoweth Family Papers, Mss. A/B937a, folder 300, FHS; Thomas Bullitt to Mildred Ann Bullitt, Mar. 23, 1864, ibid., folder 301, FHS; Cora Owens Hume Journal [transcript], June 1, 1865, entry, 2:119, Mss. A/H921 Vault C, FHS.

28. Bernard G. Farrar to Major Hunt, Mar. 8, 1862, OR, ser. 2, 1:173–174; [St. Joseph, Mo.] *Weekly Herald*, Apr. 17, 1862; General Orders No. 34, Dec. 26, 1861, OR, ser. 1, 8:468.

Chapter 9. "Slavery Dies Hard"

I would like to thank the University of Georgia Press and the Kansas City Public Library for portions of this essay that appear in Diane Mutti Burke, *On Slavery's Border: Missouri's Small-Slaveholding Households, 1815–1865* (Athens: University of Georgia Press, 2010), chap. 7, and the *Civil War on the Western Border* website at www.civilwaronthewesternborder.org.

1. Henry Clay Bruce, *The New Man* (York, Pa.: P. Anstadt & Sons, 1895).

2. See Mutti Burke, *On Slavery's Border*.

3. Jordan O'Bryan to John Miller, Feb. 6, 1854, Jordan O'Bryan Letter, 1854, State Historical Society of Missouri, Manuscript Collection, Columbia, Mo. (SHSM); John Doy, *The Narrative of John Doy* (New York: Thomas Holman, 1860). See also Mutti Burke, *On Slavery's Border*; Kristen Epps, "Bound Together: Masters and Slaves on the Kansas-Missouri Border, 1825–1865" (dissertation, University of Kansas, 2010); and Richard B. Sheridan, ed., *Freedom's Crucible* (Lawrence: Division of Continuing Education, University of Kansas, 1998).

4. See William Parrish, *Turbulent Partnership* (Columbia: University of Missouri Press, 1963); and Christopher Phillips, *Missouri's Confederate* (Columbia: University of Missouri Press, 2000).

5. Lizzie E. Brannock to Brother Edwin, Jan. 13, 1864, Lizzie E. Brannock Let-

ters, 1864, SHSM. See LeeAnn Whites, "Forty Shirts and a Wagon Load of Wheat," *Journal of the Civil War Era* 1, no. 1 (Mar. 2011): 56–78; Joseph Beilein Jr. "'The Presence of These Families Is the Cause of the Presence There of the Guerrillas'" (MA thesis, University of Missouri, 2006); Richard Brownlee, *Gray Ghosts of the Confederacy* (Baton Rouge: Louisiana State University Press, 1958); Michael Fellman, *Inside War* (New York: Oxford University Press, 1989); Thomas Goodrich, *Black Flag* (Bloomington: Indiana University Press, 1995); and Daniel Sutherland, *A Savage Conflict* (Chapel Hill: University of North Carolina Press, 2009).

6. Capt. H. B. Johnson to General, Aug. 14, 1863, in *The Wartime Genesis of Free Labor: The Upper South* (WGFL), ed. Ira Berlin, et al. (New York: Cambridge University Press, 1993), 577–578. See Aaron Astor, *Rebels on the Border* (Baton Rouge: Louisiana State University Press, 2012); and Parrish, *Turbulent Partnership*.

7. Bruce, *The New Man*, 99–100. See also Stephanie H. M. Camp, *Closer to Freedom* (Chapel Hill: University of North Carolina Press, 2004), 114–116, and Mattie Jackson, *The Story of Mattie J. Jackson*, Recorded by Dr. L. S. Thompson (formerly Mrs. Schuyler) (Lawrence, Mass.: Lawrence Sentinel Office, 1866), 9–13.

8. Bruce, *The New Man*, 103; Aug. 1862, Elvira Ascenith Weir Scott Diary, 1860–1887, SHSM. See Donnie Bellamy, "Slavery, Emancipation, and Racism in Missouri, 1850–65," (dissertation, University of Missouri, 1971); Earl Nelson, "Missouri Slavery, 1861–1865," *Missouri Historical Review* 28 (July 1934): 260–274; and Parrish, *Turbulent Partnership*, 123–148.

9. Bryce Benedict, *Jayhawkers* (Norman: University of Oklahoma Press, 2009), 155–158; Mrs. Silliman to brother [1862], Silliman Family Letters, 1862–1865, SHSM; Edward M. Samuel et al. to His Excellency Abraham Lincoln, Sept. 8, 1862, in *The Destruction of Slavery* (DS), ed. Ira Berlin et al. (New York: Cambridge University Press, 1985), 436; Mar. 1862, Elvira Scott Diary, SHSM.

10. For examples, see Bruce, *The New Man*, 99–100; Chapl'n R. M. Risk to Maj. Gen. Hunter, Feb. 25, 1862, WGFL, 564; Wylie Miller, *The American Slave* (AS), ed. George Rawick (Westport, Conn.: Greenwood Press, 1972), 11:256–257; and 1861–1865, Pauline Stratton Collection, SHSM. See Benedict, *Jayhawkers*; and David Blight, *A Slave No More* (Orlando: Harcourt, 2007).

11. General Orders, No. 3, Head Quarters, Department of the Missouri, Nov. 20, 1861, and John M. Richardson to Hon. Simon Cameron, Dec. 1, 1861, DS, 417–419; Margaret Mendenhall Frazier, ed., *Missouri Ordeal, 1862–1864: Diaries of Willard Hall Mendenhall* (Newhall, Calif.: Carl Boyer, 1985), Jan. 15, Aug. 28, Oct. 30, and Nov. 7, 1862 entries; Thos. to My Dear Wife, Nov. 14, 1862, Civil War Letter, SHSM; M. P. Cayce to Maj. Gen. Schofield, July 31, 1863, DS, 460; Major Genl. H. W. Halleck to General Asboth, Dec. 26, 1861, DS, 423–424; Major Geo. E. Waring Jr. to Acting Maj. Gen. Asboth, Dec. 19, 1861, Dec. 23, 1861, DS, 421–423; T. A. Russell to Maj. Genl. Halleck, Feb. 12, 1862, DS, 427–429. See also DS, 395–412; Louis Gerteis, *From Contraband to Freedman* (Westport, Conn.:

Greenwood Press, 1973); Silvana Siddali, *From Property to Person* (Baton Rouge: Louisiana State University Press, 2005); *WGFL*, 564; and Parrish, *Turbulent Partnership*, 101–121.

12. Capt. Wm. R. Butler to A. A. Genl. Central Division, Oct. 1, 1862, *DS*, 437; General Orders, No. 35, Head Quarters, Dept. of the Missouri, Dec. 24, 1862, *DS*, 441–444.

13. John F. Ryland et al. to His Excellency Governor Gamble, June 4, 1863, *DS*, 457–458. See also Nelson, "Missouri Slavery, 1861–1865," 260–274; Bellamy, "Slavery, Emancipation, and Racism in Missouri"; Frazier, *Missouri Ordeal*; and Parrish, *Turbulent Partnership*.

14. John R. Moore to Honble. E. M. Stanton, Apr. 5, 1862, *DS*, 429–431; Charles Jones to His Excellency Abraham Lincoln, Mar. 24, 1863, *DS*, 450–453; Charles Jones to Gen. Davidson, Mar. 24, 1863, Unentered Letters Received, ser. 2594, Dept. of the Missouri, RG 393 Pt. 1, National Archives and Record Administration, Washington, D.C. (hereafter NARA), referenced in *DS*, 453, and viewed at Freedmen and Southern Society Project, College Park, Md. (FSSP) (C-175).

15. Tishey Taylor, *AS*, 11:342–347. See also Astor, *Rebels on the Border*, and Col. Samuel M. Wirt to Brig. Genl. Clinton B. Fisk, Apr. 20, 1864, *WGFL*, 604–605.

16. Richard Kimmons, *AS*, supp., ser. 2, 6.5:293–298; Capt. Stephen E. Jones to Col. Dick, Apr. 15, 1863, *DS*, 453–454; Esther Easter, *AS*, 7:88–91; Mark Discus, *AS*, supp., ser. 1, 2:171–177; Capt. Oscar B. Queens to Capt. James H. Steger, Nov. 11, 1863, *DS*, 467–468. See Dale Baum, "Slaves Taken to Texas for Safekeeping during the Civil War," in *The Fate of Texas*, ed. Charles D. Grear (Fayetteville: University of Arkansas Press, 2008), 83–104; Bruce, *The New Man*, 102; John Starrett Hughes, "Lafayette County and the Aftermath of Slavery, 1861–1870," *Missouri Historical Review* 75 (Oct. 1980): 51–63; Nelson, "Missouri Slavery"; and Bellamy, "Slavery, Emancipation, and Racism in Missouri." See also Hattie Matthews, *AS*, 11:249–52; and John and Phoebe Hopkins, Bill of Sale, 1862, SHSM.

17. Dec. 1862, Elvira Ascenith Weir Scott Diary, 1860–1887, SHSM; William Black, *AS*, 11:32–34; Brig. Genl. Thomas Ewing Jr., to Lt. Col. C. W. Marsh, Aug. 3, 1863, in *The Black Military Experience* (BME), ed. Ira Berlin, Joseph Reidy, and Leslie Rowland (New York: Cambridge University Press, 1982), 228–230. See Mutti Burke, *On Slavery's Border*, 265–267; *WGFL*, 596–597, 604–605, 616; and Fellman, *Inside War*, 207–212. See also Harry Johnson, *AS*, supp., ser. 2, 6.5:1994–2004; Hannah Jones, *AS*, 11:214–217; and Eliza Madison, *AS*, 11:241–242.

18. Eli Andrews, NARA, M345 Reel 8, Missouri State Archives, Jefferson City, Mo. (MSA), Reel F 1137, Provost Marshal, NARA, viewed at MSA. For additional examples, Archer Alexander, NARA M345 Reel 4, MSA Reel F 1218; Henry and Lee Ashbrook, NARA M345 Reel 10, Reel F 1219; Alex Becker, NARA M345

Reel 22, Reel F MSA 1228; Whitney Fowler, NARA M345 Reel 96, MSA Reel F 1322; C. M. France, NARA M345 Reel 96, MSA Reel F 1322; William Irwin, NARA M345 Reel 140, MSA Reel F 1137, all above Provost Marshal, NARA, viewed at MSA. See Asst. Pro. Mar. O. A. A. Gardner to Maj. Genl. Curtis, Feb. 16, 1863, *DS*, 445–446; Col. Jno. C. Kelton to Asst. Ajt., Genl., Oct. 6, 1861, *DS*, 416; Brig. Genl. J. M. Schofield to Col., J. O. Kelton, Mar. 3, 1862, *DS*, 429; Eliot, *The Story of Archer Alexander*, 46–48; Henry S. Fowler/Scott [alias] pen., USCT 65E, NARA. See also Mutti Burke, *On Slavery's Border*, 268–307.

19. Excerpt from Coln. N. P. Chipman to General [Samuel R. Curtis], Oct. 16, [1862], *BME*, 72–73. See *BME*, 188–189, 236–238; Benedict, *Jayhawkers*; Jim Cullen, "'I's a Man Now,'" in *Divided Houses*, ed. Catherine Clinton and Nina Silber (New York: Oxford University Press, 1992), 76–91; John Blassingame, "The Recruitment of Negro Troops in Missouri during the Civil War," *Missouri Historical Review* 58 (Apr. 1964): 326–338; Nelson, "Missouri Slavery, 1861–1865"; and Chris Tabor, *The Skirmish at Island Mound, Mo.* (Butler, Mo.: Bates County Historical Society, 2001).

20. Anderson, NARA M345 Reel 7, MSA Reel F 1217, Provost Marshal, NARA, viewed at MSA. For information on slave compensations, see Rudena Mallory, *Claims by Missourians for Compensation of Enlisted Slaves* (Kansas City, Mo.: Rudena Kramer Mallory, 1992); and Mutti Burke, *On Slavery's Border*, 295, 367.

21. Excerpt from testimony of Col. Wm. A. Pile, [Nov. 29, 1863], *BME*, 232–236; Bruce, *The New Man*, 107–108; Mary Bell, *AS*, 11:25–31; William Fuller et al. to Maj. General W. S. Rosecrans [Feb. 1864], and Lt. Col. A. Jacobson to Major Genl. Rosecrans, Feb. 17, 1864, *BME*, 238–242; Liet. Jeff A. Mayhall to Col. Jas. O. Broadhead, Dec. 17, 1863, M435, 1863, Letters Received, ser. 2786, Provost Marshal General, Dept. of the Missouri, Records of the U.S. Continental Commands, RG 393 Pt. 1, NARA, viewed at FSSP (C-190); Thomas Vaughn pen., USCT 65K, NARA; excerpt from testimony of R. A. Watt, [Nov. 30, 1863], *BME*, 235–236; Affidavit of Aaron Mitchell, Jan. 4, 1864, *BME*, 237–238. See Hughes, "Lafayette County and the Aftermath of Slavery, 1861–1870," 54.

22. Ann to My Dear Husband, Jan. 19, 1864, *BME*, 686–687; Capt. A. J. Hubbard to Brig. Genl. Pile, Feb. 6, 1864, *BME*, 687–688; Brig. Genl. Wm. A. Pile to Maj. O. D. Greene, Feb. 11, 1864, *BME*, 242–244; Lt. A. A. Rice to Col., Mar. 31, 1864, *WGFL*, 600–601; Maj. A. C. Marsh to Col. J. P. Sanderson, Apr. 5, 1864, *DS*, 482–483; M. P. Cayce to Maj. Gen. Schofield, July 31, 1863, *DS*, 460; Martha to My Dear Husband [Richard Glover], Dec. 30, 1863; and Brig. Genl. Wm. A. Pile to Maj. Genl. Rosecrans, Feb. 23, 1864, enclosing William P. Dunning to Brig. Genl. Pile, Feb. 1, 1864, and Lieut. Jeff. A. Mayhall to Brig. Genl. Pile, Feb. 4, 1864, *BME*, 244–246; Capt. Hiram Cornell to Col. J. P. Sanderson, Mar. 28, 1864, *BME*, 688.

23. [Private Spotswood Rice] to My Children [Sept. 3, 1864], Spotswood Rice

to Kittey Diggs [Sept. 3, 1864], and F. W. Diggs to Genl. Rosecrans, Sept. 10, 1864, *BME*, 689–691; Sam Bowmen to Dear Wife, May 10, 1864, *DS*, 484–486.

24. Asst. Adjt. Genl. J. Rainsford to Brig. Genl. E. B. Brown, Mar. 6, 1864, *DS*, 479–480; Frazier, *Missouri Ordeal*, Jan. 15, Aug. 28, Oct. 30, and Nov. 7, 1862; Maj. Gen. S. R. Curtis to General, Mar. 13, 1864, *DS*, 480–481.

25. Bruce, *The New Man*, 107–108. For the end of recruitment in Missouri, see Brig. Genl. Wm. A. Pile to Brig. Genl. L. Thomas, May 21, 1864, *WGFL*, 607–608; and Lt. J. M. Gavin to Capt. R. L. Ferguson, Aug. 3, 1864, *BME*, 250–251. See also *BME*, 12, 188–189, and 236–238; Blassingame, "The Recruitment of Negro Troops in Missouri during the Civil War"; Hughes, "Lafayette County and the Aftermath of Slavery," 54; and Nelson, "Missouri Slavery, 1861–1865."

26. Richard Booth, NARA M345 Reel 30, MSA Reel F 1232, Provost Marshal, NARA, viewed at MSA. See also Sharon Romeo, "Freedwomen in Pursuit of Liberty" (dissertation, University of Iowa, 2010).

27. Jimmy S. Johnson III, "The Miller Plantation, An Archaeological Interpretation of a Northwest Missouri Antebellum Slave Site" (Missouri Department of Natural Resources, Jefferson City, 1998), 31; Newspaper quotation, Apr. 9 and 21, 1863, from Nelson, "Missouri Slavery, 1861–1865," 266–270; Bruce, *The New Man*, 108–111; Brig. Genl. Thomas Ewing, Jr., to Lt. Col. C. W. Marsh, Aug. 3, 1863, *BME*, 228–230. See also Berlin et al., *WGFL*, 579, 586–592, 595.

28. In response to William Quantrill's raid on Lawrence and in an effort to reduce guerrilla violence along the Kansas-Missouri border, General Thomas Ewing issued General Order No. 11 in August 1863 to evict the civilian population in the rural areas of Jackson, Cass, Bates, and the northern third of Vernon counties on the Missouri side. [Egbert B. Brown] to Major Genl. J. M. Schofield, July 14, 1863, *WGFL*, 576; Capt. H. B. Johnson to General, Aug. 14, 1863, *WGFL*, 577–578; Lt. J. H. Smith to General E. B. Brown, Apr. 14, 1864, *WGFL*, 602; Surg. Robt. Richardson and Capt. Theo. S. Case to General, May 18, 1864, *WGFL*, 605–607; Unsigned to Mr. E. M. Stanton, Aug. 22, 1865, *BME*, 773–774; Maj. J. Nelson Smith to 1st Lt. E. L. Burthoud, Mar. 15, 1864, *WGFL*, 589–590; Brig. Gen. E. B. Brown to Major O. D. Greene, Mar. 19, 1864, and Brig. Genl. Wm. A. Pile to Maj. O. D. Greene, Mar. 29, 1864, *WGFL*, 593–595. See Jim Downs, "The Other Side of Freedom," in *Battle Scars*, ed. Catherine Clinton and Nina Silber (New York: Oxford University Press, 2006), 78–103.

29. Excerpt from Special Orders No. 70, Head Quarters District of Central Mo., Apr. 3, 1864, *WGFL*, 601; Capt. J. C. W. Hall to Lt. Colonel T. A. Switzler, July 1, 1864, *WGFL*, 611; Bruce, *The New Man*, 114–117. See also Leslie Schwalm, *Emancipation's Diaspora* (Chapel Hill: University of North Carolina Press, 2009).

30. See Parrish, *Turbulent Partnership*, 178–207; Nelson, "Missouri Slavery, 1861–1865"; and Emancipation Resolution, Missouri State Constitutional Convention, SHSM. See also Robert W. Frizzell, "Southern Identity in Nineteenth-

Century Missouri," *Missouri Historical Review* 99 (Apr. 2006): 238–260; Jeremy Neely, *The Border between Them* (Columbia: University of Missouri Press, 2007); and Miles W. Eaton, "The Development and Later Decline of the Hemp Industry in Missouri, 1865–1870," *Missouri Historical Review* 43 (1949): 344–359. See also Pauline Stratton Collection, SHSM; J. B. Colgrove, NARA M345 reel 54, Provost Marshal, NARA, viewed at MSA, MSA Reel F 1141; and Delicia Ann Wiley [Lucinda] Patterson, AS, 11:269–276.

31. Brig. Genl. Clinton B. Fisk to Jas. E. Yeatman, Esq., Mar. 25, 1865, *DS*, 489; and Capt. Wm. Colbert to Brig. Gen'l C. B. Fisk, Jan. 22, 1865, in Berlin et al., *WGFL*, 613–614; Charlie Richardson, AS, 11:296–297. See Kimberly Schreck, "Her Will against Theirs," in *Beyond Image and Convention*, ed. Janet L. Coryell et al. (Columbia: University of Missouri Press, 1998); Melinda Discus, AS, supp., ser. 1, 2:166–170; Louis Hill, AS, 11:184–190; Smokey Eulenburg, AS, 11:109–112; F. T. Russell to Gen'l., Feb. 21, 1865, and J. H. Lathrop to Gen. Clinton Fisk, Mar. 8, 1865, in *WGFL*, 616–619; General Orders No. 7, Head Quarters 4, Sub. Dist., Cent. D, Mo., Apr. 25, 1865, *WGFL*, 622. For population statistics, see Mutti Burke, *On Slavery's Border*, 312.

32. Almost a third of the soldiers from three black regiments recruited in Missouri died while in service. See *BME*, 486–487. See also widows and orphans claims, 65th USCT, NARA.

33. Margaret Nickens, AS, 11:263–265; Peter Corn, AS, 11:85–95; Carolyn M. Bartels, *Boone County Colored Marriages, 1865–1882* (Shawnee Mission, Kans.: Carolyn M. Bartels, 1980s); Chariton County Marriage Record Book, vols. A and 1–A; Civil War Pension Claims, USCT 65, NARA; Annette W. Curtis, *Jackson County, Missouri, Marriage Records of Citizens of African Descent, 1865–1881* (Independence, Mo.: J. C. Eakin, c. 1992). See also Nancy Bercaw, *Gendered Freedoms* (Gainesville: University of Florida Press, 2003).

34. Bruce, *The New Man*. See Schwalm, *Emancipation's Diaspora*.

Chapter 10. The Guerrilla Shirt

1. *The War of the Rebellion: A Compilation of the Official Records of the Union and Confederate Armies*, 128 vols. (Washington, D.C.: GPO, 1880–1901), ser. 1, vol. 41, 4:334, 354, 726–727 (hereafter *OR*); Albert Castel and Thomas Goodrich, *Bloody Bill Anderson: The Short, Savage Life of a Civil War Guerrilla* (Lawrence: University Press of Kansas, 1998), 126–130.

2. *OR*, ser. 1, vol. 41, 4:334, 354, 726–727; Castel and Goodrich, *Bloody Bill Anderson*, 126–130.

3. Castel and Goodrich, *Bloody Bill Anderson*, 126–130. For an example of the manner in which Union officers described the guerrillas, see *OR*, ser. 1, vol. 41, 2:719. Kristen Tegtmeier Oertel, *Bleeding Borders: Race, Gender, and Violence in Pre–Civil War Kansas* (Baton Rouge: Louisiana State University Press, 2009),

85–108; Nina Silber, *The Romance of Reunion: Northerners and the South, 1865–1900* (Chapel Hill: University of North Carolina Press, 1993); Silber, *Gender and the Sectional Conflict* (Chapel Hill: University of North Carolina Press, 2008).

4. Michael Fellman, *Inside War: The Guerrilla Conflict in Missouri during the American Civil War* (New York: Oxford University Press, 1990), 148; Daniel Sutherland, *A Savage Conflict: The Decisive Role of Guerrillas in the American Civil War* (Chapel Hill: University of North Carolina Press, 2009); Barton Myers, *Executing Daniel Bright: Race, Loyalty, and Guerrilla Violence in a Coastal Carolina Community, 1861–1865* (Baton Rouge: Louisiana State University Press, 2009); Robert Mackey, *The Uncivil War: Irregular Warfare in the Upper South, 1861–1865* (Norman: University of Oklahoma Press, 2004).

5. Kristen L. Streater, "'She-Rebels' on the Supply Line: Gender Conventions in Civil War Kentucky," in *Occupied Women: Gender, Military Occupation, and the American Civil War*, ed. LeeAnn Whites and Alecia P. Long (Baton Rouge: Louisiana State University Press, 2009), 89; LeeAnn Whites, "Forty Shirts and a Wagonload of Wheat: Women, the Domestic Supply Line, and the Civil War on the Western Border," *Journal of the Civil War Era* 1 (Mar. 2011): 57. See LeeAnn Whites's essay "The Tale of Three Kates," in *Weirding the War: Stories from the Civil War's Ragged Edges*, ed. Stephen Berry (Athens: University of Georgia Press, 2011); Whites, *Kate Clark Quantrill: Girl Guerrilla* (Athens: University of Georgia Press, [forthcoming]). For other gender analyses of the Civil War, see LeeAnn Whites, *The Civil War as a Crisis in Gender: Augusta, Georgia, 1860–1890* (Athens: University of Georgia Press, 1995); Whites, *Gender Matters: Civil War, Reconstruction, and the Making of the New South* (New York: Palgrave Macmillan, 2005); Victoria Bynum, *Unruly Women: The Politics of Social and Sexual Control in the Old South* (Chapel Hill: University of North Carolina Press, 1992); Stephanie McCurry, *Masters of Small Worlds: Yeoman Households, Gender Relations, and the Political Culture of the Antebellum South Carolina Low Country* (New York: Oxford University Press, 1995); Drew Gilpin Faust, *Mothers of Invention: Women of the Slaveholding South in the American Civil War* (New York: Vintage, 1996); Kirsten Wood, *Masterful Women: Slaveholding Widows from the American Revolution through the Civil War* (Chapel Hill: University of North Carolina Press, 2004); Nancy Bercaw, *Gendered Freedoms: Race, Rights, and the Politics of the Household in the Delta, 1861–1875* (Gainesville: University Press of Florida, 2003).

6. Stephen Berry, *All That Makes a Man: Love and Ambition in the Civil War South* (New York: Oxford University Press, 2003), 12. See also Amy Greenberg, *Manifest Manhood and the Antebellum American Empire* (New York: Cambridge University Press, 2005); Lorien Foote, *The Gentlemen and the Roughs: Violence, Honor, and Manhood in the Union Army* (New York: New York University Press, 2010). See also John Mack Faragher, *Daniel Boone: The Life and Legend of an American Pioneer* (New York: Macmillan, 1993), 320–362; Paul C. Anderson, *Blood Image: Turner*

Ashby in the Civil War and the Southern Mind (Baton Rouge: Louisiana State University Press, 2002), 104–144; Don Bowen, "Guerrilla War in Western Missouri, 1862–1865: Historical Extensions of the Relative Deprivation Hypothesis," *Comparative Studies in Society and History* 19 (Jan. 1977): 30–51; Bowen, "Quantrill, James, Younger, et al.: Leadership in a Guerrilla Movement, Missouri, 1861–1865," *Military Affairs* 41 (Feb. 1977): 42–48.

7. Richard Brownlee, *Gray Ghosts of the Confederacy: Guerrilla Warfare in the West, 1861–1865* (Baton Rouge: Louisiana State University Press, 1958), 104; Eakin, *Recollections of Quantrill's Guerrillas*, 22. Also see Nicole Etcheson, *Bleeding Kansas: Contested Liberty in the Civil War Era* (Lawrence: University Press of Kansas, 2006). See Bowen, "Guerrilla War in Western Missouri," 39.

8. William E. Connelley, *Quantrill and the Border Wars* (Cedar Rapids, Iowa: Torch Press, 1910), 317–318.

9. Faragher, *Daniel Boone*, 20–21; Nicolas Proctor, *Bathed in Blood: Hunting and Mastery in the Old South* (Charlottesville: University Press of Virginia, 2002), 8–9.

10. Streater, "'She-Rebels' on the Supply Line," 88–89; McCurry, *Masters of Small Worlds*, 72. For works that discuss the household in respect to mid-nineteenth-century farm work, see John Mack Faragher, *Sugar Creek: Life on the Illinois Prairie* (New Haven, Conn.: Yale University Press, 1986); Joan Jensen, *Loosening the Bonds: Mid-Atlantic Farm Women, 1750–1850* (New Haven, Conn.: Yale University Press, 1986); R. Douglas Hurt, *Agriculture and Slavery in Missouri's Little Dixie* (Columbia: University of Missouri Press, 1992). See U.S. Federal Agricultural Census for Howard, Chariton, and Linn Counties, Missouri, 1860. According to one Union soldier named Wiley Britton, Southerners grew "small patches" of cotton on their farms, perhaps too small to be of any consequence for the census taker, in Britton, *Memoirs of the Rebellion on the Border, 1863* (Lincoln: University of Nebraska Press, 1993), 246. For an example of the guerrillas losing their clothes, see *OR*, ser. 1, vol. 22, 1:686.

11. Penny McMorris, *Crazy Quilts* (New York: Dutton, 1984), 63; *The Language and Poetry of Flowers* (Boston: De Wolfe, Fiske, 1898), 9, 18, 21, 25; Beverly Seaton, *The Language of Flowers: A History* (Charlottesville: University Press of Virginia, 1995); *Reminiscences of the Women of Missouri during the Sixties* (1913; reprint: Independence, Mo.: Two Trails Publishing, 2006), 24–27; Eakin, *Recollections of Quantrill's Guerrillas*, 22.

12. McMorris, *Crazy Quilts*; *Language and Poetry of Flowers*; Seaton, *Language of Flowers*; *Reminiscences of the Women of Missouri*; Eakin, *Recollections of Quantrill's Guerrillas*; Castel and Goodrich, *Bloody Bill Anderson*, 126.

13. Berry, *All That Makes a Man*, 12. That there are photographs of a number of guerrillas proves the popularity of this ritual.

14. U.S. Federal Manuscript Census, Breckenridge County, Kansas Territory, accessed through Ancestry.com; Castel and Goodrich, *Bloody Bill Anderson*, 11–18.

15. *OR*, ser. 1, vol. 22, 2:428, 460–461. General Order No. 10 came out on August 18, 1863, but the August 25 more radical General Order No. 11 would render it null and void. See *OR*, ser. 1, vol. 22, 2:473. Brownlee, *Gray Ghosts of the Confederacy*, 121; Castel, *Quantrill*, 119–120; Mark Grimsley, *The Hard Hand of War: Union Military Policy toward Southern Civilians, 1861–1865* (New York: Cambridge University Press, 1997), 142–151.

16. See also Charles F. Harris, "Catalyst for Terror: The Collapse of the Women's Prison in Kansas City," *Missouri Historical Review* 83 (Apr. 1995): 290–306; McCorkle, *Three Years with Quantrill*, 122–123. Gregg, "A Little Dab of History," 46, 53–54; Brownlee, *Grey Ghosts of the Confederacy*, 121; Castel, *Quantrill*, 119–120; Harris, "Catalyst for Terror," 290–306.

17. John Grenier, *The First Way of War: American War Making on the Frontier, 1607–1814* (New York: Cambridge University Press, 2005); Patrick M. Malone, *The Skulking Way of War: Technology and Tactics among the New England Indians* (New York: Madison, 1991); Guy Chet, *Conquering the American Wilderness: The Triumph of European Warfare in the Colonial Northeast* (Amherst: University of Massachusetts Press, 2003). See also Sutherland, *Savage Conflict*, 9–25; Clay Mountcastle, *Punitive War: Confederate Guerrillas and Union Reprisals* (Lawrence: University Press of Kansas, 2009), 8–20.

18. Castel and Goodrich, *Bloody Bill Anderson*, 29.

19. Ibid., 35, 36; Castel, *Quantrill*, 164–165.

20. Eakin, *Recollections of Quantrill's Guerrillas*, 22; Castel and Goodrich, *Bloody Bill Anderson*, 126; Bailey, *Confederate Guerrilla*, 48; case against Miss Mary Spencer, testimony of Miss Hattie Spencer, Sept. 5, 1864, PM Records. John McCorkle describes the scene of a similar guerrilla wedding between William H. Gregg and Lizzie Hook (*Three Years with Quantrill*, 179–180).

21. Eakin, *Recollections of Quantrill's Guerrillas*, 22. There is one photograph of a guerrilla, George Todd, wearing a Union jacket.

22. Ibid., 25–26.

23. Ibid., 36–37; Proctor, *Bathed in Blood*, 57–60.

24. Eakin, *Recollections of Quantrill's Guerrillas*, 23.

25. McCorkle, *Three Years with Quantrill*, 79.

26. *St. Louis Tri-Weekly Republican*, Oct. 28, 1864, as cited in Castel and Goodrich, *Bloody Bill Anderson*, 113–114, 154n2.

27. *OR*, ser. 1, vol. 41, 2:75–77; Fellman, *Inside War*, 139. Fellman believes the letter demonstrates Anderson's "infantile narcissism and a sense of omnipotence," but when read closely, it offers quite a bit more, especially in respect to why the guerrillas fought and fought as they did. It is important to read what the guerrillas wrote with the same measure of empathy we would grant the sources produced by a person whose morals better resemble our own. In this, I follow the advice of James Axtell, who exhorts us, "to judge each society by its own standards and values, not

those of today. We can compare individual choices of action with those made by other people in the same or similar circumstances or with other choices possible for <u>that</u> society at <u>that</u> time," and to "strive to be scrupulously fair to all parties, which is possible only after immersing ourselves so deeply in the historical sources of each society that we are as much or more at home in their time and place than in our own." See Axtell, *The European and the Indian: Essays in the Ethnohistory of Colonial North America* (New York: Oxford University Press, 1981), 210.

28. OR, ser. 1, vol. 41, 2:76.

29. Ibid., 75, 76.

30. Ibid., 719.

31. Ibid., 1:443, 3:456, 489.

32. According to James Axtell, "scalplocks, braided and decorated with jewelry, paint, and feathers, represented a person's 'soul' or living spirit." Axtell, *European and the Indian*, 213–214.

33. *Missouri Statesman*, Aug. 5, 1864, as cited in Fellman, *Inside War*, 189, 297n117; Castel and Goodrich, *Bloody Bill Anderson*, 47; Axtell, *European and the Indian*, 213–214.

34. *St. Louis Tri-Weekly Republican*, Oct. 28, 1864, as cited in Castel and Goodrich, *Bloody Bill Anderson*, 113–114, 154n2.

35. *Missouri Statesman*, Aug. 5, 1864, as cited in Fellman, *Inside War*, 189, 297n117; Castel and Goodrich, *Bloody Bill Anderson*, 47.

36. Castel and Goodrich, *Bloody Bill Anderson*, 126; Proctor, *Bathed in Blood*, 57–60; Berry, *All That Makes a Man*, 12–13.

37. OR, ser. 1, vol. 41, 1:442, 4:334, 354, 726–727; Castel and Goodrich, *Bloody Bill Anderson*, 126–130; Berry, *All That Makes a Man*, 12–13; Proctor, *Bathed in Blood*, 57–60.

Chapter 11. The Lexington Weekly Caucasian

1. *Lexington Weekly Caucasian*, Apr. 25, 1866.

2. Ibid.

3. William Young, *History of Lafayette County, Missouri* (Indianapolis: B. F. Bowen, 1910), 678–679.

4. *Lexington Weekly Caucasian*, February 26, 1870; on the career of Peter Donan, see Lewis Saum, "Donan and the *Caucasian*," *Missouri Historical Review* 63, no. 4. (July 1969): 419–450.

5. *Lexington Weekly Caucasian*, Apr. 16, 1870.

6. Kristin Tegtmeier Oertel, *Bleeding Borders* (Baton Rouge: Louisiana State University Press, 2009).

7. *Lexington Weekly Caucasian*, June 27, 1866.

8. Saum, "Donan and the *Caucasian*."

9. *Lexington Weekly Caucasian*, Apr. 30, 1870.

10. Ibid.

11. Ibid.

12. See, for example, *Lexington Weekly Caucasian*, May 16, 1866.

13. *Lexington Weekly Caucasian*, May 16, 1866.

14. *Lexington Weekly Caucasian*, Sept. 19, 1868.

15. *Lexington Weekly Caucasian*, Mar. 30, 1867.

16. Steven Hahn, *A Nation under Our Feet* (Cambridge, Mass.: Belknap Press of Harvard University Press, 2005).

17. On agriculture in central and western Missouri, see R. Douglas Hurt, *Agriculture and Slavery in Missouri's Little Dixie* (Columbia: University of Missouri Press, 1992).

18. For an excellent discussion of cultural, social, and economic life in Civil War–era St. Louis, see Adam Arenson, *The Great Heart of the Republic* (Cambridge, Mass.: Harvard University Press, 2011).

19. The classic account of Missouri politics during Radical Reconstruction is William Parrish, *Missouri under Radical Rule* (Columbia: University of Missouri Press, 1965).

20. On slavery and emancipation in Missouri, see Diane Mutti Burke, *On Slavery's Border: Missouri's Small Slaveholding Households, 1815–1865* (Athens: University of Georgia Press, 2010).

21. Michael Fellman, *Inside War* (New York: Oxford University Press, 1990); T. J. Stiles, *Jesse James: The Last Rebel of the Civil War* (New York: Alfred A. Knopf, 2001).

22. James S. Hughes, "Lafayette County and the Aftermath of Slavery, 1861–1870," *Missouri Historical Review* 75, no. 1 (Oct. 1980): 51–63.

23. Henry Clay Bruce, *The New Man* (Charleston, S.C.: Nabu Press, 2010).

24. *Howard County Advertiser*, Jan. 15, 1864.

25. According to the slave census, John R. White owned 76 slaves in 1860. See Eighth Census, Slave Manuscript, 1860.

26. Bruce, *The New Man*, 103.

27. *History of Lafayette County, Missouri* (St. Louis: Missouri Historical Company, 1881).

28. Russell to Fisk, Feb. 21, 1865, Letters Received, box 16, ser. 3537, District of North Missouri, U.S. Army Continental Command, Record Group 393/2, National Archives and Records Administration, Washington, D.C.

29. *Sixth Census of the United States* (1860); *Seventh Census of the United States* (1870).

30. Nicole Etcheson, *Bleeding Kansas* (Lawrence: University Press of Kansas, 2004).

31. Christopher Phillips, *Missouri's Confederate* (Columbia: University of Missouri Press, 2000).

32. Elaine Frantz Parsons, "Midnight Rangers: Costume and Performance in the Reconstruction–Era Ku Klux Klan," *Journal of American History* 92, no. 3 (Dec. 2005).

Chapter 12. "We Promise to Use the Ballot as We Did the Bayonet"

The author would like to thank the staff of the State Historical Society of Missouri for their support of this essay and Alison Clark Efford for her generous reading of an early draft.

1. This essay uses the term "disloyalist" to refer to anyone disfranchised by the oath of loyalty prescribed by the 1865 constitution. As Christopher Phillips has argued, however, not all people who fell into that category saw themselves as disloyal.

2. *Jefferson City Missouri State Times*, Nov. 11, 1870. Regarding the 1870 election, see William E. Parrish, *Missouri under Radical Rule, 1865–1870* (Columbia: University of Missouri Press, 1965), 309–311. See also, Perry S. Rader, *The Civil Government of the United States and the State of Missouri and the History of Missouri* (Jefferson City, Mo.: Tribune Printing Co., 1904), 535.

3. *Jefferson City Missouri State Times*, Nov. 11, 1870.

4. Eric Foner, *Reconstruction* (New York: HarperCollins, 1989), 276–277.

5. Eric Foner, *Freedom's Lawmakers* (Baton Rouge: Louisiana State University Press, 1996), xiii–xiv, xxix; Steven Hahn, *A Nation under Our Feet* (Cambridge, Mass.: Harvard University Press, 2003), 216–219.

6. Foner, *Reconstruction*, 421–423.

7. Foner, *Freedom's Lawmakers*, xiv, s.v. "Turner, James Milton"; Hahn, *A Nation under Our Feet*, 163–215.

8. Francis Newton Thorpe, *The Federal and State Constitutions* (Washington, D.C.: Government Printing Office), 4:2219, 2220–2224.

9. Ibid., 2191.

10. Brig Genl J. W. Sprague to Major Gen'l Oliver O. Howard, June 20, 1865, 14:4–5, Letters Sent to Commissioner Howard, ser. 225, AR Asst. Comr., RG 105, National Archives and Records Administration, Washington, D.C. (hereafter NARA).

11. Quote from E. OBrien to Gen. Sprague, July 7, 1865, O-9 1865, Letters Received, ser. 230, AR Asst. Comr., RG 105, NARA. See also E. O.Brien to Brig. General J. W. Sprague, July 12, 1865, O-13 1865, ibid.; E. O.Brien to General [J. W. Sprague], Aug. 9, 1865, O-120 1865, ibid.; Chaplain J. G. Forman to Capt Geo. E. Dayton, Sept. 2, 1865, F-179 1865, ibid.; and Chaplain A. Wright to Brig Gen J. W. Sprague, Aug. 2, 1865, filed with W-150 1865, Letters Received, ser. 231, AR Asst. Comr., RG 105, NARA.

12. Regarding jury service, see *General Statutes of the State of Missouri* (Jeffer-

son City, Mo.: Emory S. Foster, 1866), 597. Regarding officeholding and the vote, see Thorpe, *Federal and State Constitutions*, 4:2198, 2200, 2204, 2210.

13. Petition to the constitutional state convention now in session in the city of St. Louis Mo., Jan. 31. 1865, Missouri State Archives, Jefferson City.

14. Regarding the petition, see *Journal of the Missouri State Convention* (St. Louis: Missouri Democrat, 1865), 62–63. Regarding the attitudes of delegates toward black suffrage, see John W. McKerley, "Citizens and Strangers" (PhD diss., University of Iowa, 2008), 81–83, and Efford, "Race Should be as Unimportant as Ancestry," *Missouri Historical Review* 104 (Apr. 2010): 138–158.

15. Foner, *Reconstruction*, 27.

16. *St. Louis Daily Missouri Democrat*, Oct. 3, 1865.

17. Cyprian Clamorgan, *The Colored Aristocracy of St. Louis*, ed. with an intro. by Julie Winch (Columbia: University of Missouri Press, 1999), 85–86, n. 59.

18. Foner, *Freedom's Lawmakers*, s.v. "Bruce, Blanche K."

19. *St. Louis Daily Missouri Democrat*, Oct. 3, 1865.

20. The elected executive committee members were Henry McGee Alexander, Francis Roberson, Moses Dickson, Jeremiah Bowman, Samuel Helms, George Wedley, and G. P. Downing. Wedley, who was born in Pennsylvania around 1829, was almost certainly free as well (Wedley, George, 4th Sub District, 7th Ward, Missouri, vol. 10, Consolidated Lists of Civil War Draft Registration Records, 1863–65, Provost Marshal General's Bureau, RG 110, NARA, Ancestry.com). Regarding barbers as black politicians during Reconstruction, see Foner, *Freedom's Lawmakers*, table 11. Regarding Downing, see *St. Louis, Missouri, City Directory*, 1863, 143, Ancestry.com. Regarding Alexander and Roberson, see Clamorgan, *Colored Aristocracy*, 15, 57, 59, 62, 91. Regarding Helms, see ibid., 93–95. Regarding Dickson, see *Proceedings of the First Annual Session of the State Grand Temple and Tabernacle for the State of Missouri and Jurisdiction* (Independence, Mo.: Wright Printing House, [1888?]), 115–119. Regarding Wedley's profession, see *Edwards' St. Louis Directory* [1864], 552. Regarding Alexander and Dickson's ties to black Masonry, see William H. Grimshaw, *Official History of Freemasonry among the Colored People in North America* (1903; reprint: New York: Negro Universities Press, 1969), 246. Regarding Turner, see Gary R. Kremer, *James Milton Turner and the Promise of America* (Columbia: University of Missouri Press, 1991), 8–17, and "Saint Louis Ex-Slave, Once Sold for $50, Earns $1,000,000 Fee," *St. Louis Post-Dispatch*, July 9, 1911.

21. Clamorgan, *Colored Aristocracy*, 57.

22. Ibid., 59.

23. Ibid., 54–55.

24. Diane Mutti Burke, *On Slavery's Border* (Athens: University of Georgia Press, 2010), 309, table 1.

25. Clamorgan, *Colored Aristocracy*, 85–86, n. 59. Historian Julie Winch has

argued that Clamorgan's attack on Wells was based on business competition. Winch, *The Clamorgans* (New York: Hill and Wang, 2011), 189.

26. Foner, *Freedom's Lawmakers*, s.v. "Bruce, Blanche K."

27. *Proceedings of the First Annual Session of the State Grand Temple*, 118.

28. Kremer, *James Milton Turner*, 16–17, and "Saint Louis Ex-Slave," *St. Louis Post-Dispatch*, July 9, 1911.

29. Regarding fugitive slaves in St. Louis, see Louis S. Gerteis, *Civil War St. Louis* (Lawrence: University Press of Kansas, 2001), 273–276. Regarding Missouri's black soldiers, see Ira Berlin, et al., eds., *Freedom*, ser. 1 (Cambridge: Cambridge University Press, 1993), 2:557.

30. *St. Louis Daily Missouri Democrat*, Oct. 3, 1865.

31. Petition of the Colored Citizens of Missouri to the Honorable the [sic] General Assembly of the State of Missouri, n.d., in *A Speech on "Equality before the Law"* (St. Louis: Democrat Book and Job Printing House, 1866), 29.

32. An Address by the Colored People of Missouri to the Friends of Equal Rights, Oct. 12, 1865, in *A Speech on "Equality before the Law,"* 26.

33. Ibid., 24.

34. Ibid., 26, 25.

35. Ibid., 24.

36. Ibid., 26–27.

37. A report of the league's activities since late 1865 was published in the *St. Louis Daily Missouri Democrat* on January 15, 1867.

38. Ibid., Jan. 12, 1866.

39. *St. Louis Daily Missouri Democrat*, Jan. 15, 1867; Petition of Colored Citizens, Touching Schools, Etc., n.d., *Appendix to the House Journal of the Adjourned Session of the Twenty-Third General Assembly of the State of Missouri* (Jefferson City, Mo.: Emory S. Foster, 1865–1866), 842.

40. Margaret L. Dwight, "Black Suffrage in Missouri, 1865–1877" (PhD diss., University of Missouri-Columbia, 1978), 52–57.

41. *St. Louis Daily Missouri Democrat*, Jan. 15, 1867.

42. An Act to Provide for the Reorganization, Supervision and Maintenance of Common Schools, Mar. 29, 1866, *Laws of the State of Missouri* [1866], 177, 179, 187–188, 190.

43. An Act to Amend the Constitution of the State, and to Secure Impartial Suffrage, Mar. 11, 1867, *Laws of the State of Missouri* (Jefferson City, Mo.: Emory S. Foster, 1867), 11–12.

44. Foner, *Freedom's Lawmakers*, s.v. "Bruce, Blanche K."

45. *Saint Louis Daily Missouri Democrat*, July 21, 1868; *Edwards' Twelfth Annual Directory* (St. Louis: Southern Publishing Co., 1870), 181; Carlton H. Tandy [sic], 1860 U.S. Federal Census, St. Louis City, ward 7, roll M653_653, 233, Ancestry

.com; *Annual Report of the Adjutant General, Acting Quartermaster General, and Acting State Claim Agent of Missouri, for the Year Ending December 31, 1869* (Jefferson City, Mo.: Horace Wilcox, 1870), 7.

46. *St. Louis Daily Missouri Democrat,* July 21, 1868.

47. Ibid., Nov. 1, 1868. For a similar appeal by an anonymous black Missourian, see *Kansas City Daily Journal of Commerce,* Oct. 16, 1868.

48. *Official Directory of Missouri* [1883], 83–84; *St. Louis Daily Missouri Democrat,* Nov. 5 and Dec. 25, 1868; Parrish, *Radical Rule,* 257–258; *New York Times,* Mar. 8, 1867. For a discussion of the range of estimates for the total number of white men disfranchised by the constitution's suffrage provisions, see Martha Kohl, "Enforcing a Vision of Community," *Civil War History* 40 (Dec. 1994): 1.

49. Regarding Missouri's Germans and suffrage restriction, see Efford, "Race Should Be as Unimportant as Ancestry," 138–158, and Kristen L. Anderson, "German Americans, African Americans, and the Republican Party in St. Louis, 1865–1872," *Journal of American Ethnic History* 28 (Fall 2008): 34–51.

50. *St. Louis Daily Missouri Democrat,* Jan. 24, 1870.

51. *Springfield Leader,* Mar. 31, 1870.

52. Ibid., Apr. 7, 1870.

53. Parrish, *Radical Rule,* 289–291.

54. *St. Louis Daily Missouri Democrat,* Aug. 26, 1870.

55. Ibid., Aug. 27, 1870.

56. *St. Louis Missouri Republican,* Aug. 27, 1870.

57. Dwight, "Black Suffrage in Missouri," 141.

58. *St. Louis Daily Missouri Democrat,* Sept. 10, 1870.

59. Regarding Turner's work for the bureau and the state, see Lawrence O. Christensen, "Schools for Blacks," *Missouri Historical Review* 76 (Jan. 1982): 121–135, and Kremer, *James Milton Turner,* 25–39.

60. Regarding Turner's appointment to minister of Liberia, see Kremer, *James Milton Turner,* 53–54.

61. *St. Louis Daily Missouri Democrat,* Jan. 27, Apr. 12, 1870.

62. Emphasis added. Ibid., Jan. 27, 1870.

63. Kremer, *James Milton Turner,* 49; Dwight, "Black Suffrage in Missouri," 144.

64. Dwight, "Black Suffrage in Missouri," 146.

65. Parrish, *Radical Rule,* 304.

66. *St. Louis Missouri Republican,* Sept. 24, 1870.

67. Parrish, *Radical Rule,* 306.

68. *St. Louis Missouri Republican,* Oct. 30, 1870; Kremer, *James Milton Turner,* 49.

69. Regarding the number of voters in 1870, see Parrish, *Radical Rule,* 307.

70. Quote from *St. Louis Missouri Democrat,* Oct. 31, 1870. Regarding the Radical meeting, see ibid., Oct. 30, 1870.

71. Ibid., Oct. 30, 1870.

72. *Jefferson City Missouri State Times*, Nov. 11, 1870.

73. *St. Louis Missouri Republican*, Nov. 11, 1870.

74. Isidor Loeb and Floyd C. Shoemaker, eds., *Debates of the Missouri Constitution of 1875* (Columbia: State Historical Society of Missouri), 5:200, 203; Thorpe, *Federal and State Constitutions*, 4:2253.

75. Of Crimes and Procedure, in *Revised Statutes of the State of Missouri* (City of Jefferson: Carter and Regan, 1879), 1:225, 241, 249, 255.

76. Kremer, *James Milton Turner*, 53, 100–103.

77. *New York Times*, Apr. 2, 1880.

78. For comparison, see Michael Fitzgerald's description of black politics in Reconstruction Alabama in *Urban Emancipation* (Baton Rouge: Louisiana State University Press, 2002).

Chapter 13. "A Little Different than in Alabama"

1. Tara McPherson, *Reconstructing Dixie: Race, Gender, and Nostalgia in the Imagined South* (Durham, N.C.: Duke University Press, 2003), 1–2; Doreen Massey, *Space, Place, and Gender* (Minneapolis: University of Minnesota Press, 2001), 5; Andrew R. L. Cayton and Susan E. Gray, eds., *The American Midwest: Essays on Regional History* (Bloomington: Indiana University Press, 2001).

2. Paul A. Gilje, *Rioting in America* (Bloomington: Indiana University Press, 1996), 106. On geography and racist violence, see, for example, W. Fitzhugh Brundage, *Lynching in the New South: Georgia and Virginia, 1880–1930* (Urbana: University of Illinois, 1993); Stewart E. Tolnay and E. M. Beck, *A Festival of Violence: An Analysis of Southern Lynchings, 1882–1930* (Urbana: University of Illinois Press, 1992).

3. James W. Loewen, *Sundown Towns: A Hidden Dimension of American Racism* (New York: New Press, 2005), 198.

4. James R. Shortridge, *The Middle West: Its Meaning in American Culture* (Lawrence: University Press of Kansas, 1989), 28; Wilbur Zelinsky, "Review of the Middle West," *Geographical Review* 80 (July 1990): 323; Cayton and Gray, *The American Midwest*, 12.

5. Shortridge, *The Middle West*, 7, 132–133.

6. Eugene H. Berwanger, *The Frontier against Slavery: Western Anti-Negro Prejudice and the Slavery Extension Controversy* (Urbana: University of Illinois Press, 1967), 1–6, 97–122 (quoted passage, 101); Nicole Etcheson, *Bleeding Kansas: Contested Liberty in the Civil War Era* (Lawrence: University Press of Kansas, 2004), 2.

7. Amos A. Lawrence, quoted in Clifford S. Griffin, *The University of Kansas: A History* (Lawrence: University Press of Kansas, 1974), 21.

8. Berwanger, *The Frontier against Slavery*, 97.

9. *Junction City Tribune*, May 1, 1879. On the Kansas Exodus, see Robert G.

Athearn, *In Search of Canaan: Black Migration to Kansas, 1879–80* (Lawrence: Regents Press of Kansas, 1978), and Nell Irvin Painter, *Exodusters: Black Migration to Kansas after Reconstruction* (New York: W. W. Norton, 1992).

10. *Topeka Daily Capital*, Jan. 19, 1901.

11. Michael Lewis Goldberg, *An Army of Women: Gender and Politics in Gilded Age Kansas* (Baltimore: Johns Hopkins University Press, 1997), 9–17 (quoted passage, 10).

12. Robert Smith Bader, *Hayseeds, Moralizers, and Methodists: The Twentieth-Century Image of Kansas* (Lawrence: University Press of Kansas, 1988), 29–30.

13. Brent M. S. Campney, "W. B. Townsend and the Struggle against Racist Violence in Leavenworth," *Kansas History: A Journal of the Central Plains* 31 (Winter 2008–2009): 264. On racist violence in Reconstruction Kansas, see Brent M. S. Campney, "'Light Is Bursting upon the World!': White Supremacy and Racist Violence against Blacks in Reconstruction Kansas," *Western Historical Quarterly* 41 (Summer 2010): 171–194.

14. *Leavenworth Times*, Aug. 10, 1887; *Leavenworth Times*, July 31, 1887; *Topeka Daily Capital*, Apr. 26, 1899. On the Sam Hose lynching, see Edwin T. Arnold, *What Virtue There Is in Fire: Cultural Memory and the Lynching of Sam Hose* (Athens: University of Georgia Press, 2009).

15. *Lawrence Kansas Daily Tribune*, Oct. 30, 1867; *Topeka Daily Capital*, Jan. 19, 1901; *Leavenworth Times*, Oct. 30, 1887.

16. *Topeka Daily Capital*, Jan. 19, 1901.

17. *Louisville Times*, reprinted in *Leavenworth Times*, Jan. 17, 1901.

18. *Fort Scott Daily Monitor*, Oct. 7, 1883.

19. *Wichita Daily Eagle*, Jan. 17, 1901.

20. *Topeka State Journal*, Dec. 5, 1906; *Hutchinson Semi-Weekly Gazette*, Jan. 21, 1905.

21. *Topeka Daily Capital*, Jan. 19, 1901. On Tillman's loss of one eye, see Stephen Kantrowitz, *Ben Tillman and the Reconstruction of White Supremacy* (Chapel Hill: University of North Carolina Press, 2000), 39.

22. *Belle Plaine News*, June 8, 1911. For the acquittal, see *Wellington Journal*, Jan. 9, 1912.

23. *Leavenworth Times*, Dec. 19, 1896; *Leavenworth Times*, Dec. 22, 1896.

24. *Lawrence Journal* and *Leavenworth Conservative*, both reprinted in *Wyandotte Gazette*, June 22, 1867.

25. *Topeka Daily Capital*, Jan. 19, 1901; *Leavenworth Times*, Mar. 7, 1888.

26. *Topeka Daily Capital*, July 31, 1909; *Atchison Daily Globe*, Jan. 17, 1901.

27. *Olathe Mirror*, Dec. 31, 1896; *Emporia Times and Emporia Republican*, July 14, 1905.

28. *Atchison Daily Globe*, Jan. 22, 1901.

29. *Horton Commercial*, reprinted in *Topeka Plaindealer*, Jan. 31, 1902; *El Dorado Daily Walnut Valley Times*, Apr. 22, 1893.

30. *Fort Scott Herald*, Apr. 5, 1879; *Lawrence Daily Journal*, reprinted in *Leavenworth Times*, Jan. 24, 1901.

31. Marcet Haldeman-Julius, "Negroes in Kansas Colleges (1927)," in *Spurts from an Interrupted Pen* (Girard, Kans.: Haldeman-Julius Publications, 1931), 81, 70.

32. Quoted in Brent M. S. Campney, "'Hold the Line': The Defense of Jim Crow in Lawrence, Kansas, 1945–1961," *Kansas History: A Journal of the Central Plains* 33 (Spring 2010): 37.

33. *University Daily Kansan*, May 12, 1952; Rusty L. Monhollon, *This is America? The Sixties in Lawrence, Kansas* (New York: Palgrave, 2002), 59–60.

34. Campney, "'Hold the Line,'" 29.

35. "CORE: Report of Direction Action against Racial Discrimination at a Café Near the Campus of the University of Kansas, Lawrence, Apr. 15, 1948," General Correspondence, 1947/1948, C.O.R.E. folder, Chancellor's Office, Deane W. Malott, University Archives, 2/10/1, Kenneth Spencer Research Library, University of Kansas, Lawrence.

36. Campney, "'Hold the Line,'" 40.

37. Thomas Frank, *What's the Matter with Kansas? How Conservatives Won the Heart of America* (New York: Metropolitan Books, 2004), 179.

38. Katie H. Armitage, "African Americans Build a Community in Douglas County, Kansas," *Kansas History: A Journal of the Central Plains* 31 (Autumn 2008): 172.

39. Kenneth S. Davis, *Kansas: A Bicentennial History* (New York: W. W. Norton, 1976), 78.

40. James H. Madison, *A Lynching in the Heartland: Race and Memory in America* (New York: Palgrave, 2001), 27, 41–42; Leslie A. Schwalm, *Emancipation's Diaspora: Race and Reconstruction in the Upper Midwest* (Chapel Hill: University of North Carolina Press, 2009), 265.

41. Stephen J. Leonard, *Lynching in Colorado, 1859–1919* (Boulder: University of Colorado Press, 2002), 127; Kimberly Harper, *White Man's Heaven: The Lynching and Expulsion of Blacks in the Southern Ozarks, 1894–1909* (Fayetteville: University of Arkansas Press, 2010), 254, 256.

42. *Lawrence Kansas Daily Tribune*, June 22, 1867; *Lawrence Kansas Daily Tribune*, Aug. 5, 1866.

43. These examples and quotes come from Leon F. Litwack, *Trouble in Mind: Black Southerners in the Age of Jim Crow* (New York: Alfred A. Knopf, 1998), 284–85, 309, 534n9.

44. Stephen J. Whitfield, *A Death in the Delta: The Story of Emmett Till* (Baltimore: Johns Hopkins University Press, 1991), 25.

45. Anthony Walton, *Mississippi: An American Journey* (New York: Vintage Books, 1997), 4; James C. Cobb, *The Most Southern Place on Earth: The Mississippi Delta and the Roots of Regional Identity* (New York: Oxford University Press, 1992), 125; Joseph Crespino, "Mississippi as Metaphor State, Region, and Nation in Historical Imagination," *Southern Spaces*, Oct. 23, 2006, http://southernspaces.org/2006/mississippi-metaphor-state-region-and-nation-historical-imagination.

46. Christopher Waldrep, *The Many Faces of Judge Lynch: Extralegal Violence and Punishment in America* (New York: Palgrave, 2002), 7–8.

Chapter 14. The Quantrill Men Reunions

1. *Kansas City Star*, Sept. 11, 1898; *Kansas City World*, Sept. 11, 1898; *Independence Examiner*, Sept. 17, 1898; *St. Louis Republic*, Oct. 2, 1898. The author thanks Donald R. Hale for introducing him to many of the newspaper articles cited herein. See Hale, *The William Clarke Quantrill Men Reunions, 1898–1929* (Lexington, Mo.: Blue & Grey Book Shoppe, 2001).

2. T. J. Stiles, *Jesse James: Last Rebel of the Civil War* (New York: Vintage Books, 2002), 61–77, 80–94.

3. Michael Fellman, *Inside War: The Guerrilla Conflict in Missouri during the American Civil War* (New York: Oxford University Press, 1989), 247–264; Don R. Bowen, "Guerrilla War in Western Missouri, 1862–1865," *Comparative Studies in History and Society*, 47–49; Kit Dalton, *Under the Black Flag* (Memphis: Lockard Publishing, 1914), 95.

4. *Kansas City Daily Journal of Commerce*, Aug. 22 and 23, 1863; William Elsey Connelley, *Quantrill and the Border Wars: The Story of the Border* (Topeka: Wm. E. Connelley, 1910), 284–420; Albert Castel, *William Clarke Quantrill: His Life and Times* (New York: F. Fell, 1962), 122–143.

5. *Kansas City World*, Sept. 11, 1898; *St. Louis Republic*, Oct. 2, 1898; *New York Times*, Feb. 19, 1915; Stiles, *Jesse James*, 380–395.

6. *Kansas City World*, Sept. 11, 1898.

7. Quote from *Kansas City Star*, Sept. 11, 1898; Minutes, Oct. 15–16, 1902, Missouri Division, United Daughters of the Confederacy, State Historical Society of Missouri; Christopher Phillips, *Missouri's Confederate: Claiborne Fox Jackson and the Creation of Southern Identity in the Border West* (Columbia: University of Missouri Press, 2000), 290–292.

8. David W. Blight, *Race and Reunion: The Civil War in American Memory* (Cambridge, Mass.: Belknap Press of Harvard University Press, 2001), 1–170; Anne Elizabeth Marshall, *Creating a Confederate Kentucky: The Lost Cause and Civil War Memory in a Border State* (Chapel Hill: University of North Carolina Press, 2010), 81–110.

9. Jeremy Neely, *The Border between Them: Violence and Reconciliation on the Kansas-Missouri Line* (Columbia: University of Missouri Press, 2007), 154–170;

Brent M. S. Campney, "'Light Is Bursting Upon the World!': White Supremacy and Racist Violence against Blacks in Reconstruction Kansas," *Western Historical Quarterly* 41 (Summer 2010): 171–194.

10. Blight, *Race and Reunion*, 64–97.

11. Quote from *Cass News*, June 7, 1889; Neely, *The Border between Them*, 171–244; Blight, *Race and Reunion*, 190–205.

12. Quote from Bates County Old Settlers' Society, *The Old Settlers' History of Bates County, Missouri: From Its First Settlement to the First Day of January, 1900* (Amsterdam, Mo.: Tathwell & Maxey, 1897), 142.

13. Quote from *Belton Herald*, June 7, 1895.

14. Katie Armitage, *Lawrence: Survivors of Quantrill's Raid* (Charleston: Arcadia Publishing, 2010), 105; Blight, *Race and Reunion*, 171–190, 383–391; Neely, *The Border between Them*, 242–244.

15. Karen L. Cox, *Dixie's Daughters: The United Daughters of the Confederacy and the Preservation of Confederate Culture* (Gainesville: University Press of Florida, 2003), 8–72; LeeAnn Whites, *The Civil War as a Crisis in Gender: Augusta, Georgia, 1860–1890* (Athens: University of Georgia Press, 1995), 160–198; Anne Sarah Rubin, *A Shattered Nation: The Rise and Fall of the Confederacy, 1861–1868* (Chapel Hill: University of North Carolina Press, 2005), 215–239; W. Fitzhugh Brundage, "No Deed but Memory," in *Where These Memories Grow: History, Memory, and Southern Identity* (Chapel Hill: University of North Carolina Press, 2000), 4–15.

16. Quote from *Oak Grove Banner*, Apr. 18, 1911.

17. Daniel E. Sutherland, *A Savage Conflict: The Decisive Role of Guerrillas in the American Civil War* (Chapel Hill: University of North Carolina Press, 2009), 57–118.

18. "Memoirs of the Life of Lee Carruth Miller, M. D.," 1903, L. C. Miller Collection (C2718), State Historical Society of Missouri Manuscript Collection, Columbia, Missouri.

19. Blight, *Race and Reunion*, 255–259; Kammen, *Mystic Chords of Memory: The Transformation of Tradition in American Culture* (New York: Knopf, 1991), 101–121; Drew Gilpin Faust, *The Creation of Confederate Nationalism: Ideology and Identity in the Civil War South* (Baton Rouge: Louisiana State University Press, 1988), 21–24.

20. Mrs. N. M. Harris, "Atrocities on the Missouri Border," in United Daughters of the Confederacy, Missouri Division, *Reminiscences of the Women of Missouri during the Sixties* (Jefferson City: Hugh Stephens Printing, 192-?), 216; Brundage, "No Deed but Memory," 5–22.

21. *Kansas City Post*, Aug. 28, 1925.

22. Brundage, "No Deed but Memory," 5–22; Marshall, *Creating a Confederate Kentucky*, 82–87; Kammen, *Mystic Chords of Memory*, 101–121.

23. Phillips, *Missouri's Confederate*, 272–290.

24. Faust, *The Creation of Confederate Nationalism*, 20–22; Fellman, *Inside War*, 253–255.

25. *Kansas City Post*, Aug. 22, 1914; Frances Fitzhugh George Kabrick to A. J. Adair, Mar. 1, 1897, in George B. James Sr. Collection (C3564), State Historical Society of Missouri, Manuscript Collection, Columbia (hereafter SHSM); Cole Younger, *The Story of Cole Younger By Himself* (Chicago: Press of the Henneberry Co., 1903), 9–31.

26. Quotes from *Kansas City Post*, Mar. 31, 1923; William H. Gregg, "A Little Dab of History without Embellishment," 1906, William H. Gregg Collection (C1113), SHSM; Miller, "Memoirs," 48–63.

27. Quotes from Dalton, *Under the Black Flag*, 99, 102; *Kansas City Post*, Aug. 22, 1914.

28. *Oak Grove Banner*, Dec. 24, 1903; *Kansas City Times* Aug. 26, 1905; *Independence Examiner*, Aug. 22, 1908; Castel, *William Clarke Quantrill*, 123, William Elsey Connelley, *Quantrill and the Border Wars*, 310; *Pleasant Hill Times*, Sept. 5, 1924; *Kansas City Star*, Aug. 20, 1931.

29. Stephanie McCurry, *Confederate Reckoning: Power and Politics in the Civil War South* (Cambridge, Mass.: Harvard University Press, 2010), 263–309.

30. Quotes from UDC, *Reminiscences*, 131–132, 75; Diane Mutti Burke, *On Slavery's Border: Missouri's Small Slaveholding Households, 1815–1865* (Athens: University of Georgia Press, 2010), 269–300; Blight, *Race and Reunion*, 284–291.

31. *Twelfth Census of the United States, Population, Part One*, United States Bureau of the Census, 241; *Independence Examiner*, Sept. 17, 1898.

32. Nina Silber, *The Romance of Reunion: Northerners and the South, 1865–1900* (Chapel Hill: University of North Carolina Press, 1993), 159–195; Rubin, *A Shattered Nation*, 247–248.

33. Quotes from Dalton, *Under the Black Flag*, 251.

34. Quotes from *Kansas City Journal*, Sept. 1, 1918.

35. Quote from *St. Louis Republic*, Oct. 2, 1898.

36. Quote from Katie H. Armitage, *Lawrence: Survivors of Quantrill's Raid*, 78–87.

37. Quote from Armitage, *Lawrence*, 112; Richard B. Sheridan, "A Most Unusual Gathering: The Semi-Centennial Memorial of Survivors of Quantrill's Raid on Lawrence," *Kansas History* 20, no. 3 (Autumn 1997): 176–191.

38. Quote from Sheridan, "A Most Unusual Gathering," 189.

39. Quotes from Sheridan, "A Most Unusual Gathering," 186–187.

40. Connelley, *Quantrill and the Border Wars*, 383–384.

41. Quotes from Edward E. Leslie, *The Devil Knows How to Ride: The True Story of William Clarke Quantrill and His Confederate Raiders* (New York: Da Capo Press, 1998), 426.

42. Quote from *Independence Examiner*, Aug. 26, 1905; *Oak Grove Banner*, Aug. 14, 1908; *Independence Examiner*, Aug. 22, 1908.

43. Quote from Sheridan, "A Most Unusual Gathering," 189.

44. Quotes from Leslie, *The Devil Knows How to Ride*, 425; George W. Martin, *The First Two Years of Kansas: or, Where, When, and How the Missouri Bushwhacker, the Missouri Train Robber, and Those Who Stole Themselves Rich in the Name of Liberty, Were Sired and Reared* (Topeka: Kansas State Printing Office, 1907), 29.

45. *Independence Examiner*, Sept. 29, 1916.

46. Quote from *Kansas City Daily Journal*, Sept. 1, 1918.

47. *Independence Examiner*, Aug. 31, 1929; *Lee's Summit Journal*, Sept. 5, 1929.

48. David W. Blight, "Southerners Don't Lie; They Just Remember Big," in *Where These Memories Grow: History, Memory, and Southern Identity*, ed. W. Fitzhugh Brundage (Chapel Hill: University of North Carolina Press, 2000), 347–353.

Chapter 15. "William Quantrill Is My Homeboy": Or, The Border War Goes to College

1. "The Jayhawk," http://www.ku.edu/about/traditions/jayhawk.shtml.

2. Jonas Viles, *The University of Missouri* (Columbia: University of Missouri, 1939), 58–60; Frank F. Stephens, *A History of the University of Missouri* (Columbia: University of Missouri Press, 1962), 156–168.

3. Stephens, *A History of the University of Missouri*, 178–179. Another, though less well documented, version of the Tigers' story has it that it was not Price, but guerrillas under "Bloody Bill" Anderson, who targeted Columbia. See, for instance, "Mascot and Football Traditions" on MU's web site, http://www.mutigers.com/trads/mascot-football-traditions.html.

4. Gail Bederman, *Manliness and Civilization* (Chicago: University of Chicago Press, 1995), chap. 1; E. Anthony Rotundo, *American Manhood* (New York: Basic Books, 1993), 239–244; Kate Buford, "A History of Dealing with Football's Dangers," *New York Times*, Nov. 20, 2010.

5. David Smale, ed., *Rivals! MU Vs. KU* (Kansas City, Mo.: Kansas City Star Books, 2005), 11; John Sayle Watterson, *College Football* (Baltimore: Johns Hopkins University Press, 2000), 45.

6. [No Title], *Abilene Weekly Reflector*, Nov. 5, 1891; "Thanksgiving Football," *Iola Register*, Dec. 2, 1892; "Crown Old Missouri," *Kansas City Times*, Dec. 1, 1893.

7. Blair Kerkhoff email to Jennifer L. Weber, April 1, 2011; Blair Kerkhoff, "This Means War," *Kansas City Star*, Nov. 28, 2007.

8. Junior Class of 1895, *Savitar* (Columbia, Mo.: Press of E. W. Stephens, 1896), 69; "Victory Smiled, Then Vanished," *M.S.U. Independent*, 1900; "Missouri vs. Kansas," *Independent*, 1906.

9. Students of the University of Missouri, *Savitar: 100 Years, 1894–1994* (Columbia, Mo., 1995), 166.

10. Kyle Meadows, "The Top Ten College Football Rivalry Trophies," *Bleacher Report*, July 24, 2008, http://bleacherreport.com/articles/40626-the-top-ten-college-football-rivalry-trophies.

11. Adrienne Collins Runnebaum, email to KU Edwards Campus staff and faculty, Nov. 10, 2011; Bob Busby, "Missouri 20, Kansas 19," *Kansas City Star*, Nov. 22, 1952; "Bulging Crowd in Arena Begins Uproar after Foul by Clyde Lovellette," *Kansas City Star*, Dec. 30, 1951; Kerkhoff, "This Means War."

12. Sid Bordman, "Mizzou Ruins K.U. Hope," *Kansas City Star*, Mar. 12, 1961; Curry Kirkpatrick, "Bold, Those Tigers," *Sports Illustrated*, Jan. 29, 1990, http://sport sillustrated.cnn.com/vault/article/magazine/MAG1123100/2/index.htm.

13. Dan Devine and Michael R. Steele, *Simply Devine* (Champagne, Ill.: Sports Publishing, 1999), 204; Kerkhoff, "This Means War."

14. Frank Tankard, "Bad Blood," *Lawrence Journal-World*, August 14, 2006, http://www.lawrence.com/news/2006/aug/14/bad_blood2/; Andrew Astleford, "Fambrough Doesn't Have Anything Nice to Say about Missouri," *Missourian*, Nov. 21, 2007.

15. Kirkpatrick, "Bold, Those Tigers"; Blair Kerkhoff, "Tigers Beat No. 1 Jayhawks Again," *Kansas City Star*, Febr. 13, 1990; Kerkhoff email to Jennifer L. Weber, Apr. 1, 2011; Blair Kerkhoff, "Jayhawks Once Again Top Tigers," *Kansas City Star*, Nov. 5, 1995; "Border War: The Rivalry between Kansas and Missouri," *KCMetroSports.com*, http://www.kcmetrosports.com/MetroSports-BorderWar.aspx.

16. Students of the University of Missouri, *Savitar* (Columbia, Mo., 1996), 146–150; Blair Kerkhoff, "This Means War," *Kansas City Star*, Nov. 28, 2007.

17. There is some debate as to whether this was the first homecoming in the nation. "Mizzou Homecoming," http://www.mizzou.com/s/1002/index.aspx?pgid= 369&gid=1.

18. "Border War," *KCMetroSports.com*, http://www.kcmetrosports.com/Metro Sports-BorderWar.aspx.

19. Stewart Mandel, "War of Words," Nov. 21, 2007, http://sportsillustrated.cnn .com/2007/writers/stewart_mandel/11/21/cfb.bag/.

20. Kerkhoff, "This Means War"; "Border War," *KCMetroSports.com*.

21. "We Burned Your Town to the Ground!" *AOL News*, Nov. 12, 2007, http://www.aolnews.com/2007/11/12/we-burned-your-town-to-the-ground/.

22. "Armageddon? No. Border War? Yes," *KansasCity.com*, Nov. 26, 2010, http://www.kansascity.com/2010/11/26/2474594/armageddon-no-border-war-yes .html.

23. Rudy Keller, "Osceola Urges Kansas to Drop Jayhawk Name," *Columbia Daily Tribune*, Sept. 15, 2011, http://www.columbiatribune.com/news/2011/sep/15/ osceola-urges-kansas-to-drop-jayhawk-name/.

24. *New York Times*, Nov. 12, 2011.

CONTRIBUTORS

Aaron Astor, Maryville College, is the author of *Rebels on the Border: Civil War, Emancipation, and the Reconstruction of Kentucky and Missouri* (Louisiana State University Press).

Joseph M. Beilein Jr., Penn State Erie, defended his dissertation, "Household War: Men, Women, and Guerrilla Warfare in Civil War Missouri," at the University of Missouri-Columbia in 2012.

Diane Mutti Burke, University of Missouri-Kansas City, is the author of *On Slavery's Border: Missouri's Small-Slaveholding Households, 1815–1865* (University of Georgia Press). She also is editing and annotating the diary of Paulina Stratton, a small-slaveholding woman from Missouri.

Brent M. S. Campney, University of Texas-Pan American, is revising his Emory University dissertation into a book tentatively entitled *"'We Blacks Had Suffered on This Beautiful Land': White Supremacy, Racist Violence, and the Long Black Civil Rights Movement in Kansas, 1861–1927."*

Jonathan Earle, University of Kansas, is the author of *Jacksonian Antislavery and the Politics of Free Soil* (University of North Carolina Press), *The Routledge Atlas of African American History* (Routledge), *John Brown's Raid: A Brief History with Documents* (Bedford/St. Martin's Press), and, with Sean Wilentz, *Major Problems in the Early Republic* (Houghton Mifflin). He currently is working on a book for Oxford University Press's Pivotal Moments in U.S. History series about the election of 1860.

Kristin K. Epps, Colorado State University-Pueblo, is revising her 2010 University of Kansas dissertation, "Bound Together: Masters and Slaves on the Kansas-Missouri Border, 1825–1865" for publication.

Nicole Etcheson, Ball State University, is the author of three books: *A Generation at War: The Civil War Era in a Northern Community* (University Press of Kansas);

331

Bleeding Kansas: Contested Liberty in the Civil War Era (University Press of Kansas); and *The Emerging Midwest: Upland Southerners and the Political Culture of the Old Northwest* (Indiana University Press).

Michael Fellman (1943–2012), Simon Fraser University, was the author of seven books about the Civil War, including works on William T. Sherman and Robert E. Lee, as well as the influential *Inside War: The Guerrilla Conflict in Missouri during the American Civil War* (Oxford University Press) and *In the Name of God and Country: Reconsidering Terrorism in American History* (Yale University Press). A memoir, *Views from the Dark Side of American History*, was published by Louisiana State University Press in 2011.

John W. McKerley is currently revising for publication his 2008 University of Iowa dissertation, "Citizens and Strangers: The Politics of Race in Missouri from Slavery to the Era of Jim Crow."

Tony R. Mullis, U.S. Army Command and General Staff College, is the author of *Peacekeeping on the Plains: Army Operations in Bleeding Kansas* (University of Missouri Press).

Jeremy Neely, Missouri State University, is the author of *The Border between Them: Violence and Reconciliation on the Kansas-Missouri Line, 1854–1890* (University of Missouri Press).

Kristin Tegtmeier Oertel, University of Tulsa, is the author of *Bleeding Borders: Gender, Race and Violence in Pre–Civil War Kansas* (Louisiana State University Press), and coauthor with Marilyn S. Blackwell of a biography of Clarina Nichols entitled *Frontier Feminist* (University Press of Kansas).

Christopher Phillips, University of Cincinnati, is the author of four books—three focusing on Missouri: *The Union on Trial: The Political Journals of Judge William Barclay Napton, 1829–1883* (University of Missouri Press); *Missouri's Confederate: Claiborne Fox Jackson and the Creation of Southern Identity in the Border West* (University of Missouri Press); and *Damned Yankee: The Life of Nathaniel Lyon* (Louisiana State University Press). He is currently working on a book tentatively entitled *South of North: The Civil War on the Middle Border and the Creation of American Regionalism* (Oxford University Press). It is a social-cultural study of the Civil War experience in the Ohio-Missouri River valleys.

Pearl Ponce, Ithaca College, is working on a book based on her revised Harvard University dissertation "'To Tame the Devil in Hell': Kansas in National Politics,

1854–1858" and is the editor of *Kansas's War: The Civil War in Documents* (University of Ohio Press).

Jennifer L. Weber, University of Kansas, is the author of *Copperheads: The Rise and Fall of Lincoln's Opponents in the North* (Oxford University Press). She is also the coauthor of a children's book with James M. McPherson called *Summer's Bloodiest Days: The Battle of Gettysburg as Told from All Sides* (National Geographic).

INDEX